A Rendezvous *to Remember*

A Memoir of Joy and Heartache
at the Dawn of the Sixties

Terry Marshall
Ann Garretson Marshall

SANDRA JONAS
PUBLISHING

UNITED
KINGDOM

London ○

Paris

FRANCE

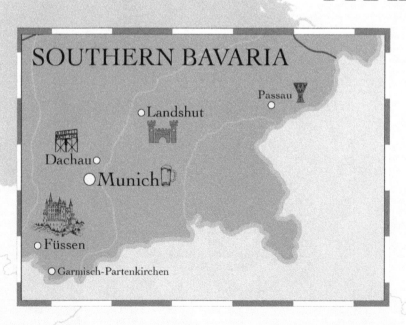

SOUTHERN BAVARIA

Passau

○ Landshut

Dachau ○

○ Munich

○ Füssen

○ Garmisch-Partenkirchen

Sandra Jonas Publishing House
PO Box 20892
Boulder, CO 80308
sandrajonaspublishing.com

Printed in the United States of America
26 25 24 23 22 21   1 2 3 4 5 6 7 8

Cover illustration: Adobe Stock/Fresh Stock
Book and cover design: Sandra Jonas
Maps: Cynthia Carbajal

Publisher's Cataloging-in-Publication Data
Names: Marshall, Terry, author. | Marshall, Ann Garretson, author.
Title: A Rendezvous to Remember : A Memoir of Joy and Heartache at
    the Dawn of the Sixties / Terry Marshall and Ann Garretson Marshall.
Description: Boulder, Colorado : Sandra Jonas Publishing, 2021.
Identifiers: LCCN 2020944339 | ISBN 9781733338622 (hardcover) |
    ISBN 9781733338653 (paperback) | ISBN 9781733338677 (ebook)
Subjects: LCSH: Marshall, Ann Garretson. | Marshall, Terry. | Political activ-
    ists—Biography. | Man-woman relationships. | Nineteen sixties. | LCGFT:
    Autobiographies. | BISAC: BIOGRAPHY & AUTOBIOGRAPHY / Social
    activists
Classification: LCC CT275 .M377 2021 | DDC 973.92092 — dc23
LC record available at http://lccn.loc.gov/2020944339

All photographs courtesy of the authors.

To Jack Sigg,
who profoundly influenced both our lives

Contents

1

Goodbye, Boulder

Terry

Thursday, 4 June 1964, Boulder, Colorado. In the final hours before Annie left for Europe, I was her faithful *domestique*. Grabbing up pages of her final term paper in progress, I raced by bicycle from her dorm, pumped uphill to her professor's office, deposited her prose, and flew back for another installment, and then another. Three trips in all. We met the noon deadline by minutes.

No lunch. Instead, I lugged her stuff out and arrayed it all on the sidewalk like a garage sale: garment bags, sacks of whatnots, boxes of books, boots, and shoes, a battered Smith-Corona portable typewriter, the AM/FM radio I gave her for graduation, bundles of letters tucked into their envelopes— all postmarked APO, all from her lieutenant waiting in Germany—as well as a carton of top secret reel-to-reel audiotape musings from the same guy.

I wedged the whole mess into her mother's Oldsmobile, as expertly as if I were a Machu Picchu stone mason. I couldn't have squeezed in so much as a toothpick.

We were left with a three-foot-high pile of *Denver Post* newspapers, months' worth that Annie hadn't read. "I'll read them in Albuquerque," she said. "I paid for them." She scrounged up rope and bundled them to the roof of the car. "No biggie. It's like strapping on gear for a campout."

But for a five-hundred-mile trip at sixty-five miles an hour? I simply shook my head.

"Goodbye, Ter." Her hand grazed my arm. No hug. No kiss. No tears. Certainly not with Mother Garretson beside her, pretending not to monitor our every move.

"Have a great trip," I managed to say.

As they drove away, I slumped onto the steps of Hallett Hall. The first newspaper fluttered free as they passed the planetarium, well before they hit the Denver-Boulder Turnpike.

We had created lots of memories here, Annie and I, all over campus, all over Boulder: those fifteen-cent burgers (for Annie, ketchup only), ten-cent fries, and spirited debates in my Ford Falcon parked at McDonald's on Sunday nights; that warm spring night when we dashed from Hallett Hall into the rain, skipping through puddles and laughing like four-year-olds, she sparkly eyed, even after the shower had soaked her curly hair into a rag mop; that fall weekend when she and two friends squeezed into my car after dinner and we drove all night to watch our Colorado Buffaloes play the Jayhawks in Kansas. She dozed through the game, despite raucous fans and unforgiving bleachers. We lost 34–6.

Throughout our early college years, Annie had been my best friend. The girl-next-door kind of friend. The friend I could meet for coffee on the spur of the moment—no shower, shave, or ironed shirt needed. The everyday friend who swapped tales with me from the books we'd read and news we'd heard. The friend who consoled me when my father was killed. The first person I called when the Peace Corps invited me to go to Venezuela.

Those were our "old buddy" years, 1960–1963, before the 1964 March winds blew the cobwebs out of my brain and I realized Annie was a girl— a captivating one.

Take last weekend (Friday night, May 29, to be exact). I converted my room into a photo studio—flood lamps, reflectors, a bouquet of flowers, borrowed bedspread, fluffy throw pillows—and coaxed her into wearing her nightie for a photo shoot. No big deal, I said. We'd shot dozens of pictures of each other for our photojournalism class, capturing close-ups in different moods and different thoughts and experimenting with shadows and light. We'd posed like nature lovers at Varsity Lake and big-time reporters at our typewriters.

Still, it took some cajoling. "I want to print a bunch of eleven-by-fourteens and mount them on my headboard," I told her. "That way, I'll finally get to sleep with you. Every night."

She glared, but a grin slowly formed. "Okay, *if* it's *The Clothed Maja* you want me to model and not that au naturel one you're always raving about."

Annie in her nightie. Wow. A silky, ivory-colored midthigh number slit up both sides to her hips, clinging so suggestively it advertised every curve and hill. We did well for an hour or so, but when she put on those come-hither looks of hers and swished her fanny? Well, I lost my focus. She did too. We didn't go all the way. She was unbending on that score. But that was a night I'd never forget.

Now she was on her way to Germany to see her West Point lieutenant, my competitor, the guy who mailed her reams of letters, hours of tape-recorded sweet nothings, and fancy gifts I couldn't match, like the hand-blown German crystal vase I had packed so carefully into her mother's car.

It didn't help that they had spent so little time together. She didn't know his foibles and annoying habits. Surely he had some. Annie knew me, though—every fiery outburst, every dirty little secret—down to the graphic intimacies of my past relationships. Worse, I had gotten so wrapped up in the joy of sex that I'd pestered Annie to take on a lover of her own (not me, by the way—I was myopic in those days). I couldn't wait for her to experience it for herself.

One thing was clear: I was in a bare-knuckle bout with one Lieutenant Jack Sigg for Annie's heart. And he wore the champion's belt. I was an amateur, better suited for a round with a sparring partner than a go at the title. Having never met him, I was flailing about in the dark. He was a shadowy phantom like those CU jocks who dominated the headlines but popped up on campus only on game days. I did know of his tight friendship with Annie's older brother. And I'd seen a photo. Jack was a stud.

Not only that, the lieutenant had the whole United States Army on his side. Annie's family was military to the core. By contrast, I was in a battle with my draft board to be classified "I-O, Conscientious Objector." I couldn't take a human life, I had told them in a letter, nor could I support a country that did. I'd pledged to myself I would go to prison before I'd go into the army. The board sent me a new draft card, stamped "II-S, Student Deferment." I was sure they would reclassify me "I-A, Available for Military Service" and snatch me up the moment I graduated. In two days.

That, too, was a slap in the face. Annie was so hot to get to Germany she wouldn't even stick around for commencement. Mine and hers.

As if all that weren't bad enough, Annie and the lieutenant were about to travel Europe together in the hottest car on the road: a 1963 Corvette Sting

Ray. They would have weeks alone. And I knew how sensual Annie could be. What if he picked up where I'd left off, leaving me to choke in his exhaust?

So, late on the afternoon of June 4, 1964, alone on the steps of Annie's dorm, I wrestled with this perplexing question: Would the foundation she and I had built over four years be enough to override my hotspur outbursts, trump the military ethos she'd grown up with, counter the coming full-court press from Lieutenant Sigg, and keep the flame alive for two years while I served my country in my own way, as a Peace Corps volunteer in Venezuela?

I flashed back to exactly one year earlier, when my girlfriend Steffi had flown to San Francisco to scout out jobs and to see if two years of letters from a former sweetheart really meant they might have a future together. She had come back aglow in his love. "But I'll stay in Colorado. *If* you're willing to commit," she said.

I wanted to say "I love you. Stay. We'll make it work." But marriage meant shackling myself to someone forever. I wanted to be free, to travel, to experience life. Oh, I had a thousand excuses. "I hate to see you go," I whimpered. She left for San Francisco the next day. I never saw her again.

If Steffi's weeklong visit to an ex-boyfriend could fan two-year-old ashes into a wildfire, what might a European summer with Lieutenant Sigg do to Annie?

Given how much my love for Annie had grown that year, losing Steffi had been a godsend. But losing love through your own timidity is like snatching up a handful of hot coals. It hurts like hell, and it's a powerful incentive not to do it again. Plus, it leaves lasting scars. Yet there I was, stoking a roaring fire, still unwilling to commit. I had told Annie I loved her, but I had choked on the M-word.

What a simpleton!

Ann

Thursday, June 4, 1964, Boulder. For an instant, Terry filled my rearview mirror, slouched on my dorm steps like a cast-off Raggedy Andy. His dejection stabbed at my heart. The image sailed quickly out of view, but not the searing ache.

Where was that guy I had grown to love? Where was that free spirit, that joie de vivre, that quirky sense of humor? Smothered. All of them. Tuesday night, in the oppressive pessimism that had fouled the air in his car, I'd told him, "This isn't the end of the world. I've been planning this trip for five months. You were my travel agent, my cheerleader—if you recall."

"Yeah, that was before I realized I couldn't live without you."

I teetered on the slippery stepping stones of my own emotions. How could I reassure him, when I felt so torn myself?

Terry and I had met at the student-run *Colorado Daily* my first week at the university, but we had known of each other in high school. He'd written to me my senior year after my essay, "Why I Want to Be a Newspaper Woman," won a statewide journalism contest. My prize: a trip to Detroit to represent Colorado at the Ford National Teen-Age Press Conference for the unveiling of their hot new model, the Falcon. Our high schools were thirty miles apart in southern Colorado's isolated San Luis Valley, and Terry had won the contest the previous year.

The Ford conference was a big deal for the students and their families, and for the local *San Luis Valley Courier*. As they did every year for the proud winner, the newspaper ran a front-page photo of me posed at the steps of a Frontier Airlines DC-3 before the flight left Alamosa for Denver, where I caught a TWA flight to Henry Ford's well-publicized shindig. In Detroit, I had my photo taken shaking hands with Mr. Ford himself.

Terry's letter was charming, from the "Dear Miss Garretson" to the hearty congratulations to the shared bond of being from the San Luis Valley to the pitch to study journalism at CU and work on the *Colorado Daily*. He even invited me to an upcoming CU-sponsored journalism workshop for high school students. And the letter was grammatically perfect. Obviously written, edited, and retyped.

The following September, I was the country mouse when I ventured into the *Daily* office to see if they needed another reporter. The receptionist pointed to the city editor. I tiptoed over. This little guy was scrunched over a typewriter, pounding so fast I expected sparks. His shirt looked like he'd slept in it. I stood there. He typed on.

"Excuse me," I said. He jerked out the page, seized a clean sheet of newsprint, and cranked it in. "Are you Terry?"

He glanced up. Oh my, such bloodshot eyes. Beyond bloodshot: the red of a nocturnal creature who could see in the dark. "Yep. And you are . . . ?"

I told him.

"Garretson? From Alamosa?" He jumped up and thrust out his hand, all business, no smile or even a mention of that letter I hadn't answered. (My girlfriend had heard he was "really conceited," so I hadn't written.)

He sent me to cover a speech. I wrote my story. He massacred it with red ink. "Rewrite," he said. Sure, he was city editor, an award-winning journalist, but I'd won the same contest, and like him, I had edited my high school newspaper. But I rewrote the story. Twice. Same thing happened with my next assignment and the next.

My writing got sharper and his edits fewer, sprinkled here and there with a scribbled "great job." We wrote a few stories as a team, not as editor and reporter. I became "one of the guys" at the *Daily*.

One school night just before spring break, as we were working feverishly toward our midnight deadline at the *Daily*, Terry cruised past and dropped a neatly folded stretch of toilet paper on my desk, meticulously typed on from top to bottom. The first item read:

EDITORS: Beginning today, UPI is initiating a strenuous conservancy campaign to save money and time. Henceforth, we will use this type of copy paper. You will benefit, as it has a practical use after having been read. This is another improvement initiated by United Press International.

The four feet of toilet paper carried a phony news story about a "sinister plot" to kidnap a Cross Arrow Ranch cowgirl (me). A made-up quote from CU president "Dr. Figg Newton" (his given name was Quigg) warned students to mind their manners and remember their morals when driving back to school after the break. He singled out "two students from Colorado's San Luis Valley"—Terry and me—"who took three days to drive the 250 miles from Alamosa to Boulder." At the time, we were *not* boyfriend and girlfriend. Terry hadn't even offered me a ride home from CU, though our ranch was only forty miles from his farm near Center.

The two of us were kindred spirits from the state's hinterlands, speaking the same argot of small-town *compañeros*, tinged with idioms from farm and ranch life. Entertaining each other with shiny nuggets from our professors, we relished the conceit of debating topics we'd never heard of in our rural high schools. We became pals, meeting for breaks at the student union, going on bike rides, picnicking, and attending plays, lectures, and concerts together. We didn't "date." We simply did things together, usually on a whim, no dressing up or trying to impress each other. Best of all, I didn't have to be on guard with him—too many guys were only after sex.

Hardly a day went by that we didn't talk. Terry spun out his secret hopes and dreams, obsessing on the Peace Corps and talking endlessly about living overseas. He pressed me for every detail of my freshman year of high school, the year Dad was commander of the US Army's port of Leghorn in Livorno, Italy.

He also fanaticized about owning a small-town newspaper, becoming a modern-day Lincoln Steffens or Upton Sinclair, exposing corruption, digging out injustice, and writing editorials to spotlight racism and poverty.

I was less sure about my future. I had declared a journalism major, but in my junior year, I took an investigative reporting lab class that required me to interview local leaders on Boulder issues. By the time I stuttered my way through the class, I concluded I couldn't be a journalist like Terry, asking none-of-your-business questions. My parents had taught me not to be rude.

So I switched to education, deciding I would teach high school kids to love great literature and, in the process, motivate them to work toward creating a better world. I, too, was inspired by the Peace Corps and wanted to join, but I wasn't brave enough to believe I could actually do it.

On the afternoon of June 4, 1964, my zany memories of Terry were undermined by thoughts of Jack Sigg and the grand adventure that lay ahead. I was a twenty-two-year-old innocent, so eager for a rendezvous with my lieutenant in Europe that I had jumped at the opportunity to take a no-frills red-eye to Paris and on to Munich. But over the past three months, my feelings for Terry had done a U-turn, snagging me in the throes of an impossible choice.

I had to find out where the airmail courtship I'd nurtured with Jack would lead. He and I had hatched the trip as a test. Were we the soul mates our letters had promised?

Or should I heed the persistent call of my best friend?

2

Hungry Lions, Circling

Ann

Summer 1961–Spring 1962, Boulder. On its face, my decision that Jack was "The One" reeked of a teenybopper's fantasy. We had never kissed, never even dated. Yet despite the absence of even a hint of carnal hanky-panky, it was, I believed, a rational, mature decision. It grew from several wrenching romantic encounters during my early university years.

The first began in June 1961 when my family journeyed to West Point to celebrate my brother Bonner's graduation from the United States Military Academy. It was a five-day whirlwind of tours, luncheons, picnics, dinners, receptions, dances, concerts, military parades, and Army-Navy sports competitions. Every cadet—all were men in those days—had to have a date. As did, my brother insisted, all visiting single women. He set me up with Geoff, a second-year cadet in his company. We were together for every event, from morning brunch until we whispered reluctant good night at the first strains of the bugled curfew. Swept up by June Week magic, we were soon plotting when and where we would see each other next.

Later that summer, Geoff spent several days at our ranch in Colorado. And over Christmas at his parents' home in upstate New York, we got pinned, a step shy of being engaged. Not long after, he proposed we marry after he graduated in June 1963. "Imagine this," he wrote. "We promenade from the Old Cadet Chapel through the Arch of Sabers, followed by a grand honeymoon after the long grind I've been through."

I was a sophomore. "Impossible. I'll still be a year short of finishing *my* 'grind.'"

"Forget the degree. I'll take care of you," he wrote.

Me, a college dropout? And a kept woman? My next letter zinged, "Think again, buster."

He fired back, "You expect me to wait until you get your PhD?"

His oozing sarcasm squelched the flame. I told him it was over. He called. He wrote. I didn't want to be mean, but eventually I quit responding.

It wounded us both deeply, but I had to get past it. I began dating again, and other romantic imbroglios plunged me into deeper troughs of pain:

Ian, a CU physics teaching assistant. After three dates, he sent flowers, talked of a ring, wrote passionate letters. "You are the most wonderful thing that ever happened to me. I love you sincerely and lastingly." I loved his English accent and his passion for our Colorado mountains. But not *him.*

Wilcox, an army lieutenant, also courtesy of my brother. He was a party guy who blitzed me with thirty-six "Darlin'" and "Sweetie" letters—none with the intellectual meat to spark my continuing interest.

Benjamin, a Colorado School of Mines engineering student. A mountain of a man with a lumberjack beard, he was soft-spoken, kindhearted, and fun. He graduated ahead of me, moved to California, and called every day, long distance. At our first reunion, I had to fight him off physically. He didn't believe that no meant NO. He begged forgiveness. Too late. He had betrayed my trust.

Charming guys all, but they squeezed me to suffocation. It crushed me to inflict heartache on them, and my studies suffered.

Here's what puzzled me: I wasn't a guy magnet. Heads didn't turn when I walked into a room. I didn't sport flashy outfits, waggle my hips, or display any cleavage. I didn't spend hours layering on makeup or have long, flowing waves like the women in the Halo ads. My hair was curly, often frizzy. And I had ten thousand freckles. If I flirted, it was wordplay, not pouty lips, batting eyelashes, or heaving breasts. On weekends, I didn't haunt the beer joints near campus, drink myself into a stupor, and later rationalize that drunken sex was the height of ecstasy.

My solution? Take matters into my own hands and preselect a mate. No more leaving the marriage question to chance. No more suffering the slings and arrows of the weekend dating game.

Once I made that decision, it didn't take me long to zero in on my choice: Jack Sigg.

My brother's best friend and roommate at West Point. Smart. Charming. And a big plus: everyone in my family liked him.

I had seen him in person only three times, but it was enough to generate sparks. The first was six years earlier, when families of plebes (freshmen) trundled to West Point to celebrate Christmas with their newly minted cadet sons. After Bonner introduced us, Jack turned to my brother and said, "Well . . . where have you been hiding this lovely lady?" He took my gloved hand in both of his and brought it to his lips for a courtly kiss. All the while, his playful blue eyes danced with mine. A warm glow, like the embers of a summer's campfire, swept through me. Wow! This guy was a college man. West Point! And I was a mere sophomore in high school.

Four years later, at his and Bonner's graduation, those embers flared again when I cruised close enough to Jack to feel the heat of him. A company commander, he was dashing in his dress whites. I was now a college girl, and when he took my hand, I held his in both of mine. I lingered. He squeezed. "It's been a long time," he said. I hoped he didn't notice my staccato breathing.

That was it, though. Soon after, Bonner unknowingly diverted my attentions by setting me up with Geoff. The sparks that sizzled in Jack's presence were snuffed out when I saw him that June Week with a dazzling girl on his arm.

My third encounter with Jack came a month later when he and Bonner made a trip to the ranch before they headed off to ranger training. I was spellbound in Jack's orbit, where the air was energizing and the conversation invigorating. Late one afternoon, when Bonner helped Dad tune up a cranky tractor, I took Jack horseback riding to my favorite spot on the Rio Grande, which ran through our ranch. We paused to let our horses drink. In the distance, the Sangre de Cristo Range had begun to glow purple-red in the sunset. "That's magnificent!" Jack said. "Nothing like the Appalachians back home."

He loved my mountains. The man had taste.

For a few splendid moments we seemed in tune.

Sadly, for the rest of their visit, I was not party to their adventures. He was a race car and I was a scooter. He left after a week, without really noticing me. Or so I thought.

Summer 1962–Fall 1963, Boulder. Now that I had chosen Jack as The One, I took the next step and sent him a "hello" letter. I entertained him with stories of college life in Boulder and asked him to tell me about Germany, where he was stationed. He wrote right back. That fall he inquired about my classes and asked me to send any papers I'd written—"not only to tell me more about you, but for my own education." I was flattered.

In one letter he asked, "How's Geoff? I haven't heard from him in months. Are you two still planning to get married?"

I told him Geoff and I had broken up and asked Jack about his dazzling date at June Week. "The 'dazzle' was quick to fade," he wrote. "Next I heard she was marrying one of my classmates . . . but I ran into him at Grafenwohr and found out that was off too. C'est la guerre."

All right! The runway was clear.

For a year, our letters grazed on the topics of the day—Cuba, the Cold War, poverty and racism at home—and on our own plans for education and our futures. Then the second week of November 1963, an extra-thick envelope arrived, bursting at the seams. He'd probably been guarding the Czech-German border again—lonely evenings there had fostered a number of long letters. But Jack's tone had changed. First, he cataloged his "faults":

Some people say I'm too ambitious, but I'm weak compared to my ability to meet my own high standards. I'm a daydreamer, a romantic prone to illusions of grandeur and happy-ever-after endings. I'm hard to live with, picky, a neatnik, a perfectionist.

He said his adviser had made him rewrite his Rhodes scholarship bio because he'd used "I" a hundred times. A Rhodes nominee? A huge honor, not a "flaw" at all. The letter wasn't a confession, but a clever rationale for why I should find him irresistible. Eight pages into his opus, I hit this pronouncement: "Why the sham before? You! You fulfill my dreams for the girl I want to marry."

Marry? The girl I want to marry! My skin tingled. My knees went rubbery. I jumped up, paced the room, flung my window open, gulped in fresh air. He wants to marry me? I raced back to my desk and read on. "I was afraid to tell you the truth. If I'm out of bounds here, please let us remain friends."

He was afraid to tell *me* the truth? Whew! I had daydreamed this declaration for nearly two years. I wrapped my arms around my head to prevent an explosion, leaped up again, paced back to the window. Marry me? Holy cow!

Jack transcended my highest hopes. In the top 10 percent of his West Point class, he was a graduate of Airborne and Ranger schools, one of the first in his class promoted to troop commander, with an invitation in hand to teach math or tactics at West Point, his choice.

Better yet, our letters had revealed his belief that a husband should be a stalwart supporter of his wife's career goals and should see her as an equal partner in achieving his. He was no "male chauvinist pig," the ultimate epithet for men too blind to recognize women's talents. A bonus: We had the same values about love (precedes sex) and marriage (a lifelong commitment). I could flourish with Jack. As the daughter of a career officer, I knew army life.

Our correspondence blossomed like a century plant, as if the seeds had been gestating all along. Jack began to sign off with "Love" and soon "All my love." His letters and audiotapes became steeped in unabashed passion. How could I resist such declarations as these:

> *I keep feeling so confident our envisioned dreams of unbounded joy will become actuality, and gloriously soon. Am engulfed by desire to be with you. Am bursting with hopefulness. I cannot fathom any course other than the beginning of a new life together. Anything else is unthinkable.*

> *I sat in my office today almost three hours preparing a speech to the troops. All I could think about was you sitting on my lap. Can't get you out of my mind. I think of you always, always.*

Soon his weekly letter count exceeded that of all the guys writing their girls in our dorm. I knew. As mail clerk, I handled every letter.

In the midst of this letter tornado, a mere four weeks later, he invited me to spend Christmas with him in Germany. He would pay. Oh my, alone with him in Europe? How bold. Shocking really. Was I ready for that? No! Besides, there wasn't time to renew my passport.

Terry

Friday, 22 November 1963, Boulder. I bounded into the CU School of Journalism reading room for a late sack lunch. Friday again. A lonely weekend lay ahead.

Inside the door, my former girlfriend Sarah grabbed me and pulled me into the typewriter lab, her cheeks stained with tears. She had broken up with me two weeks earlier, and we had been greeting each other in our classes like mere acquaintances. I'd never seen her cry. She was too tough.

"They've killed President Kennedy," she said.

That's how I found out. From Sarah. In the J-School basement. At exactly 12:42 p.m.

We held each other shamelessly, locked together as one, this time in shock, not lust.

Over that endless four-day weekend, it wasn't Sarah I comforted. Or who comforted me. After Sarah took off, I called Annie. All afternoon, she and I wandered benumbed through campus, unable to fathom the news from Dallas. Like zombies, we ended up with several other journalism students, all uninvited, at Professor Mitchell's home, crammed into his living room for four days. We sat on the floor, ate cold pizza, and stared silently into the black-and-white TV. JFK's funeral fell on my birthday. I didn't tell anyone.

Americans everywhere came out of that weekend with images burned into our minds: Jacqueline Kennedy as stoic as she was elegant. Little John-John at attention, saluting his dead father. The white horses pulling the president's flag-draped caisson up Pennsylvania Avenue to the cadence of muffled drums. The riderless black stallion, stirrups holding empty backward-facing riding boots. Lee Harvey Oswald's contorted face as he was struck by the bullet from Jack Ruby's gun. An endless spiral of anguish.

We all ached with our own personal grief. Annie's and mine was the loss of a visionary president who created the Peace Corps. After Kennedy's inauguration almost two years before, if you had asked me to state my main goal in life, I would have said, "To join the Peace Corps." JFK had touched me personally when he said, "Ask not what your country can do for you. Ask what you can do for your country." Within weeks, I had applied and been accepted to go to Colombia in the summer of 1961.

But that April, my father was killed by a drunk driver, and Mom was hospitalized for six weeks. When she got out, she was hobbled for months, both legs broken. My sister, Pam, was fourteen, and my brothers, Greg and Randy, were eleven and nine. Grandma came to help, but I couldn't leave them for two years, so I turned down the Peace Corps and spent that summer at home.

Of course, nothing was the same. Dad was gone. Mom was crippled. Grandma and I and the kids were barely able to hold our broken family together. My dreams were dashed.

After I turned down the Peace Corps, I was convinced they'd never consider me again. That was it. And now, JFK murdered. Not only my dreams crushed, but the entire nation's.

Ann

Saturday, January 4, 1964, Boulder. When I returned to CU after Christmas, a bundle of letters and two audiotapes from Jack awaited me. One tape, labeled Airmail, Special Delivery, was postmarked December 21, two weeks prior. Special Delivery? A note inside demanded, "Read this first! Make sure no one overhears what I have said on this tape!" He needed an answer, he added, ASAP.

ASAP? Too late for that!

In the last carrel at the far end of the music library, I settled in for his grand secret: "The letter from you today made me extremely happy. You are wonderful. I look at your picture and think of you hours on end. It's ruining my military efficiency."

His voice was fluid, no awkward pauses. I closed my eyes, imagining him beside me. Curiously, he began describing the carrot in his goulash soup. "The stem is old and withered where it meets the carrot, but peeking out is a sprig of green—new life!"

The man found poetry in day-to-day minutiae. I chuckled.

"This is also about new life, and it must remain a secret," he said. "I spent this evening calming a girl who is three months pregnant. I can't describe how difficult it is to try to console someone sobbing like that." He paused. "I'm telling you this because we need your help."

We? I stopped the tape. *We? He and the girl needed my help?*

What? You've gotten a girl pregnant? You, the quintessential Boy Scout grown into a West Point officer: duty, honor, country above all else? The thought hung like a noxious gas. *Okay, Ann, hear him out. At least he's got the courage to confess.*

My hand shook, but I turned the player back on. "The girl is pregnant by your brother." Jack sighed. "She's German. Bonner doesn't want to marry her, and we agree that is probably best."

An overheard conversation from Dad's office replayed itself in my mind: Dad lecturing Bonner before he left for Germany as I sat reading in the adjacent family room. "Messing with German females will torpedo your career," Dad said. "They'll yank your top secret clearance, and you'll never see it again." Memories of World Wars I and II were too fresh, he said.

Bonner responded, "Yes, sir. I know that, sir." His tone said, "Yeah, yeah, I'm not stupid."

I could see years of Bonner's sacrifices fizzle. He had stayed in the US the year we lived in Italy so he could graduate from a top American high school and get a congressional appointment to West Point. Four years of rigorous study next, followed by punishing training in Airborne and Ranger schools. He had the smarts and personality to mingle with leaders and motivate troops. He was thoughtful and considerate. I was proud of him. But at that moment, I wanted to slap him for thinking with his penis instead of with his brain.

Rooted in that stuffy carrel, I ricocheted from anger to disbelief to sadness—for Bonner *and* the girl, even though I'd never met her. *How could you, my own brother?*

Over the next two hours, I mined these additional facts: The girl, Gretchen Schumacher, had been a serious girlfriend. She loved him, but he didn't love her enough to give up his career. Distraught over her condition and Bonner's response, she had decided to have her baby in the States so her family, friends, and employer wouldn't know she had sinned.

There was more. Abandoned, the girl was sobbing nonstop. Unbelievably, having described her as a basket case, Jack asked if she could come to Boulder so she could "cry on my shoulder." He coated his request in a compliment: "If I were pregnant, I'd want to talk to you."

I snorted, right there in the library. If he were pregnant? Ha! As if asking a simple favor, he added, "Write and let me know if it's okay for her to come."

To top it off, he said Bonner hadn't told Mom or Dad. "Please don't tell them. Or Bonner. He's paying for everything, but it's better if he doesn't know I'm sending her to you." Great. Jack expected me to keep two secrets, one from my parents and one from my brother. The kicker? Gretchen would board a plane for Colorado on January 6—two days off.

Finals would begin in a week. I was buried under term papers to write, tests to cram for, and a pile of books to finish for my four English lit classes. Plus untold pages to transcribe, with dictionary in hand, for second-year Russian. I sweated through the week, polished off my papers, and headed into finals sleep deprived.

No word from Gretchen. I was a wreck. Six days after her scheduled departure, she still hadn't arrived. I swore Terry to secrecy and spilled the whole mess, including my fear that Gretchen had gotten lost. What would I tell Jack?

"She'll show up. Deal with it then," he said.

Thanks a lot, Ter!

Gretchen called on January 13, a week late. "I'm here! In America! Denver. And eating Mexican food. I love it! Jack wishes you well. From his description, you are the most amazing girl in America. When can we meet? Tomorrow?"

Well, no. I had finals. And my job. We agreed on Saturday.

I borrowed Terry's car, something I had never done. When I rolled up to her apartment, it was fifty degrees out. I spotted this petite blond perched on the porch, engrossed in a thick hardbound book. No coat. The moment I parked, she bounded over. "You're Ann, *ja*? I would know you anywhere. I've always wanted to meet a saint!" She threw her arms around me. She stepped back and gave an impish grin. "Well, maybe half saint . . . and half all-American girl."

She ushered me inside, brewed tea, and laid out a plate of *Springerle* (a German cookie), showering me with tidbits from her trip. Racing for gates in Munich, New York, and Chicago. Chatting with a grandma from Iowa sitting next to her. The boy she taught to count from one to five in German on the flight to Denver. A half-dozen funny stories, but with enough pauses to ask about my day, my classes, about Jack and me. An hour stretched to two.

This girl felt like a sister. And what a go-getter. In less than a week, she had found an apartment, moved in, made friends with a girl in the same fix, and started work at the neighborhood 7-Eleven.

She was a far cry from the sobbing girl Jack had described. No tears, no woe is me.

As for being pregnant, "Bad girls do this all the time, but not good girls. If they knew at home, it would be a scandal." Her tone was pensive, neither morose nor self-pitying. And her first request wasn't a plea for help, but "I want to hike your beautiful Rocky Mountains. Can you take me?"

A week later, Terry and I took her hiking up James Creek above Boulder. Like a mountain goat, Gretchen outpaced us. The windchill that day was twenty-something degrees. Terry and I hunkered inside a grove of pine trees and, with icy fingers, ate peanut butter and jelly sandwiches and downed a thermos of coffee. Gretchen, by then four months pregnant, raced off to the creek and slurped up icy water as if it were a summer day.

January–February, 1964, Boulder. The frozen days of winter melted in the tempo and intensity of letters zipping across the Atlantic. Jack's raves about "us" and our yearning to be together far overshadowed any actual news. Tucked among his letters awaiting my return to school was this handwritten sentiment: "May this new year bring us together and to the beginnings of a shared journey through life." That and so much more I could hardly keep pace:

December 22, 1963. *Do your folks know I aspire to be their son-in-law?*

December 24, 1963. *Income tax time is coming again. If you'd only have let me buy your plane ticket over, there'd be another deduction.*

Maybe I'll get luckier next year, and who knows, we might be filling out a joint return.

January 3, 1964. *If we [marry], we will live in unbounded joy, and could easily leave significant, respected contributions in whatever we choose to accomplish.*

We were on runaway trains hurtling toward each other. We had to meet. A trip to Germany no longer seemed indecorous. But when? Spring break? Not long enough. I'd have to wait until June, after graduation. Europe would be an ideal capstone to college and a tantalizing rendezvous. I didn't have the money, though. My job as mail clerk in the dorm paid room and board, not cash. My scholarship covered tuition and fees—$232 a year—but I was relying on Mom and Dad for spending money. I pinched every penny so I wouldn't be a burden.

Jack offered—again—to pay my airfare, but that was an obligation I couldn't accept. I screwed up my courage and wrote to Dad asking to borrow money for a cut-rate charter flight to Europe, pitching the trip as "educational" for Bonner, Jack, and me. We'd tour France, Italy, Switzerland, and Germany. I added that it would also "be enlightening for me to get acquainted with my correspondent of the past two years."

Not missing a beat, Dad wrote back, "In my day and time and your mother's, girls didn't go sashaying all over the world seeing their boyfriends. It was the other way around." He asked for a budget and in late February offered to make the ticket my graduation gift. The trip was on.

The flurry of letters between Jack and me continued, each one snapping another link into a golden chain that pulled us ever closer. He was in love. So was I, even if I was afraid to say it:

January 26, me to Jack. *I am enraptured with the magic of "us." I agree our potential is unbounded to accomplishments of tremendous benefit to many.*

February 15, Jack to me. *This morning I had a dreamlike awakening, thinking how it would be if you were here beside me. I tingled all over, shuddered in ecstasy. It wasn't the first time, but the most vivid.*

March 4, Jack to me. *My difficulty is avoiding endless repetition of how lonely I am for you, how much I want to be with you, my glorious dream of you and I becoming we and us. It can last and grow—and joyfully, I have a feeling it will.*

Through January and February, as Jack and I fired off love notes, Terry hyped my jaunt like a fast-talking tour guide. Drawing on his massive art history textbook, Janson's *The History of Art*, he said I absolutely had to see Versailles, the Louvre, Venice's Palazzo Ducale with its Tintorettos, Titians, and Guariento frescoes, and Albrecht Dürer's *Four Apostles* in Munich's Pinakothek. We fantasized over me seeing *Hamlet* at Stratford-on-Avon.

Indeed, through mid-February, Terry almost seemed to be working in tandem with Jack to fan the flames of my long-distance romance.

March 1964, Boulder. March roared in like a lion. I was student teaching at Boulder High half days, carrying a full load of classes, writing lesson plans, and studying far into the night. On the weekends, I'd trek to Denver, sometimes with Terry, but usually alone, to visit Gretchen. We never talked by phone—the long-distance charges would have eaten us alive.

Together, she and I explored the zoo, the Botanic Gardens, and the art and history museums. On hikes and huddles over tea, and in a number of soul-searching letters, we agonized over the thorny dilemma she faced as an unmarried pregnant woman. We probed all the possibilities, though as her confidante-friend, I mostly listened and never pushed for any single choice. It had to be *her* decision.

Abortion? "Never!" She was a devout Catholic. Marry the father? Not possible. My brother had made that clear. Still, she wished Bonner no ill will. She loved him.

Keep the child and raise it as a single mom? That was a burden neither Jack nor I wished on anyone. We favored adoption, so my heart had leaped in early February when she wrote, "I DID IT!" She had talked to an adoption counselor and asked me to gather family background information she would need.

But her effusive description of the counselor and the process took a right turn when she asked that I not tell Jack because "I want Jack and your brother to know about this only when I am completely sure. I can't stop thinking about this, I can't sleep, and I have these awful dreams. I must get all these doubts out of my head first."

Oh no. Not another secret to keep!

It was around this time that Terry started acting weird—making flirty jokes and brushing against me, the way guys do when they think they're being subtle.

Actually, he'd been a different person since September, but I had been too consumed with my own challenges—and joys—to give it much thought. He had come back to school with stories of an old high school flame he'd lusted after and lost over the summer. Then over the weekend before classes began, he and a J-School classmate dove into bed like newlyweds. Not a one-night fling, but every weekend and half the weeknights. That lasted a couple of months, and another girl came along, someone he'd met in Silverton. While Jack and I were exchanging love letters that fall, Terry was jumping from one steamy relationship to the next.

All he could talk about was sex, somehow seeing it as his duty to describe everything to me in explicit detail. I had no desire to hear how "marvelous" a vagina felt to a guy. I was speechless when he told me. Through the whole fall semester, Terry and I didn't meet once for coffee or for Sunday night burgers at McDonald's.

One night in mid-March, though, he fetched me off to an all-night doughnut shop, a greasy little place out of Edward Hopper's *Nighthawks*, as if we had been summoned to Potsdam by the president. We scrunched up to a mottled black-and-gray Formica-topped table, so tiny our knees clunked together.

I sipped at a cup of hot chocolate, water-based, with little globs of cocoa bubbling up and scattering sugary dust across the top. The cloying stench of deep-fried sugar nearly made me gag, but he insisted we had to talk. At this moment and in this place.

"Look, I . . . I don't know how to put this, I . . ." He stared into his empty Styrofoam cup, nervously breaking off tiny nodules from the rim, dismantling the cup until it was a half-inch high and full of confetti.

I had to be on guard with Terry. I never knew what might pop out. He rambled on. He squirmed and started to take a sip—of what? Styrofoam

BBs? He scooted the chair back. It squealed like a wounded pig. He saluted with his mangled cup. "More cocoa?"

"Nah, one's too many."

He fled to the counter and hustled back, plopping a new cup on the table.

"Okay, look, I have to say this: You've changed. I mean, I've . . . we've . . . I know this sounds stupid, but, dammit, Annie, I'm *falling* for you. You're . . ." He paused like a rabbit in the shadow of a diving hawk. "I'm crazy about you. Be my girlfriend?" He swallowed half the cup. He actually blushed.

Girlfriend?

After this stunning "proposal," he got that silly, lopsided grin of his. Digging into his pocket, he pulled out a ring and laid it like the Hope Diamond on the table. "I'm not a frat boy, so I don't have a pin. But this'll work. You can wear it on a chain like a necklace." The ring was wrapped with electrical tape, painted bubblegum pink by some long-ago girlfriend.

I couldn't stop laughing. This joke was better than those crazy "news" stories he used to spin when I worked at the *Daily*.

I scrutinized the ring like a jeweler. "Your *high school* class ring? Good Lord."

"How about my DeMolay ring? Or better yet, my super-special Lone Ranger decoder ring that set me back ninety-five cents and four box tops?"

"Nope. I've got to see diamonds, bud. At a minimum, rubies."

"Would you wear a locket? Or a broach? I've seen some nice ones at Kay Jewelers."

He was grinning like a doofus, but his tone had changed. No twinge of craziness. Jeez, he knew I was going to Germany in June to see Jack. "Uh, how about that refill? I've been broadsided by a Mack truck."

"Medic's on the way." Up instantly, he loped away. Back at our table, he said, "It's me again. My weird twin had to split." He was Mr. Cool, like nothing ever happened.

"Yep, I *knew* it was one of your jokes."

Or was it? We were pals again, but I felt warm and tender, not at all shocked. He carved new ideas about "us" in the air. Time evaporated. I lifted my hand to counter a comment, and our fingers touched, as if drawn together by magnets. Electricity sizzled. Not as profound as God giving Adam the spark of life, but palpable enough to kindle a warm burn in the pit of my stomach. The air was too thick to breathe. The doughnut shop had become a sweat lodge.

Maybe I could deal with this tomorrow or next week. Maybe. I jumped up. "We better skedaddle. I've got American lit at eight."

Terry as my *boyfriend*? Not possible. He was a great friend. I admired him. He could write. He could think. He stimulated my mind, challenged me, and pushed me to question the very foundations of my beliefs on religion, war and peace, and America's role in the world. He knew current events and loved literature and art. We could talk about anything. He had this quirky sense of humor that cracked me up. Kept me forever on my toes.

But romance? On that score, he wasn't right for me. We had kissed once, spring of my sophomore year. One night, we'd gone for a hike around Boulder Reservoir—a break from studying, like meeting for coffee, but without the coffee. It got windy and bitter cold. We squeezed into a niche in the riprap, snuggling together for warmth, and he kissed me.

Well, truth be told, I kissed him back.

Afterward, we didn't say a word, just jumped up and hiked out. A couple of days later, he brought it up. "Sorry, it was Puck and his fairy juice, not me at all."

I nodded. That was it. He remained my platonic friend. He wasn't out to see how far he could go sexually.

But now he expected me to follow that string of girls. No way would I do that.

Still, his "proposal" caused me sleepless nights and generated hours of heart-rending, mind-torturing reevaluation of our history. Besides that, what about his obsession with sex? That was one of the main reasons I'd given up on dating and set my sights on Jack.

Ultimately, I figured out that sex was an intoxicating, new adventure for Terry, like rafting or mountaineering. The previous summer, he and five friends had tackled the San Juan River in the badlands of Utah on three rubber rafts. He sent me his notes—twelve typewritten pages of vivid descriptions of swirling rapids, sheer cliffs towering overhead, emerald-green pools in barren rock, and the absolute joy of camping under the stars.

He approached sex the same way, recounting each exploit with unbridled zeal. Sometimes with Terry, you had to overlook the topic and concentrate on the enthusiasm.

What to do? My friend Julie lobbied for "the straight-arrow German guy." Her dismissiveness pushed me toward Terry. Besides, I couldn't walk away from him without exploring where we should go from here. For his sake, for Jack's, and for mine.

In the midst of my angst about Terry, student teaching, and supporting Gretchen, spring break swept in and gave me no respite at all. I had just a week to nail down a job for the fall before I left for Europe. But where? I'd endured too many frozen winters in Colorado. Albuquerque? Too close to home. California? Nah, I'd never be a "California girl" (whatever that was). Phoenix? Warm in winter. Halfway between Colorado and the coast. Rapid growth meant schools were hiring. Bingo.

I flew to Albuquerque, and Mom and I drove to Phoenix. Four interviews in three days.

Back in Boulder more than a week after Terry's professed change of heart, I laid it out for him: "You remember I'm on track for the romantic trip of a lifetime with Jack, don't you?"

"It's not too late to change your—"

"And that you've been helping me plan this trip?"

"I was a fool, I—"

"No, you were, and still are, my best friend. And best friends don't horn in on their friends' romances."

"But this is different. I've changed."

"So? What about me? You expect *me* to change on a dime?"

"Would you?" Terry's eyes lit up like the first streaks of dawn.

I backpedaled carefully. "I don't see how. Jack and I have built more than a castle in the air. We've got blueprints for a whole kingdom."

"Think about all we have. Four years of the best friendship ever. At least for *me*."

"Yeah, *friendship*, not—"

"Four years of working together. Of crazy adventures. Laughing and crying over the same things. Reading each other's minds. We're a great pair. We're meant to be together."

"But what you're suggesting feels, well, weird. It's too great a change."

Was I wrong? I didn't think so, but the question gnawed on me every waking hour in the days that followed. First, I had to admit that the intellectual exchange I'd hoped to share with a boyfriend had been there with Terry all along. And that friendship had laid a foundation of shared experiences and a let-our-hair-down knowledge of each other. We'd seen each other on both our best and our worst days. In the end, it was his incisive mind, quick wit, and passionate commitment to principles that I couldn't dismiss.

The next weekend, after burgers and shakes at McDonald's, Terry pulled up to drop me at my dorm as usual. The "girlfriend" proposal had hung in the air for more than two weeks, but neither of us had dared go near it. He didn't get out to open my door, as he always did. Nor did I make a move to leave. The lights from the dorm cast his face in full profile. We sat silently.

Finally he turned and reached for my hand. "It's time." He slid across the bench seat and kissed me—or me, him—our second "first" kiss.

After all the agonizing contemplation, it turned out to be a small step from *best* friend to *boy*friend.

Terry

Saturday, 21 March 1964, Boulder. Hot damn, a letter from the Peace Corps—from Sargent Shriver himself, offering me a position in Venezuela!

I would live in a shanty in Caracas, fighting poverty, working side by side with the locals to improve health care, sanitation, housing, education . . . everything. Three months of training to begin in June. I'd be in Venezuela by fall, speaking Spanish like a native.

I had waited so long for this and had thought it a pipe dream, even after the Peace Corps had written in November and said I'd been accepted for something the following summer. It was the first time I'd heard from them since turning them down, and the letter seemed generic—an "advance invitation"—no job description, no specific country, nothing to pin my hopes on. So, that invitation had been real after all.

I read and reread the four-page flyer Sargent Shriver had enclosed with his letter: "Venezuela: Urban Community Action." I would actually be a Peace Corps volunteer!

Then it hit me: I'd leave in June. So would Annie. Me to South America for two years, her to Europe to rendezvous with the West Point stud. God, what now?

Ann

April 1964, Boulder. Good news: Two weeks after my compressed trip to Arizona, I had a job to teach English at Glendale Union Senior High School near Phoenix. One less thing to worry about.

As my April 19 birthday neared, Terry let slip he had gotten me Turn-bull's *The Letters of F. Scott Fitzgerald*, a "must-read." And he'd made res-ervations in Denver on Sunday, my birthday, for dinner and *Becket*, the hot, new Richard Burton–Peter O'Toole movie. He asked me to "dress up a bit."

Dress up? Us? "My goodness, is this a date? A real date?"

"I got a corsage," he whispered, as if he feared I'd discover he was a romantic after all.

"Fair enough," I said. "I'll see if I can find a skirt to wear. Or my prom dress."

Late Thursday afternoon, April 16, I trudged into the dorm after a long stint in the library. A symphony of fragrances perfumed the lobby. Julie rushed up: "My God, Ann, what have you done? Promise that German guy the first three days in bed?"

What now? Julie's mouth could be as smutty as her weekend trysts. "Maybe later, huh?"

She marched me to the reception desk. "Look at these flowers. It's the flashiest let's-get-it-on offer I've ever seen. I'd go down with a guy for a week if he sent me that." She pointed to a huge bouquet of spring flowers in a sapphire blue crystal vase as stunning as a museum piece. The enve-lope read, "To my dearest Ann. From Jack." Wow, they *were* for me. No, not possible. Not from Germany.

"So open the card," Julie said. "How'd he send live flowers from Eu-rope anyway?"

This had to be a joke, something the girls in the dorm dreamed up. I hit Julie with the stink eye, but she was too busy ripping open the enve-lope to notice. I snatched it away, pulled out the card, and started to read aloud, but my voice choked off. "I've got to go."

Closeting myself in my room, I had that card memorized by dinner-time. I'm not a crier, but tears fell.

My dearest Ann: The vase in which these flowers arrived (unless the florist in Boulder double-crossed me) is the only one of its kind in the world. I had it designed and hand blown especially for you by a master German artisan. I hope you like it—because I also had him create two matching bowls, which should not be separated from the vase. So should I not be successful in my quest, you already know what your wedding present will be.
—All my love, Jack

I wrote to him that night. "I've never been more pleased, delighted, happy, ecstatic, thrilled. I can't imagine a luckier girl on earth. The flowers and vase are so beautiful I'm having a hard time keeping my eyes on this letter, even though I'm afire to share my joy with you. How can anyone be so wonderful?"

I was gushing out my love for Jack when Terry steamrolled into my mind, his eagerness for our "real date" Sunday, the way he glowed. I froze. Two guys, two irresistible guys, so distinct from one another, yet so alike, pulling me inexorably in opposite directions.

Only the night before, after a coffee date, I had embraced Terry like we were lovers. We kissed, a movie kiss, in the shadow cast by my dorm. Now I was writing this effusive letter to Jack. Worse, I meant every word, as I meant every word with Terry. But in my tight-knit family, the basic building block was *one* man, *one* woman, faithful to each other for life. Two men plus one woman? Never!

I couldn't resolve my quandary without hurting someone I deeply loved. And without forever losing one of them from my life. I ached for all of us. I had to focus on one person at a time, at least for the moment, and speak from my heart.

But I couldn't tell Jack about this development with Terry, not by letter. He would take it as a "Dear John." I had to tell him face-to-face. Somehow, I finished the letter to Jack. Somehow, I survived the night.

On my birthday, I wore my red sundress, sleeveless and scoop neck, a favorite from high school. For good measure, I dabbed a bit of perfume behind my ears, and took the dorm elevator to the lobby, instead of my normal clattering down the stairs. When the elevator opened and I waltzed into

the foyer like a debutante, Terry stammered, "Wow, you . . . you're beautiful!" I don't think he had ever seen me in a dress.

And that was the first time I had ever seen him in a tie and sport coat.
"Hey, mister. You look a lot like a good friend of mine, Terry Marshall.
Only much spiffier."

"I'm standing in for him. Chances are, he'd blow it, jab you with the
pin." He produced a crimson and white corsage and pinned it to my dress
with shaky hands.

"Can't fool me, even with the haircut. And what's this? You trimmed
your mustache." I ran my fingers over his freshly shaved chin, laid both
hands on his shoulders, focused squarely on his eyes. They sparkled. "I see
a Marshall prowling around in there."

In his scrubbed and buffed fire engine red Ford Falcon, he squired me
to a three-course dinner at a first-class Italian restaurant in Denver—with
waiters *and* cloth napkins. I told him, "I feel like Cinderella in Never Never
Land. What happened to us, Ter . . . at the doughnut shop?"

"Simple. I discovered the best thing in life. You! You make everything
smell better, taste better, look better. You make me want to be the best
person I know how to be."

This wasn't the Terry I had grown so comfortable with, a friendship
built on one-liners and wisecracks. He'd become downright charming, and
as he drove to the theater, I slid over, shoulder to shoulder, my thigh lightly
touching his, my hands clasped like a choir girl in my lap.

We got right to our seats—no wasting our money on greasy popcorn,
soda pop, or M&Ms—and *Becket* quickly drew us in: medieval England, the
debauched Henry II (Peter O'Toole) on the throne, and his lord chancel-
lor and best friend Thomas Becket (Richard Burton) constantly at his side.

Early in the story, Becket and his Gwendolen are in their bedchamber.
Gwendolen tells Becket how much she loves him, that she would follow him
anywhere. Henry intrudes and flops down beside Gwendolen on the bed
and caresses her breasts. Henry reminds Becket that some months earlier,
he had "given" Becket a peasant girl with the condition that Becket return
the favor upon demand. Becket had agreed.

I tense up. And yes indeed, Henry claims Gwendolen as payment . . .
that very night. Becket steams silently, but he consents.

In obvious agony, Gwendolen dutifully leaves Becket's bedchamber for

King Henry's. The scene shifts. Henry, grinning lasciviously, pulls open the opulent draperies of the royal bed. Gwendolen is stretched out in his bed, fully clothed. Blood pools around a dagger plunged into her chest. She has killed herself.

I grabbed Terry's arm and bowed my head against his shoulder. He leaned his head against mine. "You okay?"

"Whew, I saw it coming, but I still can't bear it," I whispered.

He stroked my arm, then held on, finally relaxing his grip as the plot thickened. But I was still with Gwendolen, holding her hand as life drained away. Grandiose music promised conflict ahead, but I couldn't focus. Terry's hand, now on my knee, squeezed rhythmically, in time with the music, and inched slowly up my thigh. Halfway up, I captured his hand and held it there for the rest of the movie.

The next day, before the glow of my date with Terry had worn off, I got a note from Jack, dated April 16. "Last night, I was seized, like never before, with this thought: 'Ann, I love you!' I want to write another letter with this single sentence, nothing else, because it is everything."

Terry

Monday, 4 May 1964, Boulder. A Western Union telegram from the Peace Corps: "The Venezuela Urban Community Action Program has been rescheduled for mid-August. We hope this will not disrupt your plans. Clennie H. Murphy, CHM Division of Selection."

Great. I had an extra two months to wait. How in the hell was I supposed to concentrate on my studies enough to graduate? And with Annie in Europe, what was I going to do all summer?

Saturday, 16 May 1964, Boulder. Heat wave! The radio said it could hit ninety today—a record high for this date.

Not a day for studies, so I called Annie, and midmorning, we drove up Boulder Canyon beyond the marked trails and hiked the creek. We were Charles Darwin on the HMS *Beagle* expedition, scrambling over boulders and logs, searching for new species of flora and fauna. We picnicked in a hidden glen and struck out on a deer path that led into thick brush. Drenched in sweat, we fought through and rounded a bend back to the creek. A flat-topped, pickup-size boulder rose from a broad, languid pool like a sacrificial altar in a moat-encircled Aztec temple. We worked our way to the pool's edge, paused like stone pillars, too awestruck to speak. I dropped my pack onto the rocky shore. I looked at Annie. She shrugged, as if to say, Why not?

In a flash, we stripped and plunged in. The water was glacial. We flailed across to the rock, clambered up, and claimed the altar as our own.

"Next time let's test the water *before* we jump in," I said.

"No kidding. But now what? We're totally exposed here."

Naked, Annie was a mermaid bathed in glistening droplets, the sun casting a golden sheen to her hair. She caught me leering, slapped her arms across her breasts, hunkered down, and buried her head against her knees, as if to make herself invisible. "Oh!" she cried out.

I was obviously turned on, but I didn't even try to cover up. "You are beautiful, you know that?"

She looked up. "All I know is there's nowhere to hide. And we don't have towels . . . or clothes. We'll have to bake dry." She stretched out on her stomach, resting her head on her arms.

I couldn't move. My mind took photo after photo. I beat back a host of salacious desires. I didn't know what to say.

"So join me," she said. "It's toasty warm down here."

I stretched out beside her. Eventually, we rolled onto our backs and then onto our sides, thrilled at our boldness. We gazed into each other's eyes. We kissed.

A twig snapped. I bolted upright. Annie flattened herself into the rock. "What if it's one of my students?" She was student teaching at Boulder High, but we were over an hour's drive from town and a hefty hike off the trail.

"Don't worry," I said. "We're alone." As if I knew.

We scrutinized the creek bank and woods and saw no one. We listened. Nothing but the babble of the creek. We braved the stream and dried off with our shirts, our eyes alert for intruders, but we were indeed alone. "Lucky us," she said.

Lucky me. I'd seen Botticelli's *Birth of Venus* come to life.

↩

Ann

Late May 1964, Boulder. My life was a treadmill on overdrive. I had been student teaching part time, producing daily lesson plans, and trying to read a novel a week for my lit class. Now, term papers loomed. Finals threatened. Visiting Gretchen and writing letters to her continued to consume hours.

Amid all that, Terry and I celebrated spring on pure adrenalin, free and uninhibited by our former fare of politics and world events. We replaced coffee breaks with romantic dinners. We went on late night strolls and to a Joan Baez concert in Denver.

One Friday afternoon we took off early because Terry wanted me to get to know Silverton, where he'd worked the previous summer—a 435-mile drive from Boulder over four mountain passes. We stayed up half the night with a new buddy, sipping wine, debating solutions for Cuba, Iran, and the Iron Curtain, and belting out folk songs, and then crashed on his living room floor.

The next day, we hiked partway up Sultan Mountain, puffing and wheezing before we made it to ten thousand feet. We munched Braunschweiger and cheese on sourdough, napped in the sun, and hiked along El Rio de las Animas Perdidas—River of Lost Souls—stopping to skip stones across the snow-fed water. Glassy-eyed, we dragged ourselves back to Boulder in time for our classes Monday morning.

In the final heady week before I left for Europe, both of us dared to whisper, "I love you."

Meanwhile, Jack's letters hit a feverish pace, each one another plaintive cry, couched in wit or silliness, but always guilt-inducing and gut-wrenching—leaving me fearful I'd lose him:

> *Just took a lethal dose of poison guaranteed to end my misery by Monday afternoon. But to demonstrate human weakness, I've kept an antidote to prevent untimely demise in the glorious event a timely epistle arrives from you.*

> *Still no mail. Efficiency has dropped to zero. Three sergeants had to hold me back from choking the mail clerk. Tomorrow I'll fool them all.*

*Will have a pistol ready with two bullets—one for the mail clerk and
the other for me. And I don't miss. What I do miss is mail from you.*

By the first of June, I was caught between an amazing young officer
enticing me to join him in Germany as a prelude to a life together and my
closest friend tugging me toward challenging, new horizons.

What to do? Jack had leaped all my mental hurdles and now proposed a
once-in-a-lifetime grand tour of Europe. We owed it to each other to follow
the silken threads we'd spun over the previous two years. The exhilarating
new feelings for Terry hadn't changed how I felt about Jack. Rather, it made
the long-anticipated trip with Jack more imperative as a foil for deciding
what was important to me in my life partner. I told Terry I simply had to
carry through with the European trip.

Besides, the plane tickets were nonrefundable.

By June 4, I felt like a lion tamer in the ring with two hungry lions,
warily circling.

3
Castles in the Air

Ann

Tuesday, June 9, 1964, en route to Europe. Under the command of "Drill Sergeant Mom," my three days at home were a postgraduate girl's boot camp. Speed-shop at one mandated mall after another. Stow away four years of academic life. Pack for Europe. Pay obligatory visits to family friends. Absorb military protocols for dress and behavior. I had no time for my final must-do task: Make a pitch to Gretchen Schumacher to give her baby up for adoption.

The day before Mom arrived to fetch me in Boulder, Terry and I had made a quick trip to Denver to see Gretchen and her new daughter, born less than twenty-four hours earlier. Gretchen hadn't decided whether to keep the child, but regardless, she said she would leave Colorado. Maybe go home to Germany. More likely to California, where her brother lived.

Even in the face of these momentous decisions, she was the same cheerful, beautiful young woman I had first met in January. I devoted full attention to her, resisting the urge to peek at the baby in the nursery. An article I'd read warned that a mother planning to give up a child for adoption shouldn't hold or even see her baby. It made the separation too difficult. I assumed the same applied to aunts. How draconian.

As soon as my plane lifted off from Albuquerque, I pulled stationery from my overnight bag. Scrawled a few words. Crossed them out. Started again. Got stuck again. Texas and Missouri and Ohio slipped by below as I tried to find the right words—me of all people, weighing in on the future of my brother's illegitimate child and her mother, after I told myself throughout the spring *not* to do it.

My letter was rooted in the fifties, when girls like Gretchen had to face societal condemnation for premarital pregnancy. Too often, the man sauntered off unscathed. Even when the guy stood by the girl, the burden of humiliation fell on mother and child. I cringed at the hypocrisy!

Nevertheless, society's prejudices were real, and my letter encouraged Gretchen to think of her and her daughter's future. Both of them would be stigmatized for life. What would the daughter say when friends asked about her father? For a woman who kept her baby, the lifelong responsibility of raising a child alone was even more troubling. "I remain convinced that adoption is the best solution—both for you, and for your daughter," I wrote.

Just before we landed in New York, I offered a vapid apology for suggesting she do what I might not have been able to do. I sealed my letter and dropped it in a mailbox in the airport.

Terry

Tuesday, 9 June 1964, Center, Colorado. Home from school, a college graduate at last. For the first time since I was fourteen, I had a summer free. I had hired on at my hometown newspaper after my freshman year of high school and worked there every day after school, every Saturday, and every summer through graduation. Two weeks out of high school, I moved to Boulder before enrolling at CU and spent the summer working at the University of Colorado Printing Services.

During college, I'd worked every summer as a reporter, one at the *Center Post-Dispatch*, two at the *Valley Courier* in Alamosa, and the summer of 1963 at the *Silverton Standard*.

It had taken me five years to graduate. After my dad was killed in the spring of 1961, Annie convinced me to return to CU that fall. I did, but my heart wasn't in it. My grades fell from As and Bs to mostly Cs. I dropped out for a semester and worked full time as a printer at the *Boulder Daily Camera*, a welcome break from school. I was also paying my own way through college. I needed the money.

This summer I had no stories to write. No deadlines to meet. My Peace Corps training for Venezuela wouldn't begin until August 10. After five years of college, I was free.

But at what cost? Annie was spending her summer traipsing around Europe with the dashing lieutenant and wouldn't get back to the States until a week *after* I left for the Peace Corps. It would be more than two years before I'd see her again.

I couldn't turn down the Peace Crops a second time. They'd blackball me forever.

But before Annie left for Europe, I told her I loved her. She said she loved me too. We even flirted with the idea of marriage. Now she was off gallivanting with Jack the Stud. If she didn't come home with an engagement ring, what were the chances she'd be there for me after my two years in Venezuela? Slim to minus ten. But what if I said no to the Peace Corps and she came home engaged to Lieutenant Sigg? I would lose both her *and* the Peace Corps.

The what-ifs were stalking me like a pack of wolves.

I had two months to fill before I left for the Peace Corps, and they would crawl by in slow motion if I spent every day pining for Annie. So I devoted my first day to building a bookcase. The second day, I dismantled an old floor lamp and attached it to my bedstead. I rounded up my two brothers—Greg, fourteen; Randy, twelve—and we raked and burned last fall's dried weeds and yard trash. After dinner, I took them to *Lawrence of Arabia*.

Day three: That night, Annie would be staying in Paris, en route to Germany. I mounted my photos of her in her nightie to my headboard and pretended I was with her in a swanky Parisian hotel room. That thought kept me panting half the night.

Ann

Wednesday, June 10, 1964, Munich, Germany. Thud! The wheels connected with the runway while I was digging for breath mints. Surely he wouldn't try to kiss me, but just in case. I gathered up my overnight bag, finger-combed my hair, and filed into the aisle. How should I greet him? What if I didn't recognize him? Where would we begin our in-person romance? As we inched toward the door, I realized I was hyperventilating. I took several deep breaths, stepped from the plane onto the stairs, and ordered my knees to stop quaking.

"Aha, Miss Colorado at last," a familiar voice boomed. "No! It's Miss

America. Welcome to Bavaria. Welcome to the adventure of a lifetime."
He was at the foot of the stairs in the bright afternoon sun. Here on the
tarmac, splendid in army greens and spit-shined shoes, with a smile that
swallowed his face. Beside him, not Bonner, but a smartly dressed man
wearing some kind of airport badge.

Jack presented his elbow as if we were about to stride into the graduation ball at West Point. "Come, *Fräulein*. Your chariot awaits. And thanks
to my new friend here, we'll be on the road in record time."

The official nodded, a barely perceptible head-erect gesture that people
in authority give to their men. "It is my privilege to meet you, *Fräulein*,"
he said, his accent obviously German. With that, we veered away from the
other passengers into a separate door, and he whisked me through immi-
gration and customs. No lines. No waiting.

At the curb, the man shook Jack's hand and turned to me. "Miss Garretson, enjoy our *Deutschland. Auf Wiedersehen*." He stepped back, executed
a snappy turn, and disappeared into the terminal.

"Wow, how'd you manage that?" I asked.

"Let's say it pays to speak German—and wear a uniform—in Germany."

Side by side, we stood awkwardly, Lieutenant Jack Sigg and I, dear
friends, yet strangers meeting as if for the first time.

"Bonner's at the border. Said he's dying to see you." Jack guided me to
his gleaming white Corvette, top down, the Sting Ray he'd written about.

What a sleek, low-slung machine, something out of the movies! He
jockeyed my bag into the tiny trunk and escorted me to my seat. Wow, I
should have worn my white gloves and ball gown—it was that elegant. This
was no mere car, but an intimate two-person capsule. I didn't *sit* in this
baby. I *fit* myself into it, strapped in, and awaited takeoff. Moments later,
we zoomed away, me a modern-day Isadora Duncan—but wise enough
not to trail a long scarf. Germany at last.

I was a wide-eyed tourist, trying to memorize every detail of the landscape
as it whizzed by. I had a 360-degree view, but every three seconds, I glanced
over at this handsome officer. Jack was doing ninety, zipping through the
curves as if an archrival were hot on his bumper. My hair whipped about
like straw in a cyclone.

He was every bit the man I remembered. A tad more muscular, perhaps.

And ruddier. Outdoorsy, a guy who spent time in the sun, but not with the red face and pasty forehead of a rancher. Ramrod straight, square-jawed, so clean-shaven his skin glowed. The hint of a cowlick swirled above his right temple, almost shaved away with his burr cut, but visible nonetheless. Bushy eyebrows. And a pointy nose—not ugly or distracting, merely pointy.

What else will we discover about each other, Lieutenant Sigg?

He caught me staring and shouted, "Great wheels, huh?" His devilish grin assured me this indeed would be a summer to remember.

Around us, suburbs encroached on verdant fields dotted with white farmhouses. A city sprang up. "Almost home," he called. He gestured ahead to a massive red-roofed white building perched on a hilltop above the city, dominating the skyline. "The castle I wrote you about, Trausnitz. Dates to 1204. Grand, isn't she?" It looked more like a grand dame hotel than a castle—no drawbridge or turrets, clearly stuccoed and painted. "And site number two on our tour: St. Martin's Cathedral." He pointed. "The bell tower is the tallest brick steeple in Europe."

Jack slowed. We rolled through an arch in a daunting brick fortification, as thick as the Great Wall. Inside, the city was a movie set ready for lights, camera, action. Pink, blue, and yellow four- and five-story buildings rose beside shiny black cobblestone streets, freshly scrubbed. The cathedral loomed before us, its tower jutting up like a gargantuan sentry.

"Welcome to old Landshut, *Fräulein*," he said. "But look quickly. I need to finish a few things at the office. We'll take the full tour later. *Deutschland* style. On foot."

"What? No drawbridge? What's a medieval fortress without a drawbridge?"

He grinned. Another thing I hadn't noticed: his cockeyed grin. "Tell you what—if it's a drawbridge you want, I'll build you one."

We glided through the old town and five minutes later pulled up to a drab barracks. No entry checkpoint or signs, but clearly an army base. Jack shepherded me from of the Sting Ray and heaved out my suitcase. "Your home away from home, Landshut's finest BOQ. My quarters and your brother's are across the parking lot, a quick sprint if you need anything."

"How racy. I'll be staying with a gang of bachelor officers?"

"Not a chance. These days, this BOQ houses female teachers and married couples."

He carried my bag like he was an orderly, not my prospective fiancé, and introduced me to a pair of young women who could easily have been dorm mates at CU. Both taught at the US Army's school for dependent children. They had agreed to put me up for the summer.

Jack raced off. I turned to my benefactors and barely mustered a decent greeting, my world swirling in fog. When I went on to explain how exhausted I was from the long flights, jet lag, and my overnight in Paris, it came out mush. One of them steered me into a bedroom.

I didn't wake up until early afternoon the next day, fully clothed in a strange bed, my brain as rumpled as my blouse. Nagging worry had offered no harbor for rest. I had to tell Jack about Terry. From the beginning of our airmail romance, we had promised to be one hundred percent honest with each other. Fie on excuses. I had broken the promise. Time to confess.

I practiced, but everything came out shallow and stupid. "Jack, something has come up I need to tell you about . . ." No! "Jack, remember my best buddy, Terry?" Ack! "Jack, I've wanted to tell you this, but . . ." No, no, no. What if he called the whole deal off?

Terry

Friday, 12 June 1964, Center. Day four at home. First, I had to finish Mom's to-do list: replace the loose board on the back steps, muck out the chicken coop, and make sure Greg and Randy finished mowing the grass and pulling the weeds from the ditch bank.

Afterward, fun and games. But you can play only so much three-person basketball on a gravel driveway, trying to fling a gritty ball through a hoop hanging by baling wire from the side of a potato cellar. Or fungo, whacking a baseball into an alfalfa field or over a sheep shed and then spending the next half hour searching for it.

Noon mail: none for me. After lunch, I wrote to Annie again—my third letter in a week—four pages, typed single-spaced. Enough! I dug out my sleeping bag and took off for Valley View, a natural hot springs at an abandoned 1920s resort in the Sangre de Cristo Mountains, forty-five miles away. I invited the boys, telling them I was going there to read Shakespeare. They hooted and raced off.

⌒

Valley View Hot Springs. Off the beaten path. Deserted, but not decrepit, and with an artesian hot-water swimming pool. No visitors. You could skinny-dip here. And you could see the entire San Luis Valley, a hundred miles north to south, from Poncha Pass to the New Mexico border, and fifty miles east to west, from the Sangre de Cristo Range to the San Juan foothills.

Nights were spectacular: a billion stars, no neon. From poolside, I could see a smattering of miniscule towns that dotted the inky valley below, each a tiny cluster of streetlights. Random headlights streaked from cluster to cluster, and here and there, a pinprick of light in a farmyard appeared. No engines, sirens, radios, or human voices. Only the occasional yelp of a coyote.

I made a fire, roasted hot dogs, guzzled a couple cans of Olympia, and spread out my sleeping bag ten feet from the pool—prelude to a hop, skip, and jump into its steamy depths in the morning. Minutes later, as at home, memories of Annie hijacked the night . . . not our May photo shoot, but the camping trip up James Creek the previous fall.

It hadn't been a ploy to lure her into a night of lechery but rather a spur-of-the-moment caper. She was my buddy. I had no romantic designs on her in those days. Saturday's forecast had been for a high of eighty-three, astoundingly hot for Boulder in October and not a day to waste in the library. Sarah, my girlfriend at the time, had snorted when I suggested a campout. She was a city girl. New York City! No interest. None.

I called Annie. She thrived in the outdoors. Besides, I missed her. Our Sunday nights at McDonald's had faded away since I'd taken up with Sarah. Annie bought in, and off we went.

James Creek wasn't Silverton. No snowcapped fourteeners or mountain-goat trails that turned your thighs to Jell-O, but instead, a shaded path along a cheerful stream, a quiet refuge in the foothills. We hiked. We splashed in the creek. We chomped thick burgers and wiped our hands on our jeans. After dinner, we emptied a bottle of wine and talked far into the night. I went on and on about Sarah and me. Probably too much detail, but Annie was as much fascinated as shocked by my sudden and unlikely partner in the loss of my virginity. All she could say was "Sarah? That older girl in J-School? Miss Lipstick? No!"

Annie was still my best friend. But something had changed over the summer. It wasn't as if she had metamorphosed from caterpillar to monarch butterfly. She'd always been a cutie, even though I teased her mercilessly about her freckles. After the fire died out, I wanted to slip into her bedroll, but I didn't tell her that. I did dare touch her foot with mine, albeit through the padding of my sleeping bag. I felt guilty, sleeping with Sarah, lusting after Annie, but desire overpowered guilt. Annie didn't notice my subtle move, I was sure. She didn't tease me about it, not once.

We finally slept. At dawn, the crisp morning air whisked away the night's illicit thoughts. We stirred up a robust breakfast, cleaned up the campsite, and spent the day hiking the hills.

That campout may indeed have marked a shift in our friendship, but only as an exercise in revisionist history. It wasn't until March 1964 that I finally realized Annie was my Juliet. I wowed her at the doughnut shop, and afterward, everything changed.

At Valley View Hot Springs that June night, Annie's image blotted out the starry sky. Before she left for Europe, we had filled a storehouse of memories. With her gone, the road to the Peace Corps at summer's end threatened to be a lonely trek through a bleak desert. With no shoes. No water. And a full pack of stone-heavy yearnings.

I had planned to spend the weekend at Valley View, hike a trail or two, and attempt an assault on 14,300-foot-high Crestone Peak. But Annie's likeness called me from every boulder and bush. I abandoned Valley View for the comfort of the farm, hot meals, and a soft bed.

And the hope that each new day would bring me a letter from Germany.

Ann

Friday, June 12, 1964, Landshut, Germany. I shivered in the frigid predawn as Jack packed the Sting Ray for a weekend getaway to southern Bavaria.

"Cold?" Jack asked.

I nodded. My cute new bolero was all show and no substance. He put the top up.

Time now to get acquainted, beyond our airmail images. And somehow I had to tell him about Terry. But after the VIP greeting in Munich and most of Thursday lost to sleep, we were wordless, cloistered side by side in his hot rod. I sneaked a peek and caught him gazing at me. "A picture may be worth a thousand words," I blurted out, "but the real thing beats a thousand pictures . . . if I only knew what to say."

He nodded sheepishly.

"You tongue-tied too, the one who can talk endlessly on tape?"

"I need my notes," he said. "What's your excuse?"

"I need my typewriter."

Our confessions broke the ice. Jack launched into an animated treatise on Bavarian farming as we whizzed through the crazy quilt of farm plots, varying in color from forest and olive green to sepia, tan, and ecru. "They're mostly small family farms," he said. "They sell their fresh meat and produce locally. Germans don't waste a square inch of land."

"So different from the American West," I said. "Our ranch in Colorado sprawled over two thousand acres, but the land was so beset with tumbleweeds, rabbit brush, and Russian thistle that our spread supported only two hundred head of cattle."

"That's the West for you. Huge tracts of land dedicated to relatively small output." He glanced over at me. "But tell me more about you. What was it like for an army brat turned cowgirl? The transition must have been tough."

"Not really. We army brats learn to adapt. As for the ranch, I loved the expanse of the valley, the sunrises, sunsets, and especially the night sky. Under a full moon, the landscape was magical. On moonless nights, the stars seemed to burn tiny holes in the sky, and it was so dark I could see forever—into the Milky Way and beyond."

"*Ja*, I remember that from my short visit. The huge sky made me feel both Lilliputian and Brobdingnagian at the same time."

I sniggered. "Whoa, that's pretty Swiftian of you."

"Just trying to talk your language, ma'am. You did major in lit, after all. But back to the night sky. It was exhilarating. Too bad we didn't 'discover' each other then." He gave a sly smile.

"I figured you were being nice to me only because I was your roommate's little sister."

"Ha! Do you recall that Bonner and I went out with a couple of girls while I was at the ranch?"

I nodded. How could I forget?

"I don't know where he dug up my date, but get this—I was secretly happy it was a bust. I thought it would enhance my standing with you!"

"If I'd only known! It could've saved me a lot of anxiety in the university dating scene." He laughed, and I was feeling more relaxed with this man than I ever expected. The miles, or kilometers, melted away.

Two hours later, the road teased the foothills of the Bavarian Alps. The azure sky played cat and mouse with the lush mountains, dipping into gorges, running up forested hillsides, and dancing on jagged peaks. Eventually, Jack turned off the main road and pulled into a parking lot. "Ready to feast your eyes on German opulence? This is Linderhof Palace, built by King Ludwig of Bavaria. One of three."

Now a tour guide, Jack spun tales of how King Ludwig had built the castles as stages for Wagner's operas, particularly *Lohengrin* and *Tannhäuser*, and that Linderhof had one of the world's first electric power stations.

In one chamber, we saw ourselves repeated endlessly by mirrors on all sides, vanishing into infinity. Jack escorted me in a circle and whispered, "Look. We, we, we, we, we . . . forever. How's that for a thought?"

Was that a proposal—after only three days? Was I ready for this? I smiled but said nothing.

Soon we were off to Neuschwanstein, zigzagging up a backcountry road through a thick forest. He entertained me with tidbits about King Ludwig: the engineering marvels in this castle, the kitchen so modern for its time, and the forced-air heating, unlike other medieval castles. And the sad fact that it was completed many years after his death.

Jack stopped at a high overlook. Ahead of us a snowy white castle perched impossibly on a spindly cliff, its spires disappearing into the clouds. "Behold! The famous Neuschwanstein!"

Truly the stuff of fairy tales. We leaned silently on the rail, shoulders touching. Softly, he said, "My castles in the air—for us—are even grander. But come. Ready for another explore?"

Castles in the air? Really? I was afraid to ask. I straightened up and hooked my hand through the crook of his elbow. "All right, Lieutenant. Lead on!"

Inside, nonstop opulence: drawing room, bedroom, throne room (never finished)—on and on, all with exquisite artworks, elaborate brocades, intricate wood carvings, and mosaics, until we were satiated. Jack sensed my weariness. "How about we find ourselves something to eat and a nice no-frills guesthouse for the night?"

"Yes, enough with King Midas of Bavaria," I said, and he whisked us off to Füssen, a village nestled nearby. We ambled down the narrow streets and tried to imagine what life must have been like for the haves—and the have-nots—in Ludwig's time.

Ah, Füssen. A bouquet of colors: pastel storefronts, red roofs, and bright window boxes, a welcome relief from lavish castles. Here was the small-town Germany I had expected—an artisan selling hand-carved wooden music boxes, an antiquarian bookseller with elegant leather-bound books in German, French, and English, a ladies' clothier, where Jack bought me a scarf "to keep your curls intact."

"Perfect choice for your warp speed hot rod." I wound the scarf around my head, gritted my teeth, and squinted my eyes like a race car driver.

He belly-laughed. "Okay, okay. Message received! I'll try to slow down."

The aroma of fresh bread lured us into a tiny café. He ordered in German, and in minutes the waitress returned. "For our special guest, we have *der haut Chocolat und der Strawberry Tart.*"

I'd written to Jack about a vivid memory from my 1957 trip there with my parents: a wild-strawberry tart, the berries picked in the morning and baked into a mouth-watering confection. "My favorite! How'd you know?"

"I pay attention to the important stuff."

After dinner, we lingered in the hall outside my postage-stamp-size room at a small inn, as awkward as seventh-graders on a first date. I expected him to kiss me good night, but he stood there, hemming and hawing about what a great day we'd had. My feet ached. My legs were wobbly. "I'm beat. I really have to turn in."

"Don't go. Please. Not yet," he said. "If you leave, I won't survive until morning."

"What, you'll change into a pumpkin overnight? How would I get back to Landshut?"

He lifted an unruly curl from my face and laid his hand on my cheek. "This is the only thing that will save us." He tucked a finger under my chin, and our lips met for the first time. He didn't close his eyes. Me either. His lips were soft and warm, and he smelled of fresh bread. But he pulled back—not far, an eyelash or two—before the kiss fully matured. "Or this."

His lips brushed mine before he moved in for a long, delicious taste. "Or something like this." He took my head in his hands, but he held back, his mouth tantalizingly beyond reach.

You're a tease, Jack Sigg. Okay, game on. I edged away. His hands tightened. He kissed me again, this time hard, pressing in. He pulled away ever so slowly, and I nibbled at his lip. We kissed until my pulse was racing. "And I thought the fairy-tale castle and storybook town were spectacular." I spread my fingers on his chest. "You, my far-more-than-friend, have made this day unforgettable. How can I ever sleep?"

"Come to my room. I'll rock you to sleep."

"Sounds tempting. But terribly dangerous, wouldn't you say?"

"I'll protect you, I—"

"From what? Your all-too-obvious desires?" *Or my own?*

He reddened. "You're right. I'm not the one to protect you from me, am I?" He held both hands up. "Good night, my dearest." He pivoted like a cadet on the parade grounds and raced off.

He left me zinging, like I had been after Terry's kisses turned friendship into a romance.

Oh, what *about* Terry? What was I going to tell him? But worse, what was I going to tell Jack about Terry? And when?

I woke up Saturday relishing Jack's good-night kisses. So far, he had exceeded my wildest hopes. Item one: He honored my wishes at the door last night with respect and grace. Item two: He knew so much about Europe, history, music. Item three: He made great choices. Where to go? Neuschwanstein, Linderhof, and Füssen. How to make me feel special? A strawberry tart.

A tapping at my door crept into my reverie, followed by a stage whisper. "*Fräulein?* Sun's up. It begs you to help light up my world." Oh, yes, Item four: He thinks like a poet.

"Be right there. Don't run off." I dressed in three minutes and creaked the door open.

He was leaning against the wall, cradling a handful of wild strawberries. "For you, my dear. They flagged me down on my morning run and said, 'Take me to your lover.' Who knew strawberries could talk?" He popped a couple into my mouth.

I kissed his fingers. "Ah, tasty. And fresh as a mountain morning!"

After breakfast we hiked into the hills along a stream to a narrow spot with protruding rocks. Jack leaped across and offered his hand. I found secure footing on an angular rock and swung toward a small boulder. The rock rolled. Jack yanked me in a hair-raising flight over the stream and caught me in both arms. Grinning, he swung me around and set me down triumphantly.

We darted off, in and out among the trees, discovering mushrooms and spying on rabbits and squirrels. At a wooden footbridge we crossed to a meadow, a riot of dainty white flowers strewn on a green carpet.

"Look! Is this edelweiss?" I fell to my knees, drawing in the scent of the Alps.

He knelt beside me. "With these guys, the magic is in the details. Each bloom is a cluster of miniature flowers. And notice its hairy stem—extra insulation against the icy air. They thrive in the mountains."

Just like Jack. And Terry. Both thrived in the mountains. I wanted to snatch them up, plant them in my imaginary highland retreat, and revel in the joy each gave me. But the rain clouds of my impending confession to Jack threatened. How could I spoil such an idyllic morning? I promised myself I would tell him later.

Back in Landshut Saturday night, Helmut, the graying proprietor of a hole-in-the-wall café, welcomed us as if Jack were a lost son returned from the Foreign Legion. Ogling me as if I were a chorus-line dancer, the man pulled me protectively to his side and seemed to lay out boundaries for Jack's behavior, supported by finger wagging and head shaking. Jack sputtered, denying whatever suggestive breeches Helmut had implied. I edged away. They keeled over in back-slapping merriment.

Helmut caught his breath. "I welcome you to my little *Gasthaus, Fräulein*," he boomed. "Jack is a good boy." He ushered us into a small dining room and bowed deeply. "*Fräulein*, excuse me. I must speak *Deutsch* to my friend Jack." After their brief exchange, Jack and I were alone, face-to-face across the table. He settled into the booth as if he were at home in his favorite easy chair. There would never be a better time. "Jack, I want—"

"I've already ordered. Helmut makes the best goulash that will ever pass your lips."

I offered a sick smile and took a deep breath. "Jack, I—"

"You know, if things don't work out in the army, we could settle in some little burg in Pennsylvania, open Helmut's first branch in the US, and serve the best goulash in America."

He had this blissful look on his face, as if here, day four in Germany, he had proposed, I had accepted, and any moment Helmut would march in with the wedding cake. *Run a goulash café? In Pennsylvania? Oh no!* "Jack, there's something we need to—"

Helmut burst in, waving a pair of wine glasses and a short, round bottle, flattened, like it had been left in the desert sun and half melted. With a flourish, he muscled out the cork, offered a sip to Jack, beamed when Jack signaled approval, and poured. As suddenly as he had appeared, this whirling dervish left us in privacy.

Now. I had to do it now. "Jack, we have to talk about—"

"I thought Germany meant beer. Wrong. Helmut swears German wines are a better drink for lovers. See this bottle—a *Bocksbeutel*, a Bavarian wine." He lofted his glass. "Here's to bright beginnings."

We clinked glasses, and quaking innards and thick tongue be damned, I barreled ahead. "Jack, I never imagined we'd have so much to explore when I started dreaming about you two years ago. I was thrilled when—"

"Hey, this is a celebration. You're making me nervous."

"I'm a bit nervous myself. Things got . . . complicated before I left Boulder. I, well—"

"I knew this was too good to be true! It's about my competitor, isn't it? That *old buddy* of yours?"

"Ah, sort of. It's so totally unexpected. Actually, I—"

"Gretchen tried to warn me. I thought she was nuts."

Gretchen? I'd never said a word to her about Terry. I swallowed hard. "I don't know what she told you, but let me explain. I—"

"Sure. Go ahead. Explain." He folded his arms and pushed back in the booth.

I soldiered on. "A couple of months ago, Terry and I went for coffee. Nothing special. We'd done it dozens of times, and out of the blue, he said he'd . . . fallen for me. I—"

"Yeah, right, 'out of the blue,' as if—"

"Darn it, Lieutenant. Do you know how to listen? This is tearing me apart. You're making it worse." I couldn't lose control or start bawling like some fluffy-headed nincompoop. I took a deep breath, crossed my arms, and returned his glare.

"Sorry. I'm listening. I really am."

"Is that a promise?"

"Affirmative," he said under his breath.

"So, Terry's going on, pretending he's some heartsick suitor. He pulls out his high school class ring, asks me to be his girlfriend. The ring still has a thick wad of tape—painted bubblegum pink—wrapped around it so it would fit some long-ago girlfriend's finger. I'm laughing. Finally, I realize he's serious. And, well, it got complicated after that. And now, we're . . . we're more than old friends."

"Exactly Gretchen's words, 'more than old friends.' I thought she made it up because . . ." A sardonic smile twisted his mouth. "Well, because she hoped she and I might get together."

Gretchen and *Jack*? I stared at him. "You mean you and Gret—"

"Absolutely not. I jumped in because Bonner abandoned her. The poor girl needed help. There's nothing between us. Never has been. I swear."

I can be naive, but everything about him said he was telling the truth. Still, Gretchen's betrayal threatened my resolve. I wanted to shout, *She's wrong. It's only you I care for!*

But she wasn't wrong. Maybe she saw it before I did. After all, Terry and I had spent hours with her. But I forced myself to confine Gretchen and Bonner's affair to a locked closet. It was Terry, not Gretchen, that Jack and I had to deal with. "Look, a four-year friendship like Terry's and mine doesn't do a one-eighty overnight. I reminded him about you, about *our* hopes, yours and mine, not only for this summer, but for life. He'd been my greatest supporter for this trip. In fact, back in January, he urged me to make love—with *you*! On our first night together."

He looked as startled as I'd hoped, but said nothing.

"If it's any consolation, this has been heart-wrenching for us both."

"Sure. It was that camping trip, wasn't it? Last October. October 4! Isn't that what your letter said . . . your oh-so-matter-of-fact letter?"

Oh no! The camping trip with Terry. Those memories flooded my mind: Indian summer. Friday afternoon. Terry had called, "Let's go camping. Tomorrow. James Creek."

Him and his jokes. Always on the wrong side of propriety. "Sure. And afterward, we could take your jet to New York for the Philharmonic. Shall I pack my high-heel tennies?"

"I'm serious. Bring Julie. This weather can't hold much longer."

"So, you're hot for my roommate. You like tall, sexy blondes, eh?"

"Nah, it's only an off-campus break before midterms. What better antidote to cramming for exams than a night under the stars with friends?" My resolve cracked. I said I'd think about it. Julie wasn't a camper, but surprisingly, she bought in. I accepted.

Next morning, Julie backed out. When I called Terry with the showstopper, he said, "So what time do we leave?"

"Go by ourselves? You and me?"

"Why not?"

Overnight alone with a man? I'd never done anything so daring. But I didn't have a good excuse. Perfect weather. Terry was safe. Besides, my dorm mother had signed a permission slip, allowing me to be out overnight. In those days of *in loco parentis*, the university acted as its students' parents, zealously guarding the virtue of its women. Coeds had to live in approved housing, with curfews and sign-out slips that detailed where and when we were going and with whom. No one ever forfeited a hard-to-earn pass to be out overnight. *Go ahead Ann, be bold for once.* So I went.

We hiked up James Creek to the trail's end and kept going, ending in a small dell near a beaver pond. As the light faded, we sculpted sleeping pads on a three-inch-deep bed of pine needles and built a roaring fire, nursing it to glowing coals. Our grilled burgers were four times as thick and juicy as our normal McDonald's fare and so delicious we sucked the drippings from our fingers.

Night fell. Within our cocoon of firelight, we settled in to a high-fidelity concert: the gurgling, cascading creek, nature's own *perpetuum mobilé*, beavers on percussion, their slaps accenting the rhythm, and wind song high in the trees dictating the melody. I propped myself against a log, knees up, philosophical and content. Terry had secreted wine glasses in his backpack. We toasted each other and gloated about the poor chumps back in Boulder cloistered in the library.

By the time we crawled into our bedrolls, I was on sensory overload. The full moon casting the trees into an army of unearthly guards over our glen, the cacophony of unfamiliar sounds, the light show in the glittering sky, the discordant pungency of forest—fragrant pine and rushing virgin stream tinged with whiffs of mold, decay, humid earth, and campfire—and that pervasive Chianti-fueled warmth inside. This night oozed passion.

"How come you're not sleeping?" Terry's whisper was an octave lower than usual.

Hmm, so he couldn't sleep either. "It's too beautiful. Too overwhelming. Too scary."

"Yeah, more than you would believe. But you're not really scared, are you?"

"Yeah, I guess. It's pretty isolated." The night sounds unnerved me, yes, but what scared me was the unsettling warmth of his presence. He was my buddy, not my boyfriend. I tried to will myself asleep, but I couldn't. I settled on trying to imagine it being Jack beside me, foot kneading mine. Luckily, Terry couldn't read my thoughts.

I had described the campout in a letter to Jack, the outdoorsy part anyway, not the romance of it. And certainly not my shameless fantasy of wishing he was *inside* my bedroll.

Now, across the dinner table from me in Landshut, Germany, Jack sat bolt upright, steely eyed. Troop Commander Sigg about to lower the boom on a guilty-as-charged private. I had no inkling last October how things would change between Terry and me. Nor that Jack thought "camping" was code for "sex." "I don't know. It was camping. It wasn't camping. It was lots of things. It's complicated."

"I'm a guy. The guy, by the way, who noticed you were a woman long before your *old buddy* did. It *was* the camping trip. I know it was."

"Well, nothing happened on that camping trip. Nothing sexual."

"Hard to believe. But it doesn't matter, does it?"

"It does to me. He was my friend, for crying out loud. I told him that. But, well, little by little, my feelings kind of began to change too. I guess I—"

"So why didn't you tell me sooner? Not lead me on like a—"

"Lead you on? And tell you what? That he offered me his high school ring? *My* feelings didn't change on a dime. In fact, I still don't know. Terry and I have so much history and—"

"So where does that leave *us*?"

"You and me? We're still the same people we were before. Whatever changed between Terry and me didn't change how I feel about you. So, here we are. I'm in Germany. With you. I plan to have a fabulous summer. Let's make it one for the ages."

"A few weeks together for us doesn't exactly level the playing field, does it?"

"Okay," I said at last. "If it makes you feel any better, he's pretty worried about you. He figures his Ford Falcon can't outrace your Sting Ray. And buying me a cup of coffee occasionally can't measure up to a tour around Europe."

Jack's face softened. His eyes gleamed. "So bubblegum pink tape on a class ring. And rejected by a high school kid?" He snickered. "Fair enough. Let the joust begin. No-holds-barred."

4

A Peek into the Cold War

Ann

Sunday, June 14, 1964, southern Bavaria. We took off again in the chilly predawn light, this time for the German-Czech border. We had a whole day before Jack had to check in for guard duty. Even so, he seemed to be racing to meet some unalterable deadline, as if he would be court-martialed if we arrived thirty seconds late.

"Can't waste a minute," he said. "You've got to experience the insider's view of the border—something most Americans will never see."

My antennae went up. "At last—the Iron Curtain. That even beats castles and quaint towns."

"Yes, ma'am. And will you ever be surprised."

We drove toward Passau, a town on the Danube merely a stone's skip from Austria, but there was no time for Austria today. We veered onto a twisty back road that led to a mountain on the border.

Walter Cronkite had painted grim images of the Cold War on my mental canvas. I pictured a forbidding wall bristling with soldiers, rolls of razor wire, lookout towers to spot escapees, spotlights for nighttime surveillance, and exhaust clouds from rumbling tanks, trucks, and jeeps.

But my real anxiety had nothing to do with geopolitics. Jack and I were about to climb a mountain together, a Matterhorn, I imagined, with perilous trails along crumbling ledges. He'd take the mountain in a few strides while I wheezed behind like a little pufferbelly. I squirmed at memories of bike rides with Terry, him on his ten-speed and me on my granny bike. Over and over, he would race ahead until all I could see was an ant-size Terry scurrying up the next hill. Today's hike promised a sorry repeat.

That was bad enough, but this proper West Point officer was also duded up like a Hollywood stereotype of a German mountaineer: deer-hide lederhosen, leather suspenders, a Bavarian white trachten shirt, a green felt hat with a feather, and sandals with white knee socks. Squelching my inner imp, I didn't sing "Happy Wanderer."

I had already blown it with the lederhosen. Last Christmas, he'd sent me a pair, size tiny-hiney. I tried to put them on, hopping around like I was in a sack race, tugging, stuffing, grunting. Didn't work. Not even close. When I told him, he wrote immediately for my exact measurements, an embarrassing array of them.

Wanting to impress him with my svelte figure, I stretched the tape measure so tight a pair of silk panties wouldn't have fit between lederhosen and skin. He sent a second pair—satiny gray suede, intricately embroidered, absolutely beautiful. Close, but still too tight to button.

Over dinner the night before this hike, he'd cooed, "Be sure to wear your lederhosen." He was absolutely beaming.

An arrow of guilt pierced me front to back. "I didn't bring them."

"You didn't br—" He jolted forward, looking like I'd sucker punched him. "Why?"

"They didn't fit. I squeezed into them, but I couldn't breathe. Or sit down. Or walk up the stairs. Plus, they were so short my fanny hung out. I was too embarrassed to tell you."

"I had them tailor-made so we'd look like locals, not tourists." The corners of his mouth twitched. He burst out laughing. "Hung out, huh? Sorry. I'm enjoying the mental snapshot."

Some miles beyond Passau, Jack edged into a grassy spot beside the road. He scooped up his daypack, and we hiked up a gently sloping, forested hillside.

"This is the way to the border?" I asked.

"Affirmative. It's not your Colorado Rockies, but you'll love it."

No, it wasn't. No rocks, ravines, or gorges. No underbrush, downed trees, or human refuse. Rather, a gathering of towering trees, politely sharing the slope. "Where's the trail?"

"We're on it. It's everywhere. It doesn't get much steeper or denser than this."

Whew, I didn't have to scramble over boulders or edge along narrow trails up rugged peaks. He still could have left me miles behind, even if he hopped on one leg. He didn't. The tang of pine energized me. The cheery voices of kids on family outings warmed the air. Jack blended in, his German getup, blond hair, and demeanor.

A man hailed him like an old friend. They launched into an earnest discussion in German, Jack gesturing and pointing, the guy nodding, questioning. The man continued on up the hill. Jack thumped his chest. "He asked for directions. He thought I was German."

"Not bad for a tank jockey," I said. "Even better for a spy. Anything else you want to tell me about your mission here?"

"*Fräulein*, I confess, my real mission is to overwhelm you with the beauty of this country and convince you to share it with me. Forever."

"Good start. But are your feet as quick as your wit? Race you to the top." I took off.

He shot past. When I caught up, he was leaning against a tree as if he'd been there an hour. "Ta-da," he said. "I present you with the Czech border. Freedom ends there."

"Where?"

He handed me his binoculars and pointed. "Over there. See? The barbed wire."

"Ha. I've climbed through plenty of barbed-wire fences on the ranch. No barrier at all. And where are the signs? How do people know?"

"Don't be fooled. Everyone knows. Our guys will run you down if you get too close. On the other side, the Czechs will shoot you if you make it across. See that long gap in the trees, that ribbon of dirt? On our side, it's green. That's what freedom looks like. The barren side? That's repression. That no-man's-land stretches for hundreds of miles. Smart people stay away."

"So this is what the Cold War looks like?"

"In this spot. Not everywhere. That's why it's so insidious. You can't always see the enemy. But you know he's there—which means we have to always be on guard."

On the mountain above this unpretentious Iron Curtain, we feasted on sourdough bread and Gouda cheese. Afterward, Jack packed up our trash, even the bread crumbs, and smoothed the dirt so we left no trace. I did a double take. In the final moments of the James Creek campout, Terry had swept away every trace of our presence with a pine bough. Were these two in the same Boy Scout troop? I loved that they were nature's guardians. But both of them?

Near the village of Grafenau, Jack pulled up to a drab, squat building in a decaying industrial park. "Here we go, milady, my best treat of the day."

I looked at him quizzically.

"Seriously," he said. "The most precious jewels are discovered in the rough."

Inside was a living daguerreotype of a nineteenth-century sweatshop. Two burly, shirtless men toiled in front of a roaring furnace. Others in sweat-stained shirts hunkered over thick, scarred tables. "Voilà! The famous crystal factory. And the artists who made your vase."

Jack's magnificent birthday gift! This stifling warehouse had no production lines, no conveyor belts, no automated machinery. Merely sweltering men bent over molten glass. "They made it here?"

"True beauty comes from men's hands and hearts, not from heartless machines," he said. "I wanted you to see true artists at work."

As if it were his own crystal factory, he waved at one of the men, gestured fingers walking, and pointed to a work station. The man nodded, and Jack steered me toward a muscular man at an open furnace, so hot it toasted my face. With a four-foot-long hollow pipe, the man scooped up a glob of bright orange molten glass. To keep it from oozing off the pipe, he turned it constantly, like honey, but this stuff was as thick as warm taffy. Resting the glob on a metal table, he twirled the pipe with one hand and rolled and shaped the glowing ball with a wooden paddle. Then he tilted the pipe downward, took a deep breath, and heaved a Louis Armstrong blast into it. His cheeks puffed out and his face turned red. A bright orange bubble slowly grew inside the molten ball.

"I tried it once," Jack said. "I couldn't make even the hint of a bulge."

The man dipped the nascent piece back into the furnace and molded and shaped it. He held his creation up, spun the pipe, deemed the shape perfect, and passed the pipe and molten crystal off to a coworker.

"Now for the kiln. This way, *Fräulein*." Jack led me toward another furnace, guiding me in close with both hands on my shoulders. "Here's how we get a two-tone vase like yours. He blows a perfect blue vase, lets it cool, and blows a clear layer inside it. This is tricky. A single bubble will ruin it. Once the two layers are married up, he'll fire it again."

Jack tightened his grip, loosened it, tightened it again, as if he had been personally involved in making the vase. "More artistry comes when Jacob there draws the design on the outer shell and his cousin cuts the design into the blue layer. Presto! The clear crystal gleams through. For the final step, they polish it. Every piece handcrafted."

Here in this grimy studio, the men who created Jack's gift gathered to greet us. To show them—and Jack—how much their work meant to me, I took each man's rough hands in mine, looked into his eyes, and flooded him with thanks. Jack translated. Unexpectedly, we were hugging all around.

As we walked out, I said, "Good job, Lieutenant Sigg. You gave me the vase all over again!"

"I'm humbled by their hard work and talent. I wanted you to meet them. And remember: That vase is a down payment. Those two bowls are still waiting for you, no matter what happens."

Really? Even if Terry was the groom? I searched for a safe, but honest thing to say, something that neither committed me to one nor betrayed the other. "I can hardly wait, I . . ." My voice failed me.

Too soon Jack had to report for guard duty. We drove to Camp Whalen, the allied outpost near the border and sat silently, neither of us making a move to get out of the car. I had been in Germany only four days, and now he would be gone for two weeks.

Jack let out a deep, mournful sigh. "Ya know, two years ago, before you wrote me that first letter, I'd given up hope of ever finding love. Some of my friends, including your brother, are satisfied with casual dating. Not me. It just made me lonelier. When my friends began to marry, the loneliness became unbearable."

He turned to face me, his eyes unblinkingly intense. "Your letters planted a seed of hope that you could be that partner I yearned for. By the time you arrived in Munich, I was beside myself with anxiety . . . worried my loneliness had conjured up an imaginary, and unattainable, woman who would be crushingly disappointing . . . or worse, that you'd be everything I'd dreamed of all these years, but I wouldn't measure up. I was shivering with both hope and fear while I watched you get off the plane." He shook his head and laughed ruefully.

"You too? I never would've guessed."

Now we were both chuckling.

"But hopefully those fears are behind us," he said. "These few days together have nurtured that early hope into a bumper crop of dreams for the two of us. Dreams to last a lifetime. I can't bear the thought of two weeks on the border. Away from you. This is going to be worse than waiting for letters."

His hand rested on the gearshift, and the hair on his arm glowed golden in a shaft of sunshine. I reached out to caress it, wanting to share the moment.

He jerked away. "You can't do that!"

I yanked my hand back. "Do what?"

"Grope me in front of my men!"

Grope? I had barely grazed the hair on his arm. I saw only two souls within five hundred yards, and they weren't paying any attention. "What men?"

"Sorry," he said. "I overreacted. In any other place, I'd smother you with kisses if we were parting for two weeks. Not here. Not where it might be seen as a weakness. Forgive me?"

"Of course," I said. But it came out tinny and insincere. I tried again. "I should've remembered: Public displays of affection not allowed. Hope the higher-ups weren't looking out the window."

He let out a bitter laugh. "They have us *all* trained, don't they? Don't worry. We'll have plenty of private moments ahead, hopefully a lifetime. I'll be thinking about you every waking moment and populating all my dreams with you. For now, though, I've got to report in."

We got out of the car and stood stiffly. He handed me the keys. "Think you can find your way back?"

I made an exaggerated point not to touch him in the transfer. "Don't worry about me."

"I do worry." His jaw tightened and he swallowed hard. "I know I offended, and I'm truly sorry." He gave me a thin smile. "See you in two weeks."

He grabbed his duffle bag, strode off, stopped, and came back. "You know one of the things I love about you? You get fired up about the same things I do. I've seen it in your eyes. We're going to make a great match!" He winked and was gone.

⟞

So there I was, alone with Jack's intimidating muscle machine. Somewhere in the hills of Bavaria. I had to figure out how to get "home" to Landshut.

I edged around to the driver's side, as warily as if I were climbing onto an untamed bronco. I sank into the driver's seat, a cockpit really, gauges everywhere. Gearshift? A knob atop a stubby rod. That would take some getting used to. I couldn't see over the dash, and my feet didn't reach the brakes or gas pedal. But I could do this. I adjusted the seat and mirrors, coaxed the car into reverse, tapped the gas, and lurched onto the road.

So how to get to Landshut? Jack had said go to Deggendorf, then turn southwest. Which way was south? Or west? I had no map. I turned left, fingers crossed, and crept down the road like a turtle. At the first fork, the road sign was a spilled quiver of arrows pointing in thirty-seven directions. I located Deggendorf and headed off.

Every intersection demanded a breathtaking last-minute choice from similar signs, but I quickly learned to home in on Deggendorf, and later Landshut. After I got the hang of it, it was thrilling to touch the gas pedal and feel the ever-ready Sting Ray leap to my command.

Jack would be proud of me. Or would he? Would he still be stinging over my small gesture—and his reaction—that had spoiled his heartfelt declaration of love?

The thing is, I knew better. After a similar encounter with Geoff three years earlier, I should have realized that the proscription on public displays of affection stretched to the outer limits of the free world. The military even had an acronym for it: PDA. Okay, I was guilty of PDA! But grope?

Another traffic circle, more multiple-choice signs. I swung easily toward Landshut. Pretty soon, I was chuckling, not only at my newfound skill at the wheel, but at my faux pas with Jack. It's not like I burped in the colonel's face. And Jack was quick to apologize for his reaction. Sincerely too. Time to forgive and move on.

Besides, military traditions came with the package. Could I live with that? Yep, I had just demonstrated I could by blaming myself for *his* crankiness. I was too quick to embrace blame or smooth over other people's shortcomings. My friends called me Pollyanna. On the bright side, I was generally a happy person . . . there I went again!

But the question hung in the air: As an officer's wife, would I be a perpetual prisoner trapped in my Pollyanna bubble? I flashed on my mom, the bright-eyed, competent hostess, knowing when to prick the bubble, when to look on in amusement. Me too? Well, life could be worse.

I pulled into the BOQ parking lot in Landshut and carefully backed the car into Jack's space. Everyone parked nose out. The on-call guardians had to be ever ready to race into battle at the drop of a grenade. I wanted any casual observers to know that Jack's car was prepared for immediate action, never mind that the owner was at the border.

The soldier loping across the quad, arms waving, made me smile. Big brother to the rescue. Bonner swooped me up in a bear hug, the sort he used to annoy me with when we were kids. He plopped his hands on my shoulders, appraising me from head to toe. "Wow, Sis, all grown up."

We hadn't lived together as brother and sister since I was in eighth grade. Over the years, we'd seen each other only during hurried vacations. Christmas at West Point his plebe year. His graduation. The week he and Jack spent at the ranch in '61. Christmas at Fort Irwin the following year.

"Jack said you'd be back by now. Great to see you."

"What, he had sentries atop the church bell tower?"

"Of course. We make it our business to know where the beautiful women are at all times." *Oh, brother.* That was Bonner, always honing his line for the ladies, even practicing on his little sister. Is that how he had seduced Gretchen? I wanted to blast him with details of the pain he'd caused my almost-sister, demand that he explain why he'd had sex with a woman he had no intention of marrying, and eviscerate him for using her up and throwing her away. But I couldn't. He was my smiling, charming big brother.

"Earth to Annie. Do you read me?"

"Huh?" I banished the roiling thoughts and sputtered, "Oh, sorry. I was just wondering how many girls you've wrapped around your finger with that line."

His eyes narrowed, then twinkled. "Whatever you may have heard is vastly overstated. But I only have time to say hi. I've got to get back to work. Dinner at seven. Be ready."

That evening, we trooped to the Officers' Club, Bonner and I, bubbling about my trip, his assignment as troop commander, the family. Out of the blue, he said, "By the way, you have a *ton* of mail. 'Bout a thousand letters from your *buddy*. Marshall, isn't it? I thought you came over to see my best friend. And me, of course."

I'd given Bonner's address to Mom and my friends, including Terry, as my only sure point of contact. "Uh, well, things got complicated," I stammered. "I—"

"You don't have to explain, Sis. Jack already told me he has competition."

"Oh, really. And what else has he told you?"

"Just guy talk. Don't worry about it."

It did worry me, but I wouldn't ask him about it. In our family, we didn't talk about our love lives. "So tell me about this dream job of yours."

"Couldn't be better. I rumble around in tanks and APCs, play war games. It's what I trained for."

"APCs?"

"Armored personnel carriers. Bigger than tanks and safer when the shooting starts. Best of all, after work, Germany is wine, women, and song. Great place to live."

I wanted to say, *Yeah, so Gretchen tells me.* But I couldn't let on that I knew.

He led me into the club like I was his girl. A table of lieutenants sprang to their feet to greet me, something I never saw at CU. The young officers were drinking and swapping stories, each a little louder than the previous. A familiar scene from my childhood, only now I was one of the grownups. I nursed a glass of wine while beer bottles piled up and the stories got more outrageous. The gathering reminded me of Jack's lament about these "guzzle fests"—too loud, too smoky, too many drunks.

As soon as they got so tanked up they wouldn't notice, I slipped away. It was past midnight when I finally got to Terry's letters. Only two? Not "a ton," as Bonner had said, his obvious gibe at my having any male friend other than one of his buddies.

The first letter, three single-spaced typed pages, dated June 5, came from Boulder. "Commencement," he began. "You missed the forty-five-minute wait before the thirty-minute march into the stadium—reminiscent of the last walk of the gladiators before the lions are turned loose—and the exorbitant cost of renting cap and gown ($3.25)." He continued, "I didn't shake hands with Dean Duncan when he handed out our diplomas."

Oh, Terry, why be so brash? And why hold a grudge for so long? The animosity between Terry and Duncan, the journalism dean, had begun two years before, when everything at the *Colorado Daily* blew up. The university president fired the *Daily*'s editor at the urging of two conservative politicians, US Senator Barry Goldwater and CU Regent Dr. Dale Atkins. Both had leveled scathing criticism at the *Daily* and the university for their "left-wing bias." That criticism and the editor's firing sparked a rowdy demonstration by 2,500 students on campus. Terry resigned in protest. Oh, he was furious. As managing editor, second in command, he took the firing personally.

Then Terry went off the deep end and wrote a scurrilous letter to Atkins, who had threatened to investigate the paper. Terry's letter ended up in the *New Conservative*, a student paper founded to counter the *Daily*'s liberal coverage.

That newspaper had published his entire letter verbatim, an angry, nasty, inflammatory diatribe, Terry at his caustic, in-your-face worst: "I learned to hate my country at the university, at this university, Dr. Atkins, the University of Colorado." It went on, condemning America, the government, our foreign policy, the people, free enterprise, religion. On and on and on.

Next time Terry showed up at my dorm, I jabbed the paper in his face before he got off his bike. "Jeez, Terry, are you serious? You 'hate America'? Do you really?"

"Dammit, Atkins—"

"What were you thinking? Sending a letter like that to a regent? Of all the dumb—"

"No, look, that son of a bitch had no right to—"

"Quit swearing! You know I hate that. Besides, where've you been? They published this Tuesday. Copies all over campus. I've called a dozen times. I—"

I stopped. Terry was slumped over his ten-speed Schwinn like he'd sprinted in from a cross-country race, sweaty, steam rising, shaggy hair a mess, his scraggly mustache drooping into his mouth. He needed a friend, not another critic. "Darn it, Ter, I've been worried."

"I'm not answering my phone. They're trying to get me."

This wasn't the Ter I knew. *That* Terry wasn't paranoid. Or rattled by crisis. He wasn't one to dream up bogeymen. Something else was up. "What do you mean, they're 'trying to get you'? Who?"

"Let's see." He held up his left hand, studying it as if he were a palm reader, and ticked one finger after another: "Dean of Men. Dean of Students. Dean of Journalism. Dean of Arts and Sciences. Dean of the Law School. The Provost. Add in their assistants and lackeys, and you've got a scary lineup. They want to kick me out of school. Dean Duncan's the worst. Face-to-face, he pretends he's my best friend, but he's after me, just like the others. The guy runs the J-School—he should defend my right to speak my mind. That's the essence of a free press!"

I'd heard that rumor about expelling him, but I didn't believe it. I put my arm around his shoulder and gave him a sisterly hug. "We need to talk, guy. Let me buy you a cup of coffee."

Basically, Terry was levelheaded, but too often, he could be a trial by fire: outspoken, bombastic, blunt, too eager to embrace controversy. He let anger and self-righteousness overrule common sense. His letter to Dr. Atkins wasn't the only example. During his summer stints on local newspapers, he had written several editorials that sent readers into paroxysms.

I had described one such editorial in a letter to Jack. "It's rare to see Terry working *with* and *within* a situation for improvement. He is powerfully fluent, but some of the trouble his vitriolic pen and wayward nature have gotten him into would curl your hair. Surely, he's doomed to a tumultuous, unhappy life, but it's impossible to separate this from his quick wit and talent. He's a tragic character. I hope I don't die before I write a book about him—his story is worth telling."

Through the months that followed, Terry and I got past all that. He didn't *hate* America. Or Americans. He believed wholeheartedly in America's ideals and railed when we didn't live up to those ideals. His passion is what made him so endearing—that and his ability to turn a solemn event into fun and games.

Case in point, his letter on the highlights of CU graduation day: "The best part was playing Batman in my graduation gown and sunglasses and scaring the tar out of Mort." I could see Terry flying off the porch, racing around the yard, long hair flopping, robe ballooning behind, and the landlord's poor dog barking and rolling over backward to get away. What a comedian. *How I miss your craziness, Ter.*

Today was June 14. He had written that letter June 5. Boulder seemed as far removed from my life as a sepia photograph of a Civil War soldier, as though eons had passed, not a mere nine days.

In letter two, June 9, from Center, he shared his thoughts while attending a friend's wedding:

No matter what happens to us and our relationship, what we have now is greater than anything I have ever experienced. I feel a calm warmth, a satisfaction in knowing that someone believes in me and in knowing someone I can believe in. I can no longer worry about you and Jack, for no matter what happens, nothing can destroy the closeness we have.

No matter what happens? That was Jack's favorite expression in letters—and even today at the glass factory. Had these two guys gone to the same love-letter school?

But each was stewing about the other guy, and at some point, I could see anguish for one of them, or both, or all three of us, lurking in the dark woods ahead. Unease churned in my belly.

And what was this? Terry's ideas about wedding ceremonies:

It was almost too much to bear to hear the minister go on about the marriage in God and ordained by God, couched in archaic biblical wording. The ceremony is so formal everyone's uncomfortable. If we need a ceremony at all (I'm not convinced we do), it would be better to have an honest, enjoyable, simple ceremony—preferably outdoors in a garden or in the mountains. Casual dress.

Jack would agree. Mr. Outdoors would love the natural setting and the simplicity. So would I. On the other hand, he might prefer the pomp of a West Point wedding. Was this one difference between them? Did it matter? What *did* matter was that Terry was writing about marriage, an about-face. That scared me. A life with Terry would be pocked with turmoil and controversy. Would I have the strength to stand shoulder to shoulder with him through the tempests?

One thing was certain: Here, in Germany, I was careening forward so fast that I had to keep my eyes on the road and my hands on the wheel, as I had done with the Sting Ray while maneuvering through hairpin curves and over dizzying mountain roads.

I didn't know where this summer would take me, but the journey itself was intoxicating.

5

Alone

Ann

Monday, June 15, 1964, Landshut. For the next two weeks, Jack would be at the border, out of contact. Bonner was chained to his desk. I was alone in Europe. Now what?

Pine for a missing boyfriend or busy brother? No way. The least I could do was enjoy the freedom they were there to protect. First thing, master the traffic. After a rocky start (the wrong way on a one-way street), I quickly got my bearings. The gearshift and I became pals. I learned to squeeze through narrow roads—paved cow paths, really—without losing any paint on the rod. I spent all afternoon whizzing up and down Landshut's streets.

The next day, I had a simple plan: Zip over to Munich, find the American consulate, and track down a notary for the Glendale High teaching contract my folks had forwarded through Bonner—stamped in red capital letters, "PLEASE RETURN IMMEDIATELY." And do some sightseeing.

Not so simple. In Munich, every manner of transportation—cars, trucks, buses, bicycles, motorbikes, even pushcarts—intruded into my comfort zone. One-way streets channeled me in unexpected directions, and a gnawing fear eroded my confidence. What if someone dinged Jack's baby?

Finally, I found the consulate: closed for lunch. Tantalizing aromas drew me to a nearby café. I settled in, pretended to read the menu, gave up, and pointed to a meat dish and drink at the next table. Lucky me, it was Wiener schnitzel and a tall glass of *Apfelsaft*—apple juice. I didn't know a word of German, but I wouldn't starve.

Back at the consulate, I introduced myself to the receptionist.

"You have an appointment, *ja?*"

"No. I just need to get a paper notarized."

"*Ja*, that would be the legal affairs office. I will put you in the queue."

"But I drove over from Landshut."

"*Ja, ja.* Please be seated."

The tiny waiting area was jammed tighter than a cattle truck loaded for market: suited men with briefcases, women with children in tow, grandmothers, students, all sitting or standing impassively. Three hours, four offices, and five harried employees later, I staggered into the sunshine, my task done. I headed back to the simplicity of Landshut.

Terry

Thursday, 18 June 1964, Center, Colorado. Finally, Annie's first letter arrived: "June 10, 1:35 a.m., Landshut, Germany," three sheets of stationery hand-scrawled on both sides. Landshut, where Jack lived—that's all I knew about the place. "I sure wish you were here to rub my back right now," she began. *Yeah, me too. Though I'd rub a lot more than that.*

"I have so much to tell you about Europe," she said. But she described her seven-hour flight from New York to Paris. Not a word about Europe. A postscript, written "Friday night, shortly after midnight," two days later: "I have been far from a mailbox, roaming around in the German boonies."

Where? Doing what? No hint. "So much to tell you," but not a word about what it was.

But wait, another add-on, this one four days later still, hasty squiggles sardined into the margin: "Suddenly went down to the Füssen area for a few days and didn't get this finished." For a few days? Nothing about Paris or Germany. And no pronoun. With Jack? By herself? Was it "we" or "I"?

"I just got home this evening," she wrote, "and happily found your letter waiting." Only one letter? I had mailed four. She closed with "I don't want you to forget I'm always thinking about you." I hoped so, but her vague hints at her travels so far didn't allay my fears. It was postmarked June 16, a week after she started it.

We had an old atlas at home. Füssen wasn't in it. I barreled into town, straight to the library. Wow, near the Austrian border. She had made it to the Alps. That's all I knew.

Ann

Friday, June 19, 1964, Landshut. As summer got into full swing that week, my two American hosts morphed from somber teachers into party animals. Every night was as rowdy as Saturday night at a CU frat house. Booze flowed. Walls shook with raucous music. I tried to join in, shouting into a din to people I didn't know. I couldn't think. I couldn't sleep.

The daylight hours, though, were grand. My hosts slept in, and I'd spent Wednesday and Thursday exploring the countryside up and down the Isar River on curvy two-lane roads with my new scarf flying, the one Jack had given me in Füssen. I gloried in wandering through small-town Germany. Solo picnics beside the river. Snacks picked off the shelves in family stores, no language needed. I merely pointed and paid. And I didn't get lost, not once.

I needed a new challenge, though. Off to Munich again.

This time, I planned to stay overnight, get acquainted with the city, and have a real adventure. I took my copy of *Europe on Five Dollars a Day*, chose a hotel near the train station, and arrived without mishap (if I didn't count getting stuck in a traffic circle for three rounds). After dinner, I headed for a nearby theater I'd read was showing the classic 1926 version of *Faust*.

I set off on foot into a narrow gorge cut into a cityscape of mammoth buildings, each more than two sprawling blocks long. *Blocks?* Every "block" was an oversized triangle, trapezoid, or tetrahedron carved by streets intersecting at random angles. Sometimes, two or three streets converged at the same corner, with only one emerging—and bearing a different name. I was a mouse in a gigantic maze. My dinky map offered no help. Soon I was hot, frazzled, and frantic.

"Maybe you are lost? Perhaps I can help."

English! Someone spoke to me in English. Her voice gave me instant whiplash. Face-to-face with a pretty blonde, I blurted, "I am *so* lost! If only you can—"

"More slowly, please."

"Oh, sorry. I want to see *Faust* . . . the movie." I showed her the tourist brochure.

"Yes, yes, it is only there. You will follow me, please?"

"Only there" turned out to be the other side of a torrent of cars, four lanes each direction. I needed a cable car to bridge the onslaught. My new guide saw the terror in my eyes and steered me to a crosswalk with traffic signals.

Bingo, I was there, albeit a sweaty wreck.

But a movie theater? This grand old building looked as imposing as the Supreme Court. Inside, thick red carpet and crystal chandeliers. Though woefully underdressed, I imagined myself in King Maximilian's court and strode boldly between gold-encrusted marble pillars framing the thirty-foot-wide entry into a two-story auditorium with velvety seats. Box seats rose up the sides to the ceiling. Balconies draped with royal blue velvet shimmered with ornamental gold leaf. White marble nymphs and muses perched in the alcoves. Across the ceiling, frescoed figures waded in blue waters and picnicked on boulders. I had already gotten my money's worth, and *Faust* hadn't begun. I collapsed into a seat as plush as a queen's cushion.

It was a silent film, dialogue written in German between the frames. Of course it was silent—it was made in the twenties. And, of course, the subtitles were in German. I tried to glean meaning from the foreign words and pantomime. But my eyes fluttered shut. The next thing I knew, the final credits were rolling. Several of the moviegoers stared at me as they shuffled out. I leaped up, hid a sheepish grin, and feigned enjoyment.

I checked my map and strode down Sendlingerstraße onto Lindwurm-straße, turned on Goethestraße, took a right on Beethovenstraße, which came to a "T" at—what was this—Lindwurmstraße? Again? Another maze! And why did they put that weird "ß" with a tail in the middle of a word? This time I turned left. And ran into Beethovenstraße *again*.

Midnight. No stores open. No safe havens. Wait, lights ahead. I started toward them. A man stumbled from an open doorway. It was a bar. He hollered, "*Fräulein!*" I dodged down a side street and waited in a dark alcove. He didn't follow. I headed away, my steps echoing through a tightly buttoned neighborhood. Dad would be furious, Mom worried sick. They would yank me back home like a runaway calf.

A car careened into the street, its high beams blinding me. A carload of rowdies jeered. Pretending they didn't exist, I turned the corner as if I had reached home. They drove on. At the next intersection, a street sign read Beethovenstraße, my third encounter with the old master. My map was too tiny to read in the dim glow of the streetlight.

A couple tumbled out of a doorway. I rushed up. "*Bitte*? Do you speak English?"

The girl's face registered surprise. "*Ja*. A lit-tle."

"I'm lost. My hotel's on Sonnenstraße." I stumbled on the *ß*. "See? Right here, on my map." I pushed it at them as if it were a treasure map. They squinted.

"Name of hotel?" the girl said.

I shrugged. She shot a rapid-fire suggestion to her boyfriend. He peered into the darkness. "*Ja, ja*," he said. She swept her arm toward a broad avenue on the distant right of a confluence of streets. "That is Son-nen-stras-se."

I got it, at last: *Straße* at the end of these street names must mean "street." That funny-looking capital "β" sounded exactly like a double S. *Wahoo!* "Which way on Son-nen-stras-se?" I said, trying to mimic her pronunciation. I pointed to the left and raised my eyebrows.

"*Ja, ja*," the guy said. Two blocks later, I crept into my little hotel and up to my room.

I had been lucky. Three Good Samaritans saved my skin. I dozed off, listing common sense rules for solo travel: Always carry a map. Stay on the main roads. Learn some German. Don't go out by yourself at night. Take a taxi—it's worth the cost. Never look like a lost mouse, even when you are one.

The next morning, I fortified myself with thick German bread with butter, skillet-fried potatoes, scrambled eggs with berries, and hot chocolate. The day's mission: visit the Alte Pinakothek, the museum Terry put on my must-see list back when he was my buddy. That part had changed, but not my marching orders to see Dürer's *Four Apostles*. After last night's tangled spaghetti walk, I opted for the Sting Ray. Sure, I could get lost faster, but, ever the optimist, also un-lost faster. I arrived at the sprawling museum in ten minutes.

Unlike the behemoth structures that towered above me the night before, the Pinakothek was only two stories high, though its footprint stretched across two city blocks. Inside, skylights channeled beams of natural light on the artists' works. At the *Four Apostles*, I felt dwarfed. At least seven feet tall, the painting—on two slender wood panels, each with two apostles side by side—loomed over me.

Saint Paul's stern gaze made me feel compelled to confess. And I wasn't a Catholic. A younger, curly-haired Saint Mark seemed to be warning him of dangers. Clearly not someone to mess with. The other two, Saints John and Peter, lost in thought, made me curious about the passage they were reading. All four looked as if they might step out of the painting at any moment. The veins on their hands, faces, and feet seemed as real as those of living men.

Back in Landshut, the blistering sandstorm of noise continued through the weekend. Jack would be gone seven more days, a prospect that left me blue. But I was an army girl, and like my mom, I would make the best of it.

In his letters, Jack had been passionate about Switzerland—so progressive, so modern, so clean. Even on our drive to Passau, he had raved about the Swiss Alps and apologized that we didn't have time to squeeze them into our schedule.

Monday morning, I bought a train ticket to Switzerland. Why not? He'd be proud of my initiative and pleased that we could share this passion, even if separately.

Terry

Saturday, 20 June 1964, Center. I had been reading the German philosopher Schopenhauer's *World as Will and Idea*, and I filled two pages of a new letter to Annie with quotes. She and I had talked a couple of times about whether it was moral to bring children into a world like ours. We had our doubts. Schopenhauer argued that "lovers are the traitors who seek to perpetuate the . . . drudgery" that is life:

> Let men recognize the snare that lies in women's beauty, and the absurd comedy of reproduction will end. The development of intelligence will weaken or frustrate the will to reproduce, and will thereby at last achieve the extinction of the race. . . . When shall we have the courage to fling defiance into the face of the Will—to tell it that the loveliness of life is a lie, and that the greatest boon of all is death?

No, I wrote her, I didn't welcome death or believe that sex was shameful. But in his writing, I found "a beauty of a man sensitive to the world about him, a man who was truly alive. Only a man who suffered great personal hurts could write as he did." This is what fascinated me about the pessimists, I said, "whether it be Voltaire, Schopenhauer, or Robinson Jeffers. After all, isn't life more than happiness, and isn't happiness more than the absence of pain?"

I was idling away the days, lonely for my best friend, waiting for summer's end so I could flee to Venezuela. Enough! Closing my letter, I wrote:

There is so much I want to say to you, Annie. You can't realize how much you mean to me. Everything I do or see I must share with you. I think of you constantly. I think about making love to you when I try to dream myself to sleep at night or when I've read something I want to share. I'm filled with the need to talk to you and know I'm yours and you, mine. All my actions and thoughts and words are interpreted in terms of you. I miss you so much.

I let the letter cool overnight, retyped it Sunday, and gave it to the mailman on Monday. All he had for me was a day-old *Denver Post*. Same story Tuesday. By Wednesday, I couldn't face another empty mailbox. I took off for the solace of Silverton.

Wednesday, 24 June 1964, en route to Silverton. Forty-five minutes after fleeing dreary, flatland Center, I paused atop Wolf Creek Pass for a drink from the rustic snow-fed fountain at the summit. Then I tackled the steep, twisting, two-lane descent into the San Juan Basin. No time to daydream on Wolf Creek—I had to concentrate on every curve and switchback.

At the bottom, I pulled over at Treasure Falls and caught my breath before cruising through the verdant valleys to Pagosa Springs, on to Durango, and over Molas and Coal Bank passes into Silverton. Every mile triggered another memory.

I had spent the previous summer in Silverton, working at the *Silverton Standard* for my friend, Allen Nossaman, who had been editor in chief of the *Colorado Daily* the year I was city editor. After he graduated from CU, he bought the *Standard* with the goal of creating a prize-winning news-paper. But the town was too small for the business to survive on subscrib-ers alone. He printed the paper on Thursday nights and spent Fridays, Mondays, and many a weekend turning out stationery, business forms, and flyers—all the printing needs of a small town. I was his partner that summer.

I'd also found in Silverton a band of eclectic but like-minded friends, who became as tightly knit a group as our gang at the *Colorado Daily*. Take John Ross, a hard-drinking bear of a man with a full beard and the pres-ence of an 1870s roustabout who taught high school math. He put me up all summer in his spare bedroom. He had restored a World War II Burma Jeep with six wheels and the roar of a tank and enjoyed taking us up trails only he believed were passable.

And Roger Craig, a wiry cowboy from the plains west of Durango. Roger owned the West's ugliest cowboy boots—screaming yellow with flaming red polka dots—so ugly they provoked fights every time he wore them into a bar, which he did just for fun.

In what little time was left after my marathon days at the *Standard*, I explored the surrounding San Juan Mountains, sometimes with this gang of adventurers, sometimes alone.

After each outing that summer, be it a solo walk up a hillside, a jeep trip, or a mountain hike, I wrote to my junior-year girlfriend, Steffi, eager to revive our dormant romance after she moved to San Francisco. I built her into each experience—sights that inspired *us* and smells, sounds, and thoughts as *we* trudged up a trail under the weight of our packs. *We* pitched snowballs at each other. *We* made love in my sleeping bag under a canopy of brilliant stars. I wove fact and fiction until I could sense her beside me, hoping she could feel it too.

Those conjured liaisons amped up my horniness, and her letters kept hope alive. But by mid-July, her new life in San Francisco had won her over. She quit writing.

The chances of meeting someone in Silverton were slim. The tour-ists left for Durango late every afternoon, and at night, the place was as desolate as an abandoned mine. There weren't any coeds—not one—and I dismissed the local high school girls as mere children. That was the sad underbelly of my summer: night after night alone, weeks without female companionship. At times I was so lonely for a woman's touch I didn't think I could survive until fall.

But then came July 27, 1963, a Saturday. I was at the Linotype, Allen at the hand-fed press. A gaggle of tourists clattered into the *Standard* office. Usually I ignored them, but that day, this gorgeous girl swished behind the counter. My God, Laura Lee Christensen!

She had been a year behind me in high school, not in Center but in Smoky Point, forty-five minutes away. She was the editor of her school newspaper, and we'd met at an annual workshop for San Luis Valley high school journalists. When I started at CU, she and I struck up a correspondence—flirty, suggestive letters. She promised to join me at CU after graduation.

I had last seen her the following summer when I worked for the *Valley Courier* in Alamosa. We went to a small-town rodeo banquet I had to cover. That was the first time I'd dared to ask her out. In high school, she was a New York Yankee, and I was a minor leaguer. She was stunning, bright, sophisticated, and two inches taller than me. After the banquet, we slipped away and talked for a couple of hours. Great conversation, but at my every timid touch, she nudged my hand away. Each time I edged in to kiss her, she turned aside.

I called her at the end of the week. Her mother said, "She moved away." "Don't call us again." That fall, I learned that Laura Lee had been two months pregnant the night of our date, and when her parents found out, they demanded she marry the guy immediately. Calling her vile names, they kicked her out of the house and refused to attend her quickly arranged wedding in Taos.

Three years later, Laura Lee showed up at the *Standard*, her throaty purr buckling my knees. "Terry! God, it's been so long." Our eyes locked, hers so intense I feared she could see my lust. Our words puffed out in whispers, as if we were captives and our kidnappers hovered nearby. I learned this much: She had divorced the father of her child and was living with her parents in Delta, eighty miles from Silverton. The "gaggle of tourists" were her two-year-old daughter, her parents, sister, and—oh no, not again—*fiancé*. They'd set a wedding date: November 9.

"Let's go!" her dad shouted.

Laura Lee jumped like a marionette. I followed her out the door. Halfway down Greene Street, she looked back and gave a seductive wave. I dashed after her, got her address, and stood rooted, watching her until they disappeared into the Grand Imperial for lunch.

I'd always been shy around girls, fearful that if I made the slightest amorous move, they'd embarrass me with a slap in the chops. But that night I mustered the chutzpah to write Laura Lee, "You can't get married. You must go to the university. And we can't part with what little we have had. I'm coming to see you. Soon."

Imagine asking this girl to call off her wedding—based on a fifteen-minute chance meeting three years after our only date. If that weren't enough, I tried to convince her we were destined to be together.

In a flurry of letters, I urged her to come to CU. She wrestled with how to raise a child by herself and still pursue her college dream. My letters went from "Dear Laura" to "My Dear Laura," and hers from "Dear Terry" to "My Terry" to "My Darling."

Two weeks after our chance meeting, I drove to her place in Delta for the weekend. Despite her parents' pit-bull surveillance and her daughter's cute but incessant need for attention, Laura Lee and I carved out time alone, talking, talking—the pain of teen motherhood and divorce, our hopes for the future, the scandal that calling off a wedding would cause. "Come to Boulder and live with me," I blurted out.

I expected outrage, but she kissed me, hugging me so tightly we melted together. I couldn't imagine myself as a father, yet we talked about day care in Boulder, about apartment hunting, and about how I would look after *our* little girl when Laura Lee was in class. When I left for Silverton Monday morning, she seemed poised to join me that fall at CU.

Our letters resumed. "No! I shouldn't," she wrote. "I can't. I must not. I won't. I've gone too far down this path to turn back. I have to stick to the course I've chosen." Still, she pleaded with her parents to postpone the wedding for college. Her mother's response: "You're a tramp!" Her father said "sure"—*if* she would pick up the phone, right that instant, cancel the wedding, tell her fiancé she'd never see him again, and "break his heart."

"I couldn't. I couldn't hurt them like that," she wrote.

I had planned to leave Silverton at the end of August and spend a week in Salt Lake City before school started. "Come with me," I wrote.

She wrote back, "We're not capable of a platonic relationship, and even if we were, no one would believe it." But she'd think about it, she said.

In the interim, I proposed a rendezvous in Ouray, a small town between Delta and Silverton.

We met on Wednesday, three days before I was to leave for Salt Lake, and spent the morning in the town park. We reaffirmed our love, revisiting the same hopes we'd expressed in Delta, but with none of the brain-wracking agony we'd wrestled with, as if we had come to terms with events neither of us wanted but couldn't avoid. We touched discreetly. No soul-searching kisses, no wandering hands.

Mostly, we tended her daughter, me scooping her up, swinging her, racing with her, hugging her, laughing. She was irresistible, but insatiable. I loved that little kid. But, God, she was a full-time job. How would Laura Lee and I ever be able to both raise her and get any studying done? I pushed that fear aside. "Come with me to Salt Lake," I said. "Just you. At least we can have one week together."

She *might*, she said. She'd let me know by Friday, the day before I left for Salt Lake.

On my way back to Silverton, a downpour pelted the windshield before I reached the summit of Red Mountain Pass. My windows fogged over. I inched into a rare pullout at the edge of a cliff, only half a car wide. I flipped on the radio and heard Walter Cronkite's avuncular voice, ". . . presenting Miss Mahalia Jackson."

The March on Washington!

Mahalia Jackson sang, "I've been 'buked and I've been scorned . . ." The crowd roared—two hundred thousand people, Cronkite said. A rabbi spoke. Martin Luther King Jr. came to the podium. Through the static, he cried, "Some of you have come fresh from narrow jail cells."

I responded, "And me from the arms of Laura Lee Christensen, a girl who loves me." The rain stopped. I sat there and soaked in every word.

King wasn't a stranger to me. His *Stride Toward Freedom* had provided the intellectual basis for my claim to be classified a conscientious objector. But I had never heard him speak. He poured similes over metaphors and wrapped them in allegories. He knew when to pause, when to repeat, when to shout, when to whisper. He boomed, "Let freedom ring from the mighty mountains of New York . . . from the snowcapped Rockies of Colorado." He called to me. Directly to me! There in the snowcapped San Juan Mountains of the Colorado Rockies.

I drove on to Silverton in euphoria. Laura Lee had rescued my summer. She loved me, and I her. If she did come with me to Salt Lake, we'd sleep together every night for a week, no question. And then she'd join me at CU. We'd live together. Life would be complete.

On top of that, King had touched me anew. I hadn't done enough for civil rights. I'd lost my way since I left the *Colorado Daily*. I'd make him proud, I vowed.

In Silverton, Friday's mail brought a brief, sad note. No, she wouldn't go with me to Salt Lake. But hope lived on. She wasn't sure she could go through with the November 9 wedding. "I think my head will split with aching," she wrote. "I can't decide. Give me until October 1."

In Salt Lake I floated in the briny water. Alone. Hiked a trail behind the university. Alone! At Temple Square's grand Tabernacle, I slipped inside and sat mesmerized as Leonard Bernstein and the New York Philharmonic recorded a Christmas album with the Mormon Tabernacle Choir. With Laura Lee it would have been the date of a lifetime. But I was alone.

When the first of October came, I knew before I slit open the familiar light blue envelope that Laura Lee's answer wasn't what I wished for. My hands shook. I stared at her handwriting to get it into focus. "I promised I'd write before October 1," she wrote, "and I've waited as long as I could, hoping to the last minute I could give you the right answer, but I can't."

The wedding was on.

"Oh, Terry, I tried so hard and prayed so much, but it's impossible." She'd tried to convince her parents she should go to school, but she couldn't. And she hadn't been able to summon the strength to call off the wedding herself. "Thank you, Terry," she wrote, "for listening and for at least giving me a hope for escape. I wish we could have done together all the things we both need to do." She signed it "Yours, Laura Lee."

I plowed on better than I had thought possible. I had loved Laura Lee, and she hadn't rejected me. We'd simply rediscovered each other too late to reverse the forces already set in motion. I'd been blessed. In only five crazy, improbable, heart-wrenching weeks, Laura Lee had taught me how to love.

But all that philosophizing aside, her letter hurt like hell!

Now, ten months later, as I drove into Silverton from Center, I feared that every step I took would rekindle some memory of Laura Lee.

I quickly discovered, though, that I was aching not for the girl I'd lost a year ago but for Ann Garretson. That night I couldn't sleep for thoughts of her. The next day, it was Annie's image that made me lose track of where I was on the trail up Kendall Peak. I was thinking about her when I drifted across the centerline at that first hairpin curve above Silverton. She was everywhere. I couldn't take a breath without her. And the damn postmaster was no help at all. Annie couldn't write me there. She had no idea where I was.

Ann

Thursday, June 25, 1964, Lausanne, Switzerland. Two weeks in Europe, and this was my first day at a beach—Lake Geneva. I'd brought my darling bathing suit, a shimmery one-piece that laid bare my back and had a plunging neckline that betrayed a bit of cleavage but kept my breasts safely in check.

Even my little brother, Jimmy, had whistled when he saw me. I'd worn it in public only once. At home the previous summer, I had glided from the pool dressing room, using every move I'd mastered in the Cover Girl modeling course that my parents had sent me to in 1960. Imagining that every stud had his eyes on me, I headed for the high board, the domain of fearless performers—guys, of course—not the piddly, inches-above-the-water springboard my girlfriends settled for.

Bounding up the ladder, I slipped on step four, bashed my shin on the metal lip, swallowed a shriek of pain, and staggered to the top. I posed like a cliff diver at Acapulco. And did the world's worst belly flop. I acted as if I had knifed into the water like a gold medalist. But I couldn't breathe. My kamikaze landing had smacked every molecule of air out of me. My gouged shin was aflame. My body stung as if I'd wallowed in a field of nettles. I was mortified. That pathetic dive sent me spiraling into sex symbol oblivion. And the wound left me with a permanent dent in my shin.

But in Lausanne, even wizened octogenarians and triple-chinned behemoths wore bikinis. If I were so clueless as to wear my old-maid one-piece, I'd probably get arrested for public *decency.* Only trouble was, I had never, ever worn a bikini. And I'd never, ever planned to. Until that day. In a Lausanne department store changing room, I glared at the image of a girl who looked a lot like me, wearing a Day-Glo yellow hint of a bathing suit. I cringed at what I saw.

Why? My tummy pooched out like Winnie the Pooh's. It wasn't fat, just *poochie*. Normally, it took all my will—and a girdle—to curb the pudginess. Dad had attributed it to poor posture. "Stand up straight, Sis. Walk like a woman."

I selected another bikini from among the colorful bits of cloth I'd arrayed on the bench. I squared my shoulders, stretched to my full height, took a deep breath, and sucked in my tummy. I couldn't make it go flat. Simply put, I was an ugly duckling, with no chance of turning into a swan.

It was just as I had always thought—except for a shining moment in my freshman year of high school when we lived in Italy. On a teen club excursion to Florence, my girlfriend Judy and I tripped merrily through the Uffizi Gallery and came face-to-face with Botticelli's *The Birth of Venus*. I stopped cold, not because of the angelic face or luscious curls, but because of her poochie tummy. She was me, at least her tummy was. Botticelli knew that girls were naturally curved, not flat bellied or washboard rippled. His art liberated me.

But back in the States a year later, my newfound confidence vanished when my girlfriends argued over who cut the most svelte profile. I again succumbed to the American narrative that girls with poochie tummies were doomed to dateless weekends.

Enough of that old self-doubt! In the tiny Swiss dressing room, I tried on a modern '60s persona—and another candidate bikini. I looked over my shoulder at my fanny. Not a bad view there, and I gave up trying to hide that poochie tummy.

But there was something worse. Far worse.

A tangle of fugitive pubic hair.

Yep, like runaway Virginia creepers, my pubic hair sprawled beyond the bikini line. For practical reasons, I rarely whacked it off. A full-scale assault was unbearable. Afterward, it itched like crazy. My panties would rub the exposed skin raw, and I'd sprout an acre of angry red bumps. As for waxing, it required nerves of steel and the pain tolerance of a pit bull. I couldn't pour hot wax on Genghis Khan storming the castle wall, let alone on the most delicate part of my body. But the hot wax is a minor part of the pain. Next you have to rip it off, along with patches of hair—as if it were invasive weeds—and layers of skin. Talk about barbaric!

Naked pubes are one of those weird notions society foists on women under the guise of beauty. The custom no doubt stems from some ancient queen who, through a freak of nature, came out of puberty as hairless as a doorknob, so she dictated that henceforth all proper women could have no body hair. Or maybe it's a throwback to the Middle Ages when crab lice infested rich and poor alike, baths were a yearly chore, and soap was made of lye and lard. No doubt it was more effective to clear-cut the forest than to try to root out the pests individually.

Okay, rest assured I didn't obsess over pubic hair. The topic rarely came up. But it did have deep roots. Seventh grade. We were learning handstands and cartwheels in PE. I couldn't do either. The teacher kept at me. She called over another girl to help and made me try again. When I threw my legs up, they each grabbed one to hold me steady. My legs splayed out in airborne splits, and horror of horrors, a bushy fringe crept from my regulation white gym shorts. That same girl sidled up later and said, "You sure have a lot of hair *down there.*" I was mortified. I had the only untamed forest in seventh grade.

In sum, in this arena, au naturel is by far a damsel's dearest friend, despite the fact that our society defines such natural growth as the hairy monster from the dark lagoon.

"Dang," I said to the image in the mirror, "if you're going to wear this getup in public, you'd better get out the sheep shears." The discussion in the next dressing room halted. Someone giggled. A different voice called, "*Mademoiselle?* You are finish, *oui?*"

Uh-oh. Must be a line out there. So what to do? *This is your grand adventure, Ann. You're in Europe. No one knows you. Go for it!*

After a hasty exit from the dressing room, I bought a bikini that afternoon, a real one, skimpy enough to make me blush. But black, a please-don't-notice-me black. I couldn't loosen up for one of those bright scraps of stretchy cloth and string shouting "Feast on these goodies" that the European beauties pranced around in.

Despite my stand on being a natural woman, I lopped off the weeds in the south forty and headed for the beach. I had to learn to do this before Jack and I took off for the French Riviera. Wrapped in a towel, I picked my way through the sea of exposed flesh like a wayward novitiate searching for a confessional. At last, a space that wasn't cheek-by-jowl with an army of strangers. I sucked in my tummy and quickly spread my towel. Feeling stark naked, I dove face-first onto it, stretched out, head in my arms, and blotted out the babble.

Oof! My breath whooshed out. Gasping for air, I raised my head to see a screeching urchin tumble off me and sprint into the crowd like one of Fagin's pickpockets fleeing a London bobby. Did the kid utter a simple *"Pardonnez-moi, mademoiselle"*? And no one nearby batted an eye. Better to be an invisible American than an obnoxious one, I guess. But still!

That was day one on the beaches of Europe. Could I survive the French Riviera?

I mailed my third letter of the week to Terry the next morning, a feat that left me both pleased and hobbled by a nagging fear that I had forsaken my sense of common decency. I was in Europe visiting Jack and thinking about Terry. I had seen girls juggle more than one guy at CU and thought them contemptible. Now, I was dancing in the same soiled slippers.

I had first written to Terry on June 10, a letter I started the night I arrived and finished a week later. I wanted to share every moment with him, but I simply didn't have private time when I was with Jack to dash off a note to Terry. Nor could I tell Terry about my best adventures: with Jack at Helmut's café and Ludwig's castles . . . roaming the streets of Füssen and sharing a finger-licking torte with Jack . . . Jack's crystal factory tour . . . hiking with Jack in the forest near the Czech border. And obviously, I couldn't tell Terry I had kissed Jack with the same passion we had shared in Boulder less than a month before.

I slithered past my adventures with Jack in a vague footnote crammed at the end of my first letter: "Suddenly went down to the Füssen area for a few days and didn't get this letter finished." As if I went there by myself on a last-minute lark. Worse, I ended the letter with "I don't want you to forget I'm always thinking about you. I'll write more tonight." I didn't write for another week. For shame.

In today's letter, I wrote to him about the beatniks I had dinner with in Zurich. They were singing their way across Europe, living off their tips as street musicians. And the two elderly men who got off the Geneva train because I'd told them it wasn't the train to Graf. I didn't know that *Graf* was German for *Geneva*. I also told Terry about my new bikini, European cathedrals I'd seen, the relics of the war that were everywhere—all kinds of things we'd talked about. He had never been to Europe, and he thought himself lacking because of it. I had to give him a full accounting after all the time he had spent making lists of places for me to go and artwork to see.

I read and reread Terry's letters—four by now, nineteen typewritten pages, single-spaced—which I'd carried with me to Switzerland, reliving shared experiences he so vividly reminded me of. Sunbathing together in Boulder Creek (naked—what in the world had I been thinking?), slurping ice cream and gooey chocolate at Charcoal Chef, reading the Sunday *Denver Post* in his apartment, and strolling the CU campus.

Meanwhile, in my three days in Lausanne, I'd stewed myself into a fine mess with my fixation on spending as little money as possible. I had opted for a hotel room with a shared bath because a private bath cost three times as much. So my bathroom was down the hall. "Shared" did *not* mean "No, please, you go first." I lurked in the hallway, trying to outrace a bevy of shadowy competitors, all of whom needed an hour or more to complete their duties.

By my final night in Lausanne, I had spent three nonstop days getting up at dawn, running around all day, and working up a sweat that would have embarrassed the racehorse Man o' War. For three days, I'd been outhustled at the shared bathroom. My need for a shower was dire. I had to be at least halfway embraceable for my reunion with Jack in Landshut. The final morning, I launched my attack well before dawn, captured the bathroom, barricaded the door, and got down to business. What was my reward? No hot water, barely enough cold drizzle for a birdbath and certainly not enough to shampoo my stringy hair.

Worse, dyslexia struck. I twisted the 7:24 a.m. departure time to read 7:42, missed my train, and wasted my tiny reserve of energy cursing my stupidity.

Terry

Thursday, 25 June 1964, Silverton. I arrived in Silverton last night at dusk and dove immediately into the yearlong BS session in the Grand Imperial bar. Today, I pitched in at the *Silverton Standard*, twelve hours' worth, helping Allen publish his paper on time.

Friday I pulled an all-day stint at the hand-fed letterpress, knocking out an order of 2,500 envelopes and letterheads. I also printed up twenty-five envelopes addressed to Annie in care of her brother in Germany—in red and black ink, which meant I had to scrub the press rollers after printing the black, re-ink them, hand-feed each envelope through again, scrub off the red, and re-ink the rollers in black. I jazzed up the envelopes with five one-inch-high dingbats, each depicting an 1880s policeman in a different pose. Ha, everyone in Germany would know Annie had a guy back home.

After a full day Saturday, Allen and the gang from the Grand Imperial bar jeeped fifteen miles up the canyon to Animas Forks, an 1870s ghost town. We gathered around a fireplace in a long-abandoned house, gobbled down beans and hotdogs, drank beer, serenaded ourselves with Pete Seeger favorites, and, as the temperature plummeted, pulled on our sleeping bags like thick lap robes and applauded the two among us who recited their own poetry.

When the full moon cast eerie shadows through the broken windows, we switched to ghost stories, let the coals die, and, huddled like spent puppies, drifted off to sleep. Two of our six were women, both spoken for, and neither of them Annie. I spent half the night trying to conjure her up inside my sleeping bag, luscious thoughts to be sure, but achingly unsatisfying, especially given the muted moans from the married couple not two feet away from me.

Monday, 29 June 1964, overlooking Silverton. The previous afternoon, I'd hiked the seven-mile jeep trail up Kendall Peak, clambering up the riprap to the summit, and then camped alone in a mini-valley below timberline. No designated campsites, no toilets or running water. Just my sleeping bag and a spot of hillside I claimed as my own. I scrounged firewood, built a fire ring of stones, charred a couple of Polish sausages from Snarky's Market, slapped them into hunks of sourdough bread, and washed them down with a can of lukewarm Olympia beer. Breakfast had been the same, minus the beer, but with an orange as a chaser. I hadn't seen another person in two days.

I was lonely but not alone, perched there on the Silverton face of Kendall, shirtless, resting against my backpack. Silverton was 3,500 feet below, as tiny as a Monopoly board from atop a high-rise office building. Even from there, the half-block-long Grand Imperial Hotel dominated the town like a giant among pygmies.

I was lounging on a hillside as plush as a Persian carpet—a mosaic of thousands of tiny white, red, and yellow flowers, each no larger than the head of a nail. Around me, a brigade of bumblebees was on a mission to frisk every single flower. I focused on one guy for ten minutes. A workaholic, he crawled up to a flower, latched on with his forelegs, pulled it to him, and dipped his snout in. He lingered only a second before buzzing on to the next one and the next. No rest. Obviously, he got paid for volume, not by the hour.

Private Bumblebee was too busy to bother me, but earlier, as I tiptoed into this botanical Shangri-La, his mates had buzzed me like a security force, circling and returning for a second opinion before buzzing back to work. They were slow, like cargo planes droning, not fast like fighter jets, and they were curious, making sure I wasn't a threat.

My only other companions had been the marmots, popping up on the rocks as I worked my way down from the summit. Neighborhood sentinels, they darted out of sight at my slightest twitch. Three seconds later, they popped up again, sounding the alarm—squealing really. Some people called them whistle-pigs. Until I cleared their territory, they rat-tat-tatted the hillside with warning calls, a constant barrage that charted my every step through their homeland.

Last night on the mountain, I remembered two things I'd forgotten since hiking up here the year before. One was the night sky, a canopy of brilliant stars, not only above but around me, a scintillating geodesic dome. Up here, above thirteen thousand feet, it was stars and moon, not a hint of civilization. I lay in my sleeping bag, marveling at the expanse, pondering the magnificence of this universe. Annie would have liked it too.

My other memory was the cold, even on the cusp of July. Yesterday, I clomped around the abandoned mine in the saddle at the base of the peak. Winter lived on there, in the form of a massive snowdrift hardened into granulated ice. In the predawn light this morning, I finally gave in to the need to pee. Outside my sleeping bag, in my briefs, teeth chattering, I expected my stream to freeze into instant icicles.

Now, nearing noon, the tourist-filled narrow-gauge train from Durango chugged into view, wending its way along the river, nearing the end of its forty-five-mile, three-and-a-half-hour run up the canyon to Silverton. From

Kendall Peak, it looked like a miniature model train. Its coal-fired steam engine puffed black smoke, but it was too distant for the sound to climb the mountain. I couldn't see inside the engine, but I knew that beside the engineer, a shirtless, muscle-bound, sweat-drenched fireman shoveled coal into the blast-furnace-hot firebox.

As the train entered town, it whistled a long, mournful howl that echoed off the mountain peaks. It transported me into the Old West, a time when men as tough as that train fireman carved the railroad bed out of the mountainside with picks, shovels, and dynamite—no heavy equipment. Between October 1881 and July 1882, they laid these tracks from Durango to Silverton, winter snow be damned.

Men mined year-round up there. At one mine, they finally built a tram to haul the ore down, and in midwinter when the trail lay buried under fifteen feet of snow, miners rode up in open ore buckets. The temperature would plummet to thirty-five or forty degrees below from December through January. How many of them lost fingers and toes to frostbite? On an earlier hike, I found a hoard of sealed ore samples stamped "The Omaha & Grant SM. Co, Durango, Colo.," dated December 28, 1877. That meant they shipped ore on pack mules to Durango for at least five years before the railroad reached Silverton.

Below me, the train arrived and sat wheezing a half block from Greene Street, the town's main drag. Some five hundred tourists poured out of the open-air cars and fanned out like explorer ants through a town that had only 849 full-time residents. They were besieged by teens shoving restaurant flyers at them. A phony gunfight in one dirt street would end when the "dead" gunmen jumped up and begged the tourists to eat at the Bent Elbow Café.

The visitors would have two hours to pick among the restaurateurs pitching them for their lunch money, window shop the six blocks of stores along Greene, and buy their souvenirs. Shop after shop peddled tourist kitsch, like key rings, mugs, shot glasses, redwood knickknacks, and mounds of cheap imports from Hong Kong and Japan.

By now, the air would be heavy with the stink of cotton candy, butter-drenched popcorn, and sizzling burgers. Last summer, in my editorial "Missing: One Ferris Wheel," I decried the hucksterism but also made the plea for a sober look at how to showcase Silverton's uniqueness—its mountains, its mining and railroad histories, its potential for winter sports. In the ensuing full page of responses from irate locals, my plea for sanity got swept away by attacks on my carnival analogy. Fortunately, they didn't tar and feather me and run me out of town on a rail, an Old West tradition that had been long abandoned, though one reader offered to revive it.

The real problem with my editorial wasn't so much the content as timing. It followed my July 4 editorial from the week before, "Old Glory: Only a Symbol." I entreated Silverton's citizens to commit themselves to the ideals America stood for—equality, justice, and fair play, for example—and excoriated those who would define patriotism as merely flying the flag, shooting off fireworks, and guzzling beer on the Fourth of July. A raft of locals interpreted it as treason. Marshall should go to Russia if he didn't like it here, one reader wrote. Another called me a Communist.

Despite the hassles, I realized after I returned to Boulder for my senior year that I'd fallen in love with Silverton—and that Allen and I shared a dream. As publisher, editor, printer, pressman, photographer, journalist, clerk, and businessman, he would succeed or fail on his merits alone. I wanted the same, my own small-town newspaper. That summer had given me a real-life taste of what that meant. I did write passionate editorials, but also dozens of news stories. I covered town meetings, made friends with politicians, teachers, miners, store owners, and plain folks and immersed myself in the town's conflicts as well as its history.

Silverton had its problems: long, isolated winters when no tourists came; the threat of avalanches that could block the single highway to Durango to the south and Ouray to the north. One did in March a year before. It swept a local minister and his two daughters to their deaths over a cliff on Red Mountain Pass.

Silverton also had more than its share of substandard houses, alcoholism, unemployment, and grinding poverty. I embraced them, not as deficits, but as challenges to confront and resolve.

But I never imagined when I left for my senior year at CU that my charming new ally from the weekend talkfests at the Grand Imperial would soon ensnare me in a life-altering moral crisis.

6

Le Grand Tour

Ann

Tuesday, June 30, 1964, en route to Paris. Today marked liberation from work for Jack, freedom from the prying eyes of his troops, and the beginning of a two-week road test of our budding romance.

But rain clouds hovered. He seemed awfully pensive, not the chatty companion I'd discovered in his audio letters. Probably still stewing about Terry. How could we move past this?

Jack waylaid my thoughts. "Our first stop is Dachau. Not the happiest spot to begin this great vacation of ours, but it's a somber reminder of my life as a soldier."

So that was it: a Nazi concentration camp. Even on vacation, the specter of war had hitched a ride.

At Dachau's main gate, a wrought-iron sign proclaimed, *"Arbeit macht frei."* Jack translated: "Work makes you free."

Inside the barracks, the beds for the prisoners were wooden platforms arranged like warehouse shelves, as if the humans housed there were miscellaneous packages to be sorted, stacked, and stored. Achingly painful photos documented the grim history: no mattresses, sheets, or pillows, despite rough-cut boards and subzero winters. I shivered, wondering how long I could have survived packed in with strangers. I'm not claustrophobic, but I nearly choked right there at that exhibit as I imagined trying to avoid the hot, foul breath of fellow prisoners, none of whom, I was sure, had the luxury of a toothbrush.

Next to me, Jack whispered, "Initially, the Nazis went after 'undesirables,' like Communists, intellectuals, homosexuals, and Gypsies, and put them to work as slaves in their weapons industry. Later on, when they started arresting Jews, they sent many of them here."

The prisoners had no place for their belongings, but there was no need. The Nazis had confiscated everything—jewelry, watches, silverware, shoes, clothes, coats, hats—all of it piled high in a macabre artwork. I stared at the emaciated prisoners in other photos, their skeletal frames outlined under their prison-striped garb, faces gaunt, eyes haunted. How could the guards look into those eyes and sleep at night? One of the exhibits said more than 200,000 prisoners were subjected to barbaric extremes at Dachau and more than 41,500 men, women, and children perished.

When Jack and I entered the low-ceiling gas chamber, images from the movie *Judgment at Nuremberg* came to mind. I conjured up my own private horror of 1944. I would have been two years old, but I pictured myself as a teenage Ann Frank arriving at that camp:

The train squeals to a halt after a ghastly five long days in a stifling, windowless boxcar, my fellow prisoners and I crammed in so tightly we can't sit. No food or water. Our "toilet" is a kerosene can, its foul contents overflowing and sloshing on the floor. The boxcar doors swing open. Guards wave their guns and order us out. We stumble from the train, blinded by the bright sun. But not all of us. When our mass of humanity thins out, the standing-up dead slump to the boxcar floor.

Shouting guards march us women and girls to a building marked Brausebad *(bath/shower). They order us to take off our clothes. I'm naked among strangers. But at last we can wash away the sickening stench of sweat, vomit, excrement, and soot from the train. Cowering, we are crowded into the shower. The doors lock behind us.*

And then an odd hissing sound. Instantly, my nose and eyes burn. I'm coughing, gagging. It's gas, not water. Impossible! I'm faint. My nose is bleeding. We pound at the door, yank the handles. No escape. Scratching and flailing, the women press in, clamber over me. I trip on a fallen child. I collapse. They climb on me, press me down, suffocate me. . . .

I gasped.

"You okay?" Jack asked.

"Not really," I said, returning to the present.

"Understood . . ."

Peering into the horrific cramped building at Dachau, I mourned the people who died there and at the other camps, along with their family members forever denied parents, siblings, and friends.

At the far end of the exhibit, a small display said that this gas chamber, unlike those at other camps—death camps—wasn't used for its intended purpose, that Dachau was a work camp, not an extermination camp like Auschwitz-Birkenau and Treblinka. Really? Was this small notice a whitewash or the truth?

As though Jack had read my mind, he said, "Many prisoners were executed by guards in other ways. They were hanged or shot when they tried to escape or when they committed minor offenses or, who knows, just because."

He touched my elbow, motioning me outside. "Other prisoners died from brutal medical experiments or typhus or the inhumane conditions. There were so many bodies, they had to cremate them. White ash billowed constantly from the smokestacks of the crematorium, and the smell of burning flesh filled the air—and the neighbors pleaded ignorance."

I shook my head, dizzy from the gruesome details.

On our way back to the car, Jack broke the silence. "Robert Burns said it best: 'Man's inhumanity to man / Makes countless thousands mourn.'"

We drove off, my mind reeling. Of course, I had read about the Holocaust, but I hadn't been personally touched by it. I had no family history, no relatives who died in the genocide. I had never met anyone with relatives who had fallen victim to it.

As the verdant countryside skimmed past, I felt a renewed gratitude for the willingness of soldiers from all over, including Jack, Bonner, and Dad before them, to do their share to put a stop to—and be a bulwark against—tyranny, even now.

Finally, Jack spoke. "Remember, not all Germans were like that. A number of Hitler's generals, like Falkenhausen and Halder, opposed him. Those two were incarcerated at Dachau. Not all of our 'enemies' were evil. Now we have to engage them. Foster our common interests."

"Big challenge."

"Yes, but look how far we've come in twenty years. West Germany, Italy, and Japan are now friends and trading partners. That's why I'm thinking Foreign Service. Big problems call for big efforts. Best of all worlds? You and me in the Foreign Service together."

He'd written that in letters, but to hear him say it now affirmed a growing bond. Leading where? Life as an ambassador's wife? Working with Jack as a USAID team? "Sounds intriguing," I said.

Near Stuttgart, Jack pulled off the road, unloaded a cooler, and spread out an army blanket. "Back in a sec," he said. He returned with his hands behind his back. "Which hand, *Fräulein?*" With a flourish, he presented a bouquet of tiny wildflowers. "Let the petals represent my tenderest thoughts. The greenery, the depth and strength of my feelings. And the fragrance, a hint of our unbounded joy. May we work together to make a difference in this world."

I tucked the flowers behind my ear. "And may we work to put an end to war."

He turned to fiddle with lunch. Had I pushed him too far? I knew we were in the clutches of war, albeit a cold war, and defending his country was both his profession and his passion. But was war the only way to solve disputes?

Late that afternoon, close to Strasbourg, France, Jack turned into a wooded area and stopped for the night by a small, grass-banked lake.

"Why don't you fix us some tea?" he said. He took out a single-burner Coleman and showed me how to crank it up. I made black tea, his favorite. I didn't drink tea, but camping was no time to get persnickety. I downed a whole cup.

Jack ambled over to the car, took out the tent, and set it up. It was teeny—space enough for the two of us only if we were on top of each other. Outwardly, he was all business, but I sensed a sinful smile lurking beneath the facade. "A one-man tent?" I asked.

"Negative. One-man, one-woman. You said you like 'cozy.' Your letter, remember?"

I had only myself to blame. After I had written about my camping trip with Terry, Jack proposed camping with me when he got home from Germany. He'd gone on a quest to find "two single sleeping bags that zip into one double."

As our letters heated up, he wrote, "Maybe a double isn't such a good idea; we'd better have a chaperone. How about your brother Jimmy?" He said he might not be able to "control" himself.

Flirtatious zeal triumphed over good sense. I wrote back,"Zip-together bags sound cozy. And let's not invite my kid brother."

But I wasn't ready to "go all the way," and tonight would put restraint to the test.

"The tent's so small. I think my pen outran my discretion."

"Bonner and I slept in this very tent during ranger training. It saved us from freezing our bu—I mean, our *toes* off. Something worrying you?" He looked at me deadpan.

"Kinda. I'm wondering how this is going to work."

"Oh, really? It worked with your *old buddy,* I hear. Same way, I suppose."

"We didn't have a tent, and we weren't close enough to touch each other. Besides, he was safe—no passions to keep in check. At that time." Oops, me and my stupid mouth!

"'At that time?' You have no idea how that thought has kept me awake at night."

He rolled the sleeping bags into the tent, laying them out side by side. Wall to wall, overlapping by at least a foot. "There. Plenty of space."

I stood there mute.

He frowned. "What's wrong?"

"Well, jeez, we're still getting to know each other. I'm a little anxious."

"*You're* anxious? I haven't slept ever since your first letters mentioned your *friend* Terry. Are you really serious about this guy?" He plopped onto the blanket, looking at me intently.

I scrambled to recover. "Jack, the most important thing is this. You exceed the person I dreamed about for years. This development with Terry has crashed into dreams you and I spun together over the past year. It's not something I sought, or even anticipated, but it's there, and I can't ignore it. At the same time, it has *not* diminished how I feel about you. Not a whit."

"Just know that every time I hear that name, a threat springs to life. I thought he was the past, that you shut it down before you came to Germany, before it—"

"Hold on. This trip is about *us*, about you and me, and what we need to do to get really acquainted in the weeks ahead." I copped a wicked grin, and I, well, I summoned my dormant feminine wiles. Nothing lewd, merely a glance and a hint of promise.

Finally, a sly smile. "Actually, I can think of a thing or two," he said.

A caution light started blinking. Guys all seemed to have the same goal—sex. And they seemed so fragile if you set limits up front, as if their manhood were always at stake. How could I make him understand that unfettered sex was out of bounds without throwing a wet blanket on our romance? "Depends on what you have in mind," I said.

"Tell you what. You call the shots on this one. I promise I won't do anything to make you uncomfortable. This is too important to commit suicide by haste."

I wanted to hug him. No, wrong message. "Agreed," I said.

At dinnertime, Jack dipped water from the lake, heated it, and set an opened can of stew in the boiling water. Soon dinner was bubbling, and the fragrance wafted through the evening air. I sopped up the gravy with chunks of bread left from our lunchtime sandwiches.

Bedtime. A new dilemma. What to wear? My nightie wasn't meant for a tent. "I know this sounds silly, but how do we do this? Sleep in our clothes? I'll look like a hobo tomorrow."

"I normally sleep in my T-shirt and undershorts and lay my clothes out beside me. Keeps them wrinkle-free. For the two of us, we can put them just beyond our heads. Wouldn't want anything to crowd us." He was enjoying this way too much.

"Easy for you. I don't have a T-shirt or boxers."

"I'll lend you mine."

Wear his undershorts? No way! But his T-shirt would be long enough to cover my vitals. "Do you have an extra T-shirt? I'll wash it as soon as we get back."

"Yes . . . if you promise *not* to wash it. I'll sleep in it every night for the rest of my life."

"Yuck!"

Flashing what Terry would have called a "shit-eating grin," he pulled out a neatly folded T-shirt. "What if you go into the tent first?" I said. "I'll change out here."

Undressing under the stars set my pulse racing. I pulled his T-shirt over my bra and panties and peered into the pale yellow triangle lit by his flashlight. I almost choked on the stench of musty canvas. "Knock, knock, any room at the inn?"

"Do you have a reservation, miss?"

"I had several, but that nice fellow outside set them at ease."

"Excellent. I've got one spot left. Here, test it out."

The sleeping bags opened toward each other. I slithered into my spot and kept my bag zipped most of the way up, but not all. I took a deep breath and let my free hand creep toward him. He met me more than halfway. "Tired?" he asked.

"A bit. I'm not used to sleeping outdoors. But you? How are you feeling so far?"

"Overwhelmingly in love," he said. "May I kiss you good night?"

How rare. I always imagined if a guy ever asked me that, it meant he was too dense to read my feelings. But Jack was keeping his promise. I tilted him onto his back and moved in. He smelled faintly of aftershave. "You'd better."

He pulled me onto him. Our lips touched, caressed, explored. He stroked my back through the T-shirt and began toying with it, inching it up. I tensed. I touched his hand, stopped his progress. "Jack, no. Not yet."

He stiffened and rolled away.

"Remember when I pooh-poohed your idea of bringing Jimmy if we go camping? Maybe we do need a chaperone. Passion could sweep us through the rapids and over Niagara Falls."

"Sounds thrilling."

"Too scary. At least for now. We barely know each other. We're headed to a place I've never been. I'm not ready to go there. We'll—*I'll*—regret it if we get ahead of ourselves."

I pulled his hand to my face and put it under my cheek, like a pillow. Eventually, he dozed off. I couldn't.

I was falling in love with him.

Terry

Tuesday, 30 June 1964, Silverton. I thought Silverton would ease the aching loneliness of life without Annie. It didn't. It merely forced me to face the truth: I couldn't live without her. But she was merrily globe-trotting through Europe with her dashing lieutenant. The all-American Boy Scout. Audie Murphy in the making. Worse, Annie loved him. She had told me that she loved me too, but the odds were against me.

Still, I wasn't about to give up, especially to some guy who was as much myth as macho man. I had to beat this guy. And by airmail, not hand-to-hand combat.

I settled into my friend John Ross's second-story corner apartment on Greene Street, got out my typewriter, and stared out at Kendall Peak for inspiration. Damn! Images of former girlfriends Sarah and Rachael cavorted on the mountainside like sprites. I had blurted out everything to Annie about my nights with both women, every sordid detail, the kinds of details that guys with common sense kept under lock and key and buried in underground vaults. What a numbskull I'd been! This was going to be like conquering Mount Everest. Alone. In shorts and a T-shirt.

After I left Silverton the summer before and rolled into Boulder, I was so lonely I jumped at an invitation to a back-to-school party thrown by Sarah Abrams, one of my J-School classmates. Classes would begin Monday, September 16, and Sarah invited everyone in J-School to her place Saturday night, all fifty of us. Normally, I avoided college bashes. Raucous music. Obnoxious drunks. Suffocating clouds of cigarette smoke. The stench of spilled beer. No chance for decent conversation at these bacchanals—not amid the mingling of sweaty bodies drenched in aftershave or perfume and pheromones dripping off the walls.

But a Sarah Abrams party was front-page news. She wasn't a party animal. She was smart, articulate, and well informed, someone you didn't challenge if you didn't have your facts straight. She was five-two and as svelte as a model, always dressed smartly in jumpers, pressed blouses, pleated skirts, pumps. Never sweatshirts or jeans. She packed her hair into a tight bun, like a stereotypical frontier schoolmarm. That made her ears stick out and her face pinched and severe, even when she smiled. And she alone in J-School wore bright red lipstick, Marilyn Monroe–style, broad and thick. Most of us were twenty-one or twenty-two. Sarah was *twenty-nine*. She exuded maturity. To top it off, she was a New Yorker from the city. She knew things I couldn't even imagine.

A Sarah Abrams party? Of course I went. Beer flowed, but Sarah served wine too, and on a table draped with a white tablecloth, she heaped plates of croissants and breads, lunch meat, finger foods, chicken and meat morsels, shrimp, and pastries. A turntable spun soft music, not wild dance stuff, but music worth listening to—Joan Baez, Pete Seeger, Dixieland jazz greats Pete Fountain and Al Hirt, and Peter, Paul, and Mary. Even some Mozart horn concerti.

We seniors huddled like sheep in a thunderstorm. After being scattered all over the country for the summer, we had tales to tell. Sarah circulated, greeting us one by one, and pulled us away to introduce us to the new underclassmen. Our eyes met now and then, and Sarah would smile or nod. She did that with everyone, but she seemed exceptionally warm toward me that night. When we talked, she laid her hand on my arm, stroking it lightly. That, too, appeared to be her big-city sophistication. She charmed everyone, guys and gals alike.

No one got drunk. Or obnoxious. At eleven-thirty, she began guiding people to the door. By midnight, there were only three of us—Sarah, me, and a jock bent on becoming a sports reporter. She had taken down her hair. It was a shimmering brown, silky and full, hanging to her buttocks. Her face was soft, not pinched at all, and she had flawless skin, her eyes sparkling with intrigue.

The jock talked on. I wanted him to go. Sarah too. Her eyes flashed it. She jumped up. "Okay, my friend, I hate to run you off, but I promised Terry I'd critique a piece he wrote on Silverton for the *Daily*. Tonight! And I'm already pooped."

She eased him out and bolted the door. "Whew, a nice guy, but oblivious."

"No lie. But what piece on Silverton? We didn't—"

"We *might* have. Quick, huh?" She broke into a grin so natural she seemed a free-spirited alter ego of the Sarah Abrams of J-School. Then it hit me—no lipstick. She hadn't reapplied it after she'd eaten. I detested lipstick, especially thick, goopy, bright lipstick. God, she was lovely!

"I don't want to leave," I said. "But if you're exhausted, I—"

She brushed her lips across my cheek. "No, sir, you're staying. I saved the last dance for you." She led me to the turntable and put on *Carmina Burana*. "I've been dying to do this all night." She cranked it up and coaxed me into a wild flight through her apartment, both of us laughing, high-stepping, flinging about like crazies. We were breathless when it ended and locked in each other's arms as if we were lovers reuniting after months apart. She fit perfectly.

I spent the night with her. We made love again before breakfast and a third time after we plowed through the Sunday *Denver Post* and polished off a pot of coffee.

How ironic that Sarah delivered me from virginity. In our three years in J-School, she had never shown the barest hint of romantic interest in me, nor I in her.

Why Sarah? Why that night?

Silverton, plain and simple. The summer had forged a new me, a guy certain he could indeed win a woman's love. In high school, girls had gone for the jocks, not for guys like me. I did play football, first-string middle linebacker, but I wasn't a star, and at 120 pounds, I wasn't big enough to try out for water boy at football-crazed CU. My memories of high school wrestling? Match after match on my back desperately trying to keep from getting pinned, the cheerleaders chanting a single cheer, "Get up, Terry, get up!"

I tried baseball one spring, but after three weeks in right field witnessing baseballs, runners, and the entire infield disappear in the daily dust storms, I opted for a printer's apron and ink-stained fingers at our local newspaper. I was first-chair clarinet in our high school band, but girls didn't flock to clarinet players, especially not the cute little saxophone virtuoso two rows behind me. She, too, preferred jocks. In college, I had scarcely dated before Steffi and I hit it off my junior year.

But my world changed dramatically when Laura Lee told me she loved me. In person. In her letters. Moreover, she sparked a flame that transformed me from a wistful wallflower into a confident suitor.

In the end I lost her, yes, but not because she judged me lacking.

On September 14, 1963, I strode into Sarah's party boldly self-assured. I was ready. Sarah must have sensed it, even if at the time I couldn't. That fall she fulfilled the fantasy I'd had since my freshman year—Saturday afternoons at Folsom Field, made exquisite by post-game celebrations in a woman's bed. With Sarah came the bonus of leisurely Sunday brunches in her apartment, as well as many a weeknight sleepover.

Boulder was nirvana: warm days, crisp nights, and a smorgasbord of guest lectures, concerts, and shows. I had classes I loved, a rewarding part-time job running the J-School photo lab, intimacy with a fascinating woman. All that was missing was a winning football team. Ever hopeful, on November 9, Sarah and I trudged yet again into Folsom Field to cheer the hapless Buffaloes against Big Eight rival Missouri. Another loss: 28–7. We always stayed until the bitter end, but that week, Sarah sat there long after the final whistle, after the student section emptied out around us. "Let's go to Timber Tavern," she said.

We had never gone drinking, not even to Tulagi or The Sink. Certainly not Timber Tavern, the hangout for locals and graduate students. "You serious?"

"Quite. We can teach each other how to cry in our beer."

Timber Tavern was dimly lit and, with its intimate booths, romantic. We ordered two glasses, not a pitcher, and before she took her first sip, she said, "This isn't working, Terry. You want me only for sex. Sex without love isn't enough."

I couldn't respond. I wasn't angry or even hurt, just flabbergasted. She was right—mostly. I did enjoy her presence, our spirited conversations, our shared meals, even washing and drying dishes together. But, yes, sex was the core of what we had. I thought that had been our understanding from the beginning.

We didn't argue or mutter sad regrets. We didn't even finish our beers. I drove her home and said good night as awkwardly as if it were a first date. I didn't go in that night—or ever again. After the shock wore off, I knew she was right. Sex wasn't enough, no matter how much pleasure it gave us. Though it would be months before I finally realized it, Sarah and I lacked what I had with Annie—a shared background, a solid friendship, common hopes, and love.

How could I have blown things so badly? Spending that fall floating in a bubble of carnal bliss, as if I were the first man to discover sex and, like Moses, was meant to convey the Word to the uninitiated. What had I been thinking, telling Annie all about Sarah and urging her to find a lover? "God, Annie, sex is exquisite. Go for it."

Now, in Silverton, less than a year later, those words had come back to haunt me. What if Annie had already taken my advice? Or, like Laura Lee, set a date for the wedding? I didn't have a minute to spare: I spent that last day of June at my typewriter. By nightfall I had drafted a letter I hoped would put Lieutenant Sigg out of Annie's mind:

Remember one night, early in our new relationship, when we walked across campus and talked of us and of marriage? You spoke of freedom, of the need to live by and for yourself. You said you wanted marriage, but not yet. And the same applied to me—so much to do, so much to learn, so many places to see. I had to live first before I tied myself down.

Annie, I was wrong, and the month away from you has proved that. Marriage doesn't fetter a man and render him a slave. Marriage means the loss of freedom only to those who do not know how to live. To you and me, who love life, who have hopes and desires, realizations of possibilities, of goals, marriage can open a wonderful and great life.

Annie, I am announcing formally and officially (since I always manage to do things awkwardly) that I am proposing to you. I want you to marry me. I want you to marry me this year, this summer, before you go to Arizona and in place of my going to Venezuela.

I can't offer much—no job, little money, a few books, no straight path to follow, no set goal, lots of unanswered questions. But I can offer a hundred different ideas and hopes, a tremendous love of life, a strange sense of humor, and one hell of a lot of confidence that we can not only make a go of it but find in each other and in ourselves a truly great existence in a world that we do not understand.

Wednesday morning, 1 July 1964, Silverton. My God, a letter from Annie! In fact, two: one dated June 23; the second, June 25. Mom had forwarded them from Center. Both letters were postmarked Switzerland, not Germany.

Skimming letter number one, I found what I was looking for: "I love you, Ter!"

Some of her news was old, from three weeks before, when she overnighted in Paris on her way to Munich. Finally, some details. "You are with me in each adventure," she wrote. I was up for that game. I was beside her— Annie *and I* took a taxi from the airport, eight lanes, cars weaving in and out like a Formula One race. *We* went to Notre Dame Cathedral—huge, marble floors, refrigerator-cold. But it was late afternoon, and the cathedral was closing, no time to linger. *We* got "only a glimpse of the beautiful windows." En route to the hotel, *we* gaped at prostitutes straight from

Irma la Douce loitering in a side street, flouting the law by flaunting their wares. Oh the irony—pious Christians at prayer within spitting distance of a brazen display of sex for sale. Ah, the French.

She mentioned my letter of June 15, about hiking the fields near Center. She'd gotten only four of my letters. I'd sent seven. Seven! She was in Zurich, but she was thinking about our spring adventures, *the two of us* at the doughnut shop, *the two of us* hiking Boulder Creek.

The doughnut shop: Me confessing that I'd fallen for her, Annie laughing like a loon. By mid-May, we were tossing around children's names like Frisbees, jokingly agreeing to honor both literature and my coming Peace Corps stint by naming our first kid Ricardo Ishmael Marshall. "Let's hope he's a boy," she said. "A girl would be mortified."

Boulder Creek: Annie naked on that granite rock, as nonchalant as if we were fully clothed in her dorm lobby, and moments later as jittery as a gazelle at a lion-rich watering hole. That was Annie—bursts of daring flirtation with the free-spirited sixties, followed by a quick retreat to the comfort of the Victorian fifties. Me too. We indignantly challenged the conservative moral code we'd been raised by, but it was imprinted in our DNA. We were neither Puritans nor free-love bohemians.

Annie's second letter was from Lausanne, Switzerland. I looked it up—southwest of Zurich on Lake Geneva.

"You spent the entire day with me, from the time I took the cable car into the exposition until I returned to my room exhausted," she said. She was brimming with enthusiasm. Around her, everyone spoke French, Italian, or German. She had lived four days as a mute, she said. "Even if there were someone to talk to, I still wouldn't be able to get along without talking to *you*."

She was traveling alone. Without her soldier and his race car. Maybe it didn't work out with Jack. I'd be so lucky.

The next morning, she was off to the beach—"I'll be able to relax in the sun for as long as I please. I haven't done that in two years."

Oh? Had she forgotten Boulder Creek so quickly? That day was far more than the memory of a nude girl. It was a turning point, an acknowledgment that our friendship had matured into love.

↩

Ann

Wednesday, July 1, 1964, near Strasbourg, France. I woke in the soft morning light. Jack was lying there gazing at me. He traced my eyebrow with his fingertips and stroked my cheek.

"Ready for new adventures, *Fräulein*? Or should I say, *mademoiselle*? Ready for Paris, city of love?" He propped up on his elbow.

"Can it top a romantic campout in the French countryside—in a just-the-right-size tent . . . as it turns out?"

"Nothing can top being with you, Miss Garretson. But think about the art! The history! The fine cuisine!" He sat up, waving his arms. Funny, I hadn't noticed his muscles before. Now I was hypnotized by how they moved under his T-shirt. He really did have a splendid physique.

"But first it's the famous Sigg fresh-air breakfast. My treat." He pulled on his lederhosen and bounded out. I dressed, finger-combed my hair, and followed. He was hunkered over the Coleman, the sun highlighting his blond hair in a warm nimbus.

He served scrambled eggs, fire-toasted bread, and tea.

I washed the dishes. After tidying up, he sidled over with a mischievous grin. "Ready for your morning bath, *mademoiselle*?"

Bathe in an arctic-cold lake? Naked? "So, *monsieur*, how do you propose we 'bathe'?"

"Well, I'll put on my swimsuit, soap up, rinse off, and, bingo, good as new. How else do people bathe? But first I'll treat myself to a real shave with hot water left from the dishes."

In the tent, I put on my one-piece bathing suit, not yet brave enough to wear the bikini. At the water's edge, I steeled myself. Cold had played havoc with me since I got frostbitten my first winter in Colorado. My hands and feet were hypersensitive, even years later. Jack was waist deep in the lake. "Is it freezing?"

"No, it's great!"

I doubted it. But fast, full immersion is the only way to beat ice water. I raced in at full speed. Surprise. It was refreshingly cool. "Wow, you're right," I said. "But what's this little animal?"

He waded over. I made a hand frog and squirted him in the face.

Our bath deteriorated into a noisy water fight—until we came together in a wet kiss. "This is better than any bath on maneuvers," he said. "Ready for a back scrub?"

"Sure!" He worked the soap into a lather at my lower back and made his way up to my shoulders. He pushed my swimsuit straps aside and, as if it were business as usual, headed for my breasts.

"Not so fast, sir. That area's off-limits to officers. Enlisted men too." I anchored the front safely in place, turned to face him, and smiled sweetly.

"Sorry. Got distracted." He soaped his chest and arms, chased the bar around inside his trunks, and dunked his body into the lake. With a hint of a lascivious smile, he handed me the soap.

Keeping a warning eye on him, I dropped the bar between my breasts, squished it around, rinsed off, and slowly backstroked to shore. He let out an exaggerated sigh.

We both dried off and dug out clothes to wear into Paris—long pants for Jack, a sundress for me. Five miles down the road, my skin still tingled. "That was fun. Thanks for insisting."

"Yes, it's great here in July. It's a bear in winter, especially with a gang of whiny soldiers."

"Do you always shave and bathe on maneuvers, even in winter?"

"Of course. Builds character. When we conquer little challenges, like shaving in ice water, it sharpens our discipline for the big ones."

In Paris, Jack wanted to stay on the Left Bank. Map in hand, I guided us down busy avenues, around traffic circles, and across bridges without a hitch. He darted through traffic like a race-car driver, in and out of openings I thought too small even for the sporty two-seater.

Parisians loved the Sting Ray. With the top down and all the narrow streets, we were close enough for them to offer words of praise. One even shook my hand as he made his way across the street. Their delight made the noise, stifling pollution, and chaos more bearable. I studied *Europe on Five Dollars a Day* and identified inexpensive hotels. Jack double-parked at the first one and ran in to check on it.

We looked no further. Jack lugged our bags up two flights to a small, airy room, the organza curtain floating in the breeze, bright and cheerful as a Renoir painting. Private bath. One bed. I shot him a withering look.

He shrugged as if it were beyond his control. "It's a whole lot cheaper. Think of it as city camping without a tent. I'll do my best to behave."

I should have asked him what "do my best to behave" meant. Had I grown up in a family where sex education was in the curriculum, I would have told him straight out that making love—*intercourse*—was verboten. We didn't have those talks in my family or say those words. Mom couldn't even say *pregnant*. Her term was a breathless "P-G." Lessons about sex were taught by metaphor, generalities, knowing looks, and moral admonitions: "Be a good girl, Annie." I assumed everyone's family was like mine, and I expected Jack not to break "the rules."

But my own libido was pounding at the door, and Jack seemed the ideal man to usher us in. Intercourse? Maybe not yet, but on the other hand . . . No. I had to convey that I wasn't going to let us go too far.

"At a *minimum*, I expect your 'best,' Lieutenant."

He snapped a salute. "Yes, sir—ma'am!"

I wasn't fooled. It would be a continuing challenge to hold that line. But I didn't push it. No need to spoil our first hour in Paris. "What do you have lined up this afternoon?"

"First, the Eiffel Tower. See the sights, stroll the Seine, find a hole-in-the-wall café. It's Paris. We go with the flow, *mademoiselle*."

Atop the Eiffel Tower, we choked on the smog shrouding the city. That and fighting the crowd on the platform took away all the fun, so we cut our visit short. Below, we gasped at the menu in the Jules Verne restaurant. Forty bucks a plate!

We scurried away. Farther down the Seine, we found Café la Palette. Comfortable. And reasonable, even with wine. The waiters switched effortlessly among French, German, Spanish, Italian, and English. At home, knowing *one* other language was a sign of education. Here, speaking several was a way of life.

"French is so sensuous," I said. "I don't speak it as well as you speak German, but I could if I immersed myself even for a short time. When I was fourteen and we lived in Italy, I quickly embraced the new sounds and gestures. Italian would have rolled off my tongue if we had stayed a second year."

"I envy your childhood," he said. "Before the academy, Johnstown was

my America. I want our kids to understand that great nations and wonderful people exist throughout the world."

Our kids? Whoa! Or did he mean his kids and my kids separately?
Didn't matter. It was a value we shared.

At the hotel, I trudged up the stairs, eyelids heavy. But this was no time
to be mentally spent. Again, what to wear to bed? Jack's T-shirt seemed
ridiculous. After all, this was Paris, not a campsite. My nightie would
cover more geography, despite the slits. Too sexy? Yep, but I didn't have
anything else. Bra? It had been uncomfortable in the tent. But sleep next
to him without one? Too risky.

In the bathroom, I ended up taking off my bra—comfort trumped
prudence—and slipped into the nightie, steeled myself, and ventured out.

Jack leaned against the headboard in his T-shirt, sheet up to his hips,
fingers locked behind his head. "Wow! You . . . you're stunning. I . . ." He
just stared. No, *leered*.

Frankly, it's a real turn-on to have the right guy look at you as if you
are the sexiest creature in the world, but at that moment I lost my nerve.
"This is all I brought to sleep in."

"It's perfect. You're perfect." Beneath the sheet, a telltale bulge threatened.

"You know what? I don't think this is a good idea after all, sleeping in
the same bed."

He dropped his arms. "No, seriously? Last night was the best campout
of my life." He paused. "But I'll sleep on the floor if you want me to."

I knew he would. That wasn't fair, though. Besides, I did want to sleep
with him. At least *next to* him. "To sleep with" held strikingly different
images for the two of us, but it wasn't the time to debate the finer points
of semantics. Unbidden, I said, "After last night, I know how delicious it
is to sleep—and wake up in the morning—beside you. We still have much
to learn about each other before . . . well, I'm not ready to make love yet.
I'm sorry."

He took a deep breath. "I guess our feelings are traveling at different
rates. Mine are at Mach speed. I already know enough. What do you need
to know?"

"I don't have a checklist or a speed limit. At Mach speed, however, you
miss the nuances." I sat on the foot of the bed. "We agree on so many big

things. It's the little things that can undermine a relationship. The further we go physically, the easier it is to overlook them. And one important thing about me is I can't rush into this. Can you accept that?"

"Maybe I'm more willing to 'overlook' whatever might come down the pike, but I also respect your need to know more about me. What do you propose?"

Glancing down, I noticed that my legs were exposed up to my panties, distracting from my message. I untucked the sheet and covered myself. "My hope is that we can sleep in this bed and enjoy being together. My expectation is that we won't make love tonight. Is that feasible?"

"Oh man, I didn't expect to fall into bed and make passionate love right off the bat. Though to be honest, I hoped we would." His eyes softened, even twinkled. "I still do. You're asking a lot. It will be the biggest battle of my life, but I want to honor your wishes. Promise to let me know the second you're ready to move forward?"

I wanted to leap across the bed and smother him with kisses. *Don't you dare, Ann. That would unravel everything.* I slid from under the sheet, turned out the light, and propped myself beside him. The city lights cast our room in a romantic hue. "I promise, soldier."

We kissed and stroked and drifted off in each other's arms.

Terry

Wednesday afternoon, 1 July 1964, Silverton. I spent the day rewriting my marriage proposal and then retyped it on high-quality bond, not on the pilfered letterheads or paper scraps I'd sent Annie over the years. I typed it single-spaced on one side of each sheet, using thesis margins instead of my normal front and back from edge to edge and top to bottom. Typed with even strokes. No letters punched into the paper or so faint they faded away. No erasures or scratched-out phrases. No hand-penciled additions. This letter had to be perfect.

I folded it into exact thirds with precision creases and slid it into one of my newly printed envelopes. At the post office, I bought an eight-cent airmail stamp *and* a thirty-cent special-delivery stamp.

"Mighty fancy envelope you got there, son," the postmaster said. "Let's make it extra special." He applied a red-and-blue "AIR PAR AVION MAIL" label and the yellow and green SPECIAL DELIVERY. "We missed the truck to Durango, but it'll go out first thing tomorrow," he added.

I headed for the Grand Imperial. Tonight, the old gang would be at the bar. We'd drink, we'd tell stories, we'd hoot and holler. And best of all, I wouldn't have to start waiting for a response from Annie until the next morning.

7
Postmark Silverton

Terry

Thursday, 2 July 1964, Silverton. The recurring nightmare woke me again last night—Lieutenant Stud, snazzy in dress blues, on bended knee, asks Annie to marry him. She's giddy. She accepts him on the spot.

No, I told myself in the dark, she wouldn't. I was positive she wouldn't. To make sure, I wrote her again in the morning, matter-of-factly, as if I were merely updating her on my comings and goings—four pages about my overnight hike up Kendall Peak. I also snuck in another plea:

> *I worry now about the letter I sent yesterday—wondering if I expressed myself well enough, if I offered enough to make you want to marry me. I worry that you will find too many objections or disregard it as a spur-of-the-moment outburst from a lonely friend, or that you are in love with Jack and remember me only as a close friend, or that you'll reject the offer (or request, or plea, or whatever one calls it).*
>
> *I know you won't decide overnight and send a reply by Tuesday, but come Tuesday I'll be expecting a reply and every day I will expect a reply, and I will be back in the mailbox routine as soon as I get home. How I wish I knew the something to say or do that would without fail assure our marriage. But I must wait, and wonder, and hope, and wait. I love you.*

For the next six hours, I devoted myself to the *Standard* before a gang of us took off midafternoon for Silver Lake. This was my Silverton: work to exhaustion and then run myself ragged in the mountains to keep my mind off Annie—what she was doing and with whom.

Ann

Thursday, July 2, 1964, Paris. Blaring horns, laboring garbage trucks, and maids jabbering in the hallway jolted me awake. I lay there admiring this guy beside me. A man of his word. We had made it through a marvelously loving night with no erosion to our pact of restraint. I leaned in for a whisper-light peck on the cheek.

He roared to life, burrowed his face in my mop of morning hair, and zeroed in with a single kiss on my lips. "Now that's a wake-up call, *mademoiselle*. Ready for round two?"

"How long you been awake?" I asked.

"Hours. Didn't want to disturb you in case you turned out to be a dream."

"Not a chance. Dreams don't get hungry, and I'm starving. How about breakfast?"

He rolled us into a full-length hug that left me tingling. And him? Clearly ready for a lot more. But when I didn't encourage him, he sighed. "Okay, I give up. Let's eat."

After showers and breakfast, we headed to the Sorbonne. He had applied for an Olmsted Fellowship, and the Sorbonne was on his list of top schools. An Olmsted would pay for graduate study and cultural immersion abroad, including language classes for the scholar and his wife. How enlightened: the wife recognized as a key partner. I wanted to be that wife.

Fortress-like, the Sorbonne sprawled over several blocks, capped by copper-topped towers aged to a pale blue. The central building was set around a long cobblestone quad. Minimal greenery. I had expected the Renaissance architecture, sure, but also expansive lawns and leafy retreats for reflection in the midst of the frenetic city. With a gesture that encompassed the quad, the dome, the spires, the cupolas, and rows and rows of windows surrounding us, Jack said, "We belong here, you and I."

"I'd master French first," I said. "Then French literature. French and British lit would make a compelling resume for a teacher. Or maybe I'd go back into journalism."

"For me it would be sociology and history," he said, rattling off a list of French sociologists he admired. Eyes sparkling, he fantasized that he would uncover a trunk of letters lost for centuries. He would analyze them and postulate a paradigm shift on the origins of the French Revolution.

As he spun his fantasy of student life in Paris, *I* became more and more *we*. "We'd rent a walk-up garret on the Left Bank, put up prints at first, and buy an obscure Matisse or Cézanne until we could afford a Picasso or Dali."

I held my breath. But he rambled on about missing out on the Rhodes and two years at Oxford. "I thought I'd won it, I really did. I was crushed."

I risked an empathetic hug. He put his arm around me. Wow. Had his rigid PDA code cracked, if ever so slightly?

Inside, we were drawn toward the library, with its brocade walls and endless rows of gleaming mahogany tables lit by individual brass lamps, all of which we could see through two-story high windows. An unsmiling guard barred our entry—no student IDs. No matter. We imagined burrowing through the dusty ancient tomes and first editions.

At noon we stopped at a small market, loaded up with a sturdy loaf of dark bread, French cheeses, a tomato, and some apples, and ambled into the Luxembourg Gardens. We picked our way among the pools and fountains ringed by red, purple, and yellow flowers, chose a shady spot in the thick grass, and ate our simple lunch while rooting for kids piloting small boats through the water. A pair of lovers sauntered by, the girl's hand in the guy's rear pocket, him patting her fanny. I elbowed Jack. "Do you want to enlighten them on PDA?"

"I know I hurt your feelings, and I'm sorry." He ran his fingers over his stubby hair. "But this GI haircut tags me as an American soldier. Too many of us have left babies behind. Besides, I want to set an example for my men. We have to show respect for all women."

I was thankful he hadn't seen me fume on my drive from the border back to Landshut. "Apology accepted," I said. "And I apologize for embarrassing you. Though I confess you warmed my insides when you put your arm around me at the Sorbonne."

"No accident. The thought of going to school together heated me up. And since ass patting—pardon my French—is *de rigueur* here, a wayward arm seems pretty tame. See, I'm more broad-minded than you thought."

"And after only one day in Paris," I said. "This place is growing on both of us."

He turned to me and flashed his lopsided smile. "Let's celebrate, declare ourselves liberated. How about a swanky dinner? Treat ourselves to Paris's world-famous cuisine."

"Love to. As long as we don't spend too much."

"Let me worry about that," he said.

Later, atop the Pantheon, we lingered hand in hand. Unlike the smoggy day before, the sky was a deep blue, dotted by puffy clouds. In every direction, Paris's landmarks jutted up in full display—Arc de Triomphe, Eiffel Tower, Notre Dame, and others we didn't recognize. We could live in Paris for years and never run out of places to visit. Inside the Pantheon, the frescoes seemed drab compared to the bright colors of the Rubens and Vermeer paintings I'd seen in Terry's art books. In the crypts, we silently honored the writings of Voltaire and Victor Hugo.

Back at the hotel, I begged for a short nap. Jack went off to arrange dinner. Thoughts of Terry wormed into my sleep. I couldn't write to him while I was with Jack, two weeks minimum. My silence would fuel his anxiety, precisely because he knew where Jack and I were. But even Terry's vivid imagination couldn't conjure up anything as damning as the reality—my cuddling with Jack in our shared bed and glorying in his kisses and caresses.

But I wouldn't have done anything differently. Not because I didn't love Terry, but because I also loved Jack. I wanted to blame Terry for blindsiding me, but I couldn't. He had opened my eyes to a world I wanted to explore. He loved me in spite of my naiveté, and he saw, before I did, what a fit we were. Meanwhile, Jack had read my thoughts from thousands of miles away and propelled me on this trip of a lifetime.

How could I have fallen in love with two men at the same time? Curiously, loving one in no way diminished my love for the other. But I could give my life, my loyalty, to only one, a commitment that could mortally wound the other.

The seventeenth-century restaurant Jack chose for dinner took my breath away—walls covered in gold leaf and a gold ceiling with intricate carvings, accentuated by a single chandelier, each light with its own tiny lampshade. A rigid maître d' whisked us through a cluster of small circular tables to a semiprivate niche.

I never could strut like a model, but after Jack pulled my hand into the crook of his arm, I confess I walked with a slight swish in the cocktail dress Mom had insisted on buying for me. He whispered, "Don't look now, but every man here is wishing he were in my shoes."

"Really? So how does that feel?"

"Scary. I need my sword to fend off the barbarians."

Ever the soldier, but tonight, I didn't mind.

The maître d' seated us in cranberry-red velvet chairs with carved wooden legs. An eggshell-white linen tablecloth reached halfway to the floor, with matching napkins and an array of silver on both sides of the nested china. To our right and left and all around were eight-foot-high mirrors, each reflecting our images from different angles. "Don't look now. We're surrounded . . . by ourselves!" I told Jack.

He nodded. "Classy company."

We delighted in course after course: onion soup, duck confit, roasted potatoes, sautéed vegetables, fruits, warm bread, and a different wine with every course—served in crystal goblets, enough to set our insides abuzz, but not so much we'd get sloshed. Between courses, we held hands across the tiny table. Openly.

With a cheese plate, the waiter delivered a special round of wine, a tribute from an unnamed diner who had penned on a small card, "*Vive l'amour! Vive la guerre!*" Were love and war two horns on the same bull? We looked around. No one made eye contact. We toasted the room.

At the end of the meal, with a flourish, our waiter presented a large plate with a chocolate soufflé for two. An elegant script, written in dark chocolate, ringed the plate's upper rim. "*Ann, Je t'aime! Jack.*" On the lower rim, it read, "Ann, I love you! Jack."

He leaned forward, eyes eager. My breath caught. This was it. He was going to propose. Here, now, with the waitstaff bearing witness, with the entire dining room gone silent. "Now isn't this an interesting surprise?" he said. "What say you now, *mademoiselle*?"

Would he fall on one knee? *Please don't!*

He winked and didn't say another word.

I waited. He smiled.

Two could play this game. "I'm shocked, Lieutenant, but this fine script is only half the story." I dipped my finger in the chocolate, swirled it around *Ann* and with arrows edited my name to the end and Jack's to the beginning.

"That's better," I said. "It's true, by the way." It was a game, yes, but I did love him. I wanted him to know. "If we gobble down the chocolate, what happens to the love?"

"It grows stronger from the inside. Here, try this." He scooped up a bite and held it out.

One bite demanded another. And another. I seized the spoon and returned the favor. Another bite. Two more. It was as intimate as kissing. Right there in public.

When the waiter brought the bill, I tried to peek at it, but Jack snatched it away. "No, my dear! Some things are mine alone."

It must have cost a fortune, probably more than fifty dollars.

Terry

Friday, 4 a.m., 3 July 1964, Silverton. In John Ross's apartment, I pounded out a letter to Annie about yesterday's trek to Silver Lake, crafted so she'd feel as if she had been with us. I was tempted to add "Sorry you weren't here. Read this and weep," but that would have been mean. Besides, I had a gnawing fear her adventures would dwarf mine.

Five of us had hiked to Silver Lake, including a cousin I hadn't seen since we were kids. Charlotte had blown into town on the narrow gauge with a college girlfriend. July 2 may have been midsummer everywhere else in America, but it was still spring in the San Juans. The switchbacks up the ridge were mountain-goat steep, made worse by a frozen avalanche as slick as hockey-rink ice. We had to chip toeholds so we could cross.

Midway, one of the guys slipped and shot past, screaming, "Grab me! Grab me!"

I lunged for him but missed. We all held our breath. He slid to a stop in a cluster of ice chunks thirty yards downslope. I started back down, but he sat up, called out "I'm okay, I'm okay," and got to his feet. We waited as he worked himself slowly across to our trail of toeholds.

"Nothing broken," he said, his voice cracking. "But I should have brought my toboggan."

"Or a parachute," one of the girls said.

After he caught his breath, we continued across, this time each of us making sure we jammed our boots into the toeholds before we moved on.

Silver Lake shivered in the shade of a legion of snow-covered peaks. The lake had begun to thaw, its surface cracked like a shattered mirror and too thin to walk on. We got there in the late afternoon, explored too long, and left after dark. Under a cloud-shrouded sky—no stars, no moonlight—we negotiated the ice field step by tenuous step with only two flashlights. Below the ice field, swirling winds whipped an icy mist into a prickly frenzy. It scoured our skin, chapped our lips, burned our eyes, and numbed us to the bone. The two girls had worn tennis shoes; their feet were soaked and frozen. Further down, Charlotte twisted her ankle, and I put my arm around her and helped her limp the last mile, plodding in tandem like wounded war buddies, our hips pressed together.

Afterward, she and I sat silently at the Grand Imperial bar, downing Black Russians until we thawed—nearly an hour. We swapped tales from our junior high years. One Thanksgiving, she and I hunted jackrabbits in our southeast forty with my .22. Another time, we cornered a rattlesnake behind the barn on their farm. In our retelling, the rabbits had multiplied to dozens, and the snake had grown to the size of a python.

We were a bit tipsy when I walked her up to her room in the Grand Imperial. We said good night and shook hands like we did in high school. Then we hugged, our first time ever. Through the night, images of my cousin ricocheted through my mind—the heat of her against me on the trail, her painful winces when I pried off her frozen tennis shoes and massaged her icy feet, and, later, her cheery laugh, her lithe frame.

I rejected those thoughts—she was my cousin!—and imagined her to be Annie. I brought Annie down the slope with me and massaged warmth back into her frosted feet, ankles, and legs. Sipped those Black Russians with her and guided her down the street and up the stairs into this very room. Ha, no self-conscious hug from Annie. Hugging, kissing, stroking were second nature to us now. Or they had been when I last saw her. But I couldn't keep Annie in focus. Too quickly her image faded into darkness.

My frozen hike rekindled other memories of winter in Silverton—the bitter cold, the mountains buried in snow, desolate Greene Street. But above all else, my week with Rachael the previous Christmas.

Oh my, Rachael: a witty, raven-haired seductress with a saunter that turned heads. I'd met her over the summer when she and her boyfriend, a CU geology grad student, were in Silverton roughing it like prospectors while he gathered data for his thesis. Rachael joined our weekend talkfests in the Grand Imperial bar. She was "Bobby's girl." Off-limits. Still, each Friday night I sat beside her at our table, consumed with envy at Bobby's fortunes. One night she told me, "Living in a tent on a rocky mountainside is the pits."

"I believe you," I said. "Would another Guinness ease the pain?"

She slipped in close and stroked my arm. "Oh, it would. It sure would, hon," she said.

We talked for hours. I didn't try to whisk her off to bed, as I so ached to do. Aside from that one conversation, I left Silverton for Boulder without spending a moment alone with Rachael.

But then came Friday, November 15, 1963, Boulder. Noon, to be precise. My last class for the week. For the first time that fall, I faced a weekend alone. Sarah had booted me out six days earlier. And Saturday's game against Kansas would be another sure loss. I stuffed my five-pound book of Shakespeare's works into my backpack and shuffled out of the classroom.

Across the hallway, a flashy girl in tight jeans and a pearl-button cowgirl shirt waved. She slouched against the wall like a rebel who'd sneaked out behind the barn for a snort. "Howdy, cowboy," she called. "You headed my way?" I looked around. "Yeah, you, Marshall. Who else you think I'm waiting for?"

My God, it was Rachael! "No Bobby here," I said. "Geology students don't hang out in Hellems Hall."

"Bobby who? I'm waiting for you, hon. And I'm hungry. I'm treating you to lunch."

She had broken up with Bobby, dropped out of CU, and moved back home to Denver. Running into me was no accident. She had talked the registrar's office into giving her my class schedule.

We ate downtown, a real lunch with wine. She scooted in beside me. Pressed against me, actually, and stroked my thigh. I squirmed. No girl had ever come on to me like that. "I could hardly restrain myself last summer," she said. "I've wanted you ever since."

We managed to finish eating, and I took her to my one-bedroom cubbyhole in a shabby Victorian near campus. We made love twice that afternoon. Saturday, we did go to the game—Kansas 43, CU 14. But mostly, we spent the weekend like newlyweds. She pranced around my apartment in bikini panties—no blouse, no bra—and stirred up meals on my hot plate that way. When she ate across from me topless, I couldn't say half a sentence without stuttering. I mock protested, and she waltzed into my bedroom and sauntered out in one of my T-shirts. Nothing else, absolutely nothing. "Okay, hon. Will this do it for you?"

Rachael wasn't ready to return to the university. She wanted to write but had no training. "What if I went to Silverton? Pitched in at the *Standard* and learned to write. Shoot, I'd even work for free if Allen couldn't pay me." *What if?*

Sunday night, I delivered Rachael to her parents' home in Denver. She called midweek. "I've worked it out," she said. "I'm going to Silverton. After Thanksgiving."

"I'll take you! You can meet Mom and the kids." Pure gut reaction, no thought of what that might imply.

Of course, I didn't know when I blurted out the offer that two days later President Kennedy would be assassinated and that I would be consumed by the gut-wrenching funeral weekend that followed. Those four days left me exhausted and mentally drained. Boulder itself had become oppressive. I could hardly wait for Thanksgiving at home. A side excursion to Silverton would renew my soul, and Rachael would be a delightful bonus.

I picked up Rachael in Denver early Wednesday afternoon and took her home to Center for Thanksgiving. Neither Mom nor the kids liked her. Not that they said anything, but Pam's melodramatic eye rolling, the boys' wide-eyed titters, and Mom's under-the-breath "tscht-tscht" told me they were shocked by Rachael's low-cut blouse and the way I enjoyed her brushing against me. They were cordial, but meals in the customarily banter-filled Marshall household were as silent as a Benedictine monastery. Each time Rachael spoke, every one of them went mute.

She and I drove to Silverton the day after Thanksgiving. John Ross was out of town, so we bunked into the two-bedroom apartment I'd slept in over the summer. Rachael was nineteen, free-spirited, and insatiable. She expressed unfettered joy in being touched. Gentle kisses to her neck and nuzzling her hair sparked deep-throated purrs, low moans, and sighs. With her in my arms, JFK and Boulder and my family all disappeared from my consciousness.

Sunday afternoon, I had to drag myself out of John's apartment for the long haul back to Boulder. Rachael stayed behind.

December pitched us into a frenetic romance by mail, three or four letters a week. At first they were filled with friendly chitchat—her settling in, events in Silverton. I critiqued her stories in the *Standard* and sent her a box of journalism texts, along with tales from life on campus. We began to write about *us*, explicit details from our two weekends together, about how much we missed each other, about what was next.

Early Christmas Eve, Rachael hitched a ride from Silverton to Durango and caught the Trailways bus to Center. My family greeted her like a teenage jezebel, but she quickly charmed them all with her hand-painted Christmas cards and her expertise in the kitchen. She also wore a bulky sweater and comported herself like a sister rather than a lover.

"Wow, great visit!" I said as we pulled out of the driveway late the next afternoon. "Mom and the kids think you're a saint."

She slid her hand across my thigh. "I am, hon. But wait until we get to Silverton."

That night, I parked beyond Molas Pass at the last switchback before descending into Silverton.

Below us was a scene unimaginable in summer: the snow-covered hamlet itself, rows of streetlights like low-hung stars shimmering on the gently falling snow. Massive Kendall and Sultan mountains, their trees buried beneath incalculable feet of snow, towered over the town like a pair of albino giants facing off for battle. "My God, it's gorgeous," Rachael said.

In town, we crunched to a stop across from the *Standard* office. Allen was gone for the week, and Rachael and I had his place overlooking Greene Street to ourselves. When we opened the car doors, an arctic blast sucked our breath away. We dashed to the entrance and up the stairs. Allen's bachelor pad was shirt-sleeves warm, as if he had stepped out for an errand. We plopped onto his sofa, pretending we had mushed in by dogsled.

Long after midnight, lights out, we stood bewitched at the bay window. Falling snow blurred the buildings across the street. Sultan Mountain disappeared into the mist. I snuggled Rachael from behind, hands clasped at her tummy. She leaned back into me, swaying to some imagined symphony. I nuzzled her hair. Then in one wild instant, we flung off our clothes and made love on Allen's white wall-to-wall carpet, as plush as a royal bedchamber.

Midmorning on Thursday, we slogged over to the Grand Imperial under a brilliant, cloudless sky. After a leisurely brunch, we hiked to Snarky's Market, filled a shopping cart with provisions, and retired to Allen's lair for a weeklong tryst.

But after only two days of carnal delight, I awoke Sunday anxious to get back to Boulder. Half my vacation gone, and I had a term paper I hadn't started and final exams the second week back. Rachael sat cross-legged on the bed, eyeing me. "Awake at last? It's the Sabbath. I'm starved. How about breakfast in bed?"

"Great. What's on the menu?"

"Me."

We eventually crawled out of bed and whipped up Spanish omelets and toast. Sitting side by side on the floor gazing out at the winter scape, we talked away the morning. She made lunch. Afterward I shouldered my backpack and headed out.

"No, you can't run off like that," she said, tugging at my arm. "I haven't kissed you goodbye." It was a ploy, but she roped and hog-tied me. We kissed and then made love again on the floor. I left Silverton late afternoon—with a four-hundred-mile trip on icy roads ahead.

The next day in Boulder, I flogged myself for having rejected Rachael's plea to stay in Silverton a full week. "I'll treat you to a *Playboy* romp," she had said.

My response: "I can't. Too much homework." Jeez, no girl had ever offered such a gift. What a wuss I'd been!

The sad irony of it all: I spent the first four days wishing I'd stayed and only three days writing my term paper.

Despite my having wimped out on her, Rachael immediately resumed her flurry of letters. By January 21, she'd sent ten. I'd more than kept pace.

Then things changed.

Friday, January 24, 1964. Three days without a letter from Rachael. *What gives?*

Saturday, January 25. Nothing.

Monday and Tuesday, January 27 and 28. Two more days with no mail. I had sent three letters since the twenty-first. Had I offended her?

Another full week, January 29–February 3. I had written three more letters, ten single-spaced typewritten pages, all with pleas for a response. No answer.

Tuesday, February 4. "And now for a long overdue letter," Rachael wrote. "We might have been, but we're no longer (I hope) in trouble."

In trouble? What?

She had missed her period. She had been to the doctor to . . . *my God* . . . to see if she was *pregnant*! But good news: "It finally came. In fact, I exploded all over my sleeping bag."

Friday, February 7. She'd been to the doctor again. "Now he's less sure I'm not in that 'delicate condition.'"

I had been firm about using condoms. I wracked my brain. Damn, Christmas night! They were in my backpack in the car, but I couldn't brave the cold to go get them. "I'll pull out," I had promised. "You'd better," she'd said. That was absolutely the only time it could have happened.

Tuesday, February 11. Another doctor's visit. Her letter had turned from *if* to *what now?* We loved being together, but we weren't *in love*. We had been up front about that. Marriage, she said, was out of the question. So was raising a child as an unwed mother or giving it up for adoption. Her conclusion: "The only solution is an abortion."

The word hit like a sledgehammer. Abortion didn't exist in my vocabulary, not even as a debate topic. I had been raised Methodist, active in Sunday school and youth programs, and though I had abandoned religion in college, abortion was *sin*, pure and simple. I didn't ask why. It just was. The church said it was.

I didn't ponder whether life began at conception or at what stage a fetus could be considered an unborn human being. Nor did I debate whether it was a woman's right to choose to be a mother. Abortion was wrong. Period.

It was also illegal.

I twisted myself into a knot, wrestling with abortion as a moral issue, as well as a practical one. Rachael was right about not getting married. We weren't in love. Like Laura Lee and her high school boyfriend, Rachael and I had been swept away by passion. Laura Lee married the guy.

Misery followed. He worked day labor jobs. They couldn't pay their bills. They fought. She left him. They divorced. And then she consigned herself to a second marriage she didn't want. Her new marriage wouldn't last, I was sure of it. No way could I let Rachael face the struggle that Laura Lee had weathered—and still faced.

My angst over the idea of an abortion had been more than I could cope with. I told Annie everything. She was disgusted that I had been so irresponsible to get a woman pregnant, and horrified because she also considered abortion a sin and a crime. Annie and I scoured my predicament for every nuance, over coffee, on long walks across campus, at Sunday dinners that lingered far into the night.

She helped me weigh the options without telling me what to do, challenging my every word but supporting me too. She wanted Rachael and me to find the best solution for *us*, even though she'd never met Rachael. Our conversations were the ones I should have had with Rachael. But Rachael was in Silverton. We couldn't talk face-to-face, and we couldn't afford long-distance calls.

Through the ordeal, I remained outwardly calm. But inside, Rachael's pregnancy dogged me everywhere—in the shower, over breakfast, on my bike, in the middle of conversations, in class.

One day I noticed the professor staring at me. A wry grin slid across his face. The class giggled. "We're discussing portraiture, Terry. I asked for your thoughts on synchronizing an electronic flash with a single flood lamp."

My thought: *How'd you know about Rachael?*

Fortunately, I kept my mouth shut. Another day, I was alone with Annie in the J-School reading room. I closed the door, and my voice shattered the silence. "What the hell am I gonna do, Annie? What?" My lip quivered. I hated that. A man had to be strong.

When I was alone, silence strangled me. I turned on the radio the instant I entered my apartment to keep thoughts of pregnant Rachael at bay. I couldn't study. Or read. Or think.

At night, memories swirled incessantly. Naked Rachael stretched out on Nossaman's white carpet. Rachael beside me as I drove, her hand performing magic. Bare-butt Rachael brushing against me as she set lunch on the table. "How's this, hon? Will this do it for you?"

Night after night, my exhausted psyche tried to alter the past: *Christmas night in Silverton. Rachael's ready. I'm eager. But this time, fireman-quick, I jump into my clothes, brave the arctic night, sprint to the car, grab my backpack, and race back. She teases on a condom. We go at it with abandon. Pure pleasure. No mess. No pregnancy.*

Worse, I was plagued by Dickensian nightmares.

Laura Lee's precious two-year-old tugs at my sleeve. She's holding her nose. She slaps a soggy diaper into my hand. "He peed again, Daddy. Make him stop." Rachael's and my naked baby is on his back on the white carpet, pee shooting up like a geyser. From the bedroom, Rachael's screams curdle the air. Damn, here comes another one. She spurts them out in litters, like puppies. I'm working two jobs, and we're mired in debt. Another one we have to give away.

One night it was Rachael curled up in a lambing pen in the sheep shed. *She's in labor, panting, but it's not working. "Hang on," I say. I kiss her cheek. It's wool! She's a ewe, not Rachael at all. No sweat, I've done this before. I thrust my hand down the passage, grab the kid by its forelegs, and drag it out. Blood's everywhere. The kid staggers to its feet. But the ewe is no longer struggling. No heartbeat. "Sorry, little guy, your mom didn't make it," I say. The kid smiles and waves. "Thanks, Dad," it says. The kid's a human! A girl. With Rachael's luxurious black hair.*

Saturday, February 15. Another letter from Rachael. She had no money, not even for a bus ticket to Denver. Time was running out. "The problem isn't going to get any smaller," she quipped. But she was also worried about us. "I can't help but feel this has ruined everything we had, or might hope to have, but I would appreciate you standing by me for the time being."

Jesus! In the *us*, I'd been consistent. It was *our* problem, not hers alone. Rachael was right. Abortion was the only solution for *us*. She was broke. "I'll pay for everything," I wrote. But I urged her to wait until we could discuss it in person.

Wednesday, February 19. "Dr. Perini says there's no doubt I'm pregnant, and if I'm going to do something about it, I'd better do it soon. To be blunt, I will leave here the day I get the money." She added, "I've been missing you something terrible, but couldn't say so for fear you would think I was trying to con you into marrying me over this."

I got her letter on February 20. A half hour later, I wired her money for a bus to Boulder.

⤙

It was thirty-seven degrees on Saturday when Rachael hopped off the bus with her ski jacket over her arm. "In Silverton, only pansies wear coats in weather this warm," she said. She kissed me, no innocent peck on the cheek either.

She didn't look pregnant. Or feel pregnant. We laced our joy at being together with a searching face-to-face discussion of whether abortion really was our only option. Without any assurances she would be safe, the risks terrified us both. But we had to do this. I tapped into the haphazard network of "a friend who knows a guy who has a friend who . . ." and got phone numbers of three abortion doctors, one in Wyoming, another in Nebraska, and the third in Kansas City. Which was the "right" one?

Sunday night, I drove her home to Denver and promised to call once I had lined up a doctor. "If Mom or Dad answers," she said, "tell them you're from CU. They think I'm going back to school. They have no idea I'm pregnant."

It took me a week to nail down the arrangements. On March 3, Rachael stayed the night, and we left at dawn for Huntersville, Nebraska, 325 miles from Boulder and 150 miles of two-lane road beyond the nearest city. Twenty miles from Huntersville, I hit a patch of black ice and spun the car in a heart-stopping 360. I crept into town at ten miles an hour, white-knuckled. The town had a tiny café, a six-unit 1930s motel straight out of the movie *Psycho*, and a medical clinic that must have been a gas station in a previous life.

Dr. Wagner welcomed us like family. Gray-haired with a kind smile, he was risking his medical license to clean up the mess we'd made. No lecture, blame, or disdain. Just quiet compassion.

We had no idea if Dr. Wagner had the skills to perform a safe abortion or if his clinic was even clean. Were his instruments properly sterilized? We didn't inspect his facility or ask for credentials. We certainly didn't ask how many successful abortions he had performed. We stumbled blindly ahead. Could Rachael be maimed or even die? We didn't know. I counted out a hundred and twenty-five dollars in advance—a fourth of the savings I'd begun squirreling away in high school when I was a printer's devil at thirty-five cents an hour.

"Can Terry come hold my hand?" Rachael asked.

"I will hold your hand, dear," the nurse said. "It's more professional that way."

Rachael forced a weak little wave and disappeared into the operating room. I slumped into a faded green plastic chair.

A sign on the operating room door read "Private. No Entry." *It morphs into neon: "Libertine boyfriends stay out / YOU knocked her up / WE fix her up." I conjure up an image of Dr. Wagner behind that door. He brandishes a three-foot-long hypodermic needle. "Spread those gorgeous gams, sweetie," he says. "You'll feel a slight pinch, and then it'll all be over." He's lying. He'll kill her. Jesus! Minutes tick by. I listen. Rachael shrieks. I smash down the door. He's poised over her, scalpel raised. No, it's a butcher knife. I flatten him with a flying tackle, wrest the knife away. "Sorry, Romeo," he says, "your hundred and twenty-five bucks is nonrefundable."*

Finally the door opened. The nurse steered Rachael out. She was dazed and unsteady. We sat her down. I held her hand. It was cold and a bit shaky. Later, in the scuzzy motel room, she was as tender as ever, albeit too sore to move. "Just hold me. I want you close," she said.

We went to the café for dinner, but Rachael didn't eat. The thought of food nauseated her. The next day, we made the long drive back to Colorado, and I took her home to Denver. That same night, she wrote, "You have been nothing short of wonderful these last two days. It lacked only one thing: You didn't get any studying done."

She wrote fondly about taking up where we had left off at Christmas. But her fear, expressed before she left Silverton, proved prophetic: "I can't help but feel this has ruined everything." The abortion had forced me to think about us as a couple, of how little time we had spent with each other, even though we'd been "together" for three and a half months. Four torrid weekends, mostly in bed. Eleven nights.

On March 10, a mere week after Huntersville, I told Rachael the blunt truth, not in person as I should have, but in a letter, in words I soon regretted for their callousness. "I know I am not in love and that the possibility of it developing into something along that line seems rather remote." I went on, "Sex without love isn't enough"—the same words Sarah had used when she cut me loose four months earlier.

Rachael and I exchanged several letters that spring. When she bled excessively one morning and her temperature climbed to 103, she fretted but toughed it out. She stayed in Denver, found a job, picked up with old friends, and made new ones.

In those letters, we revisited our relationship—our thoughts, our words, our actions. She wounded me with angry invectives and scraped the wounds raw. With talons extended, I slashed back. In our bitter exchanges, she wept. I swore. But both of us apologized for our hurtful words. More than once.

In the end, we plumbed our souls and resurrected the joy in what we'd had together and praised each other for that. Her final letter, dated June 8, 1964, came to me in Center. "I'm still enthralled with my job, and I've met someone. Ted and I are happy together, and we've made a resolution never to go to bed angry with each other."

Did she have long-term complications, physical or emotional? Did the abortion affect her ability to have children? Only the ensuing years could provide the answers. Rachael knew my family and our address and phone number, and she was no shrinking violet. She would have gotten in touch with me again if she thought there was anything I needed to know.

I never heard from her again.

Before the abortion, before Rachael left Silverton, Annie and I spent scores of hours together agonizing, not only over Rachael, but also over Gretchen, Annie's brother's girlfriend. For a bit of cheer amid the gloom, Annie and I took in a local theatre production and a couple of movies, my treat. Not dates, merely time-outs from the two crises.

Sometime during those painful weeks, I realized I was indeed in love— not with my lover, but with my best friend.

Friday, 6 a.m., 3 July 1964, Silverton. The sun rose and lit up John Ross's apartment before I could finish my letter to Annie. I had to get to work. I downed a bowl of Wheaties and a couple of slices of toast, raced off to the *Standard*, and chained myself to the Linotype. Allen always had plenty to keep me busy.

After work, he and I relaxed over dinner and drinks at the Grand Imperial. By nine, half-soused, we were both lamenting our dismal love lives. "You should have married that Annie gal when you had a chance, Marshall," he said. "I told you that in May."

Poor Allen. He wanted a girlfriend so badly, but he could be shy around women. "Yeah, and you should be sleeping with Janet Billings. Or young Miss What's-Her-Name from last summer. Or that redhead from Durango."

I had to pee, and when I came back, Allen was gone. The bartender shrugged. "You know Nossaman. By now he's up there in that eagle's nest of his, crying in that scruffy beard."

I walked the length of Greene Street and continued on to the river, El Rio de las Animas Perdidas. That was us, Allen and me, lost souls, alone in Silverton. Unlike Allen, though, I had a prospect, a damn good one. Hiking back, I caught myself humming. That was Silverton, night sky so full, so bright you didn't need a flashlight. Love really did bloom at night here. And the brilliant moon really could break your heart.

Back in John's apartment, I finished my letter to Annie. Before sliding it into one of my fancy envelopes, I scrawled a PS. "All you have to do in regard to my letter of July 1 is send me a one-word note: 'YES.'"

Ann

Friday, July 3, 1964, Paris. Like the Sorbonne, the Louvre loomed cold and uninviting. Its stone exterior and granite public square made a drab welcome. Inside, I couldn't possibly remember all the masterpieces Terry insisted I see. Nor could I relay his suggestions to Jack. Yet fewer than twenty minutes after we began the tour, as I circled the Venus de Milo, I blurted, "Terry said we should study this piece from every angle to get the full impact."

Jack's pained look stopped me short. He stood as frozen as the sculptures around us.

"Oh, Jack, I'm so sorry. I didn't—"

A muscle in his jaw twitched. I bowed my head against his arm. He jerked it away.

After the tour, we circled back to the *Mona Lisa*, pushing into the crowd to get a closer look. Jack muttered, "I know why she's smiling." His first words since my thoughtless remark.

I cocked a cautious eye toward him. "You do?"

"She has two suitors. If one doesn't work out, she can reel in the other, just like—"

It hit me like a blow to the jaw. Or was he trying to be funny? "You keeping score? If you are, you're *way* ahead."

We clumped our way back through the Grand Gallery, side by side, but not together. I ground to a halt. "Neither of us wants this. We need to talk. Let's go outside."

"Only the two of us? No third-party rivals?"

"*I* can promise not to bring him up again. How about you?"

"Of course!" He spat it out like a wad of day-old bubble gum.

Jack got his daypack from the baggage check, and we stomped along the Seine. At a quiet spot in the Tuileries Garden, we plunked down on the grass and glared at each other.

"I'll start," I said. "When I first fantasized about this trip, I was Cinderella at the ball. I ignored the fact I'm not perfect, that I do dumb things . . . like I did in there. I'm deeply sorry. Please forgive me."

He glowered.

Okay, I'd carry this by myself until he got his mind in the right place. "We dreamed up this trip to meet the real people behind the fairy tale— with our flaws and weaknesses—and to decide if we really could ride into the future together. If we—"

"I know all that. I just want you to—"

I held my hand up like a school-crossing guard. "Not finished." He snapped his jaw shut. "So far, I've found so many things to love about you. How you love learning. How you see the world. How you appreciate art and literature and history and travel. Your attention to detail."

"Well, I—"

I raised the stop sign. He crossed his arms. "We don't know yet if we can solve problems together. Will we find resolutions that bring us closer? Or ways to get even and get our way? If it's the latter, I don't want it. I don't think you do either. My comment at the Venus de Milo was thoughtless. And at the *Mona Lisa*, I blurted out that nonsense about keeping score in anger. That's not me. I hope you'll stick around long enough to find out."

"You finished?" His voice and expression were softer.

"No, I'm not." Sometimes, when provoked, I slip into a cool fog, and if I wait, I can draw out the right words. "I know I can't say the painful truths," I said, "the things that might hurt someone's feelings. I get mealy-mouthed. Okay, even devious. It's a flaw I work on constantly. But in my perfect world, we could talk to each other. If one of us did something hurtful or annoying or infuriating, we could request—and receive—forgiveness. That's the life I want with the man I marry. What I won't accept is for us to bury hurts inside and let them steam until they erupt like lava." Our eyes met. He really was listening. "Now I'm finished."

"You sure?" He was asking permission, no innuendo, no anger. "Injecting my rival into *our* trip was a kick in the gut. As bad as my anxiety last spring over how I could beat out my rivals when you were so far away. I was on the torture racks for months, waiting forever for each letter."

Guilt slammed me. His pained pleas for me to write stampeded out of the past:

Mailman let me down again today; empty mailbox is depressing . . . In a bitter mood yesterday because you didn't write . . . can't understand why you don't write more often; I remain starved for news from you. I have begun sending my letters to you from the main post office so our company clerk won't see how often I write you, compared with how often you write me.

I kissed his hand, held it to my bowed forehead. "You've laid bare another fault. I am so sorry. I have no right to ask forgiveness for my callousness—then or now." I took a deep breath. "Is there more?"

"Gretchen tightened the noose. She warned me about him. About Terry. I refused to believe her. I was a fool. She was trying to protect me. When you finally came, you confirmed it. But since that night in Füssen and on our campout, it's been paradise. Now, in the middle of this great trip, you wound me with him again. How could you?"

I couldn't look up, not until I got my tears under control. When he paused for breath, I tried to apologize, but my voice deserted me.

"I reacted poorly," he said. "I hope you know that's not me, either. Forgive me?"

Forgive him? For all the pain I had caused? No, forgive me. I'd be more sensitive, more caring, if only he would forgive me. I wanted to tell him that. The words stuck in my throat. I finally looked at him, nodded, and squeaked, "Anything else?"

He shook his head.

I had promised we would talk only about the two of us, no Terry invading our time together. But I loved them both. The less said, the better.

Except that didn't work either. Each deserved to know how much he meant to me. Even at this moment, Terry was probably haunting the mailbox, waiting for a letter. What would I tell him? *Don't worry, Jack and I are having a splendid time. At the Louvre, we saw Venus de Milo. Loved it!* Or, *Jack and I slept together in that tiny tent and in the same hotel bed. But don't worry, Ter, we didn't do anything.*

Of course, I couldn't say that. But if I didn't tell Terry about the tour, what could I tell him? I'd struggled with the same thing when Jack and I went to Neuschwanstein. I had written, "Went to Bavaria for the weekend." No pronoun, no subject. How deceptive. And from an English teacher.

I edged closer to Jack on the grass. I still had his hand in a death grip. Despite kids racing about in the garden, cars honking in the distance, and people yakking, our silence swallowed all other sound. Tears still threatened. No, sir, I would not cry. I wouldn't. I clamped my eyes shut. A shameless tear ran free and slithered down my chest. I did my best to ignore it.

At last, I found my voice. "Jack, I have no magic wand to make this less painful and no crystal ball to see what our future holds. One thing is sure, though. Being with you makes me happy beyond words. When I hurt you, it's as if I have driven a knife into my own heart."

Now he was holding both my hands.

"But we have a choice," I said. "We can dwell on misery. Or seize the moments we have and squeeze every bit of joy out of them. What shall it be?"

Just then a soccer ball careened toward me. I shut my eyes. Before it smacked me in the face, Jack caught it and threw it back to a gang of wild boys. One of them booted it back. Jack jumped up and kicked it into play. Next thing, he was sprinting back and forth with them.

"*Americain! Americain!*" one boy shouted, waving his arms wildly. "*Par ici!*"

Jack bopped the ball with his knee toward the kid, and it went high. The kid leaped and bonked it with his head back to Jack. Jack kicked wild. Another boy snagged it and dribbled it back toward Jack. With whoops and hollers, the boys delighted in targeting the willing American. The game stoked thoughts about Jack as a father . . . to our kids. I cheered him on.

Soon, Jack bailed out of the jumble and rejoined me, aglow, but puffing. "Whew, soccer isn't my sport. Hope I didn't embarrass myself. Okay, where were we? Ah yes, 'squeeze the joy.' Great idea—if it involves you and me. I apologize for being so morose."

Right there in broad daylight, he kissed me. A friendly smooch, mind you, not a passionate I-love-you *pas de deux* that melded our souls, but it was there for all the public to witness. "And now, would *mademoiselle* care to join me for a picnic?" he said.

We pulled out our cheeses, bread, and fruits, talking what-ifs as we watched the kids play. *If* we had kids of our own, Jack said, "I want museums and art galleries to be as much a part of their lives as playgrounds and ball fields and hiking trails. When I get assigned to the Pentagon, we'll take them to a Smithsonian every weekend."

His newfound cheer transported me back to Cinderella's ball. Midnight hadn't come. "And I hope you'll be a model for our kids," I said. "Show them they can accomplish whatever they set their minds to, especially our girls, like Dad did for me. You'll also teach our daughters to play sports, won't you? I was a klutz, the last chosen for grade school teams. But it's not too late. I'm sure I could learn to throw a ball or keep my eyes open when a ball comes at me. Baseball, tennis, volleyball, you name it, I shut my eyes."

"So I noticed. I'll make that my first challenge."

We moseyed beyond the park, wound up on the Champs Élysées, and ate at a sidewalk café. A strolling violinist serenaded us with "Mimi's Song."

That evening, the sunset painted the clouds in rosy and purple hues. We stood transfixed at our hotel window, Jack behind me, cradling me in his arms. As dusk settled over the city, I turned to face him. "The best shows in town are free."

We kissed. He nuzzled down my neck and across the expanse above my sundress and kissed the straps off my shoulders. "Shall we get ready for bed?" he asked.

"Is that a logistics plan? Or an invitation?"

"Which do you prefer?" He traced the line of my neck out to my shoulders.

"An invitation."

"Okay, you're invited. First, I want to give you a proper back rub."

It was a long *kissing* back rub, a long kissing *bare* back rub.

Between kisses and strokes, we changed into our nightclothes. For an encore, he delivered a soothing leg massage, from my tired feet to my panty line. My every cell saluted. "Best massages I've ever had," I whispered. "How can I ever repay you?"

He lay down beside me. His eyes lit up. My naiveté had done me in again. I held my breath.

He stared at me for a moment, eyes intense. "Let's do it again tomorrow night."

"You are a sly one, Lieutenant Sigg. A *nightly* treat, eh? Okay, deal." I felt a telltale thumping against my hip and inched out of range. "But you need to rein in your second lieutenant. If you don't want him court-martialed."

"I'll do what I can, ma'am, but he's such an independent prick, that guy. I'll give him a talking to." He looked down. "Second Lieutenant! At ease!"

8

Bumps on the Way to Saint-Tropez

Ann

Saturday, July 4, 1964, on the road from Paris. Jack and I had planned to spend the whole day at Versailles, but by midmorning, the gardens were elbow-to-elbow tourists. Besides, we'd already overdosed on opulence in King Ludwig's Bavarian castles. Before noon we were hurtling south for the French Riviera: Saint-Tropez.

By afternoon, a steady drizzle forced Jack to put the top up. No wind to snatch away our words or frazzle my hairdo. I pulled my Füssen scarf off, shook out my mop, and tucked the scarf around my bare knees below my shorts. Jack cocked an eyebrow.

"It's chilly," I said. Shivering, I rolled my shirt sleeves down and buttoned them around my wrists.

"Don't worry," he said. "I've ordered sunshine and calm waters." He started humming and then stopped abruptly. "You did pack your mono-kini, didn't you?"

"My what?"

"Your new topless bathing suit. They're all the rage in Saint-Tropez."

"Topless? You're kidding, right?"

"No. I saw it in *Sports Illustrated.*"

"That's an impeccable source. Sure it wasn't *Playboy*?"

"No, really, even feminists promote it. 'It strips away all this angst over Victorian hang-ups and permits women to express themselves freely.' One of them said that."

"You think I can't express myself? But I could if I paraded around half-naked?"

"Not at all. But you'd look great in one. You could show Brigitte Bardot a thing or two—like how to present yourself on a beach, looking gorgeous, not cheap. She lives in Saint-Tropez, you know. It's not how much you show—it's how you show it. *Hope* is what turns heads."

What a crock! Not "everyone" was wearing one. It made the news because it was shocking. And me showing Brigitte Bardot a thing or two? "Really? And what exactly do you hope for?"

"That I convince you to become the woman of my dreams, someone who—"

"Who looks hot in half a bathing suit?"

"No. One who embraces a shared future. The bathing suit's a bonus."

"Tell you what, Lieutenant. I'd love to 'embrace a shared future.' But why would I have to bare my tits to do that?" I cringed. How did that word pop out?

Jack blanched and stared straight ahead, stone-faced.

"Sorry, guy, that was crude."

"*Tits?* I don't use gutter language, Ann. Haven't you figured that out?"

"Sure. But you hit a sore spot, and my mouth outran my brain. I wasn't alone, I might add. Me in a monokini? On a public beach? Never!"

I looked for a crack in his demeanor. Nothing but the steely profile of his jaw, eyes glued to the road.

"That's drunken-sailor talk. It's not you, not the girl I've come to love. You shocked me. Pretty cheeky."

"You're right. It's *not* me. But 'cheek' isn't the story here."

For a few minutes, the rhythm of the windshield wipers was the only sound in our Sting Ray cocoon. What *was* the story? What had gotten into me? I had to think. And fast.

Sure, women's attitudes were changing. I'd read a feminist rant or two decrying society's insistence that a woman cover her breasts in settings appropriate to nudity—when nursing a baby, for example. Breasts, they argued, were natural parts of every woman's body, not sex totems to be shrouded. In fact, what was wrong with sunning naked on a secluded rock in Boulder Creek? Or skinny-dipping?

I still relished the thrill I got when my high school girlfriends and I paddled out of view on Lake Garda near Verona and liberated ourselves from our bathing suits. The water swirling around my naked body was sensual beyond belief. In fact, thinking about it made me want to do it again.

Good thing Jack couldn't read my thoughts. Derailed by my remark, he'd slowed down, and the roar of a passing Porsche on the French free-way had drowned out debate. Jack followed suit, hitting the gas, and was now in a breathtaking sprint to dominate the road—as my own thoughts on bare breasts, nudity, and sex raced ahead.

Many of my friends at CU had been active sexually. My roommate Julie huffed, "I'm not *giving out* anything. I have sex because it feels great. Why shouldn't I enjoy it as much as men?"

With one foot testing the sixties, I, too, resented the canard that a sexu-ally active woman was a "slut," yet a sexually active man was a "stud." But for me it was a hairpin turn from nudity at a secluded mountain stream to casual sex with uncommitted partners. Too many men saw partial nu-dity as a full-throttle green flag, each risqué step leading inexorably to the next. "Free love" wasn't *love* at all. It diminished the most precious gift a woman—or a man—could save for a spouse. Was I too straitlaced, cap-tive to my Sunday school mindset? Where and how could I draw the line?

Finally, I spoke up. "Honestly, bathing suits aren't the point. Society uses sex to sell everything from cigarettes to cars, and now it's the end-game on casual dates. I think we—"

He slowed down again, letting the Porsche go. "I don't think of you as a 'casual' date." He paused and added softly, "Never have."

"Good thing." I turned toward him. "I didn't fly halfway round the world for—"

"As for sex—which I prefer to think of as *making love*—sex with you would be anything but casual. More like sublime." He shot me a quick glance. "The purest expression of my love."

Whoosh! His dreamy smile whisked away the dank cloud that had settled over us. Still, I couldn't let this tiff slip away without him truly un-derstanding where I stood. "I'm sure when the time comes, it *will* be heav-enly," I said. "But here are my concerns. First, biology. Simply put, women get pregnant. Men don't." Gretchen's image popped into mind. "And sec-ond, society. Women bear the consequences—shame, birth, motherhood. Men can waltz away."

He frowned. "I'm not a rat! Besides, there's protection, so—"

"Oh, sure. The Pill. I know that line. 'C'mon, baby, it's one hundred percent safe. Guaranteed.' One hundred percent? Nothing's infallible. Bonner and Gretchen proved that."

Jack's mouth tightened. "Bonner's my best friend, but we're miles apart on that score."

"I believe that, but we can't let this delicious attraction we have for each other override common sense. What if I got pregnant? Sneak off to have our baby and give it up for adoption, as I so piously urged Gretchen to do? A shotgun wedding? An abortion?"

Memory lobbed other examples of the perils of unbridled sex: Terry and his Rachael. My dorm-mate Lila. She disappeared for months and gave up *twins* for adoption. And Terry's Laura Lee, getting stuck raising her child by herself. A smart girl, trapped into single motherhood before she could go to college. I hadn't met Laura Lee, but her story had affected me deeply. No, I wouldn't run that risk until I was certain I'd found my soul mate. "Think about it. How could I tell Mom and Dad I'm pregnant? How could *we*?"

Jack's scowl returned. "You know I wouldn't put you—us—in that position."

"Not on purpose. But I've seen too many accidental pregnancies. And I don't want gossips counting the months between the wedding and my baby's birth. Or kids chanting, 'Here comes the bride, big, fat, and wide!'" We both laughed.

"Uncle! Let's take a break and rustle up some lunch." Jack pulled into a small park near the confluence of the Rhône and Saône rivers in Lyon. Luckily the rain had stopped, but it was long past noon, and we were at least a half day's drive from Saint-Tropez. We made it quick—wolfed down cheese and brown bread and capped it with an apple for each of us. No time for tea. After we packed up, I held my breath for fear he would put the top down. Instead, he tossed me the keys. "You ready to drive?"

"Wow. Never thought you'd ask. At least not while you were in the car."

"It'll be my first time in the passenger seat. You're that special."

"Honor accepted." I swung into the cockpit as if it were my second home, turned the key, shifted gears, eased onto the busy highway, and took off. I loved driving his souped-up car. Moments later, the speedometer had swept up to eighty. "Yikes, how fast does this thing go?"

Jack glanced back over his shoulder. "Test it. Teach that Citroën a lesson." In the rearview mirror, a dinky little car was closing on us as if he were A. J. Foyt after another title.

A tiny nudge, and we shot up to a hundred. The Citroën appeared to be backing up. Sweat beaded my forehead. "Wait," Jack said. "This isn't the autobahn. The French actually enforce all their speed limits. Better slow down, especially so close to the city."

I eased back to seventy and studiously ignored the Citroën when he eventually overtook us. "So why did you buy this Sting Ray? It's so out of character."

"Not at all. It's speed and performance. This baby does zero to sixty in 6.1 seconds. Get that: Six. Point. One. And zero to a hundred in 14.5. That's a quarter of a mile in only fourteen and a half seconds. Step on it and it roars."

He showered me with details: suspension and struts, traction and cornering power, gear ratios, displacement per liter, torque and horsepower—three hundred at five thousand revs, whatever that meant. It turned out that his '63 Sting Ray marked a once-in-a-generation breakthrough in automobile technology, an engineering marvel. Here was the analytical Jack I admired.

"But I also did it for Dad. He's as proud of this baby as I am." He ran his hand over the dashboard. "You know I grew up in Johnstown, Pennsylvania, right? A steel and coal town. My folks survived the Depression on grit and wits." He paused. "In high school, I started my own house-painting business. To help out at home."

"Really? Who would hire a high school student to paint a house?"

"Someone who figured I'd do it cheap." His eyes twinkled. "Or folks who liked my dad. But pretty quick it was because I did a good job. Word got around. As for the Sting Ray, it's a statement, sure, but it also made financial sense. I'm single, no dependents." He stopped until I glanced at him. "At least for now."

I returned his sly smile.

"Yeah, it cost me a bundle—$4,400—but the army has a deal that let me buy it a whole lot cheaper than I could get it at home. If I want to sell it when I get back, I'll double my money. It's an investment—in my life style as well as my financial future."

"Sold! Can you buy me one?"

"Don't need to. You've got mine. And me."

He said it casually, not as a pitch, but as a statement of fact, and somehow that simple comment stripped away the veil of tension that had hovered between us. As we sped through the hilly green terrain, he told me about his hopes to score well on the Foreign Service exam and eventually move into work that would call on his negotiation and problem-solving skills. Someday, he said, he'd be secretary of state. We talked on and on, and the miles melted away.

But I was still torn by my own tug of war. Here I was, dashing toward the French Riviera, with this stud of a guy radiating testosterone. Tonight we'd sleep together. Again. How long before we strayed beyond the line I had vowed not to cross?

The idea of sex with Jack electrified me—both because he really might be The One and because the prelims had given me so much pleasure. What better place than the Riviera?

But I loved Terry too, and we had gone pretty far—shockingly far. What if *he* were destined to be my soul mate? How could I have sex with either guy before I'd resolved that bigger issue? Jack's tease about "sublime sex" gave me the perfect opening to lay out my concerns.

"Jack, these days together have exceeded everything I dared to hope for. But you need to know some things I haven't told you. Let me tell you *my story*—about how you came to be the 'star' of my own fantasy."

He bolted upright, eyes bright with anticipation. "The 'star,' you say? Tell me more."

"It started when I broke up with Geoff. He wanted me to drop out of school to marry him. How offensive. I quit dating and decided that I'd marry *you*."

I let him chew on that while I navigated a traffic circle. "Your letter in November opened a floodgate of letters and audiotapes. Then came your gifts. The vase was over the top. More than the vase, it was the planning and execution."

He was grinning like crazy. He started to speak, but I cut him off. "You could have sent the vase and let it go at that—like most guys. But somehow you found a florist in Boulder, sent him the vase, and had him deliver it filled with flowers. How did you find a florist from halfway around the world?"

"I didn't want it to get lost among the bounty from your other suitors. You see, I—"

"But that's only half the story. The florist left it at the front desk. By the time I showed up, the buzz was that my 'German' boyfriend was the world's greatest romantic. You transformed me from the vanilla mail clerk the girls cursed when their boyfriends didn't write into a real girl with a real boyfriend. You made us both celebrities."

"Like I've told you, the vase is only a deposit on my gift to you on our wedding day. The bowls are still to come."

Our wedding day? Was this a proposal?

Fortunately, no. He danced past the idea, like in Paris, saving me from having to come up with an answer. "They'll always be the legacy of our magical summer," he said.

He was floating. Me too, but despite myself, I made a U-turn into the rest of the story, searching for the right words about how my friendship with Terry had changed as he and I conspired to make my European adventure with Jack unforgettable. "This . . . change happened just weeks before I left for Germany. What was I to do? I still wanted to spend my summer with you."

Captive in the passenger seat, Jack fell silent. His Adam's apple dipped and bobbed, as if trying to swallow some angry tirade.

Minutes passed.

"So I'm still in the game?" he finally asked. "Care to show me your scorecard?"

I gripped the wheel. "It's not a competition. It's a journey. Of discovery. My question is, Do I measure up to either of you? And how well are we matched—our values, our life choices, our temperaments, even our quirks and oddities?"

Those questions, and my long tale, left us wrung dry. "Need a break?" I said, pulling onto a leafy side road. "I sure do."

He shot out of the car like a captive deer and raced up a wooded hillside.

Good. Go burn off some steam. The scent of pine and earth beckoned. I locked the car and hiked over to the Rhône, where vacationers were romping in the river below. When I came back, Jack was nowhere in sight.

Terry

Saturday, 4 July 1964, Silverton. Up at dawn, I chomped down a piece of toast slathered in peanut butter and piled into Allen's Scout with Roger, his wife, Ann-Marie, and their friend Janet for a long-anticipated attempt to conquer Black Bear Pass, the heart-stopping back-door entry to Telluride. We planned to celebrate the Fourth where few dared to go—a grand alternative to pining for Annie. Or worrying that she and Jack were on their "Grand Tour," whizzing along to Paris, Corvette top down, her hair flying, his hand creeping up her thigh.

A hand-carved wooden sign at the beginning of Black Bear Pass warned us: "Telluride, City of Gold, 12 miles, 2 hours. You don't have to be crazy to drive this road—but it helps. Jeeps Only." We had something better— a Scout 80. We snapped photos of each other mugging the sign, declared ourselves crazy, and took off.

At times Allen crept along, skirting boulders and ruts, rather than barreling his way through. Black Bear was the perfect antidote to loneliness and jealousy: a route through streams, over rocks and shale, and around hairpin curves, all against a backdrop of snow-covered peaks and flower-studded meadows. It was 12,840 feet at the summit, with just enough snowmelt to make the trail passable. Save for minor bruises earned on the bone-jarring rough spots, the first ten miles were on par with our four-wheeling trips the previous summer.

But when we came to a slanting patch of broken shale, the Scout tilted left and skidded a foot before the tires caught. Allen stopped. "Better hang on."

I'd already latched on like a pit bull. He inched forward a hundred yards, stopped again, and pointed directly in front of us. "Thar she is. Telluride!" The trail disappeared over a cliff into one of the puffy white clouds drifting across the royal blue canopy of sky. Telluride might have been two miles away, but all I could see was a tiny splotch thousands of feet straight down in the valley below. And no visible way to get there.

Allen anchored the fold-down windshield to the hood. "Better spot me," he said.

All four of us jumped out before he'd finished the sentence. I told myself we were simply guiding Allen down. Frankly, I was too afraid to ride. I'd heard about jeeps that had plunged over the edge. No survivors.

Good news—the trail *didn't* nosedive off the cliff. It angled onto a ledge gouged into the cliff wall, a rough, rock-strewn track with no railing and a 1,200-foot drop to kingdom come. Allen couldn't possibly back up. We had to conquer whatever lay ahead.

Roger and Ann-Marie walked in front. Allen crawled forward, and Janet and I trailed behind. Two steps into the hike, she grabbed my hand in a death grip. "This is scary," she whispered. I nodded. My heart was pounding like a jackhammer.

The trail widened and straightened out, and we all climbed back in. But then the ledge narrowed again, zigzagging down the cliff in switchbacks so sharp it took Allen three or four back-and-forth tries to jockey through each. At every turn, we hopped out and staked ourselves like sentinels to guide him. Allen peered over the steering wheel into the horizon. "I can't see the damn trail. You've got to tell me when to stop," he called. His voice was insistent, but not panicky. He'd done this before.

Roger and Ann-Marie posted themselves at the front of the Scout, each perched at the very edge of the cliff, waving him forward six inches, signaling stop, then reverse, sharp left, forward again, reverse again, left-forward again, keeping him at best merely a foot from the edge. Janet and I hung behind—eyes wide, just watching. Even that scared the hell out of me, and Janet dug her fingernails into my hand again. What if the Scout rolled when he shifted gears? Or the brakes failed?

Back in the Scout, we found ourselves nose to rock, nearly scraping the cliff's wall. After the next switchback, we were hanging out into space, millimeters from free fall, the tires bumping and skidding to the very edge. Any moment, we could have been like Wile E. Coyote, realizing we'd overshot the cliff and gravity hadn't yet kicked in. Unlike Wile E., none of us would have survived to chase again.

An hour later, we were only halfway down the towering cliff. An abandoned powerhouse atop Bridal Veil Falls hove into view like a friendly castle at the end of an arduous slog through the badlands. The trail broadened into a dirt road, wide enough for us to breathe.

Allen pulled into a wide spot and yanked on the emergency brake. I stumbled out, my legs rubbery, my nerves frayed. We hiked to the powerhouse and discovered, believe it or not, that it was both an industrial building and a palatial retreat. Allen said the powerhouse was built in 1907 to generate electricity for a mill between Telluride and the falls. The mine manager topped it off with a luxurious summer home, hiding the expense in the powerhouse construction costs.

The place was open and unguarded—no padlocks, no chains—and the five of us fanned out like Sherlock Holmes devotees, probing every niche and cubbyhole of both the manager's getaway and its basement powerhouse. Alas, we found no stashes of gold nuggets, no jewels, no secret panels, no cooked expense ledgers, no compromising letters from a sultry mistress. Not even a yellowed newspaper.

We did marvel at what had been an elegant drawing room, its bay windows suspended above the falls—at 365 feet, the tallest in Colorado. The owner had taste: hardwood floor, crown molding, a marble mantle over a stone fireplace. Standing at the window, we hovered in the air, the falls roaring beneath our feet.

Ann-Marie discovered a passageway that led to a set of rickety steps tacked to the outside of the building. On cat's paws, she tested each tread, tiptoed to the end of the house—beyond where it hung over the cliff—and disappeared around the corner. Roger followed.

I gasped. My God, what were they doing? Though my mind demanded that I retreat into the house, I shook off my fear—and my common sense—and ventured onto the shaky steps to join them. Moments later I was baby-stepping along a wet, slippery, eighteen-inch-wide plank perched above the falls, engulfed in a blinding mist. Ahead of me, Ann-Marie and Roger faded out of view like ghosts. I was floating in the fog, unable to even see my feet. I grabbed the rusted pipe railing and inched back along the catwalk and up the stairs to safety.

Ann-Marie and Roger reappeared ten minutes later, shooting the breeze as if they'd been on a Sunday stroll. "Who needs Niagara?" she said.

I managed a nod. After the idiocy of bumping and skidding down Black Bear and hanging in midair on a rickety old waterlogged plank, I knew I wasn't fearless. But crazy? Apparently.

Ann

Saturday, July 4, 1964, on a leafy side road in France. I strode into the woods where Jack had disappeared. No sign of him. Hoping hunger would lure him back, I prepared a light dinner of canned ham, sliced tomatoes, bread and cheese. He puffed up just as I finished.

I sang out, "Welcome to Chez Ann, *monsieur*! May I show you to your seat?"

"Yes, indeed. And how about a cold beer? I need it after that run. And that talk."

"You're in luck, sir. We have one beer left."

He took a long swig and finished it over dinner. After we packed up, he said, "Only one beer, but I guess you better keep driving. You mind?"

"Love to. Do *you* mind?" Driving his car was more than pure fun. It was an affirmation of his growing love and trust in me.

"You're doing fine. More than fine."

We had survived the deluge of my confession, plus dropped anchor on the aircraft carrier of sexual tension. I put my hands on his shoulders. "Remember when you said, 'May the best man win'? I'm here to say that you're a darn good contender, soldier."

Saturday night, July 4, 1964, en route to Saint-Tropez. Jack had fallen asleep by the time darkness closed in. Good, he needed the rest. When I turned from the main highway onto the road to Saint-Tropez, it quickly became a skimpy, two-lane, twisty byway through scrub-brush-covered mountains, sprinkled with intermittent stands of trees. I loved whizzing around curves through a tunnel of headlights. It kept my senses on full alert.

The map had indicated a turn onto a secondary road, and I searched the darkness for road signs. Not a one. Suddenly, a cluster of white signs sailed past. I rolled to a stop. Slowly, carefully, I backed up.

Skeeeeeer-thunk! The car tilted wildly and thudded to a stop. The engine coughed and died. Total silence. Our headlights aimed squarely at the treetops. No road.

"What? Where are we?" Jack's face lurched into view.

"I . . . I missed the turnoff."

"We're upside down! What the hell happened?"

We *weren't* upside down, I knew that much. But the steering wheel was now above me, which wasn't right. "I . . . I tried to read the signs, but—"

He butted his shoulder against the door. "The damn door's jammed. It won't open."

"I was backing up, and . . . I think we're in a ditch."

"You dumped us into a ditch?"

"I don't know. I missed the signs and—"

"Are you hurt?"

I hadn't thought about that. "I'm okay. Scared, though. You all right? I didn't realize the road dropped off."

"Damn!" He took a deep breath, expelled it. "Let's see if we can get out of here."

We threw our weight against the doors and tumbled out like rag dolls. It *was* a ditch, dry but soft and squishy. "Not as deep as I thought. We can get it out." Was that *my* squeaky voice?

I heard Jack groping his way around the back of the car. He appeared next to me, nudged me aside, and eased into the driver's seat. When he cranked up the engine, it worked. Thank goodness. He hit the gas. The wheels showered the countryside with dirt and a thick, pungent residue of decaying leaves.

He wouldn't get the car out doing that. As if he heard my thoughts, he tried again, this time with a bit of patience, rocking the car back and forth. His effort buried the back tires to the hubs. He stormed out. "Get in. I'll push."

With him behind me in the dark? "No, it's too risky."

"I'm not stupid. I'll push from the doorframe."

I was a war zone of emotions. I'd made an egregious mistake, sure, but his gunning the gas had dug us in deeper. After Dad retired and we moved to the ranch, I'd gotten stuck often enough to learn that you had to be calm and rock the car back and forth gently so the tires could grab hold. One time I buried the pickup in a bog in the northwest pasture. With patience, I wedged enough rocks and tree limbs behind the wheels to break loose. I looked like a creature from the mud fields of Flanders. Surprisingly, I didn't get into trouble with Dad. He was pleased I had taken care of it myself.

Now this. I could do it. I eased up on the clutch, nudging it a bit. No traction.

"Once more!" He grunted like a weight lifter, and we gave it another try. Nope.

Using our only flashlight, we scoured the area for something to cram under the tires. Nothing. Jack hiked up the road, leaving me standing in darkness that smothered me like a Cossack's cloak. Ten minutes later, he came back. "We're *on* the right road and *only* twenty kilometers from Saint-Tropez."

Punching *on* and *only* perforated my quaking insides. It would have been easier if he had ranted—so I could have let a few choice words fly in my defense. He didn't. And I didn't. Instead, I sounded like a crybaby. "I feel terrible. I'm really, really sorry."

"Yeah, well, that's not much help, is it?"

Ouch! The lieutenant again. After all my hopes, after surviving our ups and downs, I had dumped our romance into the ditch.

Jack took off once more, searching for some miracle. I paced in a tight circle close to the car. At first, our crash silenced the night creatures, but soon the woods chirped and rustled and growled with unseen critters. Minutes ticked by like hours.

A pair of lights darted among the trees. The flickers grew brighter. Headlights! I screeched, "Jack, quick! A car!" His footsteps pounded the road toward me. He reached into the Sting Ray, and two beams of light shot into the sky. Together we threw up our arms and waved like marooned sailors.

The car roared past. *Damn!* But then brake lights. Ever so slowly, the car backed up.

"Look out!" I shouted. "The ditch! There's a ditch!" The car stopped. The doors flew open, and a gang of guys tumbled out like circus clowns. Four of them.

Jack had never studied French, so I said, "*Bonsoir. Avez-vous un . . . ?*" I couldn't recall the word for chain. "*Un chain?*" I tried to pantomime it.

"What'd she say?" one of them asked.

"You speak English?"

"Better than you Yanks, doll." This from the burly guy in a New York Yankees cap.

Jack put a protective arm around my shoulder. "Your timing's perfect. We owe you."

"Your lucky day, mate. Looks like we sailed past the turn to Saint-Tropez."

"Wow, Corvette in the ditch," said the guy with a crew cut. "That's one bloody mess."

I winced, but I couldn't let them think Jack had done this. "It's my fault," I said. "I thought I'd missed the turn too. But this *is* the right road."

Jack and the Brits huddled at the Sting Ray. Within fifteen minutes, their combined muscle had freed the car. They shined their lights on it and deemed it roadworthy. Jack dug a glob of muck and weeds out of the tailpipe, and we were on our way.

Jack drove. In complete silence. No swearing. Not a word of blame. But an acerbic cloud saturated the space between us. I retreated into the black hole of his fury. This was about more than fuzzy-headed good intentions gone awry. It was about a man and his steed—an extension of himself. He had trusted me. And I had failed him.

Fortunately, the Sting Ray hummed along as usual. No clanking, bumping, or grinding. No audible sign of my assault on his baby.

Small comfort.

Terry

Saturday afternoon, 4 July 1964, Telluride, Colorado. Telluride had a mere 677 full-time residents compared to Silverton's bustling 849. But Telluride on the Fourth of July had two-mile-an-hour, bumper-to-bumper traffic and crowds six deep for a parade boasting a half-dozen marching bands, a slew of floats, and a massive mounted posse. A carnival was hopping, its calliope ramped up to shatter eardrums. Silverton's Fourth looked junior high by comparison.

But the festivities seemed more a pretext for rowdy behavior by a band of yahoos than a celebration of our nation's birthday. After the parade, beer cans and bottles, crushed paper cups, and piles of horse manure littered Main Street. Glassy-eyed scruff-heads staggered about, whooping and hollering, gulping Coors like it was water.

We didn't stay for the fireworks. After buying a jug of Chianti, the five of us headed into the high country and camped at Alta Lakes, accessible only by four-wheel drive and a world apart from the pandemonium in Telluride. Under a brilliant night sky unsullied by man-made light, we sipped wine, told stories around a campfire, and philosophized the night away. We flung our sleeping bags onto the ground and settled into our private cocoons.

As I drifted off, BAM! Annie shanghaied my mind. Her absence kept me awake—or, more likely, the fact that tonight she was with Jack in some quaint little French inn that dripped history and romance. He would be in the adjacent room, separated by a paper-thin wall, close enough she could hear his whispered longings. Or worse, snuggled in a tent together somewhere in the Alps. She told me he planned to take her camping. Nah, I told myself, she wouldn't put herself in such a compromising situation. But the thought of Annie beside him in a sleeping bag set me on edge. How tempting that would be.

I knew exactly how tempting, not only because of my night with Annie on James Creek, but because of young Miss Janet, who at that moment lay a foot away, her ponytail peeking out from her sleeping bag like a flirty nymph. She wasn't Annie, but frankly, she was a dish. I tried not to think about her trim figure. Even buried in a sleeping bag she was adorable. She stirred, her ponytail swished, and her face popped into view. "You awake? I can't sleep either," she said.

I had been staring. Actually, *lusting*. She must have sensed it—girls could do that. Annie had convinced me of it. "It's the night sky. Too gorgeous to waste," I said.

"Yes, that too. But I can't get Black Bear out of my mind. I was scared to death. Also at the powerhouse. I wasn't brave enough to follow you out onto those stairs."

At least she had some common sense. I'd spent the afternoon wondering how I'd gotten sucked into such foolhardy risks. But that night, I was grateful. Not only because we had seen spectacular sights most people would never see, but because I'd pushed myself beyond my limits. I told her that.

She rose on her elbows, leaned in so close the heat of her warmed my face. "Me too," she whispered. "I'm so thankful you let me come with you. You're a dear."

Had she been Annie, I would have squirmed into her bedroll and prayed that our animal instincts would take their natural course. But Janet wasn't Annie, and she and I only talked. She, too, had been repulsed by the traffic in Telluride, the crowds, the noise, the drunks. "I'm glad you insisted we get out of town," she said. "'Progress' has destroyed the charm."

We whispered on. The last thing I remember was the lullaby of her voice, soft and melodic. I tried to convince myself her presence made up for Annie's absence. I couldn't.

Ann

Sunday, 12:30 a.m., July 5, 1964, Saint-Tropez, France. At last, the lights of town flickered into view. Traffic built up as we came into Saint-Tropez. People spilled off the sidewalks. Cafés teemed. We had stumbled into a Fellini movie—women parading in Europe's finest *haute couture*, others with tops so skimpy their inflated boobs jiggled in a mad struggle to escape at every step. On some, skirts so tiny they barely hid their shameless owners' privates.

Sullenly, Jack inched through town. Eventually, he found a campground near the beach. He set up the tent. I dug out our camp stove and fixed tea. He swallowed a chunk of bread with cheese and disappeared into the tent fully clothed.

At 1:45 a.m. I sat alone in a spartan campsite. Today had begun splendidly. My stupidity erased it all. Would we recover? I couldn't muster a shred of hope. Did I dare presume to sleep in his Casbah? No choice. I couldn't sit on the dismal picnic bench all night.

I kicked off my sandals and squirmed into the tent, fully dressed, like Jack. The tent bobbed, closed in around my fanny, and nearly collapsed. Dang, I had caught my belt loop on something. I hunkered like a praying mantis, yanking at the snag. The tent heaved as if it would sprout wings. I freed myself.

Good news: He'd left space for me. Bad news: He had turned his back to me. He didn't move, but I knew he wasn't asleep. Anger steamed off his body. I lay stone still. Finally, I squiggled in next to him.

"Jack?" Barely a whisper. "I wouldn't have blamed you if you had dumped me by the side of the road. You know, 'This is the end of the line for you, kiddo.'"

Silence. Then a growl. "Well, the thought did occur to me, but—"

"I'm eternally grateful you didn't. I was—"

"—you still have a redeeming quality or two. I suppose we—"

"Can you find some way to forgive me? Can we . . ." Wow, did he say "redeeming quality"? Did that mean he could forgive me? I had interrupted him twice, and now his silence scolded me. "I wish I could show you how wretchedly sorry I am."

No answer, but he rolled to face me. He draped his arm over my shoulder and set his fingers to stroking my back. "You're a bright girl. Maybe you'll come up with something."

Yikes, our hideaway breathed sex. I had dived headfirst into that place I vowed to steer clear of. Lordy, what now? I laid his hand on my breast and held it there, feeling it rise and fall with each breath. I let him unbutton my blouse. Encouraged him, actually. Let him slip his hand into my bra. I was on my back by then. His hand slid to my shorts. He undid my belt . . . the button . . . the zipper. Could this be the night? No! This smelly tent was too cramped for love. I tensed and brought his hand to my breast again. "Do you really want me that way? Extracted as payment for my stupidity?"

"Of course not." He sighed. "Besides, I'm not in the right frame of mind." He turned away.

I snuggled up. He reached back and laid his hand on my thigh. His breathing softened, and soon his hand slid off. It didn't come back. Asleep at last.

I couldn't rein in my self-flagellation. About the wreck. About my indecisiveness. We had been to the brink of sex, and again I'd cut it off. Jack *was* the guy. What better way to atone for my egregious blunder and seal our love? Or was I right that it would have been tainted by the stink of payoff?

Was I worthy of him? I had my doubts, and for that I was thankful we didn't go all the way. But also because of Terry. What about him? How could I explain my behavior to him?

What a mess. How was I ever going to figure this out?

Dawn rescued me from a fitful sleep. I was alone in the stuffy tent. When I peeked out, the air was early-morning fresh, the midsummer sun eager at the horizon. No one in sight. To my left, the camp restrooms beckoned. I smoothed my rumpled blouse, crawled out, and raced down the dirt path. A shower in water fresh off a Norwegian glacier transformed me. But yesterday's rain had sent my hair into a frenzy of curls. Jack was about to see the real Orphan Annie.

Back at our campsite, he was flat on his back, flashlight in hand, peering up under the Sting Ray. I tiptoed past and ginned up a grand breakfast— six eggs, an onion, a bit of cheese, and half a loaf of bread. After setting water to boil, I covered the scuzzy picnic table with a towel, put a fistful of dandelions in a tin cup as a centerpiece, and hunkered down.

Ten minutes later, Jack joined me. "You're—*we're* lucky. She's okay. Let's eat."

We celebrated—tentatively—with my hearty concoction and geared up to explore this famed beach. The Moment of Truth: Could I wear my new bikini in front of Jack? I had to. Saint-Tropez was, after all, modern-day Gomorrah itself. Besides, I had paid a bundle for it.

By now a musty kiln, the tent undermined my resolve. I peeled off shorts and panties but couldn't get the tiny bikini up over my sweaty buns. Inside that five-foot-wide canvas fun house, I yanked and pulled, stuffed and squeezed. I tried it on hands and knees and then flat on my back like a capsized turtle, lifting my buns so I could stretch that snip of material over my fanny. Next, I wrestled with the skimpy top, scraping my head on the tent walls. In my mind, I heard Dad scolding my brothers and me on car trips: *Quit squirming like monkeys in a gunny sack.* I got to giggling.

From outside the tent, Jack's voice stopped me cold: "Hey, what's going on in there?"

"Don't come in. I need a sec." Choking back a snicker, I knelt like an anteater, face pressed into the sleeping bag, arms contorted behind me, and got the top fastened.

When I finally crawled out, I draped a towel over my shoulders like a timid twelve-year-old. Taking a deep breath, I stretched as tall as I could, flung the towel away, and curtsied. "Ta-dum! Am I ready for Saint-Tropez or what?"

"Well, well, well. Gooood morning. I love your outfit." He stepped toward me, arms extended, a give-me-a-bear-hug grin plastered all over his face.

"The outfit? Or all the skin?"

He stopped midstride. "I . . . no offense meant. It looks great on you. Sleek black. The design. But I'd be just as thrilled if you wore a granny dress and combat boots. You're striking. Your smile. Your hair. I didn't know you had curls like that. I love them."

He loved my curls? I couldn't believe any guy would like a wild mop of corkscrew curls. I took his arm. "Come, my prince, let's frolic on the Riviera. By the way . . ." I stood back, eyed his blue and red pinstripe trunks, and gave him a lascivious look. "I like your outfit too. Downright classy. Better than your regulation GI shorts."

Ours were the first footprints on the surf-scrubbed beach. We hunted seashells, chased hermit crabs, and stomped out notes in the sand, and then found a secluded spot and settled onto our blanket.

"So think back to January, when I was studying for finals and you were freezing at that lonely outpost on the border. Did you imagine that in July we'd be on this beach? You and I?"

"Not even in my fondest daydreams," he said. The adoring look was back.

"I never *ever* thought I'd wear a bikini. Once a prude, always a prude."

"Me too. I much prefer my baggy army trunks to this getup."

His comment invited me to appraise his muscular arms, shoulders, and chest, his taut belly and sinewy legs, the snug bathing suit. I wanted to grab him, hug him, feel him hug me. Instead, I said, "What, you don't like being girl bait?"

"Depends on the girl."

Down the beach, tiny stick figures began to dot the sand, too far away to distinguish men from women. Luckily, they remained at a distance. I wasn't keen to witness Jack ogling a parade of tanned, curvaceous, scantily clad beauties, next to whom I would be as pale as piano ivories.

From nowhere, a gray-haired man sauntered up, a leather-skinned sun worshipper who had apparently spent his entire life on the beach. A tight sliver of a sky-blue swimsuit covered the essentials, but displayed them in skintight outline. He greeted us with a burst of French. He looked expectant, but all I could manage was a hopeful *"Anglais? Parlez-vous anglais?"*

He raked his eyes over every inch of my body and sprayed me with another fusillade. I gave a befuddled shrug. He tried again, this time like one of Jack's taped letters when I accidentally put it on the slower speed, with enough gestures for a silent movie. I caught a couple of words—*le mer, les gendarmes*—and nodded appreciatively. *"Merci beaucoup, monsieur,"* I said in a chirpy schoolgirl voice.

The guy smiled broadly, bent over, and casually removed his swimsuit. Not two feet away and stark naked. I stared open-mouthed. He flashed me a thumbs-up, nodded toward Jack, and sauntered into the sea.

"You were wrong about the monokini," I said. "It's '*no-no*-kini.'"

"Know what? I bet we're on a nude beach," Jack said. "Well, when in Saint-Tropez, do as the Saint-Tropezians do." He stuck his thumbs into his trunks and tugged.

"Dare you."

"So I'm a prude too. Come on, I'll race you." We waded and swam and splashed, chasing each other like kids. We flopped on the blanket to catch our breath and raced out again. Eventually, hunger and thirst drove us to our camp. After polishing off our jug of water, we gobbled down some cheese sandwiches and napped in our tent sauna.

I woke up later that afternoon with a start. My skin was on fire. I couldn't bear the weight of clothing or even my own touch on a sunburn so horrific I opened my mouth to scream.

But no sound came out. A flaming sore throat had stolen my voice.

9

On the Road Again

Terry

Monday, 6 July 1964, Center, Colorado. I pulled into our driveway two hours past lunchtime. I'd left Silverton at ten. Four hours to negotiate Coal Bank and Wolf Creek passes was trophy-winning time. I flung open the car door and raced out to the mailbox. Empty.

Mom was standing on the back steps when I came around the side of the house.

"Hi, Mom," I said. "Any mail for me?" We didn't hug in our family when arriving or departing. Or pucker up for those awkward air kisses. We said hello and bye and waved, or sometimes we clapped one another on the shoulder.

She shook her head. "We're glad to see you too, Terry. Have you eaten?"

"Nope. I'm starvin'. Any leftovers?" I followed her into the house.

Inside, the boys descended on me like eager puppies. Greg dragged his new Boy Scout gear into the kitchen to show me—official walking shorts, sleeping bag, aluminum mess kit, and a mound of Colorado-themed trinkets to trade. He would leave Friday for the National Boy Scout Jamboree in Valley Forge, Pennsylvania. He'd never been out of state on his own, and none of us had ever been "back east." He tossed maps and pamphlets on the table, along with *Boys' Life* stories of past jamborees, and wanted me to read everything. Immediately.

The moment Greg scampered off, Randy plopped down at the table across from me and started firing question after question about California, about the cousins he had never met, about the weather and the ocean and how far we could drive in a day. He was taking off with the rest of us in two days to visit Mom's sister Gwen, Uncle Bob (my favorite uncle), and their six kids.

Pam, now eighteen, was running errands. Mom was washing clothes. "Better get your backpack in here if you've got anything you need cleaned," she said.

When I handed it off to her, she gave me a list of must-do chores: Burn the trash, mow the lawn, weed the garden, check the oil, radiator, and tires on her car, get the maps and figure out the route to San Francisco, and make sure we had enough food for the dog and chickens.

Sometime that evening, a letter from Europe appeared on my bed. I didn't see the culprit. I suspected it was all of them, Pam and the boys giggling, Mom crinkly-eyed at their mischief. *Put it on his pillow*, one of them no doubt said. *Yeah, so he can smooch it and pretend it's that girl.* They would have tiptoed out and waited in the shadows, hoping to watch me.

Annie's letter was dated June 26. She was on a train from Zurich, scribbling vignettes from Switzerland: a visit to a cathedral, dinner with a pair of beatniks, a chat with students from Vienna. Whoa, she wore a *bikini* on the beach in Lausanne. She lamented her "chalky paleness" and "overall layer of loose fat." I remembered her naked at Boulder Creek—not an ounce of fat. As for "chalky"? More like *creamy, silky, slender.* She'd be smashing in a bikini.

"I don't know exactly when I'll be able to get another letter off, so read this one slowly," she wrote. "Am going to France and Italy for a couple of weeks beginning Tuesday."

That would have been *last Tuesday*, June 30, a week ago. And not Annie alone, sightseeing. France and Italy meant Annie with Lieutenant Sigg in his flashy Corvette. By now they'd be strolling arm in arm through the starlit streets of Paris, the world's mecca for lovers. No doubt right now. This very minute.

I tossed her letter onto my dresser and bolted from the house. I needed some air.

Ann

Monday, July 6, 1964, Saint-Tropez. The sun etched pinpricks of light onto the tent walls and transformed it into an oven. My roasted skin had kept me awake for hours. I'd dozed in snatches, facedown, spread-eagle atop my sleeping bag to minimize skin contact, my head held up on a bunched-up ring of clothes. Naked, save for my panties, and too miserable to care. Every swallow shot lightning bolts down my throat. *You are some specimen, Ann: a sniveling, burned-to-a-crisp car wrecker. And not any old car. A Sting Ray wrecker.* The sunburn was just deserts.

Once we'd realized the extent of my sunburn and sore throat the afternoon before, Jack had raced off to a pharmacy and bought a couple of tubes of salve and some bitter throat lozenges. My blistered skin shuddered at the icy salve, but it eased the pain.

Jack rolled up onto his elbow. "Ready for your morning round?"

I croaked, "How'd you know I was awake?"

"I'm trained to know what's going on—even when I'm asleep." He squirted a thick ribbon across my shoulders. I flinched, then lay stone still. I didn't want him to miss an inch of skin. He finished, wiped his hands on a towel, and handed me a lozenge. "Here, suck on this. I'll whip up breakfast. Let me know if you'd like me to do the front."

Nurse Sigg was out of the tent before I could answer. And, of course, I could doctor my front myself—and preferred to. Besides, he wanted to get on the road. Military to the core: schedule driven even on vacation.

What could I wear? Nothing tight. I settled on my wilted sundress. Without the sash, it would be comfortably baggy and have plenty of breathing space. The button-up front had a high scoop neck, so I went without a bra—no straps to chafe my skin.

Jack had arranged tea, eggs, bread, cheese, and apple slivers on the picnic table. He motioned for me to sit. "How're you doing?"

"Better than expected," I rasped. I didn't tell him I couldn't swallow. Or that braless felt rather seductive. Apparently he didn't notice. Or was too polite to comment. "Nice spread."

He nodded, wolfed down his food, and headed off to pack the car.

Steaming black tea anesthetized my throat. I choked down half a boiled egg. Bread, cheese, and apples were out of the question.

I worried about the unforgiving leather seats on the drive ahead. Jack had already thought of that and spread a couple of beach towels across the seat. "A bit rough, but softer than leather," he said. "Here, aspirin—to get you through the morning."

We roared off toward Monaco. Miraculously, I fell asleep not far out of Saint-Tropez and didn't wake up until we were parked.

"Hey," Jack said. "We're in Nice. Hungry?"

"Starving. My throat's better. I think I can eat a bit now."

"Good. You didn't have enough breakfast to keep a bird alive."

At a seaside café, we people watched while waiting for our food. A striking woman in a white sheath with black accents, matching floppy hat, over-the-shoulder bag, and high-heeled sandals sashayed onto the beach. She spread out a fuchsia towel, kicked off her shoes, put her thumbs on her hips, and did a sexy wiggle dance. A pair of black panties dropped from under her dress. She flipped them into her bag with one toe. Not a shred of embarrassment.

This woman was no beach tart out to bait the young studs. Her bearing was too elegant, her clothes too refined. "Miss Chic" fished a scrap of hot pink cloth from the bag, straightened it out, and stepped into it. Wow, that thing couldn't possibly cover the basics. In a reverse wiggle dance, the bikini pursued the hem of her dress—up, a millimeter at a time—showcasing tanned legs that went on forever. Jack was ogling. I was mesmerized. Somehow she wriggled the Band-Aid-size bikini into place while keeping her private parts private.

Next, she reached into the left side of her sleeveless dress, pulled out a black bra strap, and slipped it past her elbow. What sleight of hand had she used to unfasten it? And when? She drew the other strap out, and the bra popped free. How could she possibly slither into a bikini top without exposing herself? She took a tangle of hot pink spaghetti from her bag, unbuttoned her dress, slipped the miniature triangles inside, and maneuvered the dress off her shoulders. Somehow, she slid her arms into the waiting straps and fastened the top before the dress fell onto the towel. Her bikini was half the size of mine. And she was no skinny Minnie.

"Now there's a handy skill," I said. "So perfectly, ah, *French*, don't you think?"

Jack tore his eyes away. "Uh, yes. French for sure. No doubt."

The lesson for me? *Presentation.* The woman had turned a simple change of clothes into erotic art without being indecent.

⌇

Monday afternoon, July 6, 1964, Monaco. The hotel had an oversized bed and air conditioning. "Figured you'd need the amenities," Jack said. "Besides, no low-budget options here. Or tent spaces."

After a simple dinner of leftovers, he said, "Okay, another treatment before I take on Monte Carlo."

So that was it. How could I have forgotten? He'd written that he planned to test his poker skills at Monaco's world-famous casino. Maybe what I had seen as impatience was really his laser focus on preparing himself for the professionals. As for me? I'd be on my own for the evening.

"Give me a sec." I went into the bathroom, eased out of my dress, and wrapped a towel loosely around myself. Back in the room, I lay facedown on the fresh sheets. Jack set to work.

"I'm puzzled why a smart guy like you would take on the experts at a gambling hall," I said, genuinely curious. "Is it something soldiers do to practice for the next war? Part of living dangerously?" I meant it as a joke, but it fell flat. Why was I tweaking him when he had been so attentive to my sunburn?

"Actually, we practice to *deter* the next war." His words were as crisp as tempered steel against flint. "I gamble only when we're on border duty. It sharpens my wits for battle."

"I hope you don't get cleaned out. Casinos don't give away money willingly, you know."

"It's not about cards. The guys who understand people are the ones who win."

He was rubbing the backs of my thighs so slowly and deliberately that the pain subsided. I forced myself to focus on him, not on my own budding desires. "How so?"

"I read my opponent's expression and manner. How he holds his cigarette. How deeply he drags. If he's sweating or not. What he *doesn't* say. I study his eyes. How often he looks at his cards. Each one's a tell. But I've never played against the house. This'll be new."

"So it's a science—Psychology 101. Not a game at all."

"Nope. It's war. I can see how people can get addicted . . . Someday, maybe somebody will settle me out of my single-guy perversions."

"Sounds like a challenge."

"Could be. Think about it." He ran his fingers down my sides, skated temptingly close to my breasts, and jumped up. "I'd better go before I lose my edge. Too many thoughts of—"

He cut that thought short and gave me a peck on the cheek. After a quick shower, he put on a clean shirt *and* a tie and strode out to battle kings, queens, knights, and card sharks.

A shaft of light pierced the darkness. "That you, Jack? Did you win?"

He peeked out from the bathroom. "Shhhh. Don't wake the patient." He was beaming. "Let's say that some mighty generous strangers anted up for our room."

"Aha, stories! Tell me your stories."

"About the German blowhard with an eye patch? Or the yachtsman missing his left pinky? Or the filthy-rich dandy with two gorgeous babes draped around his neck?"

"All of them, every one."

"If you insist, my dear, but let's tend the wounded first." He slathered me in ointment and rubbed briskly. It hurt, but a good hurt, like eating hot chilies—the lingering fire reminds you how delicious they were. "First, I didn't let on I spoke German, so 'Colonel Patch'—sitting next to me—recited his playbook under his breath . . ."

Jack went on until nearly three in the morning. The happy ending? He won "more than two hundred dollars," but he wouldn't say how much.

We fell asleep holding hands, me on my stomach, him on his back. Even loose snuggling set my gooped-up skin afire.

Terry

Tuesday, 7 July 1964, Center. Despite Monday's nonstop sprint from Silverton, I hadn't slept. The cacophony of two preteen boys on overdrive and the two hours I spent prowling the countryside after midnight conspired to keep me awake. Annie's letter was a record on perpetual replay: *Am going to France and Italy for a couple of weeks . . . a couple of weeks . . . a couple of weeks.* She wrote *Am.* But she was with the stud. She was hiding the truth: It was *We. We are.* Not *I am.*

A week before, I asked her to marry me, but I mailed my proposal July 1, the day after they left. She hadn't gotten any of my letters from Silverton.

She didn't know I was madly in love with her. Worse, that West Pointer was test-driving a honeymoon, chauffeuring her through Europe, romancing her every minute of every hour of every day.

As dawn peeked over the distant Sangre de Cristo Range, I sat at my desk and started a new letter, getting right to the point: "One thing that really bothers me is the thought of him touching you, kissing you. I can't dwell on that. It's too unpleasant."

I tried not to think about it. But I couldn't stop. Equally excruciating was the likely fact that I wouldn't see her for two years:

It has only been a month away from you, but with each day seeming like a month, I realize how difficult it would be to be separated from you. Two years is no longer an abstraction. It is real and long and terrifying. We have to be together. That means marriage in August or September, not two or three years from now. We need to get married before the Peace Corps, not after.

But what were the chances of her marrying me when she had Jack in hand? Slim to none. It wasn't the fact that he was a stud or a military man— or that he drove a fancy car. Annie could see past the accoutrements. What she couldn't dismiss was my own history, specifically the abortion. It was a stain I couldn't erase. Or cover up. Or deny.

Still, I had to show her how deeply I loved her, how much I wanted her to marry me, but without scaring her away.

Last spring, she had been as skittish about marriage as I had been—how it would tie us down, how we needed to be free, on and on. Merely speaking the word *marriage* had left us both in awkward silence. My plea had to be serious, but not pleading or needy. It had to be playful, not threatening. Ever hopeful, I sent her Uncle Bob's address. "Write me here as soon as you get back to Landshut," I wrote. "Tell me you have come to the right decision on this marriage bit."

Ann

Tuesday, July 7, 1964, the Italian Hill Country. After slaloming through impossibly narrow mountain curves along the Riviera, we turned north into Italy. Jack suggested another hotel night while my burn simmered down. I cringed at the expense, but we found a small *pensione* hanging off a hillside in a tiny village. As we were hauling in our gear, I banged his shin with my overnight bag. "Oops, *scusi!*"

"I wish you'd can the baby talk."

What? The word had just popped out, as it had several times in my anticipation of returning to Italy. "Excuse me? You mean *scusi*, the Italian word for excuse me?"

He looked away, as if embarrassed. We unloaded the rest of our stuff in silence.

Behind the *pensione*, we found a place in the woods to spread out our blanket. We'd picked up a couple of small pizzas and chocolate biscotti to dip in our tea. My joke that for once the tea was almost tasty didn't get a rise. Back in the room, I said, "Why don't you go explore the hills, slay a dragon or two, while I take a nap?"

He dosed me with another lozenge and aspirin and a perfunctory salve treatment. "Sleep as long as you want," he said.

What I heard: "Don't expect me back anytime soon."

The shadows in the room were long when I woke up. No Jack. A bouquet of wildflowers in a water glass sat on the nightstand—with a note. "Like these flowers, you light up my world. Sorry I was such a grump. Your Jack. PS. Come down to the lobby."

The apology and the signature swept away the gloom of the afternoon. Once we fell in love by letter, he had started signing off with "Your Jack." No comma. His note affirmed that he was still "My Jack."

On the last flight of stairs, I heard his voice—speaking German. And laughing. A woman crooned—also in German. Jack boomed, *"Ja, ja!"* I peeked around the corner. Jack and a young couple sat at a tiny table in the pocket-size foyer. Each had a glass of wine. The girl switched to English the moment I appeared.

They were on their honeymoon. He was an American second lieutenant stationed in Stuttgart, and she was a German, a translator at the American Army base there. Her belly spoke volumes, at least five months pregnant, maybe six. I thought of Gretchen and winced. I hadn't written her since my last-minute missive on the plane. I had no idea what she had decided to do with the baby, and I didn't have a follow-up address. Some friend I'd been.

After dinner with the honeymooners, I coaxed Jack into a hillside walk, despite the light rain. We talked about Gretchen. I worried that she had been abandoned by us both, her two would-be supporters. She and Bonner contrasted sharply with our cheerful dinner companions. "So our new friend married the German girl he got pregnant. Do you suppose *his* military career is over?" I asked.

"Not him. He isn't a career man."

"Do you think Bonner would have married Gretchen if she weren't German?"

Jack paused while a car splashed by on the wet street. "Germany has a long history of war, and the US Army never forgets. The lifers equate marrying a German to colluding with the enemy. To the brass, I'm tainted because I mix with locals. Too bad. I've learned a lot from Germans. Yeah, nationality was a factor for Bonner. Damn Cold War!"

Jack's rare *damn* surprised me. He so embraced military courtesy that he seldom said anything harsher than *darn*. His vitriol betrayed a frustration with the army he'd only hinted at.

"But the Germans are our allies now, at least the West Germans. Isn't it time to make peace—instead of war?"

"It's not that simple." He sighed, and I didn't pursue it. We walked on silently through streets so narrow we could have held hands and touched the houses on opposite sides.

Soon he stopped and turned to me. "Let me apologize, again, for this afternoon. I was feeling sorry for myself—you were so close but off-limits. I needed a good run."

Nodding, I took his hand. The rain began to drip down my neck. I sidestepped a puddle, and a Terry moment flooded my mind: April 1961. I was in my dorm room one evening, hard at my studies. Terry phoned. "Look out the window. Tell me what you see."

"Rain?"

"Look again. It's a warm spring rain. It's saying, 'Terry. Annie. Come out and play.'"

He and I walked for hours that night, reveling in the soft tapping of rain on tree leaves, the fragrance of newly washed lawns, the slithery hiss of tires on wet pavement, the sheen of interlocking circles of streetlights reflected in mini-puddles. I returned to the dorm tingly, water dripping from my ringlets.

Now here in this Italian village with Jack, I was *that* tingly. Was it the rain? Jack? Or was it Terry? Which was worse—the pain I would cause either man by telling him the full truth about the other or the pain I chose to swallow daily by holding back? I shuddered at the forces wrenching me in opposite directions.

"Cold?" Jack slipped his arm around my waist.

It was more complicated than that, but I couldn't tell him. "A bit chilly. I'm soaked."

"Here. Take this." He draped his jacket over my shoulders. "When we get back to the room, I'll give you another dose of the magic ointment. Tomorrow we hit Verona. We won't get more moments like these for a few days."

For sure. Dad had arranged for us to stay with longtime army friends in Verona, Colonel Ed Kirtley and his wife, Edna Mae. Over the years, Ed, a chaplain, had been stationed in almost every place Dad had been. Edna Mae had been my surrogate mother when Mom went to New Mexico after Grandma had her stroke. "You're right. Edna Mae will be guarding my virtue with bayonet fixed. Too bad. I'm enjoying your medicinal treatments. A lot."

Back in the room, my dress witlessly clung to my body like a wet T-shirt. A smile played at the corners of Jack's mouth. "What?" I demanded.

"Nothing. Just admiring how the rain makes you so . . . so lovely."

"Really? Not that I'm *not* wearing a bra? Because of my burn, by the way."

"I did notice. But I'm not keen on other men leering at you."

"Don't worry. In spite of women's lib, burning our bras and all, this is a first for me."

"I'll take that as a vote of confidence. But let's get that soggy dress off."

"Good idea, but wait a sec." The rain—or the memory of Miss Chic in Nice—had reawakened my playful side. "Let's try something new." I draped a bath towel around my neck and over my breasts. Without taking my eyes off him, I undid the top button on my dress, paused, and then undid the next and the next. Under the towel, I peeled the wet garment off each shoulder. Without the sash, the flowing dress slithered over my hips and plopped around my ankles. I flipped it to him with my foot.

He wrapped my dress around his neck like a muffler on a cold day and took a long whiff. "Very nice. In fact, nicer than Nice. You learn quickly."

"Gross! I've worn that thing three times in the past week."

"So much the better."

"Yuck!" I pulled my head inside the towel like a turtle.

He sniffed noisily. I peeked out. He had my dress pressed to his nose, peering over it like a mischievous five-year-old. I hadn't seen him happy since I'd run his Sting Ray into the ditch. He tossed the dress aside. "Okay, enough foolishness. Down, madam!"

I turned my back to him, slid the towel to my front, grasped the two ends, and clumsily stretched out facedown on the bed, arms upward, elbows out, with the towel beneath me. Clearly, I needed more lessons from Miss Chic, but Jack wasn't critical. Perched beside me on the edge of the bed, he anointed left arm and right, working out from my spine, his hands gliding once again along the edges of my breasts. Who was the tease now?

More balm, and he slid down my sides to my hips. He rested one hand on my lower back so delicately that each finger imprinted its own message. Creeping under my panty elastic, he massaged in tiny circles, each one a hair's width lower. He worked the ointment through the burn, deep into a pleasure zone beneath. Despite myself, I tensed.

He backed away, propped a knee on the edge of the bed, and massaged thighs to heels, no errant side trips.

"Ahh, you are so understanding." I sighed.

"*Understanding* is an overstatement. *Obedient* is more accurate." His voice cracked. Finally, he slapped his hands together. "Okay, let's take care of the front. Over, please."

Cautiously, I gathered the towel under my arms and rolled onto my back. He looked at the towel and cocked an eyebrow. "Do we need that? I mean, after we—"

"I'm shy. I really am."

"You're also beautiful."

"And you're a hunk, but I'm still shy."

"And too glib for a poor old foot soldier. I hear you, ma'am." He saluted—a goofy civilian wave, not a snappy West Point salute—and trailed ointment across my upper chest.

"Foot soldier? When did tank commander Sigg become a foot soldier?"

"Begging your pardon, ma'am. It was a figure of speech—for the literary among us."

The icy stuff turned up the heat deep inside. He worked the balm in above my breasts. His boyish grin was irresistible. With a quick nod and what I hoped was a seductive smile, I signaled "permission granted." He eased the towel off my breasts and traced my bikini triangles. His fingers tiptoed between them, adroitly maneuvering through the valley without scaling the slopes. He raised his eyebrows, asking approval to take the next step.

Ever so slightly, I arched. Without blinking, he planted his hands on the bed on either side of me. "I love you, you know." He kissed each nipple lightly. His face was as bright as a full moon over the Rockies, and I pushed toward him. He suckled momentarily and backed away. His hands flowed to my breasts, his breath coming in short puffs.

"I love you too," I said, barely above a whisper. "I've dreamed about moments like this."

He stroked me, fondled me, and loved me. His touch made me ache for more. At that moment, my burn was worth the pain. My misery had drawn us closer than anything we'd done—my reliance on him and his care and patience—to say nothing of the bliss of our physical intimacies. In these two days, Jack had caressed nearly every millimeter of my body and tested my resolve.

I thought I was ready. I pressed closer. But then I scraped my burned belly against his leg and lurched back. "Sorry, guy. But I can't, not yet. It hurts too much. Besides, it's late. Maybe we should get some sleep."

His face fell and his eyes pleaded. After a long pause, he said, "You're right." No argument. His restraint made me love him even more.

Deep inside, I knew my hesitancy was about more than the sunburn. Though at times I felt as if Jack and I had known each other for years, in reality we'd been together only ten days—not long enough to be certain.

And there was something else. We were in a fairy tale of our own making. Romance permeated the air and rode in the Sting Ray with us. It hovered over our every adventure and even cast a rose-colored hue over our misadventures: the ditch, the sunburn, and my hesitancies. Married life was supposed to be forever. After the glow wore off, would it still be this idyllic? I needed to know—and Jack too—if we were a match made for the ho-hum times and, yes, the hard times, as well as for the honeymoon. Only then would I be ready to consummate our love.

That night, I was content to enjoy the moment and to luxuriate in the warmth of his body next to me.

10
Flirting with the Past

Ann

Wednesday, July 8, 1964, en route to Verona, Italy. As Jack was speeding us northeast, I was speeding back in time. I was a teenager again. Fourteen to be exact. Verona was the setting for my first great international adventure.

In the summer of 1956, Mom and Dad dropped me off at the station in Livorno, along with my best friend, Judy, and we girls took the train to Verona. Our goal: Rendezvous with three school friends whose fathers had been transferred there and spend a couple of weeks in Verona and Venice, two storybook cities. By day in Verona, we frolicked at the beach. By night at slumber parties, we gossiped and told stories hours past our bedtimes, tried on each other's clothes, and paraded like models, slim and pretty and oh so feminine.

The US Army's American Beach on Lake Garda was an enclave safe from all things foreign, the perfect hangout for teenage dependents. Like other beaches around the lake, it was private, but ours was reserved for the US military. We had to show our military IDs, and not even American tourists or Italian vendors were allowed to enter.

A recreation center established for the soldiers and their families on foreign assignments, American Beach offered the essentials for American kids: a shaded pavilion anchored by a snack shack that served up hot dogs, burgers, and fries, *plus* Italian pizza and American-made ice cream—pasteurized, unlike the Italian version, which our mothers warned us would make us sick. We bought all the goodies at low prices with "script"—miniature bills for military families that America printed to stem the flow of

US dollars into the black market. Even the nickels, dimes, and quarters were paper bills. In Italian stores off the post, script was worthless.

Fortified with comfort food, we teens sunbathed, played volleyball, and, under the watchful eyes of our American lifeguards, swam, water-skied, and rowed boats along the tree-lined shores. And met boys. We swooned over "Only You" and pined for our own true loves. We jitterbugged to "Rock Around the Clock" and flirted shamelessly.

The boys tried to con us into chicken fights in the lake—boy-girl teams, girls riding atop. Older and uninhibited, our friend Marcia hooted, "What? Snuggle my ass over your pimply shoulders and pretend it's an accident each time those grubby fingers try to score? Not on your life!" The boys shriveled and slunk away.

The ultimate diversion? Waterskiing. My first try, I fell flat on my face, forgot to let go of the rope, and gulped in half the lake. After trying over and over again, I finally rode to the top of the wake. But when I pulled the handle too close, the towline went slack, and I smacked down on my rump. One day I managed a single, exhilarating circuit to the lake's center and back, capped off by thirty seconds of sheer bliss when I leaped the wake and glissaded effortlessly on the glassy surface. For a few shining moments, I'd been a swan.

Most unforgettable was our girls-only skinny-dipping escapade. For the first time in my life, I cast away my inhibitions. That day, I realized I could do things I'd never dared to do before. In retrospect, it was a major step toward womanhood.

On an excursion to Venice, we skipped across Piazza San Marco to the Loggetta at the foot of the Campanile and flirted with some American sailors on shore leave. Marcia cajoled a navy guy into letting her wear his white sailor hat. After that, he and his buddies tailed us like jackals until it dawned on them we weren't about to give them what they came ashore for. The petty officer panting for Marcia was the last to give up. She ignored him and finally kept his cap. I envied her easy way with guys—when they got pushy, she simply laughed them off.

Eight years later, I was eager to create new memories, this time with a man I could easily marry.

The downside: being cloistered during our must-do stay with Colonel and Mrs. Kirtley in Verona, cordoned off in separate bedrooms, no question. I was sure that in a previous life, Edna Mae had been mother superior in a home for wayward girls. But we couldn't possibly bypass the Kirtleys for a secluded *pensione* on Lake Garda.

Still, I looked forward to seeing Colonel Kirtley. He had always treated me like a grown-up, asking for my opinion and responding to what I said. He was also a man who would help you in a pinch. En route, I told Jack about the time he had shepherded us into an apartment near the Pentagon despite an impossible housing crunch. The Kirtleys had moved into the area earlier, and the building owner asked Ed if he could recommend someone from the waiting list for the last available apartment. When Ed spotted Dad's name—buried far down the list—he sang our praises and got us bumped to the top. "You can't go wrong if you have God's right-hand man on your side, Sis. Remember that," Dad told me before I left for Europe.

Jack's brow furrowed. "A chaplain, huh? I suppose he'll grill me about my 'faith.'"

"Nah, don't worry. They're not like that."

Jack went silent. Finally, he swept his hand toward the thick forest on both sides of the road. "We live in a beautiful, complicated universe. But simply because it would take a god to create it doesn't prove God exists."

"So?"

"So your mother told Bonner you would never marry someone who wasn't a Christian. That means *me*. What did you tell her about me and religion?"

"Nothing! But hold on. You want to talk about religion or my mother?"

"Religion. Start with religion. All religions rely on faith. Why?" He wasn't expecting an answer. I waited. "Because you can't prove the existence of God. So where do you get faith? From your parents, who got it from their parents."

"Agreed. If your parents brought you up believing a yellow handkerchief was pink, you'd believe it was pink, no matter what your friends said."

"Great example," he said. "And you actually agree?"

"Sure."

My mind jumped to one of the hubbubs Terry had ignited. One Easter vacation he went home from CU and showed up at his hometown Sunday school and challenged the kids with that yellow-handkerchief metaphor.

His "blasphemy" stirred the wrath of the minister, mortified his parents, and made him persona non grata at Center's Methodist church. Terry had laughed it off. "Wow, ten times worse than farting during the silent prayer." Jack would have laughed too, but I couldn't tell him.

More than once, Jack had written at length about religion, but what had I told him about my beliefs? Hardly a peep. Fact was, I'd never told him I had grown up with the piety of a nun. I had trundled off to Sunday school and church by myself on many a Sunday. Led the devotionals at our weekly Christian Youth Fellowship meetings. Eagerly attended summer church camp—not for the boys, but because I felt closer to God under the stars. Read the Bible every night.

At CU, though, I fell away from the church in the hurly-burly of college life. In late-night bull sessions with dorm mates—and long talks with Terry—I pondered my deepest beliefs about war and peace, civil rights, religion, and poverty, and decried the hypocrisy of political and religious leaders who paid only lip service to solving problems. College became the petri dish for a brave new perspective on the world's pervasive problems. With Sunday as the day to catch up on my studies, I simply didn't go to church. By contrast, Mom and Dad became more zealous churchgoers.

Jack's voice yanked me back. "I know I've ranted about religion. But you? I think not."

"Yeah, you sure did. I mostly agree with your premise, but I don't wear it on my sleeve."

He shot me a look, then grinned. "That's wonderful. *You're* wonderful, I mean. I couldn't marry a girl who uses religion as a crutch."

"Yes, we're in accord here, guy. But the question is, Why would Mom be commenting on your religious beliefs? Did you tell my folks you don't believe in God? That you're a heathen?" Slyly, I studied his profile to see if that would get a rise out of him.

"No. I assumed you told them. You mean you didn't?"

"'Course not. So where'd they get the idea you aren't a Christian? And that we might be discussing marriage, by the way?"

"Bonner knows I question the existence of God, but—"

"And I suppose you told him about us as well?"

"He knows I've fallen for you. But who cares? I'm not ashamed of my views. Or of loving you."

He meant it. Not sweet talk, just straight-out truth. At that moment, we both were floating down the highway. But he'd hit a touchy point—about confidentiality. He needed to understand that. "I care," I said. "I don't talk about my love life with anyone. It's private."

A sliver of memory started pestering me. Six months before, while I was home for Christmas, Bonner had written, mentioning he had some major car repairs coming up and might need a short-term loan. Would that have been a cover for scraping together the money he needed to finance Gretchen's trip to the States—and the birth? And when it got urgent, might he have called Dad, maybe around the time I had asked for help with my Europe trip? If so, I bet Mom would have gotten on the phone and asked him about Jack and me. Boy, for someone who liked privacy, I was in a pretty leaky boat—if my speculation turned out to be true.

"Don't worry," Jack said. "Your secrets are safe with me. I brought up religion only because I'm worried your folks have primed the chaplain to cook my goose."

Shifting uncomfortably in the passenger seat, I tried to be more reassuring than I felt. "No, they wouldn't be that devious. But I can see Mom getting worked up about your belief in God—disbelief, I mean. Just in case, let's make sure the Kirtleys fall in love with us. Let's be 'above reproach in all things'—as Mom likes to say."

Jack put out his hand. "Good plan, clever Ann." We shook on it.

That night at the Kirtleys, Edna Mae outdid herself with a home-cooked Italian meal: chicken cacciatore, garden vegetables sautéed in olive oil, a tossed salad, and red wine. What a refreshing break from the make-do meals Jack and I had concocted day after day.

The two of them treated us as if we, not my parents, were lifelong friends. They pressed me about my college days and waxed on about the joy of teaching and my plans for Glendale High. In a burst of questions, they asked Jack about West Point and each post since graduation. Shifting his focus to the Cold War, Ed lamented the plight of "those poor souls locked away behind the Iron Curtain." As we finished dinner, he turned to Jack. "Tell us about border duty. How are you and your men holding up under the stress?"

"Stress? Well, sir, it's deathly quiet at the border. No traffic. No people.

Not even a stray dog. It's peaceful—in that eerie eye-of-a-hurricane way. But everyone's nerves are ajangle. We're primed and loaded, our instincts at hair triggers. A wizened grandma wandering too close can throw a two-hundred-mile stretch of the border into battle alert. The US and our allies as well as Czechs and East German citizens. All of us. Everyone's always jittery. You can't sleep."

"Like Korea after the truce," Ed said. "It tests your spirits, doesn't it?"

"Yes, sir. Here's a sobering example. It's Friday afternoon, November 22, last year." Jack paused, leaned forward, and slowly looked around the table at each of us. "Bonner and I have just finished a five-day exercise at Vilseck. Beautiful day. Air's fresh, peaks capped with snow. Aside from our war games, all's quiet at the eastern perimeter of the free world."

I knew Jack's storytelling voice from his tapes, but I had never seen him in action. His voice became deliberate. "My men have packed the train—tanks, APCs, trucks, jeeps, everything. We're headed back to Camp Whalen. Not Bonner. For some crazy reason, the CO tells him to land march his men." Slicing his hand sideways, he said, "We never do that. War machines tear up the best of highways, let alone those backcountry lanes."

Ah, yes. In Landshut, I heard—and felt—a tank thundering down a city street long before I actually saw it. The ground shook. Windows rattled. Dogs howled. *One* tank. A whole convoy rumbling through German villages, ripping the roads to shreds, made no sense.

"So Bonner and his men head out by road," Jack said. "My troop goes by train. It takes us two hours. For Bonner, ninety miles at sixteen miles an hour will cost him at least half the day.

"At Whalen, my buddy Tom is duty officer. He's shorthanded, so I help drive the surveillance points, collect observations, and make sure everyone has what they need. At 19:15 hours, Tom and I break out MREs for dinner. We're shooting the breeze in the command post, listening to Ray Charles sing 'I Can't Stop Loving You' on AFN. I love that song." Eyes flashing, Jack shot me a glance. "The announcer breaks in: 'We have just received this word from Dallas, Texas . . .'" Jack's voice dropped. He was steely-eyed, grasping a make-believe mike. "'President Kennedy has been shot. He has been taken to Parkland Memorial Hospital.'"

Edna Mae, who had been piling up dirty plates at the end of the table, stopped and sank into the chair next to me.

"The radio goes to static. Then silence. No Ray Charles. No announcer. We leap for the volume knob. Nothing. AFN is missing in action." He turned to me. "Armed Forces Network is our lifeline out there. All over Europe, in fact."

Jeez, as if I didn't know.

"And no TV either. All we can do is wait. The radio crackles and we hear, 'President Kennedy has been taken to Parkland Hospital.' Nothing new. And then, 'All normal broadcasting is suspended. Stay tuned.' We're up, Tom and I. Was it an assassin? Some nut? A conspiracy?" He paused, his voice grew metallic. "The first shot in war, a modern Archduke Ferdinand? We. Don't. Know. We have to assume the worst. Protect our men. And safeguard military secrets."

Jack looked directly at me. "You may not know this, Ann, but we keep thermite, a mixture of aluminum and iron filings, on top of our safes, on everything of value. You plant a blasting cap in it and set it off, and at three thousand degrees, it'll burn the whole works—safe and everything inside—right through the floor, into the ground. Everything. If we're ever overrun, the enemy gets nothing."

That I *didn't* know.

"We begin securing all our documents, equipment, everything in the command shack that could be of value to the enemy."

Ed nodded. "And your job is to mobilize your men without creating panic, right?"

"Right. The announcer repeats the old bulletin. Fifteen minutes pass. A half hour. An occasional bulletin crackles. It's serious. It's worse. Mrs. Kennedy is okay. She's with him. The Texas governor, Connally—he's been shot too. Nothing's clear. Finally, 'President John Fitzgerald Kennedy died today at 1:30 p.m. central time.'"

Of course, we all knew what happened, but we were captivated by Jack's first-person Cold War version. Edna Mae gripped my hand. She sucked in her breath at his next words.

"This is it. We start setting in the blasting caps."

Jack swept his eyes around the table. "I direct my men to put thermite on our tanks, APCs, anything that moves. We scope out locations. Position them in the woods. Camouflage them. Prep the guns. If nothing else, we'll create havoc for the Czechs when they storm the Danube Bridge." He mapped it out on the tablecloth. "And all this time, Bonner and his men are land-marching toward Camp Whalen. He has no inkling. We make plans to disable his tanks the moment he arrives.

"Next thing we know, Czech jets buzz the border, turn back, sweep in again." He put his hands to his ears, feigning protection against the screaming planes. "The Czechs have scrambled their whole doggone air force. Our West German allies strap on their World War II helmets." He stifled a grin at the mounting absurdity. "We check and double-check our side arms. At the surveillance posts, our troops are glaring across the divide, machine guns at the ready, rifles loaded. The Czechs are armed, glaring back."

I drained my glass of wine and wanted more, but I didn't move. Edna Mae still gripped my hand.

"At the command shack, we're barraged with new reports. Huge traffic jams block the main highway nearby. Cars, trucks, horse-drawn wagons, families dragging handcarts are stampeding west in droves. I speak German, so I sprint outside, wade into the middle of the mess, and buttonhole the first guy I see. He's out of his blocked-in car, hands on hips, engine off. 'War! The American Army is moving north,' he bellows. What? This makes no sense. *We* are the American Army. The man slams his car door and stomps off. Others join him, whole families."

Jack shook his head. "I hoof it back to the command shack. Garbled voices sputter over the radio: The three- and four-stars are trying to nail down the intelligence. 'Intelligence' has fled with the German civilians. The MO seems to be 'When in doubt, scream and shout.'

"We wait. No news. Eventually, the teletype springs to life, chugga-chugga-chug. 'Urgent message for all USAREUR parties STOP All units stand down immediately STOP Do not move troops STOP Repeat do not move troops STOP.'

"So now, we're frozen in place. For what, our final stand? Custer at Little Bighorn on the Danube? Form up and charge? We have no idea. Neither do the brass. The craziness mushrooms. No clear orders. No factual assessment. We're all running around with our hair on fire. Suddenly we realize the floor's shaking. Tanks! I'd know those vibrations in my sleep."

Jack cupped his hands above his eyes as if peering into the night. "By now it's dark. The camp's ghostly. Every spotlight and strobe lit up. A line of tanks rumbles into view. They're ours. The lead tank's hatch is open, the commander standing tall. It's Bonner! They've been en route all day. He's grinning ear to ear."

Jack breaks into a full laugh. "So what's his first comment? Get this: 'Where the hell's Germany going? The whole damn country's clogging the roads. I hope that wasn't a new Mercedes I flattened.'

"I wave him down from his horse. I don't know where to start. 'They're, we've . . . the president's been shot. Killed!'"

Jack picked up his wine glass and took a long, slow drink. "In short, Colonel, when you ask about our morale, I'd say it's great. But frankly, the news rattled us all. Americans. Germans. Czechs. Everyone geared up for war." He let out a long breath.

Ed broke the silence. "And of course the whole confrontation was self-perpetuating. The Czechs were spooked by the 'American Army' on the march—Bonner and his company—so they scrambled their air force to counterattack, right?"

"Exactly!" Jack nodded. "The Czech air show convinced us the assassination was volley one in World War III, so we started repositioning our tanks and APCs. That caused the Federal German Border Guard to mass along the line, muzzles loaded. That frazzled the Czechs, so they did another flyby. The tanks and the air show sent the locals fleeing for their lives. We were all caught in a vortex of ignorance. In short, we *all* set our hair on fire. The good news—we did stand down. We didn't set off the thermite. Or charge over the bridge with everything we had."

"Or start another war," Ed said. He jumped up, refilled our wine glasses—all of them dry—and lifted his in salute. "A toast to the rewards of confusion, inaction, and what? Comic relief? Or the unseen hand of the benevolent God above."

It was late, and Edna Mae hadn't been able to tear herself from the table. But she still had dessert to serve as well as cappuccino or espresso, our choice. No proper colonel's wife sends guests off without dessert—in this case, my favorite, cherry pie. ("Special for you, dear," she said. "I remembered.") And in Italy, no proper hostess scrimps on the after-dinner liqueur.

I began to fade, but Jack went into overdrive, more effusive than he'd been all week. He and Ed were talking shop—officers in their element. Jack *was* on his way up, wasn't he?

I was about to take my last bite of pie when Jack asked, "Tell me, Colonel, how in the world do you minister to a 'flock' of soldiers from so many denominations? Aren't they at war with each other?"

I nearly sprayed cherry pie all over the table. What happened to our pact?

"Ah, Jack, that's the joy in it—dusting away the superficial trappings, the rituals and covenants and dogmas, and breathing life into the core values that unite us as Christians."

Ed had been trained in the nuances of every major Protestant faith, he said, and rattled off denominations as if they were his own children—Baptist, Methodist, Presbyterian, Anglican, Lutheran, and a number of others. He told us about unnamed commanding officers who had tried to swing his ministry toward one sect or the other and about the demands of trying to serve both officers and enlisted men. "Every day is a new challenge. That's what keeps me energized."

Despite the years I had known the Kirtleys, I had no idea what he did day to day. Silently, I applauded Jack for his ability to draw the chaplain out. The best part: no attempt at all to divine Jack's religious convictions. Or mine.

After coffee and amaretto, Edna Mae escorted us to our rooms—at opposite ends of the house. Our fond good nights? Nothing more than wistful glances. Verona or not, parting was not "sweet sorrow." After Jack's riveting account of JFK's assassination and his ebullience over dinner, it pained me to say "good night till it be morrow." I wanted to sleep with him.

Thursday, July 9, 1964, Verona. Jack and I headed for American Beach at Lake Garda to revisit the site of my giddy high school exploits. I wore my one-piece bathing suit—no bikini this time.

First thing, he snagged a motorboat, driver, and water skis. "Never tried it. I'll give it a go," he said.

Hunkering in the water, ski tips up, he signaled and rose and danced through the wake as if he'd been doing it all his life. I yearned for his athleticism, but I couldn't risk an embarrassing repeat of my 1956 debacle, especially with the breeze churning the lake into choppy whitecaps. Besides, with my sunburn still tender, the prudent thing was to sit in the shade. I watched him take three or four turns, waving occasionally to show how impressed I was.

He disappeared after a splendid run, returned in a rowboat, and waved me over to the wharf. "Cap'n Jack at your service, ma'am. Care for a cruise?"

He ushered me into the little boat as if it were the Queen Mary and rowed effortlessly, oars glinting in the sun. What a specimen—strong, but not a misshapen weight lifter, wearing the serene smile of a guy truly in his element. For him, it wasn't a chore, but life at its best. By the time he paused, we were several hundred yards from shore. The sun worshippers and splashing kids were dots on the distant beach.

Jack locked in the oars and flashed an impish grin. "Okay, my dear, I've been looking forward to this forever. Ready to go skinny-dipping?"

Uh-oh. In a reckless moment during our correspondence, I'd regaled him with my high school skinny-dipping caper. He teased me, telling me he'd found the "perfect cove" or the "ideal pond" and could hardly wait "to relive 1956 with you."

Foolish girl, I didn't really think he was serious. A fourteen-year-old's romp with her girlfriends withered next to the thought of me at twenty-two swimming naked at a public beach with my twenty-six-year-old lieutenant. Aside from the embarrassment and the message it would send Jack, I couldn't banish the specter of Edna Mae with her binoculars lurking in the bushes: *I knew it, Ed! Just wait till Dorothy and Ralph hear about this!*

"Last one in is an old fuddy-duddy," Jack said, leaping into the lake, bathing suit and all.

Whew! I concluded it was a continuation of our long-running silly joke about skinny-dipping, and I jumped in and struck off swimming. But when I turned to float on my back far from the noisy beach, I saw that Jack was still by the boat, treading water and waving me back like crazy.

"It's okay. No sharks out here," I yelled.

"No, wait! You forgot something."

"Huh?" I swam back.

"It's '56 all over again," he said. "We're skinny-dipping, remember? First, into the water, next off with the suits. Wasn't that how your story went?"

His grin mixed allure with boyish anticipation. Despite my misgivings, a part of me did want to fling off my suit. Should I heed his siren call? Or crush this lascivious notion while I could?

I bobbed up above the edge of the boat and surveyed the shore. Eight years earlier, a boatload of horny high school boys zoomed toward us at breakneck speed. Shrieking, we girls had barely squirmed into our wet bathing suits before their boat showered us in a ten-foot wake. This time, no one ashore was paying attention. Still, a nude swim with a grown man?

I teetered on a knife edge between the strict moral code Mom and Dad had etched into my internal navigation system and the thrill of intimacies I had shared with Jack.

Women's liberation and the sexual revolution had scattered the old ways like dried leaves on a windy day. I believed that women were on equal footing with men when it came to work and play. At the same time, I didn't "play" in the same arena as Julie and my other friends. To them, I was a sexual misfit. Their subtle influence, though, had greased the skids toward the sexual excursions I had taken with Terry and with Jack, both of whom stoked desires I found increasingly irresistible. So when Jack egged me on, I rose to the moment. "Think it's safe?" I asked.

"Don't worry. I'll keep watch. Need help with those straps?"

"Yeah . . . I guess."

He unhooked the crisscross straps and slipped them off. I rolled the suit down a smidge. He nodded encouragement. I peeled it over one breast. My shyness vaporized under his sunny smile, and I repressed my hang-ups enough to pull the suit to my waist.

Jack floated closer. Oh, what the heck. Shielded by the boat, I latched my fingers around his neck, and stroked my breasts up his hairy chest.

"Mmm," he said. "You trying to ignite a fire on the lake?"

"Maybe a spark or two. But wait. I'm just warming up." I paddled backward, hooked my thumbs in my suit, still around my waist, and tugged at it. It resisted.

He stroked over, cradled my buns, and we sank while he seesawed the suit down my legs, the burn now anesthetized by the cold water. He hitched it off, shot to the surface, and twirled it overhead.

"Jack!" I snatched it and flung it into the boat. "Someone could see you!"

"Guess what, my dear. No one's watching. But look at you. You're gorgeous."

I peered into the water. My breasts shimmered an anemic blue under the ripples. Below, absolutely nothing left to the imagination. But oddly enough, I felt totally free. The cool water excited every curve and crevice. I backstroked away about ten yards and then reversed course into a slow dog paddle. He whipped his trunks off, and his "second lieutenant" snapped to attention. "Whoa, that guy's dangerous. You'd better calm him down."

"He's eager, that's all." He pulled me to him and kissed me. Before I could react, he clutched my naked fanny and banged me against his erection.

"Jack! No!" As we started to sink, I shoved at him and backstroked away.

"What? Nervous?"

"You, you poked me! And not a gentle poke, either. Square in the . . . right there. That's out of bounds."

"What's wrong? I thought we were on the same page."

Naive me, foolish me—that fourteen-year-old girl from a la-la time. No, it was reckless me! In so many ways, I had told him we *were* on the same page. But this was a new book, and he had skipped too many chapters. "You *thought*? I've told you a dozen times—not yet!"

He banged his fist against the side of the boat.

Too late, I realized I'd been teasing him cruelly. I saw flirting itself as the end game—a physical embodiment of the wordplay I enjoyed so much, not a path that led irreversibly to sex. For Jack, it was a ball game: get to first base, race to second, slide into third, every twitch calculated to speed around the bases, and ultimately score, preferably by virtue of a home run.

He dived underwater and disappeared. For a long time. So long it scared me. I'd made so many promises—with daring behavior, with a look, a gesture, a sigh. No wonder he was beside himself at times, trying to figure me out. I had never considered looking at us through *his* eyes.

Finally, he erupted in a tower of water, like a whale surfacing, his body half out of the lake. "What kind of game are you playing?" he demanded.

"It's not a game." I glanced at our bodies wavering in the water and arched an eyebrow. "Look at us—naked as jaybirds! We're moving too fast. Can you bear with me as I take it step by step?" I turned my hands upward toward him, hoping he would take them.

He didn't. "Just know this—it's impossible to be 'naked as a jaybird' with you without longing for much more."

Somehow, we managed to tug our wet swimsuits on without compromising our dignity any further. Somehow, we rowed back to shore without surrendering to a torrent of angry words. Somehow, our love escaped a burial at sea in Lake Garda. All in oppressive silence. No helpful partner to fasten my swimsuit straps. No sense of shared adventure in the long paddle to shore.

We drove to the Kirtleys in silence. Jack sat ramrod straight, his hands gripping the wheel as we squealed around corners. A fracas between an indignant Jack and a defensive Ann roiled deep inside me:

Jack: *Skinny-dipping was an invitation. I thought it signaled you were ready.*

Me: *No, for me, skinny-dipping was revisiting a childhood frolic. And you went too far, too fast.*

Jack: *I've tried so hard, Ann. The first night in Strasbourg, I was beside myself with anticipation when you crawled into my tent. In Paris, I thought this must be what heaven is. In the* pensione, *I was supremely hopeful. But every time—every time—you dashed my hopes. I'm not sure how much more I'm able to take. Or willing to take.*

Me: *Why the urgency? The peak beckons, but the path itself offers so much. There's no rush.*

Jack: *Maybe not for you, but life's short, how long do—*

Me: *Not so short that I'm willing to leap a chasm to a place where we can't unravel yesterday's decisions.*

As I began to see how I had created one unfilled expectation after another, I knew I had to set things right. I said, "Jack, I am so sorry. Can you forgive me?"

The lines on his face softened. "I don't know." After a long silence, he let up on the accelerator and added, "But it's worth a try."

I wished I were wise enough, articulate enough, strong enough to do and say the right things. Truth is, I was too frazzled, too unschooled to grasp my impact on him. *But worth a try?* Yes! He was willing.

So somehow, we survived that afternoon. And somehow, we each found an uneasy truce and vague understanding of *my* sense of violation and of *his* frustration. We took a couple of steps back. Whereto, now? I didn't know.

⌒

At the Kirtleys, Edna Mae was abuzz over a "little get-together" she had planned for that evening—and too busy to notice the signs of our imbroglio at the lake. Her dinner parties were as prestigious as a base commander's annual fete, and in Verona's American military community, anyone who was anybody had to be there. She hustled us off to dress for the event.

The party plunged me into a world Mom and Dad had mastered—the casual, yet sophisticated military social, where rank and protocol ruled supreme. Guests glided about with purpose, grace, and perfect posture. Wine and liquor flowed freely. A few might drink too much, but they would never betray themselves by compromising military decorum. Even when the men sported civilian wear, junior officers addressed superiors and their wives as "sir" and "ma'am" and yielded respectfully on the conversation highway. By custom, conversations were lively, cultured repartee without controversy.

But that night, there was a big difference—my lieutenant and I were the guests of honor. Colonel Kirtley introduced Jack as if he were his own son, newly returned from battle. The guests gathered round, men talking tanks, tactics, and tinhorn dictators. The women asked Jack about life on the border. "Are you in a BOQ?" "A barracks?" "A tent?" "A foxhole?" A couple of them painted alluring pictures of their own daughters. The nerve!

I chatted with the women about Neuschwanstein, Paris, Jack's and my plans for Venice. One officer noticed my last name and asked whether I knew of a Colonel Garretson who commanded the port at Livorno in the late fifties. Before I could answer, Edna Mae piped in with tales of Dad's successes there and at Pusan and Guam, giving me some cachet of my own.

Despite our rift at the lake, Jack and I managed to sparkle at Edna Mae's party, the perfect elixir to keep us from wallowing in our separate troughs of despair. We chatted, ate, and drank until we were spent. I fell asleep on top of the bed in my Paris cocktail dress, finally waking up enough to change into my nightie at three in the morning. Jack's absence as my sleeping partner heightened my anxiety over how we could possibly mend the damaged tapestry of this relationship we had worked so hard to create. But I was grateful for the reprieve from blame Edna Mae's party had given us.

Friday, July 10, 1964, Verona. Ed and Edna Mae helped us plot out directions to Venice by way of Shakespeare's famed balcony at Juliet's house, Casa di Giulietta. It wasn't high on my list. It seemed hokey to pay homage to a real house where a fictitious teenage girl had been wooed by her equally fictitious boyfriend. But never mind. This was no time to be hard to please.

The tourist-mobbed, larger-than-life statue of Juliet was the dark brown of aged bronze, except for her right breast, shiny as burnished gold. Guys, young and old, stood in line to fondle that breast. Even some girls.

"That's so weird!" I snorted.

"Oh, not at all," Jack said. "It's better luck than the Blarney Stone. You rub her breast, and poof, you and your girl are sealed forever." He stood tall, arms crossed, sounding matter-of-fact. "I need all the help I can get," he added.

"Public fondling of a statue? Please don't," I said, ignoring the playful, wistful twinkle in his eyes.

"Never. Fondling her would be a travesty after the real thing." He chanced a sly grin.

I effected a stern look. "I hope I'm better than cold bronze."

"No question." Finally, a smile. It rivaled the shiny breast.

We hustled through Juliet's house and got back in the car. As we took off for Venice, Jack asked, "Do you think we're 'star-crossed lovers'?"

"No. If anything, ours should be a match made in heaven. Too bad you don't believe in heaven." I heaved a dramatic sigh.

"Jury's out on heaven now that I've had a taste of it. So tell me about the 'match.'"

"For all the reasons we've talked about. Values, education, politics, love. And our army lives—though that could be a drawback, I suppose."

"No. The army's clearly a positive."

"To my folks, sure, but I know how hard military life is—coping with pigheaded brass and misfit soldiers, demands on wives, the drinking, the constant moving, always uprooting the family, years spent apart. And so much uncertainty. Going off to war . . . and maybe not coming back . . ."

That thought dangled in the air, and we both fell silent.

11

Old Haunts, New Confrontations

Terry

Friday, 10 July 1964, Los Gatos, California. Our first full day at Uncle Bob's place. We had left Center at dawn on Wednesday. Taking turns, Mom, Pam, and I drove seven hundred miles the first day, all the way through the Colorado and Utah mountains to Ely, Nevada. Day two, we racked up five hundred more and arrived wobbly kneed at my cousins' place late Thursday afternoon. After staying up half the night jawing, not only with Aunt Gwen and Uncle Bob, but with all six Kocher kids, including seven-year-old Marianne, we lazed Friday away.

Saturday, 6:30 a.m., 11 July 1964, Los Gatos. Before anyone else got up, I had some time alone to start a letter to Annie—trip notes mostly: the barren landscape through Nevada, the golden hills of California, our terror of driving the California freeways. But I also told her, "I opened my Shakespeare on the way, and oddly enough, it fell to this page, Sonnet 116." I copied it into the letter:

Let me not to the marriage of true minds
Admit impediments. Love is not love
Which alters when it alteration finds,
Or bends with the remover to remove.
O, no! it is an ever-fixed mark
That looks on tempests and is never shaken;
It is a star to every wand'ring bark,
Whose worth's unknown, although his height be taken.

Love's not Time's fool, though rosy lips and cheeks
Within his bending sickle's compass come;
Love alters not with his brief hours and weeks,
But bears it out even to the edge of doom.
If this be error and upon me proved,
I never writ, nor no man ever loved.

Shakespeare was right, I wrote. True love probably can stand separation, no matter how long, "if one can stand up to the loneliness, the doubts,
the worries, the vivid imagination of what his love is doing. Shakespeare's
sonnet offers hope. So I'm hoping."

I added a few lines about the winding two-lane road over Sonora Pass,
but by 7 a.m., the Kocher and Marshall cousins were racing through the
house like Tasmanian devils. We gulped down breakfast and invaded a
beach near Santa Cruz. This was a California summer, exactly as I remembered it from our last trip in 1956.

All the kids—Pam and nineteen-year-old cousin Robert included—frolicked in the surf in a wild chase game, screeching and hooting. I retreated
to a secluded dune and sat gouging bits of bark off a piece of driftwood,
flicking them down the hillside. The sand squishing between my toes, the
waves scrubbing the shore, and the brine-scented air all transported me
to the French Riviera. Annie and the lieutenant must have been there by
then, he no doubt ogling her in her skimpy bikini while they played footsie
in the sand. The images burned holes in my brain, like staring at the sun.

"You really miss her, don't you?" A girl's voice, soft and sympathetic.

I jerked around and cupped my eyes against the sun.

"Sorry, the sun's ferocious, isn't it? I'll fix that." She glided past and
planted her feet in the sand, hands on her hips. "How's this view, cuz?
Better?"

Cousin Paula, auburn-haired Paula. Now seventeen, devilishly saucy,
and, in a two-piece orange bathing suit, as sexy as a UCLA cheerleader.
Last night, we became instant pals over ginger ale after everyone else had
gone to bed. No alcohol in the Kocher house—they were hard-core Mor-
mons. I had sensed, though, that Paula would have been open to a glass of
wine if I could have finessed it.

"Who? Miss *who*?" I asked.

"Your Annie! That's her name, isn't it?"

I hadn't mentioned Annie to anyone. Paula and I had talked politics and current events. Most high school kids gossip about who's dating whom, but Paula waxed on about civil rights marches and protests. She had read *The Wretched of the Earth* and *Nobody Knows My Name*.

But then she lapsed into Barry Goldwater's voice and countered my every argument that he would be a national disaster as president. When she saw the horrified look on my face, she said, "Got you going, didn't I? The guy's a Neanderthal. Even the Republicans aren't stupid enough to elect him."

She loved the Peace Corps. She worried about the draft, afraid her brothers would get sent to Vietnam. That was last night. On the beach, the chitchat was personal.

"*My* Annie, huh? Who says?"

"No one has to. You're a flashing neon sign. Tell me about her."

I did, more than I'd told anyone. Our whole history. Everything. She listened. No smart-ass quips. No giggling. She didn't have a boyfriend. "Mom won't let me date. But this fall, at college, I'll be on my own. I hope I find someone who will love me as much as you love Annie. And I hope I can be like her, even the skinny-dipping. It sounds so grown up." She sighed. "We better go. Sun's down. We don't want to start rumors."

I got back to my letter to Annie after dinner, but only managed a note about sitting beside little Marianne, cutting meat for her. "I really love kids. It reminded me of you, and what we . . ." I was thinking about our kids, hers and mine, but that was presumptuous. I didn't finish the thought.

Finally, it was quiet, and everyone was asleep except Paula and me. We had spent the evening with our two families, visiting and watching TV. No wonder Annie had written so few letters. She was on the go. So was I.

I had shown Paula a photo of Annie I kept in my wallet—her graduation picture, a studio pose, half-profile, eyes gazing into the future, bouffant do, every hair in place. Paula had borrowed it after dinner, disappeared into her room, and emerged three hours later with a pen-and-ink rendition on heavy art paper, remarkably lifelike. "You can put her on the wall above the bed and dream sweet dreams," she said. "I'll touch her up tomorrow and add the freckles. She'll be perfect."

We propped the drawing on the coffee table and sat side by side on the sofa. She had been drawing "forever," she said, and wanted to major in art. Vermeer, Caravaggio, Monet, and a dozen other artists rolled off her tongue as if they were classmates.

We fell silent and soon Paula nodded off. Her hair brushed my cheek, and her head slumped onto my chest. Before us, on the coffee table, Annie was looking discreetly off to the left, chin up, lips parted, but she didn't say a word. I knew that look. *It's okay, she's my cousin,* I told Annie silently. *We were talking is all, just talking. She fell asleep.* Annie stared back.

I squeezed lightly at Paula's shoulder. "Time for bed, Rembrandt. We've got a big day tomorrow." Her eyes blinked open. I pushed myself to my feet, took her by both hands, and tugged. "Come on, kiddo. Your carriage turns into a pumpkin at midnight."

"I fell asleep, didn't I? Did I snore? Or say anything dumb?"

"Nope. You were as well behaved as you are attractive."

"Disgusting, isn't it? But I get older every day. Good night, dear cuz."

I kissed the back of her hand. "Thanks for the portrait. Thanks for everything."

She headed down the hallway, then stopped and turned back. "Thanks for coming, Terry. I meant it about getting older every day. We both are. Think about that."

Nearly midnight. Alone again. Paula's drawing was a tailor-made antidote to the flammable mix of loneliness and desire: Annie—regal, determined, a portrait of promise. I cradled her in my hands and carried her to my bedroom, set her on the nightstand, and returned to the letter I had started after dinner. "You've seen the Riviera, so there's nothing I can tell you about beaches," I wrote. I didn't mention Paula but confessed I'd been "bothered" by the "fine young bods" trotting past me at the beach. "All I could think of was making love to you."

I hesitated. Annie and I had talked about making love, but in marriage, not in the throes of passion. She would wait, she told me. No ifs, ands, or buts. We had come perilously close, or should I say *gloriously close.* We had rounded third base and flirted precipitously with home. But we had never talked about our physical intimacies or written about them. These were acts of passion, expressions of love, spontaneous and unarticulated.

At that moment, it was important to make her understand how lonely it was without her, how committed I was to marriage. I imagined us making love and put it into words, removing each item of clothing, touching her and kissing her, every part of her, and carrying through to a night of glorious sex. The letter was more graphic than I had ever been with her. "Don't be shocked," I wrote. "Making love to you would be wonderful." I signed it "With all my love" and then added "I love you. I want you to marry me," as if it were some bold new declaration.

I got one of my colorful Annie envelopes from Silverton, sealed the letter inside, and added a stamp. I brought eighteen envelopes, one for each day of the trip plus an extra and a sheet of airmail stamps. Tomorrow, I'd get up early and mail it before anyone saw it. It was bad enough that Pam and the boys razzed me about every letter I sent or received. I didn't need that from the Kocher kids too.

I hit the bed emotionally spent but pleased I had finished a letter on only my second day in California. "See, you can write every day," I told the portrait on the nightstand beside me.

Ann

Friday, July 10, 1964, Venice. No camping in Venice, so a hundred strides off the Piazza San Marco, we found a tiny *pensione* with finely carved furniture, a canopied four-poster bed draped in antique organza, and a private bath, with breakfast—all for a hair under five dollars a night.

We had snacked all day on bite-size pizza, cheese-stuffed dates wrapped in prosciutto, mini-meatballs, and other delights Edna Mae had tucked into her cornucopia picnic bag. Still stuffed at dinnertime, Jack and I opted for crisp Italian bread with a decanter of Chianti. Surrounded by the cheery conviviality of a miniature bar we had stumbled on, we were rosy happy, worries behind us—until Jack asked, "Where and how shall we sleep tonight?"

Another round in the continuing skirmish. Our charming room had one bed, a marginally double bed at that. "Well, *next* to each other, of course, if that's not . . . if you're okay with that."

"Better than the floor, I guess."

"Yeah, but think about this—it's a whole lot cozier than opposite ends of the house. Two endless nights in a row."

He nodded, but conviviality had fled the bar. We emptied our carafe and downed the last crusts of bread, mothballing any hint of flirtation. After clumping up to our teeny room, we changed in silence and slipped into bed in the dark. Careful not to touch, careful not to send the wrong message or arouse false hopes, I slept poorly.

Saturday, July 11, 1964, Venice. Morning came too early. We stumbled out of bed like strangers, dressed hurriedly with eyes downcast, and swallowed breakfast in silence.

In the piazza, an oasis of calm quieted my mind. We had slipped through a crack in time to a place not polluted by swarming cars, belching buses, and noxious trucks. I nudged Jack with my elbow and whispered. "Listen. Hear that?"

He cocked his ear and looked around quizzically. "No. What?"

"No waspy Vespas terrorizing us at every corner. No cars at all, in fact. Even the air smells scrubbed—if you don't get too close to the canals."

"Yes. Peaceful, isn't it? Just what we need." With a single gesture, he took in the sprawling Piazza San Marco before us. "The enormity of this piazza puts things in perspective, doesn't it? Life's problems seem minute next to the Campanile, the basilica, and the colonnades."

I nodded. "I like the way you're thinking. Is this a sign of happier times to come?"

"I hope so. Happy is better than morose."

"Agreed." I didn't dare push him too far, too fast. Ambling through the piazza, we chuckled at the ubiquitous, feathery knots of pigeons—sweet-cooing beggars competing for goodies scattered by eager tourists. "You'd think people would realize this isn't an international bird sanctuary," I said.

"Or that ten thousand pooping birds leave a nasty legacy for cleanup crews," he added. "So let's leave this bird latrine behind and see what else we can discover."

We struck out to explore Venice, eyes alert, like wary big-game hunters. Minutes later, the meandering lane ended in a cul-de-sac. We backtracked, but angled off to a canal. No bridge. We backtracked again, turned left instead of right, and ended up back at our *pensione.*

Jack smiled for the first time all day. "Well, aren't we the intrepid pathfinders?"

A break in the morning's regret over our first night in Venice?

Nope. We went back to trudging again, silent, in parallel worlds. Deep into the maze, where the pathway narrowed, we lingered atop a picturesque footbridge. I leaned on the white wood parapet and peered into the canal. Jack did the same, nestling his shoulder against mine. My emotional antennae sprang to attention. I had to jog us out of our malaise. "How'd you sleep?"

"Didn't."

"Me either. This isn't what we want. I still love you, you know."

"Loving you is my curse."

"Your curse? Really?"

"If I didn't love you, I could walk away . . . but I can't." He looked at me, his hangdog face absolutely mournful. "You still want me around?"

"I . . . I won't let you go," I said. "Our Lake Garda calamity wasn't an *end*, but a discovery. We've been gone what? Ten days! If we can't navigate the ups and downs of two weeks, there's no hope for a lifetime together. I might as well throw myself off this bridge."

"You wouldn't. Not onto that dead fish." He scrunched his bushy eyebrows toward the canal below.

"Phew! You're right—it'd be a stinky grave. I want this story to have a sweet ending."

"Me too." He offered his hand. "Okay. We're in Venice—almost the end of our trip. Let's make the most of it!"

Good ole Jack. Back to his enthusiastic self. I accepted his olive branch, and we bounded across the bridge. Together. A couple again.

It seemed that every corner deli had a master chef in training. We loaded up on pastries bursting with meat, cheese, and crisp veggies, plus two blood oranges, and searched the byways of the Giardini Papadopoli for a picnic spot. Settling into a stand of trees, we devoured our goodies, all the while scouring Frommer's *Europe on Five Dollars a Day* for every single "you can't miss this sight" in Venice. Monday night we'd be back in Landshut, in the land of army demands. If not on the border, Jack would be at his desk under the colonel's thumb.

From the array of Frommer options, I latched onto Murano Island. "What say we find out how they make Murano glass? It's a far cry from 'our' Bavarian crystal, but it's so intricate, so colorful, so tiny! The factories offer free exhibitions. And the hourly ferry is forty-five lire round trip. That's only seven cents."

"Great! You know how I love demos. And bargains."

We scrambled for the next ferry and spent the waning hours of the afternoon in the spell of master glassblowers creating these spidery gems. We trooped from factory to factory until hunger and weariness drove us back to Venice. On the boat, Jack asked, "So what do you like better: Bavarian crystal or Murano glass?"

"They're both amazing. But my Bavarian vase is the gift of a lifetime, no matter what." That brought a sunny smile.

At Piazza San Marco, we settled on the retaining wall and laughed at each other eating the uncontrollable cheese strings from our fried mozzarella sandwiches. A band struck up, and we enjoyed a ringside seat for a free evening concert. Well, some of us, anyway. I fell asleep, Jack's arm enfolded around me. At some point, he woke me enough to guide me back to the hotel, where I tumbled into bed without brushing my teeth.

Sunday, July 12, Venice. Reading from Frommer's over breakfast, I said, "Hey, listen to this. 'Most Venetian museums are free on Sundays.' Shall we tour the Doge's Palace and the Torre dell'Orologio?"

"Yes!"

"Soak up Venetian art at the Gallerie dell'Accademia?"

"Of course. Let's visit them all!"

Hours later, my feet were dragging, and I couldn't keep up. "Ready for a rest?" Jack asked. We stopped long enough to eat two gelatos and then took off again, winding our way through a dozen tiny art galleries. Further on, shops selling miniature watercolors captured every nuance of this fabled city. I halted at one. "Hey, there's our bridge: Dead Fish Crossing."

Jack squinted at the painting, then sniffed it. "Nope, can't be. Smells more like the fresh laundry flying above the canal than our fishy friend."

At the Grand Canal, a sprawling watery boulevard, we caught a *vaporetto*, one of those chugging water-buses. "Where are we going?" I asked.

"Doesn't matter," he said. "We're going to float along, rest our feet, and imagine life in one of these grand old homes on the canal."

I smiled, and in my head, I painted a picture of Jack and me and a flock of little Siggs at our ankles exploring the byways of this charming city. That thought kept me warm despite the cool breeze blowing off the canal.

Eventually, we wound up at the Lido, a slender barrier island between Venice and the Adriatic Sea, where we meandered at water's edge. Looking at the ships in the distance, I said, "What must it have been like, sailing the seas with Marco Polo?"

"It must have been awful. Think about traveling in one of those creaky old sailing ships and trekking overland on what, a camel?"

"Difficult yes, but imagine the adventure of traveling to new lands, meeting new people. It would be like our grand tour, multiplied by a hundred."

We ate on the beach, watching the dipping sun paint the clouds gold and black over Venice. As we cuddled on a dawdling *vaporetto* en route back to Piazza San Marco, dots of light twinkled on, grew brighter, and cast long reflections in the canal. Around us, tenor gondoliers materialized from the dark, serenading the lantern-lit lovers in their holds. The melodies, I told Jack, seemed more romantic wafting across the water at night.

On the ride back, as our days together paraded through my mind, I told him this truth: "If I live to a hundred, this summer will be etched forever in my heart—extraordinary places all, now uniquely our own."

The two small lamps with old-fashioned lampshades cast our room in a cozy hue. Jack wrapped his arms around me and whispered, "You know, Venice is the most romantic city of cities. Tell me that tonight's *the* night."

I wanted to say yes, but I couldn't. "Let's play it by ear. Better yet, by touch. For starters, I'm going to give you an old-fashioned, time-tested cowpoke massage. On yer belly, soldier!"

"Yes, ma'am!" He dived angle wise across the bed.

On our last night, I wanted him to totally unwind before he plunged back into the Cold War. Hunkered on my knees at the foot of the bed, I pulled each calf into a hug, massaged his ankles, squeezed and tugged each toe, pressing into his soles to relieve the aches from walking all day. Pinch-walking the muscles on the backs of his legs, I continued up to his shorts and skated underneath to his fuzzy buns. His small grunts of satisfaction emboldened me, and I straddled his fanny to get a better angle on his back. His buns tightened beneath me, and from deep inside a delicious glow spread through my thighs and tummy.

"I like where you're headed," he whispered.

"Hang on. More to come."

I tugged off his T-shirt, tossed it aside, and worked my hands into the cranky muscles in his back, slipping his undershorts down a bit for a deep massage on his tailbone. Hugging his sides with my knees, I told him, "That's how a cowgirl hangs on to a stallion."

"Don't worry. This old horse is tethered to the spot."

When I stretched to reach his arms, my hair tumbled over his head, and I snuggled into his neck. Slowly, he turned over, and little by little, we lost sight of the massage and concentrated on each other. For the finale of this long, slow crescendo, he slipped off my nightie and panties and dropped them beside the bed, and I removed his undershorts.

He tapped at the gate, gently but persistently. My body burned with desire. I wanted him, but I tightened up. I couldn't, even in that most romantic city.

Instead, I grasped his eager second lieutenant—in affirmation, not denial. "Relax. This moment's for you," I said, though I fully accepted the hand slowly inching up my inner thigh.

Our eyes homed in on each other. I stroked him and squeezed him. He stiffened, rose up into my hand, wouldn't hold still. Suddenly, he threw his arms over his head and shuddered. I took my own pleasure in it too—how wondrous that a few loving strokes could both inflame his zealous instrument and tame it into a spent shadow of itself.

Afterward, we lay pretzeled together, his leg looped lazily over mine, my arms wound through his. "You okay?" I asked.

"More than okay. Ecstatic."

"Still doubt me?"

"Not at all."

"Any more questions, sir?"

"How about an encore?"

Terry

Sunday, 12 July 1964, San Francisco. After breakfast, we were sitting around talking and watching the news when CBS Channel 5 announced a protest march against a predicted hands-down win for Senator Barry Goldwater at the Republican National Convention. It was set to open Monday at the Cow Palace, San Francisco's convention center.

Paula and I glanced at each other. We couldn't resist.

Mom shook her head. "You kids are nuts."

I don't know how Paula convinced her mom and dad to let her skip church and come with me. But my cousin could have charmed Goldwater himself into voting for President Johnson.

An hour later, she and I plunged into a crowd of black people and fell in behind a guy with a four-year-old on his shoulders and a pregnant wife at his side. We weren't the only whites—there were scores—but whites were clearly a minority. The parade wasn't floats and bands marching in step. Rather, a slow-motion stream of folks flowed up Market Street, as if en route to church, most of the men in suits, ties, and hats, others in dress shirts and sweaters, and women in Sunday dresses. No hippies, scruffy longhairs, or disheveled malcontents. And no jeering segregationists showering us with insults.

I'd seen protests only on TV—in Birmingham, Jackson, and Detroit—and in photos of the 1963 March on Washington. Being inside a protest was a new world for me. There were no blacks in Center—not one. In high school, no team in our league had black athletes. None. At CU, we only occasionally saw a black person on campus. A handful starred on the football and track teams, but the basketball squad had only one. We had one black guy in my freshman- and sophomore-year dorms, but I'd never spoken with him.

That first step onto Market Street was tough. I was nervous. No, not nervous—scared, my heart racing. I glanced furtively at the faces around us. No one frowned or snarled or called me a honky or flipped the bird. Beside me, Paula stepped out as confidently as if joining a group of classmates. This was a meandering crowd of like-minded protesters, nothing to fear.

Paula and I strode along, waving her calligraphy signs like beacons. Hers read "Civil Rights in '64 / Ho, Ho, Ho, Barry Must Go." Mine was less flamboyant: "Civil Rights, Yes / Goldwater, No." I took Paula's hand and squeezed it. She beamed and squeezed back. "Me too, cuz. This is great, isn't it?"

I wasn't one who worshipped heroes, but JFK and Martin Luther King Jr. came close. I had read King's *Stride Toward Freedom* enough times that I knew every detail of the 1955–56 Montgomery bus boycott. I had followed news of the Birmingham protests in the spring and summer of 1963 and toyed with going to the March on Washington in August. When the four little girls—Denise McNair, Carole Robinson, Addie Mae Collins, and Cynthia Wesley—were murdered in the Sixteenth Street Baptist Church bombing that fall, the news hit me like they were the children of family friends.

But I had done nothing to further the movement—no marching, no protesting, no sign waving, no contributions, nothing. For me, in Center and at CU, civil rights had been a national news story, not something that involved me personally.

What had drawn me to King was his essay "Pilgrimage to Nonviolence" in *Stride Toward Freedom*. In it, he calls for a "philosophy of nonviolence," defining nonviolence as a force for peace, not a cop-out for the cowardly. As a force, it seeks to win an opponent's friendship and understanding, not to defeat or humiliate him. King urges us to attack the force of evil, not the persons doing the evil, to accept suffering without retaliation, and to avoid both physical violence and violence of spirit.

"The nonviolent resister not only refuses to shoot his opponent," King writes, "but he also refuses to hate him." Christianity should tackle both social injustices *and* man's spiritual enlightenment, he asserts. He weaves in Niebuhr's critique of pacifism, Gandhi's belief that pacifism confronts evil by the power of love, and the ancient Greek distinctions for different kinds of love—*eros, philia,* and *agape,* "love seeking to preserve and create community."

To me, King's philosophy applied to both military service and civil rights. He articulated my own turmoil as I wrestled with my belief that the draft, military service, and war itself were immoral. His essay formed the intellectual underpinning for my case that the draft board should classify me as a conscientious objector on *moral* grounds, not religious ones.

King made me a believer in nonviolence and heightened my awareness of civil rights. Though I knew little about prejudice against blacks, the cause felt right, largely because my rural hometown of Center had a history of discrimination. Not against blacks, but against Mexican Americans, who made up sixty percent of the population. They were segregated into a sixteen-block barrio fronting the railroad tracks. Anglos ran the town, owned the businesses, and held every seat on town council and school board. In the barrio, poverty was the norm.

As a high school student who lived on a farm, I knew nothing about the conditions in the barrio. That changed my junior year when I dated Angela Archuleta, the daughter of a farm worker. In Center, Anglos didn't date "Mexicans." But I thought I was immune to that taboo—after all, I had been class president every year since eighth grade, and Angela was a top student, a cheerleader, and the prettiest girl in school.

On our first date, we strode into the all-Anglo Masonic Hall for the year's premier social event, the Valentine's Day DeMolay Sweetheart Ball. No Mexican American—girl or guy—had ever been invited to the Sweetheart Ball. Classmates gasped. Chaperones sputtered. Angela and I danced the night away. Afterward, parked on a lonely dirt road three miles out of town, we enjoyed our first kisses. By the next morning, town gossips were peppering the telephone party lines with rumors and slurs.

That gutsy girl opened a window into a world I had been blind to.

Now, on this bright July morning in San Francisco, we marched into Civic Center Plaza, no longer a loose menagerie, but a pulsating mass gulping for air, Paula and I in a sea of heads and shoulders. Half a football field away, a tiny figure popped up on a temporary stage. A disembodied voice rattled over the loudspeaker, "William Scranton, governor of Pennsylvania!" stretching it out as if he were a prizefighter entering the ring.

Scranton laid into Barry Goldwater—clearly a fugitive from Dante's eighth circle. We cheered, we clapped, we waved our signs. But the Goldwater juggernaut had locked up the nomination before the opening gavel.

A string of celebrities paraded to the lectern—Jackie Robinson, James Farmer, Henry Cabot Lodge, Jacob Javits—and each boomed his support for freedom, equality, and opportunity. Again, we cheered, we clapped, we waved our signs. Two phrases later, we did it again.

And then Nelson Rockefeller came to the mike and blasted Goldwater. We cheered. But he launched an attack on Democrats. We booed. He went on and on. The sun got hotter and hotter. A sickly cloud of perfume and aftershave and cigarette smoke and BO settled over us. My eyes burned. Rockefeller finished. We cheered, thankful that he was done. My feet hurt. People mopped sweat from their faces. We needed towels.

Finally it was over—two hours of political fire and brimstone. The beehive we were in expanded, giving me room to wriggle my elbows and talk to Paula.

"I've got to pee," she said.

"Me too." We worked our way toward a bank of portable toilets. In the milling crowd, two women were dissecting Rockefeller's diatribe phrase by phrase, laying it out like English teachers diagramming a page-long sentence. Ahead, someone told a joke, and his circle burst into laughter. A toddler wobbled past. His mother shot by and caught him by his waistband. He screeched in joy, and she scooped him up, hugging him as if he were a teddy bear. We were a family of thousands, assembled to oppose an anti–civil rights, whites-only Republican Party that wanted to drag us back to the "good old days."

Paula overheard two black guys talking about a protest march. "They're with CORE," she said. "They're gonna picket the Cow Palace. Right now." Her eyes grew big. "Why not? It's boring at home, and we do have these signs."

Indeed, why not? "It would be a crime to waste your art," I said. "Let's go."

We were seventy strong—I counted—shuffling in an amorphous loop outside the main entrance to the Cow Palace. We waved our signs and bounced them up and down. Across from Paula and me, the chairman belted out "Jim Crow Must Go."

I had no idea who the chairman was or how he got that position, but he was the loudest, no question, so we shouted our response, each word sharp, clear, and as loud as we could make it: "Jim. Crow. Must. Go." Again. Over and over.

Aside from Paula, I didn't know any of these people. But as we marched and shouted and waved our signs, the faces became familiar. "Freckle-face" handed me a bottle of water. I took a drink and passed it on. "Stretch" popped a joke and we all laughed. "Princess" said she was hungry. "Little John" hollered, "I'll order a pizza." We applauded. We were friends, even if we didn't know each other's names. We shared a cause. We were working together as one.

Not long into the afternoon, a band of hecklers sidled up to within spitting range—twenty college kids, all scrubbed preppies. They, too, had signs, printed professionally, not homemade—"Barry in '64 / Goldwater for the US of A;" "Young Republicans / Adore Goldwater;" "True Americans / Vote Goldwater." Plus bright campaign buttons and festive hats, the whole works. They chanted, "Go Barry, Go! Go Barry, Go! Go Barry, Go!"

Our group had thirty-one blacks, thirty-nine whites. A handful were older men and housewives, and two or three looked like high school kids. We were integrated. The Goldwater kids were all whites, every one of them.

The chairman boomed, "Who should go?"

"Goldwater!" we shouted.

"Who?"

"Goldwater!"

"Louder," he hollered, like a high school cheerleader.

"GOLDWATER!"

"Go where?"

"Back to Arizona!"

"Louder."

"ARIZONA!"

We drowned out the preppies, but they were like horseflies, intent on annoying us. A couple of them, no doubt both first-string tackles at USC, bellowed: "Take a bath, hippies!" "Try work, not welfare!" "Go to college, creeps—make something of yourselves!"

We sang. We marched. We alternated between football chants and civil rights songs, as spirited as if we had come from a Southern Baptist revival:

Oh freedom! Oh freedom!
Oh freedom over me
And before I'd be a slave I'll be buried in my grave
And go home to my Lord and be free.

The song went on and on, some verses expressing a painful recollection of what it had meant to be a slave and now to be treated as a second-class citizen, and others expressing hope for the future. It wasn't just a song but a powerful hymn to lives I had known nothing of:

No more moaning . . .
No more weeping . . .
There'll be singing . . .
There'll be glory . . .
And before I'd be a slave I'll be buried in my grave
And go home to my Lord and be free.

When we moved on from "Oh Freedom" to "We Shall Overcome," I knew I had finally joined the civil rights movement. Pete Seeger and Joan Baez—two of my favorite folk singers—had recorded it. I had their albums, and I'd memorized the words and the tune.

The singing transported me into the crowd at the March on Washington, arms linked, bodies swaying, a hundred thousand people joined as one. Today I had become one with my fellow picketers, one with the whole movement. Tears came to my eyes with each verse. I blinked them back:

We'll walk hand in hand . . .
We shall all be free . . .
We are not afraid . . .
We are not alone . . .
The whole wide world around . . .
We shall overcome some day.

As the afternoon wore on, we began to slog through the songs like dirges. My legs ached. Paula was dragging. Picketing wasn't fun and games; it was damn hard work. And frankly, the naysayers were getting to us, those sanctimonious Republican preppies. I wanted to bust one of them in the chops, especially the USC stud who would lean in close like a drill sergeant, puff out his monstrous chest, and literally spit his chants in our faces, but I didn't—the guy was twice my size. But oh, how I wanted to. My anger shocked me: how could I profess to be a devotee to Martin Luther King Jr.'s philosophy of nonviolence? I didn't retaliate. None of us did.

But we and our Republican gadflies weren't alone. A nutcase with a bullhorn shadowed us for an hour, proclaiming, "The only way you'll find freedom is through accepting Jesus Christ as your Lord and Savior." He punctuated his rambling sermon with "Jesus is the answer! Repent! Forsake your evil ways!" and on and on. A weird guy—we didn't have street preachers in southern Colorado—but in a way he became a welcome diversion for our retinue of marching friends and Goldwater antagonists, as if he'd been sent by central casting to lighten our day. In the middle of one rant he hollered, "Fornication is an abomination to God!"

Fornication? I glanced at Paula.

She mouthed *It is, you know,* and burst out laughing.

Crews from all three networks—CBS, ABC, and NBC—descended on us as if we were bigger news than a five-alarm fire. At first, I was thrilled. So was Paula. Neither of us had ever been on TV. But the cameramen moved in close enough for us to trip over them, and then they backpedaled to catch the whole picket line. A gang of photographers joined in. One guy shuffled backward in front of Paula, snapping frame after frame. I calculated the angle of his lens—the bastard had focused in on Paula's breasts and legs—leering as if he could see through her blouse and miniskirt. "Hey, you!" I yelled. He scurried off.

In the end, we picketers outlasted newsmen, Republicans, and the preacher. Our seventy dwindled to forty. The chairman gathered us around. "You've done great. Mission accomplished," he said.

We shook a few hands, wished our new comrades well, and headed for home. Paula and I were zinging. We had been part of a cause bigger than ourselves. Best of all, we were at the core of the day's news, not looking in through a one-eyed, one-way television set.

At the Kocher home, Paula and I were celebrities. "We saw you on TV! We saw you on TV!" my brother Randy shouted. "I saw you with that sign." He danced around the living room, waving a pretend sign. Everyone had seen us. We were on the six o'clock news on all three networks.

Over dinner, we talked politics—the Republican convention, really. After Aunt Gwen's blackberry pie, Uncle Bob tapped his water glass. He twiddled his thick, black mustache—he did that when he wanted to be profound. He nodded at Paula. "I'm disappointed in you, girl."

The table went quiet. He homed in on me. "You too, nephew. You talked my little girl into this, didn't you?"

I squirmed. Uncle Bob was not one to cross. He had been an officer in the navy and had a master's degree—my only relative who had gone to college.

"That convention doesn't start till tomorrow," he said. "You know what that means?"

Silence from us all. Paula withered.

Uncle Bob leaned forward and glared at Paula, then me. "Well?"

"No, sir," I said.

"Didn't think so. You didn't confront the real delegates, the right-wing fanatics who stole the party from the few Republicans who've got some common sense. You should have saved your picket line for tomorrow. And you should be blocking the doorway, poking your signs in their mugs, not out in the parking lot."

He grinned—a wide-face, sparkly grin that set everyone laughing.

"I'm proud of you two kids," he said. "You're true Kochers and Marshalls both."

Ann

Monday, July 13, 1964, Landshut, Germany. On the road near Landshut, a US Army jeep shot past. It sprouted half a dozen military caps and associated arms and legs. Jack straightened up—as if he ever slumped. "What the heck?" His voice turned as crisp as a new cadet's salute.

A huge khaki truck—the kind they call a deuce and a half—trundled by, laden with troops. Jack got whiplash trying to see who was in it. "Where do they think *they're* going?"

The men in the overloaded truck shouted out a ditty I remembered from childhood. An image of ragtag little boys with wooden rifles marched stiff-legged through my mind:

We're in the army now,
We're not behind the plow,
We'll never get rich a diggin' a ditch,
We're in the army now.

But now the song meant work. Duty. An end to mirth, frivolity—and touching.

A tank rumbled toward us on the main road. Jack snarled, "What the hell's going on?"

"What's wrong?" I asked.

"Too much military activity. These men should be in the field, not here." Instantly, my jovial Jack had morphed into Li'l Abner's grumbly Joe Btfsplk, lacking only the dark rain cloud over his head. He spun a sharp right and beelined for his office, skidded to a stop, jumped out, started to walk away, but stuck his head back in the car. "Sorry. Be right back."

He loped across the lawn and hailed another lieutenant, who began waving his arms, gesturing toward the office and the motor pool. Jack put a clenched fist on his hip, kicked a pinecone, checked his watch, and shook his head. Turning on his heel, he marched back to the car, hurled himself into the driver's seat, and gripped the wheel. The muscles in his jaw knotted. "Bad news. After a year of dillydallying, we're moving out. Home. Back to the US of A. Next week. Can you believe that—*next week!*"

For a moment, I stared. I had come for the summer, and now they were ripping him away. They couldn't! What would I do? We weren't ready! "That's horrible. You sure?"

"Yeah, horrible for us, even worse for me and my men. We have to pack up everything here *and* at the border. We've got seven days, maybe ten."

"A week? Jeez, I—"

"The worst is"—he sat tall, every inch the officer, despair clouding his eyes—"we're leaving for the border in two hours. I don't know for how long. A fine end to a fine time, huh?"

I studied his face. *We did have a fine time, overall, didn't we?* But no time to think about that. "Guess you'd better dump me at the BOQ so you can do what you have to."

"I'm not 'dumping' you anywhere. I'll get you situated with the teachers. And, yes, I've got a truckload to do before we head out." He jammed the Sting Ray into reverse.

Ten minutes later, after a peck on the cheek and a barely audible *bye*, he was gone.

I was alone, surrounded by the relics of our "honeymoon"—half a loaf of dark bread, two apples, a bag of peanuts, dirty clothes, dirty dishes, well-used towels, assorted sandals, and even, it turned out, his lederhosen. I picked them up and hugged them to my chest.

If nothing else, I would sleep with them tonight.

12
Politics East and West

Ann

Monday afternoon, July 13, Landshut, Germany. I moved our travel rubble to my room and relived precious moments—a picture postcard of the Sorbonne, a poker chip from Monte Carlo, a paper napkin from a *pensione,* the cork from a bottle of wine in Venice, and, sifting out of everything, sand from Saint-Tropez and the Lido. Too many memories. Too many unsettled questions. I needed to figure out what Jack meant to me. Equally important, what did I mean to him? And where did Terry fit? I couldn't sit there and stew in my mementos. My wild side urged, *Get away! Take off. You wanted to see Berlin. Do it!*

I dug out my train schedule and found a connection that would get me to West Berlin the next morning. Why not? I salvaged my sundress, a skirt, shorts, a blouse, and underwear from my dirty clothes bag, crammed them into my overnight case, scribbled a note to the teachers, and turned to leave.

Rap, rap, rap. Someone at the door. I opened it a crack. Jack!

"I have an hour. May I treat you to dinner?" He still looked preoccupied, his brow furrowed, but never mind.

"Wow, of course. The gods must be smiling on us. Guess what? I've cooked up an adventure—Berlin! I'm leaving tonight."

"Great flexibility. An essential quality for an army wife." He used the same tone—as if checking off all the things he had to do before moving.

I smiled, thinking, *How about for an army girlfriend?* Wisely, I bit my tongue.

"It'll be a humble meal. Not like Paris. More the real me."

"Perfect. The real you is the best deal in town." He whisked me off to his BOQ lair. Here was the bachelor as chef: a can of tuna, a gob of mayonnaise, a sprinkle of dried onion bits, a pot of stout black tea, and my lump of leftover bread. He ate standing up, packing at the same time—as if he'd have to make a quick getaway before the door burst open and the shooting began.

"I'll be back Friday night," I said. "What's your schedule? Will I get to see you again?"

He shoehorned his gear into his duffel bag, so tight it was wrinkle-free. "We've got a mountain of work, but I'll try to get back Friday or Saturday night. Then four, maybe five days in Landshut. I'll order the commander to set aside the evenings for us. For you and me alone."

"*Order* him? You will, huh? Every night, just the two of us?"

"Every night! Except for the going-away shindig Monday. I'll parade you past every drooling officer on the base, show them that patience, hard work, and good luck pay off."

I couldn't resist. I leaped to his side and hooked my arm through his. "A trophy girlfriend, exactly what I've always aspired to be. I'll bleach my hair."

"No, that's not what I—" He paused, cocking his head. "Would you? And could you put on some bright red lipstick and fingernail polish?"

"Ha! I'll buy some in West Berlin. And purple eye makeup too."

"Purple eye makeup?" Finally, the first ray of sunshine broke through since we had driven into Landshut, a belly laugh actually. "Yeah, that would be perfect."

"Tell you what, soldier, I'd love to meet the brass, swap stories with your buddies—and spend as many evenings with you as possible. Deal?"

He nodded and disappeared back into his unseen checklist. Our hour evaporated like a raindrop on hot pavement. We didn't exchange a single tender moment—not a kiss, an embrace, even an accidental touch—until I slipped up behind him and hugged him while he was tidying up his dresser. "I'll miss you," I whispered.

He turned and with both hands pulled my face to his and lingered a good eight seconds. His eyes were so intense I was melting inside. Slowly, deliberately, he kissed me, imprinting it for all time. "I'll miss you more," he said, hugging me as if to stave off his departure. "But you'll come visit me in Johnstown on your way home, won't you? My family's part of the package."

"Sure. Your mom invited me, you know. You'll meet me at LaGuardia?"

"Of course." He cinched his duffel bag. Mentally, he had already left.

Two hours later, I hopped on a train in Munich and girded myself for the trek to the Hanover exchange—about eight hours away, plenty of time to get some perspective on my feelings.

Was I really in love? Or had I been swept off my feet by memories of the elegant side of army life and by flitting around Europe in a Sting Ray? No, I concluded, I loved this man. Most of our difficulties were the product of my own carelessness—or naiveté. Still, could I be an army wife like Mom? That refrain ran over and over in my mind until the clickety-clack on the tracks dissolved into the fog of a vertical sleep . . . *army wife, all my life . . . army wife, all my life . . .*

Somewhere east of Hanover, I awoke in time to connect to the "express" and my adventure through Communist East Germany en route to the free-world oasis of West Berlin. Before long, curiosity urged me to peer into that forbidden territory. But opaque shades covered every window. An armed guard prowled the aisle, and the interior of the car was lit up like a prison yard. When the guard turned away and lit a cigarette, I lifted the corner of my shade, skittish as a Peeping Tom on parole. My watery twin stared back—the interior glare and inky night shrouded Communist Germany in mystery.

Eventually, the train slowed to a crawl. The conductor, with the guard in tow, tromped through announcing, presumably, the name of the burg where we were stopping. As soon as they were out of sight, I dared another peek. Nothing. No flashing railroad crossings, no traffic, no shops. A single streetlight on the platform moseyed past my peephole, and next, a naked bulb inside a bare station.

Below my window, two uniformed guards drifted past—close enough that I could have tweaked their hats if the window had been open. I dropped the shade and took a deep breath, trying to calm my thumping heart. Seconds later, two guards boarded my car. I slumped in my seat, whipped open *The Feminine Mystique*, and acted as if I were totally engrossed.

They paused at my row and fired a fusillade of German. I looked up blankly, "What?"

"You ticket," one of the guards growled. "Und passport."

I handed them over.

Scowling, he thumbed through my passport. "Americahn-ish?"

I nodded and hoped that looking out the window wasn't a capital offense.

He squinted at my passport, eyed me again—for three long heartbeats—scribbled something, and handed it back.

"*Dankeschön.* Thank you," I said, trying to sound businesslike, but my words clattered into the aisle like marbles.

They moved on, but the train lingered at the station forever. I was frazzled with worry they would come snatch me away.

When I finally returned to my book, I realized I'd been holding it upside down.

Tuesday, July 14, 1964, West Berlin. Late morning, I emerged sleepless and hungry into the blinding sunshine of a bustling city. I found a hotel on the famous Kurfürstendamm, rented a room for $1.50, and, over lunch, scoped out how to get into East Berlin.

As a Westerner, I wasn't allowed to go into East Germany, but I could visit East Berlin on the other side of the Berlin Wall. On the other hand, Berliners couldn't move freely between the east and west sides—not since August 1961, when the Soviet Union colluded with East Germany to slam the door to such interchange, purportedly to keep out "Western fascism" and also stem the hemorrhage of East Germans fleeing to the West.

What was it like for East Berliners to be detained in a modern-day fortress? Were they aching to be free? But my jittery ride through East Germany caught up with me. I lay down for a short nap and awoke with the city's neon lights illuminating my tiny room and a distant clock striking midnight. I pulled on my nightie, curled up, and went back to sleep.

Wednesday morning first thing, the fragrance of fresh bread and ham lassoed me into a nearby coffee shop. After that, I plunged into the busy streets of a warm and balmy West Berlin. The place teemed with men and women in classy business suits, elegant shoppers in high heels toting colorful bags, and frenetic tourists succumbing to the lure of souvenir shops. Tempting, all of it, but I was on a mission.

I set off for Checkpoint Charlie, the nexus between the free world and Communism. This infamous spot turned out to be a nondescript white clapboard guard shack squatting in the middle of Friederichstraße. No more than eight people—ten, max—could have squeezed in at any one time. As the line inched through the shack, the guard standing outside snapped his rifle to his right shoulder, to his left shoulder, and back to his right, and then he banged his heels together. I slammed to a halt and looked around warily.

I'd spent enough time on army bases to know that this heel-clicking guard was merely doing his job. For him it was routine.

Beyond the guard shack, an austere no-man's-land barricaded East Berliners from West. The barren strip, two hundred feet wide, was studded with waist-high chunks of broken pavement, construction rubble, and those pointy hedgehogs—huge angular obstacles made of catawampus iron I beams capable of halting a tank in its tracks—like jacks, but on a scale for the children of a giant. Tangled barbed-wire fences stretched out of sight in both directions.

Across the divide, keeping a weary vigil, was a five-story apartment, clearly a survivor of World War II. Its bricks were in various stages of disintegration, and the black-hole windows—those few not bricked over—shouted "Vacant!" But wait, did I detect snipers lurking? How many would-be escapees had been shot from those very windows?

It was one thing to have seen the endless strip of denuded land that separated sylvan Germany from Czechoslovakia near Jack's outpost, but quite another to be within sniffing distance of these tough-guy guards at the menacing gap between East and West Berlin. I was beginning to understand why the Cold War was so hot for Jack, Bonner, and their men.

Shaking off my qualms, I strode into Checkpoint Charlie as if I did this every day and bought a one-day visa, then marched into East Berlin and a crash course on "the enemy."

From the CinemaScope movie that was West Berlin, I'd parachuted into a grim two-dimensional black-and-white photo. Few cars. Eerily empty streets. Drab buildings in need of face-lifts. Blank windows, no curtains, no lights. No store signs. No window displays. No colors and lights and hype to tempt consumers. How did people know where to buy food or clothing . . . or anything?

Then it hit me. No need for signs. Or window displays. In a Communist society, the state owned everything—resources, means of production, services. That meant only one "brand" and no competition. People didn't—couldn't—choose from among competing products.

On that East Berlin street, a few men in gray work clothes and women in shapeless dresses scurried past, eyes fixed to the ground, trying to avoid attention from the ubiquitous, unblinking, uniformed men safeguarding intersections and entrances to important-looking buildings. Pistols on their hips and rifles on their shoulders, they didn't crack jokes. Or even smile. I, too, avoided eye contact with those stone-faced centurions.

Hairs on my neck prickled. I was skulking about in a war zone, as nervous as a cat burglar on a police station heist. Why was I risking my personal freedom to experience these differences firsthand? Jack had warned me, "They aren't nice people. Don't call attention to yourself."

I could have gotten swept up in a police dragnet, and no one would have known. Jack and Bonner were busy at the border, not waiting for Pippi Longstocking to waltz in from her escapades. My folks had no idea I had inserted myself into Commie land. And Terry was probably gallivanting around California with his cousins. It could be weeks before anyone noticed I was missing. While I was locked away in some gulag, pounding rocks, Jack might not figure out until winter where I was and come for me—*if* he saw fit to. After all, getting mixed up in my harebrained scheme could torpedo his career. But by that time, I'd be frozen to death.

I'd also entered East Berlin on a practical mission—to load up on juicy examples of propaganda. In my first year of teaching, I wanted to motivate all students, not only college-bound kids who grew up as readers. I would immerse them in real-life language and issues of the day and let them discover how important English was to their lives. Communist propaganda was the perfect vehicle: newspapers, handbills, and manifestos we could dissect as a class. But I didn't see a single newspaper dispenser. And no flyers, no posters, no propaganda at all.

After an hour in East Berlin, I was anxious to flee the dreary place, but I had promised Terry I'd visit the Pergamon Museum, a spectacular collection of Middle Eastern artifacts from Turkey, Babylon, and ancient lands I'd never heard of. Using a minimalist map I'd found at my hotel, I tracked it down, asking directions each time I bumped into someone—a challenge in East Berlin, where few people spoke English. Or admitted they did.

Many wrong turns later, I dragged up to the titanic entryway, collapsed on a stone bench, and decided I couldn't bear another grueling museum crawl. Gathering my energy for the hike back to Checkpoint Charlie, I was struck by a grand idea. I'd buy a museum postcard for Terry to prove I'd been there.

Inside, I chose the best from a beggarly selection: a drab black-and-white postcard that squeezed three poorly rendered photos of uninspired buildings onto one card. But never mind. It was East Berlin. Terry would love it, especially since it had been two and a half weeks since I'd written. I couldn't let him dangle anxiously another five or six or eight days. When I paid, the cashier asked in halting English if I wanted stamps.

"Can I mail it here?" I asked.

She furrowed her brow. I pantomimed writing my card, stamping, and dropping it into an imaginary slot.

"*Ja, ja!*" She pointed to a padlocked box on the other side of the lobby.

"Yes! *Ja, ja, danke.*" I did a happy dance and bought the stamps. She almost smiled.

I hunkered on a bench and scrawled my note in green ink, pretending I was a Berlin correspondent. "Miss Ann Garretson is still alive and kicking, despite the fact she hasn't been heard from for over two weeks." My breezy note belied my pent-up loneliness and my wish that we could have explored East and West Berlin together. But I knew that the mailman in Center, Colorado—not to mention Terry's brothers and sister—would scrutinize every word for mushy innuendos. They would get no such fodder from me. Still, in print half the size of the disclaimers on an insurance form, I added, "God, I miss you!"

I bounded over to the mailbox, kissed the card, and deposited my missive. Somehow, that tiny success generated new energy. I peeked into the museum. It was cool inside. I wandered from exhibit to exhibit, lightfooted, stunned by the grandeur of the Ishtar Gate, with its blue and gold mosaic, and by the monumental Pergamon Altar.

Alone, amid the exquisite pink and gold and black mosaics of the wraparound Aleppo Room, I regretted mailing my postcard so hastily. No matter, Terry would be delighted with any word from me, especially on a card festooned with DDR stamps from behind the Iron Curtain.

By midafternoon, I'd made it to Checkpoint Charlie with only half as many wrong turns. In the museum, and along the way back, I kept my eye out for any written literature that would fulfill my propaganda mission but saw nothing. Gradually, I realized that if I did see anything in writing, it would be in German. How would that be helpful? What was I thinking?

The guard shack was as forbidding as it had been that morning. But while I wilted in line, tired, hungry, and thirsty, I spied a pamphlet—in English—touting the kind of propaganda I wanted to share with my students. Lying by itself on a counter was a white pamphlet with bright red letters: "You're right, Senator Fulbright." A small, blurry black-and-white photo in the corner seemed to be of our own Senate Foreign Relations Committee chairman, J. William Fulbright. Unobtrusively, I tried to read the smaller print upside down. It seemed to be saying he supported the right of East Germany to close the Berlin Wall. *What? Really?*

I wanted it. I was afraid to ask, afraid the East German guards would detain me, afraid the Americans at the other end would lock me up as a spy. I waited. I watched. When no one was looking, I snatched it. Yep, I *stole* it and stashed it in my purse. And over the next twenty minutes, I nearly disintegrated from anxiety as I smuggled my booty through both the East and West Berlin checkpoints.

Terry

Thursday, 16 July 1964, Los Gatos, California. We were abuzz—Kochers and Marshalls both—over Barry Goldwater's call to arms that night: "Extremism in the defense of liberty is no vice!" In a landslide, the Republican National Convention had anointed Goldwater to oppose Lyndon Johnson for president. His battle cry was no slip of the tongue; he smacked us in the face with it. Pausing between each word, he shouted, "Liberty—is—no—vice!" Delegates applauded, cheered, whistled, and blew air horns in approval—for a thunderous sixty seconds. All of us watched it on TV.

Paula and I just shook our heads. Who decides what's extreme? Who defines the defenders of liberty and the desecrators? Goldwater had done a backflip into the 1950s. Worse, the "cream" of the Republican Party—delegates from Maine to California—agreed. They leaped up, mounted hypothetical horses, and formed a modern-day posse ready to ride out of the Cow Palace and lynch any American who disagreed with them.

We truly were in for it—a spare-no-mud presidential campaign.

The very next morning, the local newspaper, the *San Jose Mercury*, carried two articles that confirmed my fears. From page one:

Sen. Barry Goldwater Wednesday called President Johnson "the biggest faker in the United States" and "the phoniest individual who ever came around."

And then from page five:

Republican presidential nominee Barry Goldwater issued a victory statement last night vowing to "conduct a vigorous campaign" against President Johnson, but one based on issues and not personalities. "I assure you it will not be a personal attack," he said of his campaign plan against Johnson. "It will be confined to the issues only."

The contradictory passages brought laughs from the whole family. But this wasn't a joke. I had bought and read Goldwater's *Conscience of a Conservative* (fifty hard-earned cents) and Phyllis Schlafly's *A Choice Not an Echo* (seventy-five cents wasted), and I was convinced Goldwater would be a catastrophe as president.

Further, I objected to Goldwater's position on civil rights, and not because I thought him racist, as many liberals claimed. He argued that racism and discrimination, while evil, were matters to be solved in men's hearts, not by government intervention. Morality couldn't be legislated, he said.

In Martin Luther King Jr.'s book *Strength to Love*, I'd found a clear rationale for rejecting that argument:

Let us never succumb to the temptation of believing that legislation and judicial decrees play only minor roles in solving this problem. Morality cannot be legislated, but behavior can be regulated. Judicial decrees may not change the heart, but they can restrain the heartless. The law cannot make an employer love an employee, but it can prevent him from refusing to hire me because of the color of my skin.

Goldwater also argued that any legislation on civil rights should be the dominion of the states, not the federal government. To me, the civil rights movement had demonstrated that the states were a major part of the problem, not the solution, and that the mantra of "states' rights" was code for preserving the status quo. Civil rights had to be protected and enforced nationwide by the federal government, not relegated to the states for an uneven patchwork of potentially conflicting, oppressive laws.

In one sense, Goldwater's nomination seemed ideal. Here was a candidate with a clearly articulated philosophy of conservatism. I could vote against him because I didn't buy that philosophy, not because of any of the thousand other reasons Americans vote for or against a presidential candidate. We did have a choice, not an echo—as Phyllis Schlafly so astutely put it

As much as anything, it still rankled that Goldwater had taken on the University of Colorado in 1962, forcing my untimely departure from the *Colorado Daily*.

That school year had promised to be stellar. Back at CU after having dropped out for a semester, I'd been promoted to managing editor of the *Daily*, second in command. Editor-in-chief Gary Althen and I planned a lively, hard-hitting campus newspaper that would earn national recognition.

On the Saturday before classes began, Annie and I went out for coffee. She was back in town after the summer working in Albuquerque and adapting to her folks' new home. They had sold their ranch and moved to the city. We chatted on as if it had been a week since we'd last seen each other, not three months. We splurged, sundaes—hers chocolate, mine strawberry. My treat: $1.02. But she sat fidgeting like she was counting the seconds until I drove her back to campus. "What's with you?" I said. "You're not listening. You got a hot date tonight?"

"No. I'm excited for you, Ter. I really am. It's that . . . well . . . I don't think I can help at the *Daily* this fall. My schedule's brutal—Russian, math, two lit courses, and Intro to Education—I'm going to switch from journalism to English."

It didn't surprise me. We'd talked often about teaching high school—she English, me history. Still it was a blow. She knew how to write, and I had hoped she'd help train the new crop of freshmen. Besides, I liked having her around. She was fun. She knew how to banter.

The next night we were back to old times—dinner with Annie at Twin-Burger, $1.43. Her treat, but she scowled. "How come when it's my turn to pay—"

"Okay, tell you what," I said. "Next week, we'll eat here again. I'll pay. Shakes *and* fries."

"I'll bet."

I snickered, but her retort turned out to be prophetic. The following Sunday night I ate half a cold pizza in the *Daily* office. Only five issues into the school year, and the paper was under attack. In our September 21 issue, when we threw down two gauntlets that enraged CU football fans, alumni, the Board of Regents, Colorado's Republican politicians, and, eventually, yes, US Senator Barry Goldwater, the resulting controversy battered my psyche and threatened my college career.

Gauntlet one. Editor Althen took on Big Eight football in an editorial. The previous year, our Buffaloes had won the Big Eight football championship—CU's first ever—and fans had been delirious. But in April, the National Collegiate Athletic Association (NCAA) sanctioned CU for illegally paying some of its athletes. The NCAA report ignited a furor, and the Board of Regents fired the coach. The uproar escalated. In his editorial, published the day before the 1962 season-opening game, Althen wrote:

> We hope the Buffaloes lose tomorrow's game and all those that follow. Only then, when the glory of the conference championship has been lost in a string of inglorious defeats, will the University see the idiocy of supporting an exorbitant weekly circus in the name of an institution of higher education. University officials could work toward making all teams in the conference either strictly amateur or strictly professional—or abandon football completely.

Dr. Dale Atkins, a CU alum, athlete, and candidate for the Board of Regents, blasted the *Daily* in the Denver media for "its defeatist attitude." I interviewed Atkins on Sunday night and wrote the lead article for Monday's issue. Atkins told me, "If I'm elected, I will investigate the student newspaper policy, its organization, its advisers, its political bias, and incomplete coverage."

Atkins wasn't alone in his outrage. In the coming weeks, campus sports fans and alumni rallied around the football flag as if it were Old Glory and we at the *Daily* had trampled it with feces-encrusted boots. My God, from the uproar, you'd think we had murdered the school mascot, Ralphie—a fifteen-hundred-pound buffalo—in cold blood.

Gauntlet two. In the same issue, we published a lengthy polemic on American politics by student Carl Mitcham, a stinging critique of Senator Goldwater's political philosophy as expounded in his books *Conscience of a Conservative* and *Why Not Victory?* Near the end of Mitcham's hundred-inch-long essay, he wrote:

> Goldwater is the victim of forces outside himself, not because of fate, but because of the nature of violence. His delusion is his passion. Read for what he is—not as an abstraction or depersonalized politician—Barry Goldwater is a fool, a mountebank, a murderer, no better than a common criminal.

In Denver, Atkins condemned the *Daily* and the university as a hotbed for left-wing radicals. From Washington, DC, Senator Goldwater demanded that CU President Quigg Newton apologize for Mitcham's words. By the end of the week, the CU Board of Regents had voted to investigate the paper.

Newton apologized. Goldwater scoffed, calling CU a "haven for un-American ideas," and charged that Newton wasn't qualified to be a university president. In response, Newton excoriated Goldwater for "unforgivable meddling in the affairs of the University."

Pressure mounted. Newton asked the Board of Publications, the *Daily*'s governing body, to fire editor Althen. The board refused. The Denver newspapers and radio and TV stations all headlined the story. In mid-October, Newton himself fired Althen.

At that instant, I became acting editor in chief. A second-semester sophomore, I was propelled into the most prestigious position on campus for a student journalist. But the *Daily* had become the handmaiden of university administrators and Denver politicians. I couldn't accept that. Nor could I turn my back on Gary Althen. Two *Daily* staff members resigned in protest that day—city editor Stefanie Wiercinski and I. The others stayed on. "We do not believe we should be silenced," they wrote in an editorial, "and that we should not silence ourselves."

Steffi's response, "That's bullshit! They're gutless. They disgust me."
I agreed.

Only a month into the school year, I had given up my coveted position—not just its prestige, but the opportunity to hone my journalism skills, which would have propelled me into a bright future. I was out of a job, without income, and, to put it mildly, damned angry. The only bright light in my life was Steffi. We began seeing each other socially—coffee breaks at first, like those with Annie. Then movies, CU basketball games, dinner dates. All mixed in with late-night phone calls, strolls across campus, Sunday drives, good-night kisses, intimate touches, and passionate embraces.

In November, Colorado Republicans swept the election: governor, US senator, state house. To top it off, Dale Atkins won a seat on the CU Board of Regents.

And that meant he was going after the *Daily*.

At the root of the assault lay a national right-wing campaign that was far larger than the paper. Led by Goldwater, conservatives preached that colleges should teach America's greatness, not point out its faults. In his missive to CU President Newton, Goldwater had written, "I have spoken with groups of some 250 colleges and schools in this country, and this is the only one where the Socialists seem to have the ability to do what they want without censure."

Goldwater and Atkins attacked the basic tenets of what a university should be. Clearly, Atkins didn't understand those tenets. So the day after the election, I sat down at my typewriter and explained them to him in a personal letter:

> *The university is the meeting place of ideas, a place where one has an opportunity to find the truth, whatever that truth may be. This, above all, is its function; and this, above all, is the function that you and other misguided patriots are inadvertently trying to destroy.*
>
> *There are those of us at the university—who attend not to prepare for life within your society, but to find whatever it is we seek: the nebulous, perhaps unattainable, truth—of life, of ourselves, of our relations with others, of the very idea of existence. These goals are paramount. They cannot come without prolonged questioning and searching.*

I had talked to Atkins in October. He didn't listen. He was like a farm mule—you had to smack him in the face with a two-by-four to get his attention. So my letter had to be strong:

> *Yes, I hate the United States, with its base hypocrisy and undercut-ting rottenness that defiles and debauches the beautiful land that I love. I hate the people who are the United States; I hate their ideas, their actions, their goals, everything about them. I see a people cor-rupt and base; I see false goals and materialism; I see worship of your false God; and belief in your rotten free enterprise. And I detest it all, Dr. Atkins. I see the university as the only bastion of worth left in a society corrupt and despoiled—and I see you as one who would destroy that worth.*
>
> *I shall continue to subvert your dirty Americanism. I shall con-tinue to move to overthrow the perversion my country has become, for I detest it. I look forward to your term on the Board of Regents—for my subversion is yet to begin.*

Somehow, the *New Conservative*, a campus newspaper created that fall to counter the *Colorado Daily*, got a copy of my letter. In mid-November, on page one, they headlined my tirade. A week later, they reprinted my entire letter, verbatim—the letter Annie so vehemently upbraided me about, the letter that taught me that for most people, *hate* is mighty strong language. And when you add *America* as the direct object, it's the worst of the four-letter words.

Yes, the letter was hot. I should have asked Annie to edit it. I didn't. I had foolishly let the *Daily* controversy push her away when I needed her most.

Nearly two years later, in sunny California, Barry Goldwater actually did me a huge favor—he eradicated my qualms about supporting Lyndon Johnson in the November 1964 election. Though I feared President John-son would plunge us deeper into Vietnam, I believed Goldwater would precipitate a nuclear war.

Goldwater had hammered Kennedy and Johnson for being "soft" on Communism, for opening a hotline with the Soviet Union, for failing to "remake" the United Nations. He demanded the US "get tough." His attacks on our foreign policy brought back memories of the 1962 Cuban Missile Crisis, which happened during those weeks of the *Colorado Daily* brouhaha.

October 22. Monday. President Kennedy on TV, calm but stern. The rumors were true. Soviet troops had streamed into Cuba—nearly forty thousand of them. American spy planes had photographed bomber bases and missile launch sites under construction on the island, plus actual missiles. Soviet nuclear missiles within range of every major American city, with launch sites activated. Unimaginable!

The president said, "It shall be the policy of this nation to regard any nuclear missile launched from Cuba against any nation in the Western hemisphere as an attack by the Soviet Union on the United States, requiring a full retaliatory response upon the Soviet Union."

A full retaliatory response. My God, he meant war! Nuclear war.

He had declared a quarantine around Cuba. The US Navy would blockade the island and board any ship transporting weapons to Cuba. The US put its fleet of B-52 long-range bombers—armed with nuclear weapons— in the air around the clock. An arsenal of midrange B-47 bombers sat armed and ready for takeoff on fifteen minutes' notice. American missile sites were put on high alert. On Thursday, October 25, the Soviet tanker *Bucharest* passed through the blockade unchallenged. Soon after, a Soviet SAM missile shot down an American U-2 spy plane taking photos over Cuba, killing the pilot.

I'd seen *On the Beach* and read the book. We were doomed. I gassed up my car and left Boulder for home. I'd be safer there—no bases or missile sites or weapons plants in the San Luis Valley to attract Soviet nuclear bombs. But if worse came to worse, if it were a worldwide nuclear holocaust, at least I'd die with my family.

I spent the last week of that October in Center. The *Colorado Daily* faded into the past. In Center, no one talked about the football team's latest win, potato prices, or whether we could finish harvest before the ground froze. Every conversation—in Skeffs' Grocery, Walker's Clothing, the post office, on the street—was about Nikita Khrushchev, SAC bombers, ICBMs, U-2 spy planes, Polaris submarine ballistic missiles, and Soviet Divina surface-to-air missiles. About first strike capability and MIGs and F-102s.

Every night at six, our whole family fell silent in front of the CBS evening news, and Mom didn't start dinner until after Walter Cronkite signed off.

I drove into town every day that week. Same topic at Center High, and Sunday at the Methodist church—Mrs. Bemenderfer cast aside the topics in her Sunday school lesson plan. We talked about war and death and our chances of getting into heaven.

None of us knew it then, but in Washington and Moscow, diplomats and politicians were meeting around the clock, drafting secret messages, proposals, and counterproposals.

November 2, Friday. President Kennedy on TV again. Khrushchev had agreed to dismantle the bases in Cuba. They would crate up their missiles and ship them back to the Soviet Union. In response, the United Sates would remove its ballistic missiles from Turkey and Italy, the ones pointed toward the Soviet Union. And America pledged never again to invade Cuba.

Crisis over. War averted. We'd all live after all.

I drove back to Boulder in time for classes on November 5. I tried not to think about *On the Beach*, but I couldn't get the strains of "Waltzing Matilda" out of my head, particularly those last moments together for Gregory Peck and Ava Gardner before he returns in his submarine for the voyage that will bring certain death in radioactive America . . . and before she dies in Melbourne in the approaching nuclear cloud. How could we be sure insanity wouldn't prevail? That no one with a wild hair would press the button, send a missile aloft, and unleash Armageddon?

Since that week, I thought we had forever averted the threat of nuclear war. But now, two years after that near cataclysm, "Waltzing Matilda" again shrieked at me like a chimera from hell. If a levelheaded president like JFK could have brought us so close to nuclear war, I was sure that Goldwater would pitch us over the brink. His bellicose acceptance speech proved it.

Annie hadn't heard of Goldwater's nomination, I was sure of it. Had she been there with me, we would have dissected his speech and mulled over what his candidacy meant for America's amped-up meddling in Vietnam and the Republican Party platform (which had rejected a plank affirming the constitutionality of President Johnson's new Civil Rights Act).

I spent the morning writing to her, six pages' worth—half of it filling her in on Goldwater's nomination, the other half taking her on a tour of San Francisco with me. At the end I wrote:

An advertisement in the concert program last night reads: "The Ham-
ilton is offering a limited number of brand-new redecorated and beau-
tifully furnished apartments on lease . . . one bedroom townhouses
from $360 (a month)." Marry me and let's move to San Francisco
and watch the fog roll in and the sun set over the ocean and the city.
Better bring a few coins of your own.

She would laugh at the thought. My senior year, I had rented a room
in the basement of a suburban ranch-style home for forty-five dollars a
month—triple my outlay when I'd lived in the furnace room of a decrepit
old apartment building.

Annie hated the eight-by-fifteen-foot concrete cell that fronted the monstrous old furnace. No linoleum or rug, merely grimy unpainted cement.
Two-burner hot plate. Tiny sink. No bathroom, just a toilet one foot from
the furnace and a showerhead mounted on a pipe behind the toilet. I had
to straddle the toilet to shower. My single bed completely filled the adjacent "bedroom." The furnace-room suite cost me fifteen dollars a month,
and it was more than cozy warm during the grip of winter.

Ann

Thursday, July 16, 1964, West Berlin. In a crowded little coffee shop I enjoyed
the last bites of my scrambled eggs with *Preiselbeeren* (cranberries)—my new
favorite breakfast. My only task was to rest from the stress of my foray into
East Berlin. Rest from all-night train rides, past and future. Rest from the
emotional jangle of Terry versus Jack that had kept me on edge for weeks.
I'd play tourist until my train to Landshut that evening.

First stop, the Kaiser Wilhelm Memorial Church—famous before World
War II for its architecture and famous afterward for its devastation. It
had been left unchanged for more than a decade before they built a rueful
monument to the mayhem of war. I felt dwarfed by the single remaining
war-damaged spire that dominated Kurfürstendamm Avenue and grieved
silently above the hurly-burly of this street below. At least five other spires,
which apparently had housed belfries, were gone. Such an architectural
beauty, destroyed because it was in the path of war. Sure, some things
are more important than preserving beauty—like life and liberty. Still . . .

As I strolled into the sanctuary, I wondered what Jack would have done had he rolled into Berlin in his tank and seen the enemy lodged in the belfries, firing machine guns and bazookas at his troops. For two weeks, we had marveled at the extraordinary architecture across Germany, France, and Italy. But I was sure he wouldn't have hesitated to take out enemies hiding inside a church, to blow them—and the church—to smithereens.

How could he? How could he not?

And what would Terry do? Nothing. He'd be rotting in jail for refusing to go to war.

Two men. So much alike, yet worlds apart on this fundamental point. I could see both sides, but I didn't have the courage of either of them. Not Jack's, for his willingness to face men firing at him, lobbing mortars, dropping bombs, intent on killing him and his men. He'd fight to the death.

Or Terry's, for his *un*willingness to kill another human, period. His was a different kind of courage, a commitment to principles so powerful that he would endure society's scorn, to become, for many, the enemy in our own country, to go to jail, to shame his family, to be forever tarred not as courageous, but as a coward. And most likely, whether or not he got drafted—and had to face the consequences—he'd continue to oppose war.

In my heart, I would choose peace over war, life over death, so I was wracked with this question: How did I fall so far from my family tree?

A memory from first grade in Honolulu flashed in my mind. Bonner and his fourth grade buddies decided to "have a war." They conned us little girls into collecting ammunition for them—three-inch-long dried tropical bean pods, hard as nails, with dart-sharp points at each end. These tan beans fell from trees in every yard, providing an abundant source of harm. Flattered by the big boys' attention, we girls ran off to do their bidding.

But then in my mind, I heard Grandma's voice: *You could put someone's eye out with those!* I deserted the munitions-gathering crew and wandered off to play on the swings. Before long, the combined forces of the big boys and their little conscripts surrounded me on my swing. Every one of them—including my friends and my own brother—threw pods at *me*.

I swung higher and higher to dodge their missiles, and fortunately, none connected, not physically. Though the wounds to my feelings weren't all that deep, they were indelible. Simply put, I knew that war was a bad idea. I was right. They were wrong. That certainty followed me into adulthood.

Sitting in a pew in that enormous church, I asked myself, Could I support Terry's choice if he went to jail rather than to war? The thought scared me. And what about the "lesser" things, his challenges to authority, for example, like that scurrilous letter to Dale Atkins. That letter could come back to bite him. Another thing was his passion about the state of world affairs—like that time during the Cuban Missile Crisis when he jumped into his car and drove home to dodge the bombs or, if worse came to worse, to roast with his family. How long until he joined some of those antiwar protests I'd read about in the paper? Explain that to my family and friends!

Dang, thoughts of Terry and Jack had commandeered my mind, even in this peaceful place. Again. I fled from the church into a nearby shop and headed for the women's accessories—something, anything that wouldn't remind me of either one.

Friday, July 17, 1964, Landshut. Bonner met me with a boisterous nuzzle, a gesture he used in childhood both to annoy me and to express affection without betraying that he loved his freckle-faced sister. At least, that's what I told myself. "Sorry, Jack's at the border," he said. "You're stuck with me till tomorrow." Then he peppered me with questions.

Did you climb the Eiffel Tower?

"Of course."

Did you see nude sunbathers at Saint-Tropez?

"Yep, you shoulda been there."

How were the Kirtleys?

"They treated us like long-lost family."

Did you and Jack sleep together?

What? I looked at him deadpan. "Yep."

He didn't pursue it, and I didn't tell him we didn't have sex. *Stew over that nugget, brother.* If it burnished Jack's stature, so be it. Still, it must have been tough to protect his little sister from his best friend, and his best friend from his little sister. *Ha!*

That evening, we joined several lieutenants with wives or girlfriends for dinner at the officers' club, where the tables huddled around a polished dance floor. As drinks flowed, the group got rowdy. Next thing I knew, everyone at the table was comparing noses—actually feeling each other's noses, a stupid drinking game. When the group whooped over their discovery that Bonner and I were the only ones with cold noses, I pulled him up to the dance floor. "Save the Last Dance for Me" offered a perfect exit. He was a great dancer, and we changed the atmosphere as the other couples followed us onto the floor. We danced, changed partners, and danced until my feet ached and my eyelids drooped.

Bonner walked me back to the teachers' quarters, angling past his room for my mail. "I shouldn't have to tell you this again," he said. "Don't import your own men when you come to visit me."

He handed me a bundle of envelopes, all from Terry, all addressed in print-shop font, not typed or handwritten, and as gaudy as circus flyers. My name, emblazoned in red, was flanked by Greek columns. Scattered over the front were black and red Keystone Kops. One letter was festooned with a sticker—"AIR *PAR AVION* MAIL"—and an eight-cent airmail stamp, *plus* a thirty-cent "Special Delivery" stamp and sticker. Bonner was as steely eyed as a gunslinger. "And don't break my best friend's heart."

Good heavens, was this the pot calling the kettle black? "Breaking Jack's heart would hurt me far more than it would hurt you," I told him.

I retreated to my room, lined up Terry's letters, and opened the special-delivery one—four typed pages. The first page:

I have told you many times I love you. It has been said truthfully and honestly, but I have sometimes wondered if I was attracted not by you, but by love. Could it be love of love, with you as a vehicle rather than as the end? I hoped not. I am now positive it is you, not the abstract concept, whom I love.

I could picture him, hunched over his typewriter, pounding away, so insistent that I believe his every word. At the top of the second page, I gasped.

Annie, I am announcing formally and officially (since I always manage to do things awkwardly) that I am proposing to you. I want you to marry me.

You can exist without me, and me without you—if not forever, at least for twenty-four months. Twenty-four months is only a bit of time in retrospect; but, dammit, in the present, it will be an eternity. Annie, we can make it without each other, but I want so much more

*than just to make it. I want us to have that fulfilling life together—
and there now seems little reason to postpone it for two long years.*

Marry Terry? Now? What about the Peace Corps? And my job in Glendale? I read quickly, determined to finish before tears spilled.

*It has been only a month, but seconds have seemed like hours; the last
time I saw you belongs to some hazy past of long-gone years, not a
mere thirty days. Darn you, you have become an integral part of me—
life means you, and us; it does not mean being separated from you,
especially for twenty-four long months. I don't think you have found
more in Jack than you have found in me. At least, I hope not. If you
have, forgive my intrusion—but don't forget what I have asked of you.*

    *I have never asked anyone to marry me, so I hope this is okay. I
tried not to mess it up. And I hope this doesn't shock you too much.
I am completely serious, completely sober, and completely sure this
is what we should do. Besides, I love you, even if you do have eighty
million freckles.*

Forgive my intrusion? Oh my. He had inserted himself into the heart
of my dilemma and then asked forgiveness for nailing it. I did love him.
But I loved Jack too.

    Terry's letter was so tender, so perceptive, and so . . . funny, so typically Terry. *Where's the drum roll, Ter, and the post horns?* "I want you to
marry me." *Where's the bended knee? And the entreaty? Shall I edit this for
you? No, no, it's so . . . so you.*

    Oh, I missed him so much. But I had no one to turn to for advice. He
had hijacked my best friend, my confidant.

    And tonight, somewhere along the German-Czech border, was the
Other Guy—the one who had squired me around Europe for two glorious weeks, the one I would see tomorrow morning. He would read this
news in my face. What would I tell him? What would I tell Terry? A silent
scream wracked my insides. *I don't know! Don't pressure me! Either of you!*

    I jolted awake at 2 a.m., my curls stuck to my neck, stiff with salt, the
lamp blazing, and Terry's letters, save for the one lying on my chest, still
lined up patiently.

The second letter transported me to Silverton, beneath the achingly blue sky framed by mountains too massive for the speck of town below. He took me on his escapades, every day a different heart-stopping adventure—an ice-encrusted lake (in July!), a flower-studded high meadow, a jeep caper down a cliff on a narrow ledge, suspended thousands of feet above the valley. I shivered with excitement and fear. Fear for Terry. And myself. I was a wimp compared to the outdoorsy penchants of *either* of these guys.

In each letter, Terry hummed the refrain of his persistent question:

July 2, Silverton. *How I wish I knew the one thing to say or do that would assure our marriage.*

July 4, Silverton. *All you have to do in regard to the letter of two days ago is send a one-word note: "Yes."*

July 7, Silverton. *Unfortunately, as you sit down to read these accumulated letters, your mind will be filled with thoughts of your trip and of your companion—hardly the time to consider seriously any such request as the one I have made and must repeat again.*

July 10, Los Gatos, California. He quoted Shakespeare's Sonnet 116: "Let me not to the marriage of true minds / Admit impediments." *Shakespeare's words offer hope. So I'm hoping.*

Midway through this letter, holy cow, he described—in mortifying detail—making love to me. I couldn't read it. It was too private. But I pressed on, fighting to suppress my anger. *Some things you just don't commit to paper, Ter!*

Here we were again, like last spring, Terry barging into my romance with Jack, asking me to fall in love with *him*. On top of that, he had injected sex so explicit that it conjured up the string of messy relationships he'd paraded in my face: Laura Lee, Sarah, and Rachael—an engaged, divorced mother he lobbied to live with him; an older woman he wanted only for sex; and a young would-be student he got pregnant who ultimately had an abortion (an *illegal* abortion). He was making it impossible to overlook his transgressions.

Enough. I skimmed the letter and, with trepidation, opened the last one. July 13, also Los Gatos. No sex. Thank goodness. This was about the Republican National Convention. Finally, space to breathe and delight in his antics. Oh, and there he was—picketing and protesting the Republican platform, just as I feared. How typical. But how exciting it must have been to march with like-minded people. I lingered over every word and imagined the passion of the crowd.

Perversely, I looked for the words of love that gave me so much pain. What was wrong with me?

He ended with a plea for me to call so we could talk about marriage. How? The teachers didn't have a phone. Find a pay phone? And tell the operator what? *I'd like to make a collect call to Terry somewhere in America. And can you speak English?*

And if I did manage to track him down, what would I say? *I don't know, Ter. I can't decide.* Call to tell him that?

End of letters. I reunited each with its fanciful envelope and buried them all in the bottom of my bag. I didn't want any nosey roommates skulking around my room while I was gone and snickering over the juicy tidbits.

An hour later, I had cooled off, set aside the sex talk, and turned my thoughts to Terry's proposal. I lay in a warm glow. After all was said and done, I thought how lucky I was to have Terry in my life, making me feel so full, so alive, sharing his tales, standing up for bedrock principles—despite my ire at his unrelenting campaign to get me into bed.

A second thought chased the first—how incredibly lucky I was to have Jack embrace me in such a short space of time, filling me with joy through this improbable airmail-turned-grand-tour romance. I would be fortunate to marry either one.

13
Farewell to Our Sting Ray Summer

Ann

Saturday, July 18, 1964, Landshut. I startled from a deep sleep to straight-up awake at nine, gobbled a bowl of Rice Krispies, and allowed myself an hour and a half to wash Paris, Saint-Tropez, Verona, Venice, and Berlin out of my dirty clothes. Bonner said Jack would pick me up at five. Before he arrived, I had to figure out how to break the news of Terry's proposal. No way could I credibly feign a life-is-normal mien. My eyes would telegraph the news. Worse, Jack would sniff it from a mile away. I needed solace—the tranquility of the Isar River.

The Isar mesmerized me with its undulating Salvador Dalí reflection of the old town fort. The image lured me over the bridge, through the arch between the massive battlements, and into the town plaza. Wandering the shiny cobblestone streets, I happened upon a footbridge over the Kleine Isar, a narrow offshoot of its "mama" river. The Kleine offered another Dalí, a tidy, German neighborhood shimmering across the smaller river. There, I communed with sixteenth-century muses, hoping they would offer rhetoric for my coming encounter with Jack.

It had to be a news report. *Here's the latest from my end.* Not to angle for a counteroffer. And not to give Jack the impression that a deal with Terry was sealed. The key message: You haven't been knocked off your steed, and the joust isn't over.

Promptly at five, Jack bounded into the teachers' quarters like he'd been promoted to general. "You look fantastic, Miss Garretson." No embrace, not even an air kiss. But his eyes smoldered with coded smoke signals. We quickly escaped, and Jack steered us out of town. "I know a cozy *gasthaus* down the road. No soldiers. No emergencies."

En route, he laid out plans for our final three days together, leading up to Tuesday's departure ceremonies on the parade grounds. Sunday, we'd go to Helmut's for lunch and hike Jack's favorite hill afterward. Later that evening, he'd whip up dinner for my hosts and a few friends. Monday night, the shindig for the departing officers at the club. "It's a command performance." He sighed, as if resigning himself to torture.

I chuckled. I was all too familiar with the army way. In fact, I enjoyed the elegant functions, the mingling, the dancing—though not the drinking, the raunchy jokes, and the occasional crude attempt to cop a feel. "Don't worry," I told him. "We'll escape to the dance floor, put our arms around each other, and outfox the PDA cops."

"You know those 'PDA cops,' as you call them, are really inside my head."

"Sadly, yes. At the same time, I appreciate those guys inside your head and the respect they, and you, show. It's so different from most guys. Makes me love you even more."

Minutes later, he pulled off the highway onto a side road and parked in a grove of trees.

"Speaking of putting our arms around each other . . ." He took my face in both hands, and we kissed, as best we could, across the console. "Been dying to do that all week," he said.

"Nice start, but that gearshift's an unforgiving chaperone. Meet me outside." I scrambled out, and we cannoned together in front of the car for a probing, insistent kiss, as fervent as if he were a shipwreck survivor rescued after years adrift.

"I've missed you so much," Jack whispered into my hair. "The week crept by as slowly as a lifetime."

His words jolted. They were almost identical to Terry's.

"What's wrong?"

"Uh, it's a little chilly out here." This was *not* the time to tell him about Terry.

He pulled me close, and I snuggled into the heat of his body. "Thank you for not slathering your face and lips with makeup," he said. "And thank you for being the real you."

Over dinner I regaled him with timid-mouse stories about East Berlin and thanked him for his own steadfast service on the border. He asked about the previous night with Bonner. I told him about the drinking and the nose game—how annoyed I was that I almost got sucked into it.

"I know. You get caught in the moment. I'm not proud of this, but I've gotten drunk more than once with the gang at the club. I try to stay away. Sorry I wasn't there to save you."

"That's army life. You can't avoid it."

"They didn't get drunk at the University of Colorado? Party U, as I recall."

"*They* did, yes. Some of them, particularly the freshmen, newly untethered from mama. But I've never been drunk. Nor have the people I hung around with. But drinking's a way of life in the military, isn't it? You know—'have another drink; it could be your last.'"

His eyes narrowed. "That's harsh. Every workplace has good points and bad. But I do get razzed for avoiding the drinking crowd. Glad to know you avoid them too."

Conversation faltered. The fifty-pound rock of Terry's proposal teetered on my back.

He stared me down. "But that's not what's on your mind, is it? What's eating you?"

I took a deep breath. "Well, things have gotten more complicated. I—"

"Your old buddy again! What now?"

"How'd you know?"

"Special-delivery letters don't go unnoticed. Not ones gigged out for Carnevale."

So he knew. "What else did your spies tell you?"

"Wrong question. How about our promise to be honest? What do *you* have to say?"

"I got those letters last night and read them *after* I got back from the club. Did your spy tell you what the letters said? Do you want to know?"

He folded his arms, tilted his chair back. "No . . . and yes."

"Terry proposed. He wants to get married. This summer."

Jack blinked. The defiance in his eyes vanished. Slowly, he brought the front legs of the chair to the floor. "What are you going to tell him?" His voice sounded as tight as violin strings.

"Nothing. He's half a world away. I don't know what to tell him. The

only sure thing is this: I am *not* getting married this summer. To anyone."
I sucked in my breath. This was a truth I hadn't articulated—even to myself—until now.

"When were you going to tell me? Or were you?"

"Let's start with when I *wasn't* going to tell you. Not in front of the
teachers, when you picked me up. 'Oh, by the way, Jack, Terry proposed—
just got the letter last night.' And it wasn't an appropriate topic over dinner, when we were so happy to see each other. And certainly not when you
said almost exactly the same thing Terry said about how the time crept by
last week. 'Funny, Jack, that's what Terry tells me!'"

He jolted back like I'd smacked him in the face. "He said that? The
same thing?"

I nodded.

"So he attempts to steal my girl by stealing my lines? He'll try anything,
won't he? I guess we have more in common than the same girl."

"You'd be amazed." I shook my head, tried—and failed—to keep a
straight face. We both snickered, unable to squelch it.

"But you're right. There's no good time for bad news." He took my
hand, fiddled with it, and then looked at me, the light gone from his eyes.
"I knew this summer was too good to be true."

"So, you're thinking . . . what? It's over between us? Don't be such a
pessimist, guy."

"All I know is what I read in your face. And that he has a huge head start."

"Really? Can you see into my heart? See that I love you deeply? See the
struggle between you, my dream come true, and my closest friend? Can
you see the pain? Can you feel my agony in knowing at some point I will
deeply hurt at least one of you?" I paused to regain my composure. "But
maybe you're right. Maybe it is less painful for *you* to walk away from *me*."
Tears lurked; I willed them back. "But before you flee, know that I'll always
be grateful for these weeks together . . . Now, excuse me."

I dashed ahead of the tsunami of tears and lingered in the ladies room
until it was over. When I returned, I was a wreck, eyes red, nose redder,
despite my efforts to wash away the evidence.

When I slid into the booth, Jack took my hand, held it to his face, and
kissed my palm. "You okay?" he asked.

"Not really. But I'll survive."

Jack said nothing. We finished dinner and drove back to Landshut in silence. At the teachers' door, he kissed my forehead. "See you tomorrow. Nine sharp." He didn't linger.

What was the point of being honest if he clammed up? It was just another problem to unravel. I slept poorly, furious at Jack for giving up, furious at Terry for expecting me to marry him this summer—as if marriage were a simple walk in the rain.

Sunday, 8 a.m., July 19, 1964, Landshut. Someone pounded at the door. Jack! An hour early. The teachers had gone to mass. I was eating breakfast, and my hair was a fright.

"Wow. You look wonderful," he said.

I eyed him suspiciously.

"Seriously, I love the natural you. And I apologize for last night. I might have given the impression I had thrown in the towel."

"Indeed."

"Well, I haven't. I tied up that sorehead and threw him in the closet. I was angry. Not at you but at my unseen rival. I'm on my best behavior today. I promise."

"Does this mean we're still on for lunch?"

He kissed me square on the mouth. "You bet—and more."

That morning we avoided serious conversation by visiting his favorite haunts a final time—the entry to the old walled city, the lederhosen shop, charming back alleys, and St. Martin's Cathedral, where we nestled in a back pew. The calm of the place mended my frayed mettle. Jack whispered, "You don't have to be religious to appreciate the serenity of this church." He gestured. "And the architecture and stained glass."

I agreed. For today, I would immerse myself in the moment and refuse to be battered by either-ors. I'd focus only on Jack.

Lunch at Helmut's radiated all the antic joy of my first meeting with this wild-man proprietor, only now I was part of a prodigal couple welcomed home. "Jack, my friend, my son. You are gone so long! I worried . . ." He slipped into German and they both laughed. Jack later translated, ". . . that you had run away to marry your *Fräulein*!"

We took a last hike into the nearby hills. A lady hike, with me in my sundress and sandals and Jack in his lederhosen, of course.

Dinner with the teachers, their boyfriends, Bonner, and his date introduced me to chef Jack at work in a real kitchen. A simple meal—burgers and fries—but his style was meticulous: hamburger richly seasoned and massaged into identical patties, and tomatoes, lettuce, cheese, and onions arranged in a colorful artwork. He cut the potatoes into precise strips, fried, drained, dried, and fried them again. I tasted one. "Wow, light and crunchy. You are a master!"

"My special secret," he said. "The double frying makes all the difference."

After dinner, he and I strolled under a lopsided moon and chatted about his next assignment. First, a debriefing at Fort Belvoir of his stint in Germany. "Then, not sure. Probably stateside."

Normally, he said, the army didn't send men directly from one theater to another—from the German-Czech border to Vietnam, for example. "My thinking has been to volunteer for Vietnam one of these days. As an adviser. It's safer and the best route to promotions. And maybe I can have a positive impact before the firebrands spin it all out of control. But this news about my rival throws a wrench into the works. I need to rethink everything."

I listened, only listened. Was he agonizing over proposing himself? Lamenting that Terry had beaten him to the draw? Expecting a signal from me, thinking he had made his case plainly enough? As he rambled on, I gasped inwardly at the thought of Vietnam. We paused near the BOQ in the shadow of a tree. "So you're *not* volunteering to go to Vietnam?"

"Not yet, but probably sometime." A simple statement, neither apprehensive nor eager, merely a fact of life. With Jack, the specter of war would be a lifelong resident in the household.

He pulled me to him and tucked my head under his chin. No matter what happened between us, I didn't want him to go to Vietnam. Everything I had heard made me doubt whether the United States should be there, from last year's horrifying self-immolation by the Buddhist monk to the CIA-backed assassination of President Diem. Jack's very presence in Vietnam would put his life at risk. But I couldn't tell him what to do any more than I could prevent rams from crashing headlong into each other.

PDA be damned, I kissed him a kiss to remember. He kissed me back, a full-body hug that left me pained because we couldn't spend our last private night together.

Terry

Saturday, 18 July 1964, Los Gatos, California. We Marshalls—Mom, Pam, Randy, and I—took off early for Eureka in Northern California to see Mom's younger sister, Clarice, an aunt I'd never met. After high school, Aunt Clarice had joined the Women's Army Corps and got to see a bit of the world. She married, settled down, and somehow never got reunited with the rest of Mom's family. Mom said there was no animosity, just distance and separate lives. At long last we'd get to meet the mysterious Aunt Clarice, soldier, world traveler, and family anomaly—apparently she was six feet tall.

We started out in the wrong direction—south. Uncle Bob had insisted. "You absolutely have to see Carmel. It's picturesque perfect." Uncle Bob didn't give advice—he issued orders—so we circled around the bay to Monterrey and then drove on to Carmel. We window-shopped, and Mom even let the kids get ice cream cones . . . before lunch! While they were indulging in that rare treat, I started a letter to Annie.

I pretended that California was as exotic as Europe—to bring her thoughts back to the States. "You would love Carmel," I wrote. "A wonderful little town—no neon, no garish signs or billboards, quaint little shops with quality goods instead of schlock. Even the service stations blend in architecturally."

That afternoon, at the Humboldt Redwoods, we cruised the thirty-two-mile Avenue of Giants as if we were on a Sunday drive, oohing and aahing at one towering sentinel after another. We hiked into the shadowy forest and tried to measure one of those monsters by linking our hands. The four of us couldn't stretch even halfway around it.

Earlier, we had maneuvered the car through Chandelier, a drive-through tree with its own name. Pam jumped out and snapped a photo. Randy asked why people would carve the heart out of a tree so we could drive a car through it, "Why didn't they just make a road around it?" No answer from any of us.

In Eureka, we spent the evening chatting with a passel of cousins every bit as delightful as the Kocher gang. Aunt Clarice was at least six feet tall, and Uncle Al at least six-four. I had never met anyone so tall. Despite hitting it off with the Keister kids, by the time we finally trundled off to bed, I was missing Annie more than ever, and wrote to her with a new confession:

I've been hit again with a desire to have children. One of my Eureka cousins has a ten-month-old boy; the other, a two-year-old girl. I can't think of anything greater than giving you a child we could raise and love and share—in a couple of years after you've taught for a while and I've gotten my MA. (I hesitated to mention this for fear I'd send you running, but I'm so far out on the limb now that this can't make much difference.)

Last week, in Chinatown, I saw some beautiful silk shifts with splits up both sides that I wanted to get for you. Since then I've been noticing women's clothes. I want to marry you, buy you a fancy wardrobe, and just sit around the house admiring you. We'd spend all our money on books and sexy clothing for you (and maybe a pair of socks for me once in a while).

On Sunday, US 1 back to Los Gatos proved to be a narrow, winding trail that zigzagged through the hills along the coastline—slow going, but welcome relief from the seventy-mile-an-hour speed limit on California's open highways. Each time we stopped along the way, I continued my letter to Annie.

It's our kind of place: rocky shore lines; crabs scurrying from their sunbathing atop the rocks to dark hideaways beneath them; slippery rocks blanketed with tiny snails. In the quiet pools left isolated when the tide goes out, we discovered hundreds of beautiful plants, sea anemone, sand dollars, an occasional starfish.

It's a wonderful world, but empty when I can't share it with you. My desire for you creates a dull pain that never goes away. I thought before we left Los Gatos that if I were on the run seeing things, doing things, I could put you out of my mind and enjoy myself. I can't. I hope you're going through the same thing so you can understand what it's like.

Damn, what a mean-spirited thought. I didn't really hope she was as painfully lonely as I was. She couldn't be. She had Lieutenant Stud. But maybe, I hoped, maybe she missed me too. I didn't try to black that sentence out or, as I should have done, start the page over.

"We're leaving in a day or so and plan to be home by Friday," I wrote. But I meant, "I'll be in Center by the end of the week. Write me there, not here. Or better yet, call me." She was a whiz at reading between the lines.

Ann

Monday, July 20, 1964, Landshut. I still had no answer to Terry's proposal, but I couldn't postpone a reply any longer. Ever since high school, the right words had flowed when my fingers connected with a typewriter, so I borrowed a portable from one of the teachers and began:

> *Silverton, more than any other thing, brings me close to you because it typifies a way of life. The only thing I've figured out for sure this summer is that a woman marries far more than a husband. She weds a way of life she must also love.*

I knew I would choose peace and the tranquility of the mountains as a way of life—if I could only cut the powerful sinews that bound me to the military. Could I turn my back on my parents, my brother, and my life so far? That, in a nutshell, was the challenge. But I couldn't even say it out loud.

Breaking my pledge not to mention Jack, I told Terry how he and Jack were so much alike. Why not share the heartache I had subjected Jack to? I had to make Terry understand how difficult the decision was. I asked for more time, promised to call when I could, but concluded, "Something catches inside me with the thought of marriage right away."

Before noon, I addressed my letter to Terry in California, marched to the post office, and paid thirty-eight cents for an airmail special-delivery response that was totally inadequate.

That night, decked out in his dress blues, Jack ushered me into the reception line at the officers' club as if he were introducing his new bride. I'd trotted out my sexy cocktail dress with matching shoes and bag—still trailing delicious memories of Paris and Verona. I wanted to look good for Jack.

Everyone, from the colonel on down, closed ranks around him, each telling me Jack was a go-getter, a star, a soldier's soldier—as if I needed to be convinced. *You can always count on him to do what he says. He's a problem solver. He's a real team builder. His men would follow him anywhere. When we invited him for dinner, he helped clear the table*—this from one of the wives, as if such a man were as rare as a pearl in a clam.

Late in the evening, a tipsy major sidled up and clapped me on the shoulder. "That Jack's a warrior. He tells you what he thinks, no matter who you are. He'll be a four-star someday." Pressing in, the major burped whiskey breath in my face and stroked my arm. When his hand advanced to my shoulder, I edged back. He pulled me into his chest. "Let's dance, sweetheart."

Jack elbowed him aside. "Sorry, sir, she promised this one for me."

He swung me onto the dance floor. "What he didn't tell you is he and I had a run-in last winter after I busted a guy for stealing from the noncom club. Get this. The thief took off, but I tracked him through the snow. The major there, soused, as usual, called *me* on the carpet. 'I'll get your sorry ass, Sigg! You're history.' On and on. I went over his head to the colonel, who already had him in his crosshairs. 'Major Hooch' backed down."

"Thanks for rescuing me. He's an octopus, eight hands, foul breath."

"He thinks he's Don Juan. His wife puts up with a lot. Forget him . . . How about we get some fresh air? Go for a walk?"

The night was too breezy, and we wound up in his room in the BOQ. In one day, his cozy space had been stripped—naked walls, bare shelves, empty closet, no stereo, the bathroom echoing around his toothbrush and razor. It had become a way station for dozens of identical boxes, neatly labeled, stacked five high in tidy rows, along with two stout duffel bags.

"Whoa. No sign of you left!"

"All my worldly goods, except the Sting Ray, packed and ready to go." In front of the dresser, he wrapped his arms around me, bear hugging me from behind.

"It's so final," I said. "Once the boxes and bags are gone, you could disappear without a trace—like we did from the party."

"Yeah, you're right. Who cares if we're missing in action and eyebrows go up?"

I kicked off my shoes. We cuddled on the bed and never made it back to the reception. When he walked me home, he asked me to come to the ceremony the next day.

"Wouldn't miss it, but I'm warning you, Juliet had it wrong. Parting is *sorrowful* sorrow. I hope I can maintain decorum."

Jumbled emotions wrecked my sleep. A decision that had begun to congeal—to marry Terry—had dissolved under Jack's low-key, full-court press. He wasn't pushy at all, merely his wholesome, enthusiastic, loving, irresistible self.

Tuesday, July 21, 1964, Landshut. Early morning. Barely light. A rumbling rattled my room. Watery eyes. I knew that smell—diesel exhaust. I stumbled to the window. Across the parking lot, soldiers swarmed the BOQ like an invasion of ants, hauling boxes and duffel bags into belching trucks. The Sting Ray crawled up a ramp onto an auto transport. Soon, I would be left alone.

How to say goodbye? There wouldn't be a time or place for a proper farewell. But I had an idea—I could send part of myself, a lock of hair. The thought yanked me from the window. I penned several versions of my parting note before I lit on this:

> *My dearest Jack,*
>
> *Your departure leaves me less than whole, for you are taking part of my heart with you. I know you can't hold it in your hand when you think of me, so I'm sending this lock of hair that you can see, touch, even sniff (if you're so inclined—heh), to remind you of our extraordinary summer—and to hold us till Johnstown.*
>
> *No matter what happens, part of me will always belong to you. With my deepest love for all you have shared with me, and for the better person I have become by knowing you.*
>
> *Yours,*
>
> *Ann*

I snipped a curl, tied it with a few strands of hair, and, in case he really did sniff it, dabbed shampoo on the cut ends. I popped the note and curl into an envelope and sealed it.

Running late, I speed dressed into my best skirt, jacket, blouse, and hose, my dressy sandals, and the white gloves Mom had insisted I take. At the parade grounds, I linked up with two wives I had met, and we found a good roost as the military band struck up. The troops paraded in, the men singing, "Over hill, over dale, we have hit the dusty trail . . ." The chorus of male voices belting out "And The Army Goes Rolling Along" gave me goose bumps.

Everything I loved about army life flooded my mind, especially the camaraderie among the men, but also among their families. We army brats shared a special bond of independence that made us confident beyond our abilities and kept us grounded in the midst of the constant shuffle from post to post. Scenes from a dim past played in my head: young Annie romping like a wild child with her chums, exploring old battlements and climbing banyan trees in Hawaii; attending school on Governor's Island in the shadow of Manhattan; living inside a full-fledged, water-filled moat at Fort Monroe; and frolicking around Rome, Venice, and Verona with my pals.

I was proud to be part of that tradition and imagined myself embracing this familiar life. I'd be equally proud to introduce children into it.

The wives and I clapped as each company filed by. When F Company marched past, I got a lump in my throat. Jack and his troop outshone them all. Fact! Not a biased opinion. The lump almost burst when the men's voices softened for this stanza, the way they always did in my childhood memories:

> But if fate me should call, and in action I should fall,
> Keep those caissons a-rolling along.
> Then in peace, I'll abide, when I take my final ride,
> On a caisson that's rolling along.

By the time my attention returned to the current moment, the colonel was droning on that these men had acquitted themselves heroically. Kept the world safe for democracy. Remained ever alert in their lonely vigil on the border. On and on.

Afterward, I bobbed through the forest of green uniforms, searching for my own iconic figure. I saw him working his way toward me. Finally, we were face-to-face. "Splendid," I said. The ceremony? The parade? The music? Or this striking man before me? Well, all of it.

"You liked that stirring speech, eh?"

"Nah, too short." That made him laugh. "Actually, the commander of F Troop caught my eye. Did you see how he and his troop conducted themselves?"

"Must have missed it. Tell me about it."

I hooked my gloved hand through his elbow. "Sorry, you had to see it for yourself."

"Maybe next time."

"Maybe so." My thoughts turned anxious. "How long do we have?"

"Half an hour, max. My troop and I are ready. The only loose end left is you."

"Beware the loose end. She might lasso you and take you to her secret hideout."

"And have the whole army after us? Sounds exciting."

"Yeah, but they'd win, wouldn't they?" I pulled out the envelope with my lock and the note. "Why don't you take this to remember me by?"

"What's this? Okay to open it now?"

"Up to you. Immediate gratification or deferred?"

A spiffy soldier appeared, clicked his heels, and saluted. "Lieutenant Sigg, sir!"

"What is it, sergeant?"

"Everything is buttoned down, sir! We're moving out."

For an instant, Jack's eyes clouded. "Very good, sergeant. Be right there."

Jack slid the envelope into the inside breast pocket of his uniform. "I'll keep it close to my heart. Let it tantalize me until I get a private moment. See you in Johnstown?"

"Hope to survive that long," I said.

14
High-Stakes Gambling

Terry

Thursday night, 23 July 1964, Reno, Nevada. Mom and I deposited Pam and Randy in our hotel room and ventured into Harrah's Casino. My God. Banks of flashing lights, the seductive sound of bells and whistles, the scent of riches with every spin. We each bellied up to a slot machine with twenty dollars in coins and agreed that when the money ran out, we'd stop. If we didn't strike it rich first.

Before me, reel one in the whirling dervish display spun to a stop: 7. Reel two: 7 again! My pulse skipped a beat. One more and we would be set for life. Reel three spun, slowed, and crawled to a stop. Cherries. Damn! I inserted another nickel. This time, a lemon, another lemon, and . . . a melon. Around me, these bandits whistled and sang and spewed coins like candy tossed in a parade. But mine gobbled coins as if it hadn't eaten in a month.

What a cunning creature! When my stash got low, the vamp spit out a deluge of nickels. My riches grew to twenty-seven dollars. Then thirty-two. I started stuffing coins in as fast as I could. Beside me, Mom was feeding her machine just as feverishly. Minutes later, whir, thrump, bing-bing-bing! My pile dropped to sixteen dollars, and in a flash, my machine gulped every last nickel. It winked at Mom's machine. Poof! Her pile vanished in a melee of sounds and flashes.

Leaning back, Mom threw her hands up in surrender, but she was grinning like a ninny. "Your dad used to say gambling was a waste of good money. Don't tell the kids—or Reverend Wisehart—but that wasn't money wasted at all. It was great fun while it lasted."

We tromped up and down Virginia Street, lit up noonday bright with neon, and checked out other casinos—Horseshoe, Primadonna, Nugget, Cal Neva—and ended up back at Harrah's for the late-night adult show. A small-town gal, Mom was not a partier. A big night for her had been the monthly pinochle klatch she and Dad organized—four couples, best of friends, potluck, two beers max, gossip, tall tales, and cutthroat pinochle until midnight. She hadn't been out on the town, not even to dinner or a movie, since Dad was killed three years before.

Scrunching up to one of the tiny cabaret tables, we ordered Black Russians—"Wow, Terry, these are yummy!"—and settled in, front row. There I was, rubbing knees with my mother, as close as a hot date. The lights dimmed. Chatter died out. The orchestra roared to life. Out strutted the "girls" in high heels and skimpy, spangle-covered, skintight, low-slung half bikinis. And naked from head to hips! Not even sporting those tiny tasseled pasties I'd seen on Bourbon Street when a carload of us drove from CU to New Orleans one spring break. That steamy tease had nearly set me off, especially the girl who swung her tassels like tether balls in opposite directions simultaneously.

But this troupe bested New Orleans. The stage sparkled with topless beauties, bare breasts bouncing, nipples front and center. These girls danced. And pranced. And kicked their heels so high I got an embarrassingly close-up peek at that hidden wonderland. Their tight little bikinis veiled their privates, sure, but so snugly that no detail was left to the imagination. I was afraid to twitch for fear Mom would catch me letching and box my ears. It wasn't just the sex on display that blew me away, but also the dancers' enthusiasm, their energy, their athleticism. They were in better shape than I'd been when I wrestled in high school.

As we filed out into the street, I couldn't say a word to Mom or even look at her.

"Well," she said, once we had broken free of the crowd. "That was quite entertaining. Those girls are beautiful, aren't they? So graceful. Too bad we have to leave tomorrow."

Friday morning, not far out of Fallon, US 50 narrowed to a lonely track through an uninhabited land. Pam and Randy had zonked out before we made it through Fernley. Riding shotgun, Mom hung on for a half hour and then drifted off. Silence. A two-lane road. No traffic. No radio reception. No scenery. Thoughts of Annie laid siege to my mind.

Three weeks had dragged by since I had proposed. To be precise, twenty-four days. No answer. Not a letter. Not a card. Not a call. She had been back in Germany nearly a week—time enough to have read my every letter a hundred times.

The reason for her silence? Obviously, she had rejected me. She was serious about the lieutenant. I couldn't blame her. She knew every detail of my lurid past with women.

But it was more than my sexual history that doomed me. Annie had grown up Christian, in a family of Republicans. I had, too, before I'd turned left down a path that was anathema to Annie's mom and dad. No doubt she realized that life with a peacenik would be impossible for an army girl. I stewed over that truth for miles as the bleak desert rolled by.

How did I turn out so different from the rest of my family? No mystery there. It was the *Colorado Daily*, damn them! The *Daily* had brought Annie to me, but it had also radicalized me and sent her running. It had transformed me from the buzz-cut, churchgoing, Boy Scout, Boys State, DeMolay, straight-A teachers' pet I'd been at Center High School into a shaggy-haired, left-wing, confront-anyone-in-authority muckraker.

The *Colorado Daily* plunged me into national and international issues. We covered the campus news, but we defined ourselves as crusaders on the front lines of a nationwide student movement for social change. In the spring of my freshman year, I was promoted from volunteer reporter to wire editor, a paid position. My job? Select the best stories from our United Press International news service and produce a daily page to keep CU students abreast of world events.

We reported on the Cuban revolution as if it were on campus, our stories pro-Castro, pro–Che Guevara, indignant at the US economic blockade. We lionized Martin Luther King Jr.; celebrated the freedom riders, sit-ins, marches, and boycotts; decried police brutality and mob violence against civil rights demonstrators in Anniston, Montgomery, and Jackson. We at the *Daily* believed America was gasping its last breath.

Mom and my brothers and sister didn't know about those stories or the angst they caused me. All Mom knew was that I'd been managing editor at the university and that "something had gone wrong." *Terry, what an honor.*

We're so proud of you. That was Mom—she always managed to see a good side to everything. I glanced over at her. Even asleep she wore a faint smile.

That same semester at CU, the required Makers of Modern Journalism class introduced me to the pre–World War I writers who exposed the sordid underbelly of America. Lincoln Steffens's *Shame of the Cities* unmasked the slimy world of political corruption. In *McClure's Magazine*, Ray Stannard Baker dug into exploitation in the coal mine industry. And Upton Sinclair's *The Jungle* grabbed me by the collar and forced me to wallow in the stench of meat-packing sweatshops of Chicago. The American history I had learned at Center High had been sanitized, polished, and distorted, its blatant evils expunged.

In the School of Journalism reading room, a dingy hideout in the basement of Hellems Hall, one entire wall was taken up with shelves of magazines and newspapers from around the country. I discovered a raft of publications I'd never heard of: the *Nation*, *Saturday Review*, the *Atlantic*, *Harper's*, the *New Yorker*, the *New Republic*. The basement reading room, cold enough to require gloves, sweaters, and scarves in winter, was an Aladdin's cave of intellectual treasures.

At the Marshall house, our only magazines were *Reader's Digest, the Saturday Evening Post, Field & Stream, Ladies' Home Journal*, and *Boys' Life*.

And CU's giant Norlin Library seemed like El Dorado compared to Center's one-room thrift shop of a town library. What a thrill to prowl shelf after shelf, floor after floor, discovering one nugget after another. No more Hardy Boys and Zane Grey for me. When I stumbled onto Sinclair Lewis, I devoured all his books, especially *Elmer Gantry*: How could I ever walk into the Methodist church again without being disgusted by the hypocrisy of organized religion?

Then Thomas Wolfe. Couldn't get enough. He spoke directly to me in *You Can't Go Home Again*. Alone, through the night, Wolfe's George Webber would walk the streets of Brooklyn, his mind in turmoil, seeking to make sense of the world. For me, it was Boulder's streets—solitary walks from midnight to dawn. One night, propelled by Wolfe's prose, I, too, pounded in anguish at a brick wall until my knuckles bled. It brought only pain, not relief.

George and I shared the torment of trying to figure out who we were, the despair of loneliness, and, at the same time, the joy in living. And though I railed on about America's flaws, Wolfe articulated my own underlying faith in my country:

> I believe that we are lost here in America, but I believe we shall be found. And this belief, which mounts now to the catharsis of knowledge and conviction, is for me . . . not only our own hope, but America's everlasting, living dream.

As Mom and the kids slept, my mind floated free. The miles sped by. On days like this I could drive for hours without stopping, as I had done from Silverton to Boulder and later from Silverton to Salt Lake.

Now, Burma-Shave signs flew past: HARDLY A DRIVER / IS NOW ALIVE / WHO PASSED / ON HILLS / AT 75 / BURMA-SHAVE. Along the roadside, hills appeared, then trees and mountains. Inside the car, my mind served up a kaleidoscope of memories from CU.

It wasn't books alone that sent me off on a different track at the university. Or the *Daily*. Or my classes. It was life itself.

Faith in my country had been shattered late in my freshman year when the Soviet Union shot down the American U-2 spy plane. What? America had been spying on other nations? Our country had been lying to us and the rest of the world? Eisenhower was more than a president or war hero. He was a favorite uncle, wise, experienced, a proven leader, the antithesis of a wheeler-dealer politician. Mom and Dad had voted for Ike in '52 and '56. I still had my prized "I Like Ike" button. If I couldn't trust Ike, how could I trust any American politician?

A year later, we invaded Cuba. The Bay of Pigs. The CIA mucking around in another foreign land. More US skulduggery. More official lies.

And in the US itself, the ruthless backlash to the civil rights movement erupted across the country. At the start of my junior year, federal marshals had to escort James Meredith through angry mobs of whites so he could enroll at Ole Miss, the first black ever to do so. Night after night, nothing on the news but sit-ins, protest marches, boycotts; rioting mobs attacking blacks, burning cars; demonstrators beaten and dragged away. TV brought the brutality of discrimination into my sheltered life.

Considering I had grown up on a farm in the boondocks, maybe it shouldn't have been a surprise that the university totally changed my life.

Center had a two-block business district and a single traffic signal. For entertainment we had a pool hall on Main Street and a drive-in movie three miles out of town. No radicals. No socialists. No protests.

We didn't talk politics at dinner. Or debate issues of the day. Or sit around reading great literature. No child or spousal abuse in our home. No alcoholism. No drugs. Mom and Dad were respected and active in the community: the Methodist church, the Veterans of Foreign Wars, the American Legion, and the Masons and Eastern Star. In the summer we camped out and fished for trout. We were the Anderson family in *Father Knows Best*—parents nurturing carbon copies of themselves. Kids growing up in a Norman Rockwell painting.

We lived on a farm, but we weren't farmers. Dad had been busy building the Marshall Produce Company, begun by Grandpa Fred in the thirties, and he and Mom rented a farmhouse not far from his warehouses. Marshall Produce bought potatoes in bulk from farmers and shipped them to wholesalers that stocked grocery stores throughout the West.

Mom was a housewife raising four kids. Then a widow at forty-one. She didn't have time to ponder whether America was a racist, oppressive society. She had kids to support. After Dad was killed, the business transferred to his partner. Mom had to start from scratch and find a job—and she did, as a secretary at a local Department of Agriculture office.

Annie and I felt much the same way, but she was a gentle soul, not given to radical outbursts. Now, in the silence of a lonely day, speeding across Nevada toward the hinterlands of Utah, I realized I'd shot myself in the foot with my lust and politics.

No doubt, Annie had "come to her senses" in Europe. This image flashed through my mind: Annie and the Stud in his white Corvette, waving to the crowd, a "Just Married" banner and strings of tin cans trailing behind.

I finally faced the truth—Annie loved Lieutenant Sigg. All that was left for me was memories.

Saturday, 25 July 1964, en route to Center. Near Grand Junction, Colorado, the radio came back to life: the Top 20. We sang along, even Mom. "The Girl from Ipanema," "Everybody Loves Somebody," "The Little Old Lady from Pasadena," and on and on for miles.

We hit farmland and talked crops and reprised my high school trips to Grand Junction—our state semifinal football game in nearby Palisade my senior year, the DeMolay state conventions, the all-state band concerts I'd played in.

Late that afternoon, when I pulled into our gravel driveway, I swung too fast and wide, nearly skidding into the irrigation ditch, and crunched to a stop inches from the backyard gate. I leaped out and sprinted to the mailbox. It was packed so tight I had to pry everything out.

In the kitchen, I went through the mail like a pirate digging up his loot. Voilà! News from long-lost Annie—two letters and a postcard. I skimmed the card:

East Berlin, July 15, 1964—Contrary to popular belief, Miss Ann Garretson is still alive and kicking despite the fact she has not been heard from for over two weeks. Our Berlin correspondent spoke with her briefly this morning in front of the Pergamon Museum and she promised that one TM would have a letter within 3 days. This was all she was able to say as she was totally exhausted.

No signature. Not even her bold, sweeping initial *A.* Communist East Berlin? Wow! But that was ten days ago. Was she alone? Or with the Stud? No hint. At least she was the old *Colorado Daily* Annie, budding journalist with a fake news story. A good sign.

Upstairs in my room, I slit the letters open, the skinny one first—a single sheet with one hand-scrawled paragraph. Landshut, July 22. Only three days ago.

Ter, am on my way to Scandinavia for a week or so, then back here for a day or two and on to London. I have encountered nothing that can change my feelings for you, and I miss you more and more. I sent a letter to you in Los Gatos but doubt if you received it before you departed. It wasn't a very good letter because it didn't tell you how much I love you. I'll write again when I arrive.

I read it. And read it twice more. "I have encountered nothing that can change my feelings for you . . . It didn't tell you how much I love you." *Yes!*

The other letter, special delivery, had been sent to Los Gatos and for-warded to Center. Uh-oh, the one she warned me about. I slit the envelope open as delicately as if it were a bomb and a careless motion would trip a trigger and blow my life to pieces.

Two pages, dated July 20, Landshut. I flipped first to the end: "I love you, A." *Yes!* I skimmed through. "Jack has not, by the way, proposed." Thank God!

I read her letter line by line. She didn't list them, but it was clear that six letters from me had been waiting for her in Landshut. She wrote:

You speak of Silverton and I am transported there with you, doing all the great things you describe.

You must know I share wholeheartedly with you the desire to be together this year, and yet something catches inside me with the thought of marriage right away. Jack and I have had some very good times together, but we have also discovered more incompatibilities than you and I ever had because of a mutual stubbornness. Even so, Ter, I still cannot give you a definite answer right now.

I read the last line again and teared up. My mind went blank. When I returned to life after who knows how long, I refolded her letters, put them in their envelopes, and buried them under my T-shirts in the dresser. No cursing. No crying. No "woe is me, my life is over."

I clumped downstairs. I didn't have time for girls. I had work to do—check the chickens, feed the dog, carry in suitcases, put things away, help rustle up some dinner.

My attempt to blot out Annie's crushing rejection failed. By 8:30, ev-eryone had collapsed. Pam and Randy hadn't even turned on the TV, but merely trundled off to bed. By 8:50, I was at my typewriter. Calm. Rational. Intent on convincing Annie that she was wrong, that, as King had put it at the March on Washington, "Now is the time."

I didn't need to tell her I loved her. I'd written it over and over. She had too. "I love you," her latest letter declared. She wanted us "to be together this year." She loved Silverton as I did, recognizing that it represented a lifestyle that she, too, wanted. How could she possibly conclude "I still cannot give you a definite answer right now"?

A nightmare tormenting me for weeks caromed through my mind: Annie and the Stud leap from his Corvette and sprint into an opulent sultan's tent, flinging off their clothes as they run. Inside, she's naked. He's naked too—save for his sword, dangling from his red West Point waist sash. They sink into a palatial bed: silk sheets, rose petals, sultry music, flickering candlelight, incense wafting. Instantly, arms and legs entwined, they're one, more exultant than Rachael and I were in our wildest moments. Argh! I couldn't stand the thought.

I reread Annie's letters and card, scouring between the lines. The card had an odd smudge in the bottom corner, nearly obscured by her handwritten "MIT LUFTPOST": a green squiggle, so small I needed to read it with a magnifying glass—the one I bought when I was working on my Boy Scout Insect Study merit badge. Ha, not a doodle at all, but a declaration: "God, I miss you!"

Annie never said "God"! When talking about religion, yes, but never as an expletive. So what was this?

Dammit, don't lie to me, Annie! Do you want to be together or not?

I jumped up. Tiptoed downstairs. Plugged in the coffee pot. Devoured a bowl of Cheerios while the coffee brewed. And crept back upstairs to the typewriter.

Obviously Annie didn't fully realize how deeply intertwined our lives had become, how much I loved her, or how pressed we were for time. She needed to say yes. Posthaste, not in some nebulous future.

Peace Corps training would begin in Berkeley on August 14—two days *after* she would arrive back in the states. I'd leave for Caracas November 3. It boiled down to this:

I don't think I could go on for two years with the loneliness and frustration I've felt these fifty days. My life now is thoughts of you, of plans for this next year, of the many things we must do together. It's inconceivable that I leave for two years without your going with me. But if I do go to the training, I'll go with full determination to succeed and be sent to Venezuela; I can't do it any other way.

We needed to talk. But how? Last week she was in Berlin, then Landshut, and now, on her way to Scandinavia. Where in Scandinavia? I'd never track her down. "Call me collect. I'll be at home," I wrote. Waiting by the phone. I didn't tell her that.

I reread my letter. It was all doom and gloom. I needed to lighten it up and make her laugh. So I told her about Reno, about playing the slot machines, drinking Black Russians with Mom, trying to act like a cultured theatergoer but wincing at one raunchy joke after another, and going bug-eyed when the topless dancer flounced up to our table and squiggled in so close her nipples grazed my cheek. I'd been so flustered that I jerked back like I'd been jabbed with a cattle prod. I confessed that much to Annie. I didn't tell her I'd nearly creamed my jeans.

After four single-spaced pages, my eyes burned. I ended my letter with a request I figured would clinch the deal: "If you do decide to marry me, would you mind being the best man? You are my closest friend."

Ann

Sunday, July 26, 1964, Copenhagen. When I spilled out of the train station into the Copenhagen sunshine, the fragrance of bakery-fresh bread reeled me into a small café. Famished after my overnight ride, I ordered whole wheat, two slices, still warm, and slathered them with soft butter. The nutty taste sparked indelible memories of Mom timing her bread baking to coincide with our arrival home from school.

Two couples, one young, one old, at different tables, were rat-a-tatting in Danish. The older man acted out an animated story, interrupted frequently by the woman's wisecracks, which sent them into gales of laughter. I imagined Terry rolling out yet another goofy tale in fifty years—and me forever young in his presence. A sense of humor, yeah, that was a biggie. For life, and for love.

The younger couple were going at it as if he were Jack the Ripper, and she, judge, jury, and executioner. He turned his hands upward, eyes begging, and pleaded a soft defense. His murmur provoked vituperation. Could that be me, with either Terry or Jack? No. Neither had ever done anything to anger me so. I felt for the guy. And the girl. But I had my own challenges to confront. In love with *two* guys? Did I love them equally?

How do you measure love? In drops, like honey? In bunches, like flowers? Either way, Terry nearly won me over when he wrote that he wanted me "as a lover, as well as a friend, to share the millions of small things, the great emotions, and frustrations, and also the beautiful physical love that comes from your sensitivity, your awareness." But Jack prompted the same response when he said, "My love for you has exceeded what I felt was safe. I'm finding no limit to the pool." I'd have to forgo a lifetime with one guy or the other. How could I bear it?

Maybe love had different grades, depending on its "impurities." Did true love even have impurities? Or was true love the fodder of romance novels? Dad had told me—after he and Mom suggested I was too critical of former boyfriend Geoff—"You can't always change them, but oftentimes some accommodation is in order."

What accommodations would I have to make with Terry? Or Jack? A few came to mind, like restraining impetuous outbursts—from both men. I cringed as I thought about Terry's "I hate America" letter—and equally about Jack's fury at having to work "with swine" when the major tried to dance with me. Hotheads, the two of them!

And what about my own flaws? Either one would have to deal with my Pollyanna tendencies, which I constantly struggled to rein in.

Scarier yet, how would I survive as a conscientious objector's wife who might have to visit her spouse in jail—or as an army officer's wife who had to put a lid on her beliefs about peace over war?

Tearing myself from the bakery, I strolled Copenhagen's freshly swept streets.

But the pesky questions persisted. Could we judge the quality of love by its origins, like we do with "clover honey"? Would love be more lasting if a guy came from a cohesive family? Terry's parents were happily married until his dad was killed. After months in the hospital, Terry's mom recovered from compound broken legs and ribs, got a job for the first time in twenty years, and was raising Terry's three younger siblings in junior and senior high school. Single-handedly. How resilient. How powerful. I liked her and his siblings. They all had a quick wit that bound them together.

I hadn't met Jack's parents, but he had confided in them when he hatched the scheme for Gretchen's trip to America. Before she decided to go to Denver, they were willing to take her in without judgment. How generous. Presumably, both Terry and Jack had learned the give-and-take of love from parents who had married for life. That was essential.

Pausing by the Nyhavn Canal, I latched on to this truth: Marriage was about more than love. My husband had to see me as an equal. Both Jack and Terry stood tall on that score. Jack *expected* me to get my degree. How gratifying that he asked to read my college term papers—so he could learn from me. During our travels, we had fantasized about pursuing advanced degrees and even serving in the Foreign Service—together.

And Terry had always treated me as an equal at the *Daily*. Sure, he edited my work mercilessly. But he demanded the same critical eye from me toward his work. In those last fraught weeks before I left Boulder, we had shared dreams of teaching, joining the Peace Corps, and maybe someday owning a small-town newspaper—all of it together. And on life's challenges, he had always sought my advice, probably more than he now wished.

I checked my map and headed for my chosen dollar-a-day hostel. Ah, yes, frugality. That was another gauge. If anything, both Terry and Jack were more tightfisted than I was. Terry reached the nadir when he lived in the dismal furnace room of that apartment house in Boulder. As for Jack, I still snickered, recalling a rambling audio letter when he finally said, "Well, I guess you can tell I've run out of news, but I hate to waste the rest of this tape."

After four years, I really did know Terry. We got along perfectly. I loved his sense of humor, and I loved being with him. And Jack? Even before we fell in love, he and I explored our values—and our flaws—through our letters and found our values to be in sync. Flaws? How could you objectively discuss your own flaws with the person you hoped would love you forever? Really, I had to spend the summer with him. And guess what. Big picture, we *were* compatible!

In a clatter of high heels, two women strode past, trailing cigarette smoke that assaulted my eyes and nose. Ah, yes, another important detail. Luckily, neither guy smoked.

Darn, I'd lost my thought. Ah, flaws . . . Jack's flaws. His PDA rigidity had set me off. But that wasn't the man speaking; it was the army.

Maybe love worked like electricity. The real thing excited a palpable buzz, like that night in the doughnut shop when Terry and I touched fingers. That same electricity set my soul afire when Jack smoothed on the salve after I toasted myself in Saint-Tropez.

I loved both men and for many of the same reasons. That was the di-

lemma. It was too much to contemplate. I shoved both guys aside and zeroed in on my hostel.

At the hostel registration, a lanky blonde in the check-in line towered a
full head above me. "You are from America?"

"How'd you know?"

She pointed at my overnight case. "So big."

It was a monster compared to her tiny backpack. I felt like a klutz.
"Long trip. All . . . all summer," I stammered.

"Yes, and a long distance, much farther than Sweden," she said.

She chose the bunk next to mine, and we settled in like new college
roommates. With no fixed itinerary other than a party in Germany, Agneta peppered me with questions. "You are a student? Going where? Where
have you been?"

An instant travel buddy, she proved to be the perfect guide. First stop:
the famous amusement park, Tivoli Gardens. "Over here!" she hollered,
motioning me to the wooden roller coaster, charmingly built into a rocky-
looking mountain. I hung on for life as we whooshed across the park. From
there, we staggered to the Ferris wheel, and I calmed my stomach as we
floated above Copenhagen. We explored every corner till I dropped, and
she revived me by introducing her favorite Danish treats in the food hall.

Monday night I squeezed out time to scrawl the long-delayed letter to
Terry, telling him that the joy of travel had been diminished by his absence.
More importantly, I confessed:

When I returned from Berlin, I thought I wanted to marry you.
Then in the last days before Jack left, my feelings toward him did an
about-face. Now my emotions are a jumble. I know I shall never love
you any less, but Jack has made me reassess my feelings toward him.

Terry would be distraught with this news, but I had to be honest. Ironically, as I scribbled out the letter, my feelings turned another somersault. I
added, "I am so eager to see you I can hardly contain myself." Still, I wrote,
I couldn't make a decision before I saw him again.

The next day, Agneta and I took the fourteen-cent ride out to see the

Little Mermaid statue. We cavorted in the sea at the foot of the famed bronze perched on a boulder in the water a few feet offshore. On our last night in Copenhagen, Agneta and I clambered up the ancient tower Rundetaarn for a breathtaking view of the city. Agneta's raison d'être was to "enjoy." No serious talks. No hand-wringing about boyfriends.

As we prepared to leave Copenhagen, Agneta invited me to go with her to her party that night—in Gladbeck, Germany. She planned to hitch-hike. I imagined endless hours of cars whizzing past . . . *Someone finally screeches to a stop. Two friendly guys. We jump in. We're off. Their smiles turn to leers. The car swerves onto a dirt road. They brandish stilettos. Okay, girls, off with the clothes.* "Is it safe?"

"Of course, if you know how. I do it all the time."

Hitchhike? Never. My cautious self puffed up like a bullfrog with mumps. *Don't you dare. Insanely dangerous!*

"Come with me," she said. "I leave this morning."

Thinking of the money I'd save, I blurted, "Why not? Let's go."

Sporting bright aqua culottes and a matching blouse, I stood as tall as I could beside Agneta, waving my arm like I was washing a seven-foot-high window—the European way to thumb a ride. I felt foolish, but Agneta insisted. "Yes, yes, like that. Always smiling. You have to smile."

We had a ride within minutes, a neatly dressed businessman, mid-forties. Agneta took the front seat and chatted with him in Danish. After he dropped us off near Hamburg, our next ride was a couple of young Germans headed for Düsseldorf, and Agneta immediately switched to German. We cruised into Gladbeck in under four hours.

The party, hosted by someone Agneta had met on an earlier adventure, was as warm as a class reunion. Germans mostly, all our age, and fluent in English, though they lapsed into German often enough to make me wish for Jack. We ate brats and sipped beer (no one commented when I dodged the beer)—a gathering of worldly friends exchanging ideas, not a frat bash where booze was the ticket to sex. We stayed the night, Agneta beside me in our sleeping sacks amid several new friends on the floor of an extra room.

The following morning, Agneta headed east to Berlin. Me? South to Landshut—on my own. Before we parted, Agneta laid out her rules: "Look your ride over before you get in. If anything seems suspicious, wave them on. Never hitchhike at night. Never hitchhike in France, Spain, or Italy. Those men are perverts." That ruled out the three non-English languages I could navigate in. Was I supposed to ask for their passports?

On the opposite side of the road, Agneta smiled and waved as her ride whisked her away.

On my side, an Opel stopped. Two men. With a cheery smile, I asked, "Landshut?"

They looked at me, puzzled, and then splattered me with German. Good. They passed Agneta's third test. "München?" They *had* to know Munich.

"München! *Ja, ja.*" The passenger opened the back door, motioning me in.

I took a deep breath and we were off. I pulled out my Berlitz dictionary: "*Mein* . . . name . . . Ann . . . *Ich* . . . *gehen* . . . Landshut."

The passenger snatched up my dictionary. "We . . . brothers. We . . . go . . . Nuremberg."

I checked my map. That would get me three-quarters of the way home. Excellent.

"We . . . holiday . . . wives . . . stay . . . home." Uh-oh. "We . . . own meat shop."

Butchers? Before I could worry about being hacked to mincemeat, they were entertaining me with their newest purchase: spray deodorant, something they had clearly never seen. Passenger brother squirted the driver under his arms, behind his ears, on his crotch. Then he reached over the seat, lifted my arm, zapped me, and cackled wildly.

They shared their lunch with me on the road—cheese and some sausage-like lunch meat on bread. I got them back on track after a wrong turn at Frankfurt (they were clueless about maps). "*Nein, nein,*" I said. I thumbed my dictionary for "wrong way" and "turn around." We wasted ten minutes on that mistake. Finally, "*links, links*"—left, left—guided us to the autobahn.

The next six hours were mine alone. Not Jack's. Not a time I wished for Terry. I managed a huge challenge by myself—as I had done in Munich, Lausanne, and Berlin. I had a memorable adventure at the same time. I was discovering the real me, the girl who was her own person. I could make it on my own.

As I waved goodbye to my new German friends, I asked myself, Why get married at all?

⟶

Saturday, August 1, 1964, en route to Munich. I was on the road again after a day in Landshut. This time the charmer behind the wheel, my brother Bonner, was careening toward Munich, extolling the night ahead: "Hofbräuhaus is Munich's most famous beer hall. You'll love it, Sis. It's the perfect place to meet local women. Or in your case, men."

The nerve. Was he trying to undermine his best friend by introducing me to other men? Was this how he betrayed Gretchen? Somebody needed to set him straight about the pain he caused every time he broke a girl's heart. But what to say? *Oh, by the way, Bonner, this charming girl looked me up in Colorado. Turns out she was carrying your child, and she's still madly in love with you.* No, it couldn't be me, not his little sister. Besides, I promised Jack and Gretchen I would keep their secret. Jack had to tell him. Or Gretchen herself.

Our dirndl-clad *Fräulein* at Hofbräuhaus fit my mental picture of a German beer-hall girl: stout as a fireplug, with a ruffled apron dress cradling plenty of cleavage and brown corkscrew curls bouncing with every step. I didn't notice her football-tackle-size hands and arms until she plopped five one-liter steins of beer on our table. *Five.* Delivered with one hand. She had five more in the other.

Bonner's eyes twinkled. "Don't you love it?" His manner was so infectious, I almost did. But I'd never consumed a whole glass of beer at one sitting in my life, let alone a gargantuan stein. I had ventured into Tulagi in Boulder once my freshman year. The waiter had served a pitcher the size of that stein for our gang of four. I'd choked at one measly glass.

Bonner had done his best to initiate me into the world of alcohol. "Men notice a woman who drinks Scotch," he advised. First, Scotch sours—the sugar and lemon cloaked the nasty taste of the whiskey. Then Black Russians—sweet and warm to the insides. Beer? He'd skipped that lesson. On August 1, 1964, he set out to fix that oversight. I took a sip. Yech, as bitter as it was at Tulagi!

"No, Sis, you don't *sip* beer." He guzzled half a liter. Slurped the foam off his lips. I took a swallow and did my best not to gag. Smiled gamely. Thumbs-up from my brother.

The drinking hall was as long as a football field. Revelers cozied together at communal tables running the length of the room. The arrangement yielded instant new friends to our left, to our right, and across the table. Soon they were pounding the table rhythmically, singing along with the oompah band on the stage. A few more swallows and the alcohol anesthetized my taste buds. The German to my right—I never got his name—denounced "the overbearing American occupation of Deutschland."

"Oh really?" I said. "I thought our countries were working together to protect Germany from the Communists."

He launched into a diatribe on American bases in Munich, Heidelberg, Frankfurt, and too many other German cities—and the "thousands of GI's chasing our women." Fueled by beer and testosterone, he touched my arm to make each point and let his hand linger. His earnest charm waylaid common sense. The atmosphere worked its spell, and I finished the whole liter. Seconds later, five more steins clanked onto the table.

At my left, Bonner had engaged a gorgeous Italian in a hand-slapping game I had seen so many times. He held his palms upward, and she rested her hands, palms down, on his. Like lightning, he swatted the back of her hand before she could pull it away. His eyes capturing hers, he stroked her hands and offered his hands for round two.

I turned away. My drinking partner leaned closer and asked, "Have you seen US military bases in Germany?" (Of course I had). And "What do you think of the US presence in Germany?"

"The no-man's-land on the border seems to show how our countries are cooperating on shared goals," I said. "What do *you* think?"

With a sheepish smile, he said, "Well, yes, yes. Maybe I over-speak myself. Here's to you, *Fräulein*." He clinked my stein, and I sipped yet more beer. In fact, the beer had made me effusive. I egged him on.

Meanwhile, every half hour, the lederhosen-decked-out band marched through the room, blasting our eardrums with horns and accordions. Oh my goodness, my brother was marching backward in front of them as if he were the director. I took another slug from the second liter.

The room grew fuzzy. Bonner came into focus beside me, shouting, "Time to go! Now!" My second stein was empty. Mr. Politics urged me to stay. He'd show me "the hidden Munich." We'd get to know each other as fellow human beings, not Germans and Americans. He'd deliver me home, all the way to Landshut. I looked to Bonner for guidance. He shrugged. Gosh, Mr. Politics was engaging! Oops, he remembered, he didn't have a car. That settled it. I left with my brother.

My only memory of the drive home was flashing blue lights—a German police car. Bonner swore, words I'd never heard him use. "Calm down, Bonner. You don't want a ticket."

When the cop walked up, my brother turned on the charm, flashed his magnetic smile, said something (pleasantly) in German, and crawled out of the car. Meanwhile, I stumbled into the woods and hunkered down to pee. By the time I got back, Bonner and the cop were leaning against the car, chatting like best buddies.

"Wow, so what happened?" I asked when he pulled out into traffic.

"Oh, it started out badly. He said he had been following me for 'kilometers.' And I was driving all over the road." He shifted gears, pausing for effect. "But once I showed him my military ID, we clicked heels together and exchanged war stories. The best part?" He grinned. "No ticket."

"Your German was impressive."

"I've managed to learn just enough to keep me from falling into the abyss."

At the teachers' apartment, common sense took over—despite the careening room bent on dumping me out of bed. I'd read that the human body took one hour to process an ounce of alcohol. I had downed two liters. Half a gallon. Thirty-two hours of misery ahead? No way. I staggered to the bathroom, knelt over the toilet, stuck my finger down my throat, and rid myself of the stinking beer.

I had behaved badly. I had given Mr. Politics the idea I was "open for business," despite the fact I bristled each time he trashed my country. Would I really have gone with him if he'd had a car? He didn't plan to take me straight home, no question. Surely I wouldn't have, but where was my cautious self when I needed her?

Only one evening out with Bonner and I'd lost my inhibitions. Appalling. Would I behave that way the next time I was in a drinking crowd?

⸺

Terry

3 August 1964, Center, Colorado. Monday again. Ten more days ahead, trying to find things to do to keep me sane while I waited for that letter from Annie—or a trip to Berkeley.

No more chores left. Last week I mowed the lawn twice, spent two mornings pulling weeds overgrowing the ditch bank, and mucked out the chicken coop. I even reshingled the little outbuilding we used as a chick brooder. Put in time with the boys, shooting hoops, chasing baseballs, and supervising them as they murdered beer cans with my .22. But mostly I read: *The King Must Die, The Agony and the Ecstasy,* and Michener's *Hawaii.*

After breakfast, I retreated to my bedroom and started *Nobody Knows My Name,* but I couldn't concentrate. My calendar kept glaring at me. Only ten more days!

But ten days until what?

Until I got a yes from Annie? A letter that declared *I love you—of course I do. And, yes, I want more than anything to marry you. Go buy a ring. Find a preacher and have him at the plane when I get there.* We'd marry. We'd move to Arizona. In a month, she'd begin teaching at Glendale High. I'd find a newspaper job and we'd begin the good life.

Or ten days until I plunged into a ten-week Peace Corps boot camp in California? I'd study Spanish six hours a day. Learn Venezuelan history and culture. Master the principles of urban community development. Undergo a physical regimen that would make my high school football practices seem like a romp in a meadow. Then I'd leave the States on November 3 to spend two years in the slums of Caracas.

The plane ticket the Peace Corps sent had me leaving Denver at ten in the morning on Friday, August 14. Mom would drive me to Denver, but we'd have to go up the day before to get there in time. Annie planned to leave Europe for New York on Wednesday, August 12—at best, we'd have a chance for a quick "hi, howdy" over the phone, but she hadn't told me her flight times. I wrote to her mom last week and got a note back on Saturday. She didn't know exactly when Annie would fly into Albuquerque, only that she had mentioned "making a short side trip in the East before returning home."

A "short side trip"? To where? And why? It didn't matter. No way could she get to Denver before I left. If I used that plane ticket, I couldn't see her before I left for Berkeley. If I sent the ticket back, I'd forfeit my last chance at the Peace Corps.

I started to write her a quick note, make one last plea. I got as far as "Dear Annie" when I realized she'd never get the letter—she was on her way to London, and I didn't have her address.

I knew at that moment I was willing to give up the Peace Corps for her. Until that point, I'd been unable to articulate the possibility. I *could* send the ticket back.

My logic and my dreams compelled me to go to Berkeley.

My gut told me I couldn't leave without Annie.

The week before, I had written her three letters, each expanding on my conundrum. In each, I spun a new twist on the same argument. They were logical, eloquent, and persuasive.

Our love is so strong, I know we'll survive. Take as much time as you need. If you can't see your way to marry me next month, we can marry when I come back.

Ten days from Berkeley, I finally admitted to myself that my optimism had been bullshit. If I went to Venezuela, I'd lose her—if I hadn't already. But if I didn't go, she could come home, shake my hand, and say, "Sorry, old buddy, I'm engaged to Jack." I could lose both her and the Peace Corps. I was stuck. I wanted to marry them both. And next week. An impossible dream.

Back at my typewriter, I explained my dilemma to the Peace Corps. It was a gamble. I had to warn them I might not show up in Berkeley and at the same time let them know I was still devoted to the Peace Corps.

I addressed my letter to Mr. Clennie H. Murphy, Classification Officer, Division of Selection, Peace Corps, Washington, DC. I'd never talked to him. He was a name at the bottom of a form letter. I could see him in my mind's eye—a bleary-eyed bureaucrat with three-day stubble who had the power to make me a Peace Corps volunteer. Or crush my dream.

Clennie Murphy reads my letter. He frowns. He goes to his filing cabinet and digs out my first invitation to Colombia. "This guy's fucked up," he says. "He doesn't know what he wants." He has two rubber stamps on his desk:

ACCEPT and REJECT. He picks up one. Bam! REJECT. He staples my letter to a copy of my invitation to Venezuela, signed by Sergeant Shriver himself. He swivels around, stuffs my whole file into a black filing cabinet that doesn't even merit a label. "Shit, I've got a week to find a replacement," he says. He grabs a handful of applications off a foot-high pile in his inbox, opens the first one, spreads it out, and smiles. "No sweat. This guy from Philly will be a lot better anyway."

Yeah, that could be the outcome, but I owed them a heads-up.

I finished my letter, edited it, retyped it, and got it to the mailbox as Mr. Carter pulled away from Coffman's farmhouse a quarter of a mile down the road. I waited and handed it to him personally, hoping he would reward me with a thunderous *YES!* from Annie.

He didn't.

15
Last Act in London

Terry

Wednesday, 5 August 1964, Center. Two days later, I was leaning on a shovel at the ditch bank, pretending to irrigate the spuds, when Mr. Carter slid to a stop at our mailbox. He rooted among the letters in the passenger seat, pulled together a bundle, and handed it through the window. "Sorry, son—bills and a newspaper. Nary a peep from Europe."

I tapped my hat brim. No words needed. He pulled away, stopped, and stuck his head out. "Don't need to guard that beat-up old mailbox, son. No one's gonna steal it." He roared off.

Eleven days since I got Annie's postcard and letters. Nothing since. Zilch. In eight days I'd fly to Berkeley. I wanted to call and get a definite yes or no, but I had no idea where she was.

I had replayed my options a thousand times. It was simple. If she said yes, I'd cancel Berkeley, marry her, and move to Arizona. If she said no, I'd bid a teary farewell and take off for Venezuela. But I had no option for protracted silence.

After lunch, I tried to read. I couldn't focus. Plus, the boys were at me like horseflies: "Take us to town. Take us swimming. Take us, take us . . ." Mom said I was acting gooney. "Why don't you help out at the *Post-Dispatch* until you leave?" she said. "They'd love to have you."

I had worked there two summers before. Now, though, my mind had flown Center for good. The town council and school board, with their endless bickering over minutiae, were irrelevant, as were the Jaycees, the VFW, the annual PEO flower show, and projections for this fall's potato crop.

But Mom was right. I couldn't spend the next eight days draped over the mailbox. "I'll think about it," I told her.

What I was really thinking about was Annie. No letters was a bad sign. On the other hand, she was in Europe. She'd be up at five, racing until midnight. That was Annie: always trying to do more than humanly possible, always behind. She didn't have a minute to sit, let alone write.

Finally, I was clearheaded. She was going to say yes, I felt it. I didn't have time to help the *Post-Dispatch* or sit around and mope. If I wanted to marry the girl, I had to get a job—in Arizona—so I could be close to her. I slammed my book shut. Ten minutes later, I was doing sixty-five on graveled County Line Road, bound for Alamosa.

At the college library, I dug into *Ayer's Directory of Newspapers and Periodicals*, the catalog of every newspaper in America. It listed two weeklies in Glendale—the *Herald* and the *News*. I'd write to them both, as well as to the nine other papers in the Phoenix area. Annie expected a husband with a future. I wouldn't disappoint. I'd get a job *before* she got home. I copied the names and addresses and on the way home sketched out an application letter in my head.

By late Thursday morning, I had typed all eleven letters, each error-free, each with an individually typed copy of my resume. I was slouched against the mailbox when the familiar grimy Dodge Dart showed up at six minutes before noon. "Sorry, son, no mail for—"

"Morning, Mr. Carter. You can save me a trip to town. Would you mind?" I handed him the bundle of letters. Not even reading the envelopes, he reached over the seat and dropped them into his box of outgoing letters. "I'm hopin' you'll have better luck tomorrow," he said.

Ann

Wednesday–Sunday, August 5–9, 1964, London. I was back in the English-speaking world where I could understand and be understood. Sort of. In the airport, I had asked another passenger the time. His four-syllable answer: "Ba ha pah eh."

I stared at him: "Huh?"

"Ba ha pah eh."

I mouthed each sound, rolling them around my tongue. At last I got it—"about half past eight"—though I wasn't sure until I saw the huge wall clock across the corridor. I made my way to the London Underground station—the Tube—and got off at Sussex Gardens, where I found my hotel. Thank goodness the signs were in English!

Yet in some ways this country was more foreign than Germany or France. Though everything seemed familiar, some things were life-and-death different. Like crossing the street. When I got off the Tube, I spied my hotel across the road. I looked left. A break in the traffic, so I stepped out. A horn blared. Brakes squealed. I whipped my head around. A Jaguar was barreling toward me on the wrong side of the road. He swerved, roared past, and shouted, "Watch where ye' goin', Yank!" *Yank?* How'd he know? After that, I came to a dead standstill at every crossing, reminding myself the Brits drive on the wrong side of the road.

But I embraced the quirky accents and traffic and soon was navigating the super-clean, super-streamlined Tube and bright red double-decker buses. The price for my small hotel included "porridge" for breakfast—better than paste, though not much. Midday, I picked up fish and chips for lunch—on par with fish-on-Fridays in the grade-school lunchroom, but the "chips" turned out to be chunky fried potatoes. Not bad.

A frenzy of sightseeing took me to Buckingham Square, Westminster Abbey, Big Ben, the Tower of London, and Hampton Court, all with my mind transported to my coming persona, Miss Garretson, English teacher. *This month we're studying Shakespeare, kiddos. Come with me. Imagine you're wearing your Sunday go-to-church duds. We sweep into the grand Aldwych Theatre like princes and princesses. We're right there, front row, when Lady Macbeth wails, "Out, damned spot! Out, I say!" She can't erase what she's done. We feel and see her pain.*

I did see a Shakespeare play at the Aldwych, but it was *Merchant of Venice*, not *Macbeth*. Instantly, I was in Venice again—with Jack, my hand in the crook of his elbow.

At Hyde Park, the main attraction was a plaza where anyone with an opinion was free to hold forth. People brought actual soapboxes, jumped on top, and raged about religion, politics, and the price of liver. I moseyed from one public rant to the next. They shouted at hecklers, and hecklers screeched back. For all our talk about free speech in the United States, I couldn't imagine Americans opening themselves to public potshots that way. Something else to share with my students.

The torture display at the Tower of London left me queasy. Religious dissidents had been hung from manacles, stretched on the rack, and crunched like walnuts. I squirmed equally on the Tower Green, where Anne Boleyn, queen of England, had been beheaded. Horrifying. I kept moving, faster, faster to escape the grisly specters.

Actually, the real reason I was running like a mad woman was avoidance. I knew I should call Terry, but I couldn't say the one word he wanted to hear.

Terry

10 August 1964, 5:58 a.m., Monday, *Center*. I was in dreamland, and somewhere in the fog, the damn phone was ringing off the hook. Then clomp, clomp, louder and louder, footsteps tromping up the stairs into my brain.

"Terry, Terry. It's for you. *Long distance*," Mom hollered. "*Overseas!*"

I stumbled downstairs. "Hello, hello?"

"I have a reverse-charges call for Terry Marshall from"—the woman on the phone had the same stuffy British accent the queen had, and it was six o'clock in the morning, for crying out loud—"Ann Garretson. Will you accept the charges?"

"Annie? Is that you?"

"This is a collect call, sir. Will you accept the charges?"

Her again, the Brit. "Collect?"

"Yes, sir. Will you accept—"

"Sure. Yes. Of course. Put her on. Annie?"

"Hi, guy. How are you?"

"Annie? Can you hear me? I—damn, it's good to hear your voice. Where are you?"

"Yes, but you have to speak up, Ter."

"It's good to hear your voice. Where are you?" The phone line echoed my every word, as if I were in a wind tunnel and the words were blowing back into my face. I was shouting over my own voice. Mom and the kids were staring at me like witnesses to the Hindenburg. I backed into Mom's bedroom, stretching the phone cord to its limit.

"London, and I've—"

"Can you hear me, I—"

"I'm in London, I—"

Our voices lagged behind our thoughts. Her voice came, and I interrupted her, waited, tried again, interrupted her again, then got stuck in an awkward silence. "When are you—"

"Yes, I can hear you. I'm leaving . . ."

Finally, I figured it out. I had to wait for my words to reach the other end of the line—after all, it was five thousand miles—and for her to respond and for her words to make it all the way back.

"I'm fine," she said. "Lonely. Dying to see you."

Exactly what I needed to hear! "Me too. You're in London already?"

Yes, and she'd seen *Merchant of Venice*, one of our favorites, and by the Royal Shakespeare Company. It was neither the Globe Theatre nor Stratford-upon-Avon, but she had been there too, and the play was "wonderful, so British. You would have loved it. And this fabulous bookstore—Foyles—just marvelous and huge and oozing so much history I expected to run into Dickens or Percy Bysshe Shelley around every corner, and . . ."

Take a breath, Annie, take a breath.

But she didn't. She told me she'd hiked across the London Bridge and witnessed the changing of guards at Buckingham Palace and rubbed elbows with the rich at Harrods and the British Museum, and . . . "I'm dog tired. I can't walk another step."

I wanted to tell her how much I loved her, that I could hardly wait to see her, but the boys were leering in, bouncing past, popping into sight again. Mom shouted, "Boys! Git!" Footsteps thumped into the kitchen. The boys tittered and raced past again. I could barely make out what Annie was saying. I couldn't hold off any longer. I had to ask her, despite all the nosey little ears: "About my letter. My proposal. Will you? I've got to know."

A sigh. Silence.

"You still there?"

"I don't know, Ter, I don't know yet. I—"

"But you love me, that's what you said."

"I do, I do, but . . . well, it's complicated."

"I've got to leave for Berkeley Thursday. That's three days. I've got to know, I—"

"I need time. I can't decide here, like this. I need to spend time with you. Am I still welcome in Center? Could I come?"

"Why don't you move in? I'll show you how welcome you are."

"Terrrrryyy!"

"Just kidding. You are, you know. But when? Your mom said you were going to spend some time on the East Coast."

"I leave for New York on Wednesday. A couple of days there. By the weekend."

"No, that's too late. I'll be in Berkeley on Friday." Silence again. "You still there?"

"I can't make it before the weekend, Ter. I really can't. I promised Jack's mom in May I'd visit them in Johnstown on the way back. I told you. Remember? I've got a ticket to Denver Saturday, then on to Albuquerque on Sunday. I could change it and fly to Alamosa Sunday. That's the earliest. Can you call the Peace Corps and go late? Next week sometime?"

Go late? Tell the Peace Corps I'd waltz in next week? Jesus! "I—damn! I guess, but—"

"You'll work it out. I know you can. I'll call from Denver. I will. I have to see you. I love you, you know. I've really missed you. I'm missing you right now."

"I . . ." My voice tightened up. I couldn't breathe. She did that to me: She said *I love you* and my mind went to mush. God, what a relief to hear her voice. "I love you too," I croaked. I did love her. I simply wasn't good at saying it, not out loud. With witnesses.

"I've got to run. I'm on my way to the airport. I'll call. I love you. Bye."

"Bye," I said. "I love you, I miss you, I—"

The phone clicked. She had hung up.

I must have hung up the phone, but all I could remember was standing in the hallway like a dunce. Four sets of eyes peered at me from the kitchen doorway.

"What'd she say? What'd she say?" Greg said. Or Randy—they were both jabbering.

"She wants to come to Center as soon as she gets back. That's it. Let's eat."

"Come on, you were on the phone for twenty minutes," Pam said. "And long distance. From *Europe*. Collect! Boy, that's going to cost us."

"Well?" Mom said.

"She's fine. Having a great time. She's in London and dying to come see you guys 'cause you're so cute, all of you—and me, if I'm still here. That's it."

"Nuh-uh!" one of the boys said. "I bet she said 'I love you, sweetie puss' or something yucky like that."

"Kissy kissy," the other said, smacking his lips.

"All right, knock it off, you two," Mom said.

"Would you mind making waffles this morning?" I asked Mom, hoping that would quiet the peanut gallery.

"It's not Sunday," Randy said.

Greg pointed to the wall calendar. "Yeah, see. It's Monday."

We made it through breakfast, despite their objections that we never had waffles on Monday. In fact, the boys scarfed down more than their normal fare—as Pam duly pointed out.

By seven-thirty, the boys had used up their supply of banter on Annie's call and took off to hunt rabbits. Mom left for work. Starting time was at eight, but she made it a point to be at least fifteen minutes early every morning. Pam did the dishes and then turned on the vacuum cleaner in the living room—she'd taken over housecleaning when Mom went to work full time. I closeted myself in my bedroom to record as much of our call as I could remember. "I don't know. I need more time," she'd said, but her tone was upbeat. She did love me. Said it straight out. She wanted to marry me, but she couldn't get the words out.

And if she'd told me about visiting Jack's parents, I'd forgotten. Damn. I needed a secluded spot to figure out what to do. I grabbed my reporter's notebook and hiked off for the haystack in the southwest forty.

An hour later, I ended up two miles from home at the abandoned cattle-loading chutes behind Marshall Produce. In high school, the cattle chutes had been my Walden Pond. And my lovers' lane. Beyond an old shack that marked the end of the property, a one-lane rut of a road snaked through a thicket of tall bushes roughly paralleling the railroad tracks. I'd parked there many a night with Angela Archuleta after ball games and school dances. The bushes swallowed up my old red '48 Ford as if it were a Tonka toy. At night, lights off, we were invisible.

While my mind whirled, I hiked the tracks a bit, tossed rocks at a beat-up old beer can, and herded a few make-believe calves into the loading chute before I settled into a tiny pocket in the bushes to think. In this Brer Rabbit thicket, I could focus. Despite what she said, maybe Annie was going to Johnstown to plan their wedding. Maybe I'd already lost her.

Nearby, a meadowlark gave me hope with its cheery greeting, *chupp-chupp, wheedle-e*. I responded. She sang for me and fell silent. I never did see her. For a while, a magpie perched on a fence post and scolded me for invading his territory—no sympathy from him. A jackrabbit appeared in the rutted roadway, stared, then bounded into the weeds. None of the other thicket dwellers cared about my dilemma—not the busy ants, the stink bug, or the grasshoppers. Or maybe they did, maybe their mere presence helped me realize what I had to do.

I trudged home too late for lunch, made a cheese sandwich, went upstairs, and typed a short letter—a telegram actually—drove to the Western Union office in Monte Vista, and sent a missive to Mr. Clennie H. Murphy Jr., Division of Selection, Peace Corps, Washington, DC:

10 August 1964. Re: my letter of 3 August. Am turning down invitation to Venezuelan project. Will not report 14 August for training in Berkeley. Airline tickets being mailed today to Washington. Apologize for last-minute decision and any inconvenience to you, but feel entering training now would be mistake.

16

Bombshell in Johnstown

Ann

Wednesday, August 12, 1964, Amsterdam. My last day in Europe. In an hour, I'd be flying to the States, and tonight I'd be in Johnstown, Pennsylvania, with Jack, at his parents' home. After that, I'd see Terry in Center—if he could postpone his Peace Corps training. In May, when I had accepted Jack's mom's invitation to visit on my way home, I thought he would be in Germany. And Terry in the Peace Corps.

How was this new "plan" supposed to work out? Two days in Johnstown to scrutinize Jack's family and maybe two days in Center to negotiate Terry's proposal? Then choose the "best offer"? How brazen.

Equally troubling was the distinct possibility it would be one visit, not two. I promised Terry I'd call from Denver. What if the call brought only a sad, brief update from his mom: *He's gone, dear. I took him to the airport in Denver on Thursday. Didn't he tell you?*

I couldn't do a thing about that now. When I stopped at American Express to change money, I didn't change my Denver–Albuquerque plane ticket to go see Terry. Too risky until I knew whether he would still be there on Sunday. Even if he were, he'd be leaving the next day for the Peace Corps. What then? Ricochet from double jeopardy to double loneliness—put on my mourning cap and go teach high school in Glendale while Terry made peace in Venezuela and Jack made war?

A pox o' both your houses—I had a plane to catch.

Wednesday afternoon, August 12, 1964, New York City. Jack swept me up at the LaGuardia gate in a bear hug so powerful I couldn't breathe. "At last, at long last. How was your trip? As endless as it was for me? Three months? A year?" Question after question. He didn't pause.

He tucked me into the Sting Ray, and on the way to Johnstown, I introduced him to my Swedish friend, Agneta, and took him with me on that madcap drive through Germany with the butcher brothers. He roared with laughter over the deodorant caper. "I love your independence, your self-confidence—to set off without being able to speak German."

I told him how the *Merchant of Venice* in London had taken me back to our days in Italy. What a great listener—nodding, chuckling, eyes intent. I'd pause, and he'd whisper, "What else? Where did you go next?" And "The Thames. Tell me about the Thames. Is it like the Danube? The Rhine? I never made it to London, you know."

Late that night, at 85 Osborne Street in Johnstown, his mom put her arm around my waist and whisked me upstairs to a slanted dormer room overlooking the backyard. She and Jack's dad embraced me as if I were their own daughter, returned from distant lands.

After the eleven-hour flight from Amsterdam and the five-hour drive from the airport, I slept until noon Thursday. Jack, his parents, and I talked away the afternoon. Before dinner, Jack's father, Bud, gave me a tour of his garden as if it were the grounds at Versailles. His small garden was bursting with summer's yield of peas, green beans, onions, carrots, sweet peppers, and tomatoes. Blackberry and raspberry bushes sprawled across trellises.

He paused at a stand of corn. "You want a feast, girl? This is it. First, you start up a fire and put on a pot of water—as close to this cornfield as you can get. While it boils, you get your plates, your salt, your pepper, your butter, your knife. Have 'em ready. Once that water's boiling, you harvest the exact number of ears you're going to eat, then you race back, shucking the cobs as you run. Don't worry about the husks—you collect them later. Then you plunge that corn into the pot the moment you get there. You leave it just a minute or so, then slather it with butter, salt, and pepper, and you've got a feast for a king. You want seconds? You go back and harvest more."

Seconds? I had fourths. Corn was my entire dinner.

Bud and Peggy Sigg's white frame house whispered *You're home now*— overstuffed olive sofa, matching chair and ottoman, the secretary's desk and wooden chair, the high-fidelity record player with a generous library of

33 rpm records. The living room was a tableau from an earlier era, maybe when Jack was born, twenty-six years before.

On Friday, Jack's parents—like not-so-subtle matchmakers—sent us off on a bike tour of Johnstown, and we pedaled toward the Carnegie Public Library. While we paused to rest on our handlebars at the Conemaugh River, Jack blossomed into tour guide, historian, and barker, casting his hometown as a case study of an industrial American city.

"Dad was an engineer for Bethlehem Steel's Conemaugh and Black Lick Railroad. In the boom years of the steel and coal industries, we lived comfortably." Jack paused, scowling slightly. "In the bust years, you see, we all contributed, scraping by as best we could, with help from the union. That's when I became an expert house painter." He smiled at a memory.

"But enough about us. Here's a bit of history you don't know. Eighty years ago, the city's steel barons—the likes of Andrew Carnegie and Henry Clay Frick—frequented the South Fork Fishing and Hunting Club in the steep hills up above town, there. Kicking back at the clubhouse, they snagged fish from the private lake they created by damming the Conemaugh.

"In 1889, biblical rains fell, if you'll excuse the religious reference." He glanced sideways, looking for a rise out of me. "The river swelled, and on May 31, the dam collapsed. Rushing down the hillside, the waters rose to the third floor of city hall, splintered the building, and swept it away. The flood obliterated our town. More than 2,200 people died."

I tried to imagine an entire town mourning so many family members and friends.

We stitched a zigzag trail past historic buildings. Our destination, the local library, was an elegant three-story structure built after the flood. Andrew Carnegie donated funds to rebuild it. "Johnstown's library was the fourth of our country's many Carnegie libraries," Jack said.

At a grassy spot nearby, we spread an oilcloth, laid out the picnic Peggy had packed, and imagined ourselves back in the German countryside, this time with fried chicken and potato salad rather than lunch meat and cheese. We snacked on homegrown cherry tomatoes, freshly plucked sugar peas, and peaches, slurping the juices off our chins.

"You're so passionate about this town," I said. "I love it."

"Love me, love my town." He smiled. "This world would be a better place with more people like the folks of Johnstown."

Our bike tour was interspersed with cheery conversations with people along the way. One, his high school English teacher, pronounced him, "My smartest student ever." Two people whose houses he'd painted in high school declared his work "the best paint job" and "the best deal in town." They all praised him, the local boy turned West Point man.

Jack was charming, confident, thoughtful. I imagined myself embracing and being embraced by these people. "How grand to have that sense of community," I told him. "I never had that."

"Sure you did. Yours was mobile, that's all. The army's a huge family. Think about the Kirtleys." He was right. "And speaking of family, how's Bonner?"

Two thoughts collided. First was Jack's use of "Bonner," my brother's middle name. His friends called him by his first name, Ralph. Did that make Jack *family*? It felt like it.

The second thought was Hofbräuhaus and that wretched ride back to Landshut. "Uh, we had our moments."

"More stories for the family lore?"

"Maybe not. Some are better exorcised." I spilled the sordid story of the bacchanal at Hofbräuhaus—everything except the close call with Mr. Politics. "I drank more beer that night than in my whole life," I confessed. "Good thing the German cop didn't ask *me* to walk the line."

"You mean you were drunk? Not Supergirl, not the girl with willpower of steel."

The word *drunk* clanked like a cowbell in church. Sure, I'd had too much, but never for a moment had I applied the D-word to myself. Drunk was to my life like a fan dance would be to a nun. "I didn't see myself as drunk. But you're right. Now I'm more disgusted than ever."

"You were with your brother, not some predator. You got drunk and gained some wisdom. Nothing lost. Not even your virginity."

My virginity? "Is that still stuck in your craw?"

His Cheshire grin evaporated under my glare, but he looked so chagrined that I steered us past as quickly as I could. "No, sir," I said. "Getting drunk is not normal. Not for me."

"We all do things we aren't proud of. You're not permanently flawed. More important is what you choose to do with it. Wallow in your mistake? Or learn from it?"

He wasn't getting it. It was the fact that booze was as common to an officer's life as snappy salutes, spit-shined shoes, and the ever-present threat of war. "It's not what I learned, but what I fear: a lifestyle where drinking is the norm, where that temptation repeats itself."

"You know that's not who I am. Together we can slay that dragon. We can. I have such high hopes for us."

He was so earnest I would have marched down the aisle then and there if he had asked me. I trusted him. And if I wanted him to trust me, I had to cough up the rest of the story. "You're right. But I haven't told you the worst part." I spit out the rest, how I'd swallowed a line from that flirty German guy. "My judgment failed me completely. What if I had gone with him? I may well have been robbed of that *virginity* you seem so preoccupied with—or my life."

Jack tensed. He started to speak, but I waved him off. "Would Bonner have left me to that guy? Probably. He was on his way to the door. Talk about impaired judgment."

No hint of a smug grin now. "Well, that is serious. I'll talk to him."

"No need. I'm the wiser for it. Let's not dwell on it when we have so little time."

"Agreed. I apologize for my uncalled-for remark." He took my hand, kissed it. "Friends again? Better yet, more than friends? A lot more?" He leaned in toward me. I expected to kiss, but he paused, sighed, and looked away as if distracted by an unseen intruder.

We were off balance. Was it him? Or me? Why did he seem so distant?

I couldn't read his mind, but at least I could cheer him up. "Absolutely. Far, far more than friends, Lieutenant Sigg. But we've been gone too long. Should we head back before your folks send out a search party? By the way, what do your parents know about us?"

"Mom's already grilled me about our grand tour." He pulled me to my feet, wrapped me in a bear hug, and kissed me—no peck on the cheek. "You belong here. Mom and Dad agree."

"So do I." I meant it. I wanted to be at his side, part of his family and his community.

Dinner conversation Friday night flowed like a mountain stream through our times in Europe—Jack's two years, our two months. Bud and Peggy played tag team bringing us up to date on the headlines in America: Mickey Mantle hit a 461-foot homer. President Johnson signed the Civil Rights Act. The Gulf of Tonkin Resolution authorized full-scale war against North Vietnam.

The Gulf of Tonkin! We all fell silent. I exchanged looks with Peggy. Bud turned to Jack. "That resolution sounds serious, son. What do you make of it?"

"It is serious, Dad. I've been thinking about duty in Vietnam. I need to do it sometime, might as well be sooner than later." He tried to skip it into the conversation like a pebble on a still pond, but it landed like a mudslide, damming the stream of chitchat.

Peggy caught her breath. "Oh, Jack, no! That Tonkin stuff means war."

"That's what I'm trained to do, Mom. Can't shirk my duty."

"But now?" I asked, my voice barely above a whisper. "I thought we . . . now, Jack?"

Jack focused squarely on me. "I've thought about this a lot. Might as well go while I can do some good, before Communism spreads its tentacles to another Asian country."

This wasn't a spur-of-the-moment conversation stopper. He was a soldier facing war. I leaned in. His mom and dad faded away, as if Jack and I were alone, negotiating our future. "So, have you already signed up?"

"Yes. Combat zone duty is essential if I'm going to move up the ranks. I'll be an adviser to the Vietnamese army. A teacher, not a dogface leading the charge up San Juan Hill."

Whoa. He *had* decided. Duty and career first! Was this a warning shot to me—a tangible illustration of the life of a soldier? And a soldier's wife? Was he driven to the decision by training and inclination? Or had he concluded things weren't going to work out for us, and Vietnam duty would put a dramatic end to things? "When do you leave?"

He was sitting ramrod straight now, that West Point stance I had seen on the parade grounds in Landshut. "Early next year. After I finish counter-intelligence at Fort Holabird and three months in Monterrey learning Vietnamese. Then Saigon." He spoke in a monotone, as if he would divulge no more than name, rank, and serial number.

We three pelted him with questions. How long—a year, two? Just you?

You and Bonner? Where would you be? Saigon? The countryside? A Vietnamese military school? Behind the lines? Out in the jungle?

As if we could build a barricade of questions against the inevitable.

Saturday, 2:20 a.m., August 15, 1964, Johnstown. Jack's bombshell explained so much: his distraction the last two days, maybe even why he hadn't proposed. Silly me. I thought he was bugged about Terry's proposal. If that were the case, why hadn't he made a counter proposal? All night, conflicting thoughts swarmed me like a flight of Valkyries:

Maybe he believes he already proposed.

Oh, sure. Like he simply "forgot" he hadn't!

No, he laid out his case in "the girl I want to marry" letter and then lathered it up with foamy dreams of living in Paris, going to school together, raising kids—our kids—fanciful visions trailing overhead in sparkling bubbles. Only hours ago, he said we could slay that alcohol dragon together. No doubt—he's committed.

Yes, but we agreed the summer was a trial run. When did that change?

We survived Saint-Tropez and Lake Garda. And the letters, the gifts, the trip, the romantic Paris dinner, the shared love have spoken volumes.

Is he supposed to get down on his knee?

That thought made me grin.

Well, sure. A little drama would be swell.

That's silly. He loves you. You love him. Better yet, get down on your knee and beg him. He's worried it's over between you two.

That's ridiculous. He has his rules—a man proposes, a woman accepts.

But what about this single-handed decision? Shouldn't he have discussed it with me—before he signed up? Or at least with his parents? Did he see it as his decision alone? Okay, so we're not married or even engaged. But still, it doesn't bode well for a lifetime together as partners.

Before dawn, Jack slipped into my room. "Morning, princess. How'd you sleep?"

"Poorly. No, actually miserably. Nothing serious, though. Vietnam . . . more Vietnam . . . a bit of Vietnam. Are you bringing better news? A new plan? Or at least a good morning kiss?"

Better than that, he lay down beside me. Kissed me. Stroked my hair and whispered, "Don't worry. I won't be in the line of fire." I wanted to lambaste him for not consulting me before he decided. But what was he supposed to do—ask his "maybe-yes, maybe-no" girlfriend for permission? No, I didn't have that right. But would it have been different if we were married?

He laid his arm across my chest and pulled me close. "We need to leave for the airport by seven. What time do you want to get up?"

"Five. Stay with me till then?"

"That was my hope."

I didn't fall back asleep. Neither did he. We lay there spooning, him behind me, his hand clasped tightly to my breasts as if to imprint them forever in his mind. Or maybe we did sleep—not long, a few minutes at most, but long enough that we had to rush through breakfast, wave good-bye on the run, and race to the airport in Pittsburgh.

Taking a deep breath, I broke the silence above the roar of the Sting Ray. "I love your parents—and not only because they were so welcoming. Clearly, they adore each other, and you. That's how a family should be. It's how my family is, and—"

"That's what I want for you and me."

"That's the ideal. But are we really meant for each other? How can we know?"

"How could you doubt? We have so much to live for."

"*We?* We who?"

"You. Me. *We?* Remains to be seen. What are you going to tell my rival?"

I dug deep for the right words. "No clear answer. If I didn't love you, the answer would be easy. But I do love you. And now you're telling me you're headed off to war."

"And vice versa? Where are you headed?" His eyes begged for a no to Terry.

"To Denver today. After that, I'm not sure. Terry may delay his departure to Peace Corps training so we can sort things—"

"You're going to see him on your way to Albuquerque? When did you decide this?"

"I haven't *decided* anything. I won't know until I get to Denver if he's even going to be there," I said. "He's probably already left for Berkeley."

"So help me understand: You're hoping to go see my rival today. Then what?"

"If I see him—tomorrow—we have to put this proposal thing to rest. All I know for sure is I'm not ready to make this big decision about either of you. Not immediately."

He was quiet for too long. "One reason I signed up for Vietnam now is I thought he would be safely on ice for two years. Long enough for *us*—for our relationship to fully bloom," he said. "Our pen-pal romance worked wonders. But now Vietnam could kill any future for us." He sighed that mournful sigh. "So after you see him tomorrow, or not, then what?"

"Home to Albuquerque, collect my stuff, and head to Arizona. I have to. I signed a teaching contract."

At the airport, we raced to the gate, arriving with only minutes to spare. Panting, I turned, hugged him tightly, and whispered, "Thank you, Lieutenant Sigg. I'll never forget our Sting Ray summer, for as long as I live. No matter what happens."

He kissed me, a passionate kiss.

I cocked my eyebrow in surprise.

He winked. "No man goes off to war without kissing his girl goodbye."

17

Conundrum in Colorado

Ann

Saturday, August 15, 1964, Denver. At Stapleton airport, I commandeered the first phone booth, dropped in a dime, and dialed zero. My hand was shaking. I gave the operator Terry's number. Four rings. Five. *Come on, Ter. Be there. Please.* Six . . . seven . . .

"Marshalls." His mom's voice.

"We have a collect call from Ann Garretson. Will you accept the charge?"

She did. "Terry's outside," she said. "I'll go get him."

He postponed the Peace Corps! At least I'd get to see him, if only for a day or so. But then what? Jack's warmth was still buzzing in my mind.

"Annie?"

"You're there! I knew you'd figure out a way to see me before Berkeley. When do you leave? How much time do we have?" Silence. "Ter?"

"I'm not going, Annie. I sent the plane tickets back. I'm moving to Glendale."

Oof. No! A double-whammy kick in the gut. First, he would never get another chance at the Peace Corps, not after he'd already turned down Colombia. And it was my fault. Second, I still couldn't give him an answer. I needed space to breathe, to think, to come to my own conclusion. By myself. Without either guy around. I couldn't tell Terry that, not after this news. Now a decision would be even harder with him where? *Next door?*

"I . . . I don't know what to say. Do you still want me to come?"

"Jesus, Annie, you're why I'm still here. What are you thinking? Frontier has a morning flight to Alamosa. It gets here at ten. They've got seats. I already checked."

I didn't think. I didn't hesitate. "I'll be on it," I said. "See you tomorrow."

Terry

Saturday late afternoon, 15 August, 1964, Center. I hosed down, scrubbed, and vacuumed the Falcon, then parked it in the potato cellar so it wouldn't get dusty. In the fading light, I scoured the countryside to assemble the perfect bouquet for Annie's arrival at the Alamosa airport Sunday morning. First, to represent our farm's crops: a backdrop of forest green alfalfa, a spray of golden-tan malting barley, and a smattering of flowering Red McClure potato vines. And then to brighten it up: three cheery sunflowers from the barrow ditch, a fistful of daisies from Mom's flower garden, and a softening pallet of pale green milkweed.

"Oh, for heaven's sake, you can't give her weeds in a coffee can," Mom snorted. She offered her china vase, rearranged it all, and scolded me again for not ordering roses.

Sunday, I was up at dawn. I showered, helped Mom fix breakfast, did the dishes, changed my sheets, and tidied my room. It was 7:30, still two and a half hours until Annie would get to Alamosa. I dusted off the Falcon, outside and in, checked the tires, trimmed my mustache, and brushed my teeth: 8:15. I took a hard look at my bouquet, combed the southwest forty, and found replacements for the potato flowers, then showered and brushed my teeth again: 8:45.

"I better go," I told Mom at 8:50. "That plane comes in early sometimes."

"Yeah, you'd better," she said. "It takes almost half an hour to get to the airport."

I drove County Line Road at thirty miles an hour to keep from kicking up dust and still got to Alamosa twenty minutes early. The airport was small—one runway, one plane at a time, no coffee or gift shop, a waiting room the size of a doctor's office. I wandered out back, searched the sky, and went inside a couple of times to pee—waiting always set my bladder on overdrive.

I spotted the DC-3 circling in from the Sangre de Cristos before the ticket agent did. It zoomed past on the runway, slowed, and crawled back. Greeting this two-engine plane wasn't new to me—I'd been first on the tarmac before, snapping photos of dignitaries as they stepped out onto the stairs.

This time, I had imagined a grand cinema reunion: *We sprint across the tarmac toward each other. She flings herself into my arms. Her legs lock us into a licentious embrace. Our kisses go on forever.*

Instead, I stood there like a doofus, Mom's vase with my ragtag bouquet clutched in my left hand as my right hand snaked out for a handshake. "Damn," I said. "It's good to see you."

She shook my hand. "Good day, sir."

That was Annie, always quick with a smart-aleck retort.

"And what's this? A bouquet!" She picked through it. "Let's see. Some weeds. Beer barley. Cattle feed. Potato flowers. Oh, Ter, it's lovely! And so romantic."

I never knew when she was spinning an extended joke. "Really? You like it?"

"Natch! What better welcome than symbols of farm life in the San Luis Valley?" She laid her hands on my shoulders. "Thank you for waiting, Ter. For not leaving for the Peace Corps. I was afraid you'd be gone. You're not angry with me, are you?"

"We have to go together." I forced back tears. "Damn, what a long summer!"

"I know," she said. "Tell me about it."

At home on the farm, we began like skiers inching up a mountain slope, anchoring each step so we wouldn't slide backward. We chatted under the cottonwoods at Coffman's pond, hiked the fields, and cuddled atop the neatly stacked alfalfa bales in the southeast forty. We followed the railroad tracks to the old cattle chutes beyond Marshall Produce, and by midafternoon, our words were tumbling out like boulders in the spring runoff. Sometimes speech became impossible because the thousands of saved thoughts logjammed in our brains.

Then we'd kiss. And hug. And off we'd go again—to Paris, Silverton, San Francisco, the Bavarian hills, London Bridge, a lake near Juliet's house in Verona. And, oh yes indeed, she'd marveled at the Venus de Milo and the Winged Victory of Samothrace in the Louvre, as well as the Dürer masterpieces in Munich.

She was the Annie of late May, but with ten thousand new freckles. She *had* been in the sun. The freckles enhanced her charm—she'd never been an alabaster-skinned Botticelli fit only for a pedestal. She pulsed energy and wielded her wit with épée-like precision. Best of all, she was as responsive to my every touch as she had been in June.

Nevertheless, beyond every joyous affirmation, shadows of disquiet hovered. Each time they swooped in, we artfully dodged. We didn't acknowledge that marriage proposal of mine—or her non-answer. Nor did either of us dare mention *his* name, that summer companion of hers.

By eleven that night, the house was quiet, the family asleep. Annie and I were wired still, but her eyes started to droop, yawns coming midsentence. My thoughts drifted to one pre-finals night in Boulder, us dining in a real restaurant, not McDonald's. Her words had gone to mush, and she dozed off at the table. That was Annie, full-out until she hit empty.

"We'd better turn in," I said. "You're about to crash."

Her eyes popped open. "No, I'm not. The night's young." She flashed a phony smile.

"Yeah, and I'm in Caracas too. Come on." I helped her to her feet.

She readied herself in the bathroom. We had only one, at the end of the hall beyond Mom's and Pam's bedrooms. Annie tiptoed out and whispered, "Tuck me in?"

Wow, she'd put on that clingy nightie, the one I'd photographed her in last May. "Why, of course," I said, as if settling a girl into my bed was part of my nightly routine.

I shadowed her up the attic stairs to my bedroom and, with a flourish, drew down the clean sheet. "Your bedchamber, miss. Silk sheets. Down-filled pillow."

"No rose petals? No lute?" she said. "But I've got you. That's all I need." She eased into bed and patted the edge. "Don't rush off. I haven't seen you in *years*."

The moon was nearing full, and the glow streaming through the window was bright enough to read by. Her silky nightie gathered in the light as if to showcase rather than conceal the wearer. I seated myself gingerly beside her, my thigh touching her leg. She didn't scoot away. "I love you," I said. "I even put it in writing."

"Yes, I read that—more than once. Wrote it myself too, if I recall."

"You did—though not nearly often enough."

"I'm sorry. I'm a terrible correspondent, but I was on the go, and—"

"Doesn't matter now. You're here. I'm here. That's all I've asked for."

"That's all? You sure?"

"Well, a few other small things—a kiss or two. And a lifetime."

She arched an eyebrow. "Oh really? Some of those letters suggested a whole lot more. In quite vivid detail."

Damn, I shouldn't have been so explicit. But she wasn't pushing me away—she was playful Annie again, teasing. "Yeah, it shocked me too. I meant it, though."

"Tell you what, let's start slowly and see what develops." She held out her arms.

I yearned to dive in with her, but my bedroom shared a wall with the boys' room. No insulation. Open doors. And both boys had ears sharp enough to hear a mosquito tiptoe across the ceiling. Besides, we had too much ground to make up and that looming question to answer. None of that mattered—she was asleep before I could have made it to first base. "Sleep well," I breathed. I disentangled myself and snuck downstairs to a dreadful night on the sofa.

Monday, 17 August 1964, en route to Albuquerque. Not five minutes from home, speeding down a backcountry gravel road, Annie unbuckled her seat belt and moved over beside me on the car's bench seat. "At last, you and me. Alone." She squeezed my knee.

I flinched, tightening both hands on the steering wheel.

She flashed an impish grin. "Relax, Ter, it's a long drive."

Yeah, sure. Relax. I eased my hand onto her knee, inched my way up her thigh. She leaned closer. "I want to say yes, I do, Ter. But I get scared, like I'm on the high dive and I jump before I'm ready and, oh no, they've drained the pool. In Germany, alone, hitchhiking and on the train, I couldn't speak German, but I told myself, *You can do this, Ann. You can travel by yourself.* And I did! At the same time, I kept thinking that it would have been so much better with you. It's like that now. I need to be on my own—in my own apartment, not a dorm—challenging myself, making my own decisions. I never have. But I want to be with you too and share every moment with you. I do love you."

I squeezed her thigh. No words needed and none possible.

"I feel terrible about the Peace Corps. Please don't hate me for it. Maybe you could still go, maybe it's not too late. You should call them."

"Do you want me to? Without you? For two years?"

"No, absolutely not. But what if you've torpedoed your last chance?"

"I'm still committed, but I want to go with you. Together."

She went silent. Then she laid her hand over mine, pressed it into her inner thigh, more affirming than a breathless kiss. "I've thought a lot about that too. I want to."

It *was* a long drive to Albuquerque, six hours. For most people it took four. We stopped in Española where the highway crossed the Rio Grande, stretched our legs, and skipped a few rocks across the river as we had done in Silverton in May. In Santa Fe, we lunched on green chili burritos, a leisurely Sunday-night-in-Boulder kind of lunch, as much chatter as meal.

As we neared Albuquerque, she pointed ahead to a pull-off on the side of the road. "Let's stop for a minute. Over there in that grove of trees."

I finessed the potholes and rutted trail and parked out of sight of the highway. "Well?"

"No emergency. I wanted a few more minutes alone with you is all, no distractions. Mom will be the sentry on duty, and Dad may lock you in the garage tonight."

"Tell them I'm wearing a chastity belt. Stainless steel and welded shut."

"Whew, I was hoping. You're dangerous. But seriously, once you get to know Dad, you'll like him. He'll like you too."

"I bet. Like a lion likes Christians."

"Tell you what. Let's forget Mom and Dad for a moment. I was so tired last night, I know I disappointed you. Your bedroom was so romantic too, with you beside me in the moonlight. Hold me—like you did at the haystack yesterday afternoon."

Snuggled together, we gazed out at the Rio Grande—in mid-August, more a shallow creek than one of the nation's grand rivers—like us, unhurriedly wending its way from the San Luis Valley to Albuquerque. We sat silently. Back in May I would have been pawing at her like a satyr, but this touch seemed a meshing of souls, not lust at all.

She sighed. "We'd better go. My folks are waiting. They'll worry."

"How about a parting kiss?"

"Of course," she said, and I planted a hearty Bronx cheer behind her ear. She screeched. "What a relief! The same ole Ter after all."

Monday, 17 August 1964, Albuquerque. The Colonel and Mrs. Garretson were hovering curbside when I rolled to a stop. Annie's mother whipped the car door open and greeted Annie like she'd been freed from Stalag 17.

The Colonel didn't look like a colonel at all: no uniform, no snappy salute, no brisk orders. He wore slacks and a polo shirt and greeted us with the smile of a fun-loving uncle. "Mighty good to see you two. Come in, come in." His handshake wasn't bone crushing, nor was he posturing like a tough guy opponent before a wrestling match. Rather, friendly and welcoming.

They ushered us in—Annie to her old bedroom, me to a spare single bed in her little brother's room—then summoned us to the den. Annie's mom poured sherry from a crystal decanter. The Colonel hoisted his glass. "To the safe arrival of our wandering girl. And her escort." We clinked glasses, and Annie's mom launched into a "Flight of the Bumblebee" string of questions: Bonner and Germany and some old friends in Verona and "Oh, did you make it to St. Mark's Square, it's one of my favorite places, and—"

Annie held up her hand. "Come on, Mom, we've got more than five minutes. Let's take one at a time."

The Colonel smiled. "Right, Sis. Let 'er catch her breath, Dorothy." He turned toward me. "Here, Terry, try this." He offered chips and a bowl of salsa.

"Oh, Ralph, don't—"

The Colonel flicked his hand, and she stopped midsentence.

The Test! Annie had warned me. Her dad served a Hades-hot mix of minced jalapeños to every guy she'd ever brought to the house. Every one of them had either cried out in pain or half choked.

I took a chip, scooped up a mighty bite, and popped it into my mouth. The den went silent. I love hot salsa. But, oh shit, a dragon had blasted fire down my throat. I blinked back tears and, as calmly as I could, chomped the chip to death and swallowed a four-alarm fire. I looked the Colonel in the eye and forced a smile. "Mmm, delicious." Then I took a second chip, ladled up as much salsa as it could hold, and dispatched it as if it were a sugar cookie.

All three of them stared at me. The Colonel's eyes twinkled. Her mom shook her head. Annie smiled sympathetically.

Over dinner, Annie's mom shifted into an attentive, delightful hostess. She could have passed for Annie's striking older sister. Petite, two inches shorter than Annie, slim, graceful, charming, and a skilled raconteur. Each time conversation lagged, she rekindled it with a witty comment or a well-chosen question. She and the Colonel adroitly worked me into the discussion, asking about Silverton and CU, as if I were a long-lost nephew, all while refilling our wine glasses and urging me to take seconds. She even commented on my stints at the *Valley Courier*: "Didn't you write that wonderful story on the Manassa Pioneer Days?" she asked. "You caught the very essence of cowboy-country life!"

I'd written that feature four summers ago. "You remember that?"

"I saved it," she said. "You write beautifully."

Mrs. Garretson insisted that Annie relate every detail of her brother's life and duties in Germany and then effortlessly interlaced those reports with parallel tales of the Garretson travels when the Colonel was stationed in Italy. No one mentioned that Annie had traveled Europe with Jack the Stud or that he was the reason she'd gone there in the first place.

At evening's end, Annie and I had a quiet moment after her parents went to bed—time for a delicious kiss wrapped in a loving embrace in her dad's hideaway office off the den. "They like you," she said. "Dad's impressed."

"I did my best. But oh, I'll need reconstructive surgery on my seared tongue."

Ann

Monday night, August 17, 1964, Albuquerque. The streetlight illuminated a swath of the aqua wall in my bedroom, along with the flowery bedspread, the vanity mirror, and the matching miniatures of laughing square dancers, all decor that Mom and I had worked with juicy delight to assemble for my very own room—when I was in sixth grade. My family had moved five times since then, and Mom had recreated that original look after every move.

This familiar place had always enfolded me in comfort. But I wasn't a little girl anymore. The past two days had been a replay of my summer, teetering from one precipice to the next, only this time trying to shield Terry from mention of Jack. Worse, I had declared my love for Terry as avidly as I had for Jack. I struggled with my behavior these past months, hurling painful words at myself: Tramp. Jezebel. Minx.

I never intended to fall in love with two men, to subject them both to deception and heartache. I had been looking forward to the isolation in Arizona so I could sort out my feelings—by myself. All I'd gotten so far was a change in scenery. Plus, I had regressed from independent world traveler to prodigal child returned home.

On the positive side, Mom and Dad had bent over backward to welcome Terry. And Terry had passed Dad's jalapeño test—my only boyfriend ever to succeed. The trouble was, I had never *told* them he was my boyfriend. Nor that Jack was also my boyfriend.

Years earlier, Mom and Dad had exhibited too much eagerness to know all the details about boys I dated and too much interest in steering my preferences, which rarely matched theirs. My reaction? I built a vault around my love life. They had more or less backed off, but every time they did drop a comment about a boyfriend, I changed the combination lock on that vault. Now here I was, facing my most momentous decision ever, and I hadn't told them either man was a potential life partner.

But they must have constructed their own theories about both guys. They knew I'd traveled Europe with Jack and had visited both Jack and Terry on my way home. They treated Terry as if he were still my buddy while artfully steering the conversation around any mention of Jack. I was grateful for that. But very likely, neither man qualified, in their estimation, to be married to the precious child who used to occupy this girly room.

I didn't want them dabbling in my decision. What did I want from them? I didn't know.

Terry

Monday night, 17 August 1964, Albuquerque. I couldn't sleep, not with Annie in the next room glowing in the moonlight. I lay there three feet from fifteen-year-old Jimmy, him on night watch, pretending to be zonked out.

Annie and I had spent a day and a half together since she stepped off the plane. We'd talked for hours. The signs were positive. She hadn't mentioned Sarah and Rachael, my bombastic editorials and the scurrilous letter to Atkins, my left-wing politics, or the fact she was army and I was a conscientious objector.

A few shadows darkened my spirits: her comment that she had never lived alone, her realization that traveling solo had given her a desire to make it on her own, and her chilling declaration that she was "not quite ready for marriage." But I couldn't help dismissing those as footnotes, not key themes. Her passion—the lingering kisses, embraces, touches—far outweighed her doubts. We had picked up where we left off in June, constrained only by the fact that we'd been cloistered in our parents' homes. Had we been in my apartment in Boulder . . . oh, that thought nearly set me off.

Despite my best efforts to remain hopeful, a menacing chimera lurked under my bed in Jimmy's room—that lieutenant she had left behind.

On the way to Albuquerque, I had dared ask Annie if he had proposed. Her eyes narrowed. Whiffs of smoke curled up and singed the roof of my car. "No, he didn't," she said at last, her words icy. "But, yes, we had some great times together."

For an hour, we had driven in silence. I didn't bring *that* up again or the question I didn't dare ask: *Did you have sex with him?* I'd read in *Playboy Letters* that after having sex for the first time, girls glowed and acted differently—a spring in their step, a change in how they comported themselves. Mostly, I thought that was bunk, but still, I couldn't help studying her as intently as an artist with a model, trying to grasp every nuance of her body language, words, tone, what she didn't say or do. She did have a tan, that's all I could see. Best of all, she was as loving as if we had fallen asleep for these ten weeks, awakened side by side, and set off hand in hand on some grand new adventure.

For a week, I had worried I had blown it by turning down the Peace Corps, that she'd come back, reject me, and all I'd have would be shattered dreams. Now, there I was, ready to take off in the morning for Phoenix to find a job so we could be together.

She hadn't said yes, but more importantly, she hadn't said no.

18
Great Expectations

Ann

Tuesday, August 18, 1964, Albuquerque. Over breakfast of poached eggs, toast, and cantaloupe, Mom chatted with Terry. Wasn't he due to leave for South America for missionary work?

I held my breath.

"Venezuela," he said. "With the Peace Corps. It's a government program to help underdeveloped countries. But I've changed my plans. I hope to go next year."

"Really?" Mom said. "What will you do in the meantime?"

"See if I can get on at a newspaper . . . somewhere in the Phoenix area."

The cogs of conversation ground to a halt. Mom and Dad exchanged looks. Mom frowned. "Oh, maybe you'll wind up close to Annie. She's going to Glendale."

"I sure hope so," Terry said, poker-faced. "I miss our Sunday nights at McDonald's."

No one choked. Dad quickly finished and excused himself. Mom jumped up to tidy the kitchen.

An hour later, as I bid Terry goodbye at the curb, he said, "Well, that was awkward. So when are you going to tell them I have designs on becoming your roommate?"

"Well, not *then*. Mom's sure going to stew over that!"

"She'll get over it." He snaked his hand around my waist and pulled me toward him. "Wish me luck on my job search." He leaned in for a kiss.

I reared back. "Not in front of the neighbors. And Mom!"

"Come on, Annie. No one's looking. No one cares!" He jerked away.

"Fine! See you in Glendale." He yanked the car door open, flopped in, slammed the door, and sped off.

Dang! Why did he always push the limits and then shut down if he didn't get his way?

Questions about Terry hovered in the air until noon when Mom and I had lunch while Dad was at a meeting. "Kind of a big surprise, Terry moving to Phoenix and all," she said.

Everything I had practiced deserted my brain. "He's more than a good buddy, and—"

"Oh, Annie, he could really complicate things for you!"

"My life is already pretty complicated, Mom. In fact—"

"Don't let him box you in, not before you—"

"Don't let him move to Arizona? Call the highway patrol to stop him at the border?"

"A girl needs to . . . you could put a stop to it. Tell him—"

"Tell him what? That I don't care for him? Can't do that, Mom. It wouldn't be true."

"But Terry? Is he *right* for you? In all the important ways: morals, religion, background?"

Bam. There it was—thumbs-down on Terry. That I could respond so calmly surprised me. "That's the sixty-four-thousand-dollar question, Mom, something I have to figure out."

"We just want the best for you, sweetie, that's all. But please, above all else, you can't be allowing him to smooch with you. Certainly not in public!"

Wednesday morning, August 19, 1964, Albuquerque. At last, a day to myself. No Terry. No Jack. I stretched, turned over, and was about to drift back to sleep when my bedroom door creaked open. A shaft of light punctured the semidarkness.

"Annie? Time to go shopping." Mom's voice, as joyous as a meadowlark. Jeez, 6:20. I pulled the sheet over my head.

"Up and at 'em, sleepyhead," Mom said in a stage whisper. "Dillard's has an early-bird sale on fall clothes. The bargains go fast."

After a bowl of All-Bran, a piece of toast, and a three-minute shower, I dashed off with Mom to her favorite mall. At 6:55, she was chattering away, me dragging behind. I hated shopping. She embraced it as a fundamental component of healthy living, like her daily walk.

At Dillard's, a hat display waylaid her. I hadn't worn those things since my high school churchgoing days. "Do you like pink or beige?" She plopped the rosy one on my head. "A woman is never out of style with pink."

Oh, such a brim. Perfect—if I had a horse in the Kentucky Derby. Surprisingly, the hat looked fetching on that girl in the mirror. But still. "How about a pillbox?"

"A good brim minimizes the freckles. Scarlett O'Hara would snatch this one up."

"Okay, a brim"—damn my freckles and Scarlett—"but beige. It'll go with more things."

Mom led me into a jungle of dress racks, her practiced eye spotting *possibles*, deft hands plucking out *potentials*. "See. Great prices." Eyes sparkling, she draped seven over my arm. "Try these—I'll keep looking." The hatbox banged my knees all the way to the fitting room.

As the first dress settled over my shoulders, Mom slipped in, looked me over, and shook her head. "Try this sheath. Basic black. You can dress it up or down. And only twenty dollars, down from forty."

I yanked off dress number one, speed tested the rest, and found two that worked, just as she rushed in with another load, laid them out, and dashed out again.

She pressed on, her delight at our savings outracing my horror at the soaring cost. "Now shoes. Teachers need dressy heels and comfortable flats." By the time we agreed on two pairs of "perfect" heels, we had turned the shoe department into the Gettysburg battleground of footwear.

Next came gloves. Purse. Girdles. Bras. Stockings. Apparently, she had inspected my entire college wardrobe and couldn't find a thing that wouldn't embarrass me as a teacher.

In Dad's career, Mom had been an essential partner as he rose to post commander. The brass called her whenever they had an impression to make—like when Bess Truman barnstormed into Livorno. How did she manage to get the former president's wife to carry on like a personal friend? "Simple," Mom told me once. "We talked about our daughters."

Still, I chafed at being her Barbie, at being dressed to fulfill her aspirations. On the other hand, she was an eager, helpful valet, a trusty escort in unfamiliar territory. By the end of an exhausting day hoofing through two malls, Mom outfitted me with a wardrobe of suits, dresses, blouses, and skirts that guaranteed I'd be a fashion plate at Glendale High.

The next day, I shoehorned remnants of my college years into the closet, under the bed, and into the garage.

Terry

Wednesday, 19 August 1964, Glendale, Arizona. I eased into a parking space near my first prospect, the *Glendale News*, readied my résumé and portfolio of published articles, and swung the car door open. Whoosh! A blast furnace singed my eyes and lungs. Time and temperature on the bank marquee: 3:14 p.m., 106 degrees. Jesus, what was I doing there? In August!

In Colorado's San Luis Valley, we melted if it hit ninety. In Silverton we baked at eighty. I stifled an impulse to throw my panting Falcon into reverse and head for the mountains.

Forty-five minutes later, I had a job: reporter for the *News*, $4,500 a year, with grand prospects ahead. A country town for decades, Glendale was booming. Population now twenty-eight thousand, a new shopping center, a college campus under construction, and classrooms being added overnight to the public schools. My new boss would complete the paperwork to buy out the competing *Glendale Herald* by November 1. We'd become the *Glendale News-Herald*, expanding from weekly to biweekly and then to a daily within a year.

I'd work five days a week, covering city hall, police, courts, local politics, school board—all the major hard-news beats. The paper was delivered Thursday mornings. On either Thursday or Friday, I could pursue in-depth, investigative stories of my own choosing.

By nightfall, I'd found a house—not an apartment or basement cell, but a *house*—a charming one-room bungalow, at $60.10 a month, in an elderly couple's backyard, an easy stroll to the newspaper office on the town square. The next morning I'd head back to Center, pack, return the following week, and begin my newspaper career Monday morning, August 31.

Annie would be coming that week. I called her.

"A job and a house? On your first day?" she said. "I'm impressed."

So was I. We were on our way!

Ann

Friday, August 21, 1964, Albuquerque. In the midst of my countdown to
Arizona, Mom insisted I visit Cindy Gomez, the daughter of a friend of
hers. Cindy had recently given birth to her first child, and upon greeting
me, she launched into a tale of the delivery, as if it had been a big-screen
spectacular.

"Oh, Ann, it was so exciting. I knew it was time, but Howard dawdled
and dawdled, and we barely made it to the car when my water broke—oh
my, like a rainspout in a cloudburst *down there*. The car's a mess. By the
time we got to the hospital, I had dilated six centimeters. Did you know
you open up ten centimeters *down there*? That's four inches!" She formed
a circle with both hands and held it between her legs. "Amazing, isn't it?"

Gretchen had gone to the hospital by herself. When Terry and I visited her, she had spoken lovingly about her baby. No gory details, just un-
restrained happiness at having brought a child into the world. Watching
Cindy cuddle her baby, I sensed the angst Gretchen must have felt. She
hadn't decided whether she would give it up for adoption. Having a child
should be a time of joy, not emotional pain and shame.

"Isn't that amazing?" Cindy said.

"Huh, what?"

"My episiotomy." With a grimace, she adjusted her derriere on her
doughnut pillow and gestured downward. "I needed only four stitches."

"Stitches? For what?"

"You know, they cut you *down there*. And after that, the baby squirts
right out."

The image jolted. *A masked doctor hones his scalpel, slices her tender
underside, and then drops his tool of torture to catch a squirming baby!*
Something else Gretchen didn't mention. I was not ready for this marriage
thing. "Oh, yeah, Cindy. Yes. Really amazing."

"Being a mom is fantastic, though. This little tyke is such a delight."
Fiddling with her blouse, she tugged it up and snapped open her bra. An
engorged nipple popped free. She maneuvered the baby to her breast. "There,
there, baby, you *are* hungry, aren't you? Have some mommy juice." The
baby latched on. Cindy winced, "Go easy, sweetie." The baby went after
it like a starving calf. Cindy looked up and beamed. "See what I mean?"

⟶

Sunday, August 30, 1964, Albuquerque. Two weeks at home had taxed me more than my final month at CU. The nonstop drudgery of shopping, packing, and visiting family friends was interspersed with snippets from my parents' favorite aphorisms. Both worried that I look like a lady—not like a ragamuffin in sweatshirt and frayed shorts:

Dad: "Don't parade around looking like monkeys in a gunny sack." (Translation: *Always wear a girdle. Buns—or breasts—that jiggle in public are indecent.* As if anything on my five-foot-five, 110-pound frame could jiggle.)
Me: "Don't worry, Dad."

Mom: "Do you have a razor? New blades? Shaving cream?" (Translation: *A proper lady never leaves the house with underarm or leg hair.*)
Me: "Thanks, Mom, I'm all set."

I had just one last detail to manage before I left for Arizona: buy a car. With Dad as my broker, I bought our neighbor's 1954 Bel Air, for an affordable $65.94 a month. What a beaut—a rich cinnamon with white stripes over the rear fenders.

My final night at home, Mom and Dad took me to dinner at the Kirtland Air Force Base Officers Club. I donned my new sheath (undergirded by my new "corset," new bra, and new stockings), necklace, and heels—and engaged in witty conversation with their friends. After dessert, Dad rose, bowed, and offered his hand, "Sis, may I have the honor of this dance?"

We had danced together twice: after my eighth-grade graduation in Livorno in 1956 and at Bonner's West Point commencement in 1961. This dance was bittersweet—my father's last embrace before his daughter's ship sailed he knew not where. He had equipped me with the skills and confidence to flourish on my new voyage, trying to set my course just so, but too late he saw my bearing was to the left.

I ached as I drifted from my safe harbor. At the same time, I welcomed the next adventure, while he was left with only hopes and memories.

I knew letting go was harder for him than for me.

⟶

Monday, August 31, 1964, Albuquerque. I left for Arizona, not alone, but with Mom beside me. "You don't want to drive out there by yourself, honey." She would talk to me, drive if I got tired, and help me find an apartment. "Besides, I hate to see you leave." I couldn't say no.

That afternoon in Glendale, we circled through town once, and the moment we toured the Maryland Club Apartments I knew I'd found my new home. Close to Glendale High. Furnished. One bedroom. Cozy kitchen. Well kept up. A complex that pulsed with teachers and young professionals. I could lounge around the pool with colleagues on weekends, join in activities—like the luau planned for September—designed to turn these apartments into a real neighborhood. The rent, though, almost killed the deal: $119 a month.

"Oh for heaven's sake, Annie. You're a professional now, not a student. If money's a problem . . . with your car payments and all, Ralph and I will—"

"No subsidy needed, Mom." I didn't mean to be so short, but enough was enough.

In our time together, Mom laid out their expectations for my behavior as a teacher—in softball questions, offhand remarks, and hints seeded into our zigzag conversations. Sex lay at the core of their worries, lurking underground, verboten as a discussion topic. She warned, "Don't do anything that would reflect badly on yourself or your upbringing." In Mom-speak, *Do not invite men into your apartment.* Corollary: *Do not have sex.*

In June, their worry no doubt had been Jack, in Europe. Now, it was Terry, too close for comfort, living in the same town, though she never mentioned either name. An awkward threesome dinner with him on Tuesday seemed to reinforce her fears. On Wednesday, as I drove her to the airport for her flight home, she campaigned—in her sweetest voice—against my having anything to do with him. He wasn't right for me, she said directly, forcefully, openly.

To my astonishment, she resumed her crusade with a letter that weekend. She wrote:

> *I am not intending to lecture you—just advise. Ralph and I are in*
> *accord on this. Teachers <u>must</u> be perfect examples of propriety. They*

must shun all "appearances of evil." Things you might have done as a student will be strictly taboo now. You can't be having Terry in your apartment, helping you grade papers, and such. In fact, he shouldn't be hanging around all the time—it won't look good. A teacher can lose a job for any little act of impropriety. And, Ann, <u>please</u> don't ask him to the apartment luau. It's an opportunity for you to meet others. You will lose other opportunities if he is too much in evidence. You have plenty of reasons to keep him at a distance, in that you <u>need</u> to be busy with your teaching.

With your charm, personality, beauty, wit, background, you can command the best. Stick to your high ideals, your religious beliefs— and don't be swayed by superficial things (such as a "gift of gab" and a jolly time you can have with someone). Look deeper and see the real man. Don't let yourself get indoctrinated by any screwball ideas someone else might have, but study both sides of a question and make your own decisions.

*Oh, yes, one more thing: you have been used to good things that money can buy in life. Find yourself a **man** who can take care of you.*

The conversation and her letter stung me to the core. I had enough trouble sorting out my feelings for the two men I loved without her inserting herself and Dad into the mix. I took her jab about "your religious beliefs" as a shot at Jack. Her machine-gun attack not to "let yourself get indoctrinated by any screwball ideas" was a direct attack on Terry. Okay, his politics were out of step with theirs. "Screwball ideas," however, put us on two different planets, with no hope of finding common ground.

"Find yourself a **man**"—the word *man* heavily underlined and typed over twice on her 1939 black Remington standard typewriter to make it boldface—wounded me profoundly. In Mom-speak, it reeked of a double slur—Terry wasn't able to "take care" of me. And he wasn't tall enough. Male height was a big deal in my family. Dad was five feet eleven, but according to Mom, my grandmother refused to believe her only son was a hair under six feet—the height of a "real man." Terry was five feet five, same as me—not tall enough in their estimation to "measure up."

I didn't tell him this. I didn't want him to be hurt or embittered by it. Nor did I want him to know my parents were "size-ist"—in my view, as untenable as being racist and a nasty denial of Terry's intelligence and capabilities.

As for needing a "man to take care of me"? That was a retreat into prehistory. Women's liberation was about fighting for equal footing with men, not dependence on them. Betty Friedan had pointed out in *The Feminine Mystique* that women in American society abandoned their own professional lives and goals in deference to their husbands' careers, and that was precisely why so many housewives felt unfulfilled and dissatisfied.

Both Mom and Grandma embraced those outdated attitudes. Before Mom married Dad, she had been working for New Mexico's US Senator Dennis Chavez, alternating between Washington, DC, and Santa Fe, but she gave up her career to spend her life as an officer's wife.

Similarly, Grandma—Dad's mom—told me a woman should never have her own income. It would "spoil" her, make her too independent. Ironically, Grandma managed a two-thousand-acre ranch after husbands one and two died and left her to raise my dad, three stepkids, and a niece. By herself. She was the most cussedly independent and powerful woman I knew.

For me, there would be no "marriage versus career" choice. I intended to have both. And I didn't need a husband to "take care of me." My starting salary at Glendale High would be $4,800 a year, and Terry would make $4,500 at the *News*. So what?

Mom and Dad had aspirations for their only daughter to "marry well." Someone tall. Handsome. Educated. Someone who could support me. A man on his way up.

I was a dutiful girl. I didn't want to disappoint, except for one small detail. We were haggling, in our oblique ways, over the rest of my life, not a hunk of meat. My decision had to be more than skin deep, measured by more than the number of inches to the floor, more than a checklist of the "right stuff." Who was out of step with whom? Was I wrongheaded? Or were they?

Given that I loved both men, it was about the best match of our goals and values. And the wrenching decision of what path I would choose for my own future.

19

A Decision at Last

Ann

Thursday, September 3, 1964, Glendale. Terry bounced into La Cocina Café like Tigger on catnip. He dropped the first fresh-off-the-press "Terry issue" of the *Glendale News* on the table. I scrutinized all eight pages, one by one. "So where are your bylines?"

"No bylines this week. No lurid exposés, no breaking news, all piddly stuff."

"Okay, let's see. You did the lead story on next week's election, right?"

"Yep."

"And the high school and college news? Building permits? Foiled teenaged burglars? Miss Mexican Fiesta royalty? And the installation ceremony for the new postmaster? What a scoop! How about the editorial 'Auto Drivers: A Dying Race'?"

"Yep, yep, yep, yep, yep—and nope. You won't catch me writing a cotton-candy editorial like that. I have plenty to say about drunk driving, but this isn't it."

I read the conclusion aloud: "'So we think the millions of words will be wasted—like these we've written,'" I mocked in my best sing-song. "'Good drivers will pay attention. Poor drivers will go on being poor drivers.'" I snorted and tossed it aside. "*Worse* than cotton candy. It's a permit to drive drunk. They shoulda asked you."

"No kidding. Never mind. I'll save my fire for the future."

"You wrote all of page one! What'd they do 'before Terry'? They paying you enough?"

"Enough for what? Where else could you interview the key politicians, the police chief, the gorgeous Miss Mexican Fiesta, and, yes, the postmaster? All in the first three days on the job. Plus, get paid to do it."

"Hey, you even squeezed my name into the Glendale High new-hires story. How embarrassing." I skimmed the rest. Twenty articles in his first week, the majority of the newspaper. What a talent.

Over my first-ever quesadilla at La Cocina, I prattled on about my orientation at school, my new colleagues, the principal. We didn't run down until after nine. "I gotta go, Ter," I told him. "Another long day of orientation tomorrow—can't afford to fall asleep."

"Stay a while longer? Better yet, let's adjourn to your place?"

His eyes were puppy hopeful, but I was beat. Besides, I had to digest the thick binder of school rules and policies we'd been given as "homework"—pages and pages on attendance, tardies, discipline, grades, lesson plans, reports, and deadlines.

He walked me to my car, tried to kiss me good night under the streetlight—right there in downtown Glendale. Not this again! "Hey, let's save that for private."

"Jeez, Annie. Don't be so uptight."

"This is diff—" Too late. His lips had drawn into a line, and his left eyebrow dropped into a scowl. "Sorry, guy," I said to his back. "See you tomorrow?"

He tossed a surly "Sure!" over his shoulder and disappeared around the corner.

Managing Terry around my job was going to be a challenge. Visions of student gossip cavorted through my mind: *Did you see Miss Garretson necking with that guy from the newspaper? ¡Eeeeejole, hombre!* It would undermine my authority. Ugh. I sounded like Mom.

I was still tormenting mental worry beads when I picked up my mail—advertisements, flyers, and two letters. One from Jack. The other from Terry, sent to Albuquerque, forwarded by Mom. Wow, seven neatly typed pages from Terry, dated August 29. And six handwritten pages from Jack, dated September 1. Both error-free. How did they manage to lay their thoughts on paper so perfectly? I always second-guessed my own wording, backed up, crossed out, started over. I skipped to the last page of Terry's letter:

Regardless of what happens to this relationship of ours—whether you decide to marry me or not—I will have gained a new, important outlook, which is far greater than either of us. This, of course, is aside from the great personal gains I have had because of being loved and being able to love.

Let me hastily add that this in no way decreases my desire for marriage, or alters my inability to see any other life but one with you. I want you now more than ever before, but I want you now so that you too can find and share with me what I have found. I hope, then, that you will soon reach the same conclusion.

Oh my, another Terry heart-grabber. I flipped back to the beginning. He bewitched me with descriptions of sunset and nighttime in the desert: "The clouds turn purple, then black, and with the red shining through and around them, they become grotesque, unknown forms guarding the sinking sun. Hundreds of bugs and beetles hum and croak and sing and twitter in the darkness." I wanted to be there beside him.

I turned to page two:

I have grown to want to make love to you very much. Nothing excites me more than seeing your pale, white breasts against your lightly tanned body, or feeling again the softness of a woman. I have wanted you for a long time, of course, but before this summer, it wouldn't have been right. Only when you blushingly told me you wondered what making love with me would be like did I know that you were ready for lovemaking.

Not again! He launched into two pages on having sex with me, even more explicit than his letter from San Francisco. After that, a four-page monologue on love—based on Martin Luther King Jr.'s essay in *Stride Toward Freedom* on *eros, philia,* and *agape.* I loved that about Terry, always reading, thinking. But the sex was too much. He was obsessed with it. *Back off, Ter!*

The letter smoldered. I pushed it away, but not before an image from my high school days threw me into a stinging sweat. My senior year, my boyfriend had declared, "I love you." I was aghast. I liked him a lot, but I was too young to be in love. I wrote him a two-page letter explaining why I couldn't say "I love you" back. I planned to give it to him on our next date, but changed my mind—better to tell him face-to-face. Not wanting anyone to read it, I tore the letter into a mound of confetti and threw it all into my wastebasket. When I got home that night, Mom was asleep on my bed, something she occasionally did so she would know I had gotten home safely. In the semidarkness, I saw it: My confetti reassembled on the carpet, like a puzzle.

Now this letter from Terry sent through Albuquerque. Oh no! Mom didn't steam it open, did she? I examined the envelope. No signs of illegal entry, but that didn't quell my raging anxiety.

I laid Terry's scorcher aside and turned to Jack's letter. It started out chatty, about Terry not leaving for the Peace Corps and the value of volunteers bringing international awareness back to the United States. He said he would join if he were a civilian. At the top of the last page:

> But on the other aspect of Terry's staying, the rival side, well, no man could ask for a better opportunity to throw out his complete line than I had on our European tour. So if my impression was not sufficient to last over time and distance, then it was not of the proper sort in the first place. C'est la vie.

"C'est la vie"? Something deep inside stung, exploding the sparkly dream I'd nurtured for two years. It was an ominous depth charge signaling an end: f-f-f-f-thud. "C'est la vie"? Just like that? Where was his passion? Not sufficient to last? He didn't believe that. Why would he say it? To hurt me? Well, it did, Lieutenant. It did.

I read on. "Now that you've bought a car, I'll have to find somebody else to keep the Sting Ray while I'm at war." He signed off, "Miss you. Love, Jack." Overall, his letter reflected the warm current that had connected us. I was sure he loved me, deep down, but he was marching off to war—no *we* in that declaration. Did I say or do anything on our trip that sent him there? Could I have done anything to make it different? If we had decided to marry, would he still have put in for duty in Vietnam?

Two letters, so opposite, each infuriating in its own way. Terry, sex-crazed and bombastic, crashing into the most private of acts by putting it on paper. And Jack. So defeatist. Preoccupied with war. Unable to think straight about us, about what we'd shared. But "c'est la vie"?

Those pesky thoughts doomed me to a sleepless night—until I hit on a solution: I didn't have to marry either one, not immediately, not until I was sure what I wanted.

It couldn't be right for them—either of them—until it was right for me.

Sunday morning, September 6, 1964, Glendale. My focus was so clear. I couldn't marry Terry or Jack. Not right away. I had to tell them, but how could I carry it off without hurting either of them?

I started with a letter to Jack—a trial run—writing was easier than stuttering things out face-to-face with Terry. Still, my letter was awkward. After Johnstown, I wasn't sure he actually wanted to marry me. But I couldn't leave things up in the air. I told him I couldn't marry anyone right now (so he would know it included Terry), because my first priority had to be my teaching. I couldn't be worrying about planning a wedding or learning how to be a wife or fearing an inevitable call to duty from the army.

Then I had to face Terry. By midafternoon, I was pacing my living room—long before he picked me up for dinner, jittery as a fourteen-year-old on a first date.

At La Cocina, Terry went on about the upcoming week's stories, his plans for turning the *News* into a "real" newspaper. All I could muster was the occasional "uh-huh" until he stopped midsentence and cocked his head. "You're too quiet. What's up?"

I finished chewing the last bite of my quesadilla. "Ter, I can't do it, not right now," I told him—gently, lovingly, but emphatically. "I'm simply not ready to marry *any*body."

Instantly, he clammed up, a gloomy replay of Jack as stone statue in Landshut, when I first told him about my feelings for Terry. "I don't mean forever," I said. "I need time on my own so I can be sure, that's all."

His eyes clouded over and then glistened. "Let's get out of here." He paid the bill. Dropped me off like a hitchhiker. Didn't open the car door. Didn't say good night. Didn't walk me in.

Now what? He had to understand my decision. Love wasn't the issue. I did love him. I simply wasn't ready to marry. Europe had taught me that.

While I had loved the time with Jack, I also took pleasure in (and was amazed by) what I did by myself. I didn't need to depend on my family or a husband.

Terry

Sunday night, 6 September, 1964, Glendale. My mind was reeling. She turned me down. We were talking, chatting like normal. She went silent. Then bam. "No, Ter, I can't."

Was it Jack? I didn't know. She didn't mention him. She did say "your military views" and "I need to be on my own." I couldn't remember what else. It didn't matter, the exact words. It was over. Right there in La Cocina, halfway through a burrito. Our first week together in Glendale, and it was over.

What the hell was I going to do now? In Glendale, Arizona. Alone.

Ann

Labor Day, September 7, 1964, Glendale. On my last day to plan for my first week of teaching, I tried to be super-organized—not a strong suit for me. With three classes of regular senior English and two "decelerated" classes, I'd have to scramble to keep up. As a first-year teacher, I had no reservoir of lesson plans, no notebook full of tips and tricks, no experience. I'd have to create each day's lessons on a blank slate. To top it off, Glendale High was growing so fast I didn't have my own classroom. I'd have to troop from room to room, lugging my materials with me. I refined my first day's lesson plans over breakfast.

But I couldn't concentrate. Pulsing images of Terry and Jack sailed past, tugging, pulling, pleading, scolding, offering up fond memories and tempting pleasures.

And now, I was paralyzed by a new fear. Marriage was forever. How could I possibly know whether I would love either of them forever? That I wouldn't change or they wouldn't?

And finally, I feared disappointing Mom and Dad. But I resented the pressure from all sides. From Mom and Dad *not* to marry Terry. From Terry *to* marry—now—and dive immediately into bed. From Jack, who,

though now distant, circled overhead like a hawk waiting for an opportunity to swoop in.

What was I to do?

Terry

Monday, 7 September 1964, Glendale. I awoke a stranger in a foreign
land, an orphan abandoned in the desert. Last night, she dumped me. My
Peace Corps dreams were dashed. Hopes for marriage squelched. Friends
nonexistent.

At least I had a job. Or I would until the draft board caught up with me.

But no time to mope. Deadlines loomed. I ran a hose from the coffee
pot to my bottomless cup and pounded out one story after another—bios
of the eight candidates from Glendale who were running for statewide offices in the primary election, plans for a new junior college in Glendale, a
burglary, a new well in a local park. Every article would run on page one.
Lunch? A peanut butter sandwich at my desk. At night I collapsed, too
tired to fret over former girlfriends and their twisted logic.

That got me through Monday. Then came Tuesday. And Wednesday.

After we put the *News* to bed Wednesday night, I trooped with the rest
of the staff over to La Cocina for their ritual post-production quesadillas
and Dos Equis celebration. By bedtime, I was too loop-legged for anything
but instant sleep.

Thursdays at the *News* were a midweek respite, as relaxed as Sunday
mornings. I rolled into work at nine-thirty. Turned on the lights and made
the coffee. Read a few press releases. Thumbed the *Arizona Republic*. Somewhere between the front-page news that President Johnson had ordered
the FBI to probe the nation's string of recent race riots and the devastation caused by Hurricane Dora, I realized that Annie hadn't said, "I don't
love you," or "No, Terry, I'll never marry you." She'd said, "I'm not ready,
Terry, I'm just not."

That slow-to-come insight got me through the first week.

Tuesday, 15 September 1964, Glendale. Nine days since I'd seen Annie.
Nine days since she'd destroyed my future. Before the school year started,
both of us had signed up for a class on the Arizona State Constitution at

the local community college—she because it was required for teachers new to Arizona, and I because it would help me cover local and state politics. It didn't make sense to drive there separately, so I worked up the courage to call her.

Not a simple call, though. No "hi, howdy" would do. With Annie you had to open with a puzzler or something that would make her laugh.

"Hi," I said. "Happy anniversary!"

A long silence. "Terry? Is that you? And whose anniversary might that be?"

"Darwin's—1835. On this day the HMS Beagle dropped anchor in the Galapagos."

Silence again, and then, "Dang. It slipped my mind. Meant to bake a cake."

"Never mind. How about we celebrate? Can I buy you a drink?"

Another pause. "Deal."

We met for Cokes after school at La Cocina and circled like boxers in a rematch, tossing around softball tidbits from our new lives. As our initial awkwardness dissolved into normal banter, I ventured, "Do you want to carpool to the Arizona Constitution class tonight?"

"Of course," she said. "It would be crazy to drive two cars downtown."

An awkward half hour, but at least we talked. Even laughed once or twice. I paid. Twenty cents. It was a start, and it gave us a reason to see each other at least once a week.

Early fall 1964, Glendale. My promised five-day-a-week job quickly burgeoned to six, then seven. I filled my days and nights with work. I didn't date. I didn't have time. Besides, as for girls, all I wanted was to win Annie back. My night life? Other than the Tuesday-night Arizona Constitution class, it was city council, school board, "Goldwater for President" rallies, reelect Johnson rallies, Democratic powwows, Republican powwows, weekend festivals.

I camped out one whole weekend with National Guard troops playing war games—sprinting through the desert, diving into the dirt, firing on pop-up enemy targets—and produced a full-page photo essay. I crept into John Birch Society rallies and collected right-wing propaganda—a screed on the Supreme Court, "Nine Men Against America"; Joseph McCarthy's

"America's Retreat from Victory"; and pamphlets on CIA clandestine operations in Bolivia.

My boss urged me to join the Birchers, saying he would give me a day a week for as long as I needed to write an insider exposé. No, too slimy! I wasn't a spy or an undercover man. But when he asked me to write editorials, I jumped at the chance and wrote the paper's endorsement of Lyndon Johnson over what's his name, that local guy—Arizona Senator Barry Goldwater.

I also covered Glendale High and became as familiar with the sprawling campus as Annie was. I shot a group photo of all the new teachers—Ann Garretson front and center. I wrote a feature on the cross-country team (how long-distance runners deal with the pain) and one on the marching band (the many hours of practice needed to perform so precisely each Friday night).

I did a "teen of the week" feature: the kid who organized a "Teens for Goldwater" club (step one, he hoped, to becoming Arizona's senator); the boy out deer hunting who bagged a cougar from ten feet; the girl with a Julie Andrews voice who played the female lead in the school production of *Carousel*. I was on hand with my camera at their final rehearsal when John Rait—who played the male lead on Broadway—strode in from the wings, shunted aside the befuddled student playing Billy Bigelow, and joined her in a tear-jerking "If I Loved You." He kissed her as passionately as he had kissed his own Julie Jordan on the Broadway stage.

And when the *News* merged with the *Herald* in October and we became the *Glendale News-Herald*, I did a full-page photo essay showing local folks reading the first combined issue. Not accidentally, Miss Ann Garretson was one of those "randomly chosen" readers.

Ann

Early fall 1964, Glendale. I plunged into teaching with the fire of Carrie Nation and Margaret Sanger. I'd teach these kids to love literature and to write with passion. That first day, I hauled 140 papers home to grade. I wrote comments on every one. It took me three nights. Even if I limited myself to five minutes each, it meant at least ten hours of work—on top of creating new lesson plans daily. One month into the school year, piles of ungraded papers had mushroomed, commandeering every horizontal surface in my apartment, threatening to bury me.

I had requested the decelerated classes (as they were called) during my job interview. I wanted to work with kids who needed extra help. Thus began my education in real life. My decelerated classes were the same size as my regular classes. Too many students for one-on-one tutoring. And they were not longing for my benevolent touch. They were less motivated and less able to express themselves—the products of eleven years of our society's not-so-benign neglect. Many lived in poverty and faced crippling conditions at home, like the kid who crept in late, half an hour or more, every morning for my eight o'clock class.

Sometimes Felipe didn't show up at all. I should have called him aside and asked him how I could help him arrive on time. I should have done everything possible to open his eyes to literature, to worlds he had never imagined. But I didn't. Rather, I pleaded and scolded. He shrugged and made jokes. The class laughed. I became impatient and aggravated.

It wasn't until the end of the school year that his counselor mentioned over lunch that before Felipe came to school each day, he carried his father, a double amputee, out to the car and drove him to physical therapy. I was stunned, then haunted that my harangues had added to his burdens, that I hadn't taken the time to understand his challenges or didn't have the maturity or teaching experience that would have prompted me to find out.

Most students in my decelerated classes were Mexican Americans. I liked them. They kindled warm memories of my own Alamosa High classmates—kids who opened a small window into a different culture for me, where extended families wrapped their children in a mantle of love and humor. At the ranch, my cousin and I used to pile our siblings into the pickup and go hang out at the little store at Las Sauces, a Mexican American settlement a short jaunt down the road. We shared a common love of wide-open grasslands under endless blue sky.

The appalling truth was that being Mexican American in Colorado and Arizona branded kids as less capable, even when they were really bright. Too many teachers had accepted that racist stereotype, and by the time the decelerated students arrived in my senior English classes, they were perilously behind their Anglo peers.

The system had failed them. I didn't know how to change it.

↜

In addition to the required Arizona Constitution class, I signed up for two more college classes: Modern Literature and Transformational Grammar. What was I thinking? Fortunately, Terry and I managed a reconciliation around our Arizona Constitution class and met for "study dates." That helped a lot, but the other two classes were eating me up.

Soon, the passion for our new jobs overshadowed all else. Early on, Terry scooped the big city *Arizona Republic* on Glendale's controversial new city employee union. The union president invited him to their meetings. Terry came back with tales from the garbage men about abysmal working conditions—low pay, antiquated equipment, and an epidemic of debilitating back injuries. Together, we honed his drafts, me pressing him for details, pointing out errors, and suggesting alternate wordings.

In less than a month, Terry became the paper's primary editorial writer. I read those drafts, too, toning down his sometimes vitriolic rhetoric.

On top of his weekly newspaper production, he helped me catch up on the mountain of work that came with recording grades, tracking progress, and even lesson planning.

He, too, aspired to teach someday. One night I cried out in frustration, "How can I ever get these kids tuned in to Victorian lit?" We kicked ideas around. "Make it a game," he said.

At school, I split the class in half, pitting one team against the other, telling them it's their version of TV's popular *GE College Bowl*, and then began firing questions. By Friday, hands were shooting up so fast I couldn't tell whose went up first.

Sharing the excitement and challenges of our work brought us ever closer—the *Colorado Daily* all over again, only better. As Halloween approached, our enthusiasm spilled into and revived our Sunday night dinners and led to an occasional movie or hike in the desert.

We got together at my place, never his. I'd been to his quaint one-room cottage once. That was enough. When we first entered his "home," he flipped on the light and banged the wall.

"What's that about?" I asked.

"You have to wait for the cockroaches to scatter. There's a million of 'em."

"Roaches?" I hesitated.

"Yeah, this is the desert. What do you expect for $60.10 a month? They won't hurt you."

"But they're filthy!"

"Yeah. But it's the scorpions you have watch out for. Last week, while I was dressing, I dropped my shoe and a three-incher scurried out."

That was another thing: Though Terry and Jack were both skinflints, I knew Jack would never stoop to live in such a dump. Nor would I, regardless of which one I married.

To humor Mom, I squeezed in dates with a few other men. I wasn't looking for someone "better than" Terry or Jack, but a date now and then seemed a good test of my judgment. So when I was asked out, I accepted. Each was a one-shot ordeal:

The air force pilot, first lieutenant. Training at Luke Air Force Base on some new supersonic fighter jet, he soared through the skies at Mach 2.3 (1,751 miles/hour). He swore he could fly faster and with more agility in his cape than in his plane.

The corporate lawyer. Not yet a partner and dealing mostly with real estate transactions, but he'd be a famous trial lawyer someday, he was sure of it. He didn't converse—he delivered points, counterpoints, and closing arguments.

The up-and-coming oilman. Every well he drilled apparently spewed gold bullion, not oil at all, so much that he had to build his own King Midas vault. Nonstop talk about money got boring halfway through our only date.

I couldn't generate any more interest in their jet planes, legal cases, or oil wells than they expressed in my teaching career. Plus, they all smoked, and I came home smelling like an ashtray. Worse, every single one seemed interested only in sex, money, liquor, and sex.

Each fiasco endeared me even more to both Terry and Jack.

Terry

Wednesday, 28 October 1964, Glendale. Damn draft board! For two years, they had stalked me like a coyote on the scent of a wounded fawn. They had refused to classify me a conscientious objector, but at least they had deferred me from the draft while I was a student.

Now this. Today's mail brought SSS Form 223: "Order to Report for Armed Forces Physical Examination." The draft board ordered me to show up at the Rio Grande County Courthouse in Del Norte, Colorado, on Wednesday, November 18. Then they threatened me:

> If you fail to report for examination as directed, you may be declared delinquent and ordered to report for induction into the Armed Forces. You will also be subject to fine and imprisonment under the provisions of the Universal Military Training and Service Act, as amended.

In March, before I graduated, I had informed them I'd been accepted into the Peace Corps. They'd responded with SSS Form 300, "Permit of the Local Board for Registrant to Depart from the United States," granting me *permission* to leave the country until October 1, 1966—as if those old fogies on the draft board had any right to bar me from leaving.

When I moved to Glendale, I wrote to them that I wasn't going to the Peace Corps after all. I sent my new address, a copy of my April 1963 letter asking to be classified as a conscientious objector, and a request for SSS Form 150, "Special Form for Conscientious Objector." I'd heard that draft boards wouldn't even read CO requests unless they were filed on that particular form.

In response, they jerked my II-S student deferment and reclassified me I-A, "Available for Military Service." They also sent the CO form. I had read the form carefully the first time they'd sent it and decided I couldn't fill it out. It was too bureaucratic, all black and white, no shades of gray. Take question five: "Under what circumstances, if any, do you believe in the use of force?"

This time, I had to give them an answer. I responded with a short lecture:

The term "force" could carry several meanings, and thus is vague. If one believes (as do Mahatma Gandhi and Rev. Martin Luther King Jr.) that love, as applied through nonviolent resistance, is the use of force, I must say I believe wholeheartedly in the use of force.

Every question was rooted in a preconceived bias that to be a conscientious objector, you had to be a card-carrying member of some government-sanctioned religious faith.

Question 1: Do you believe in a Supreme Being? ☐ Yes ☐ No.

Question 2: Describe the nature of your belief which is the basis of your claim . . . and state whether or not your belief in a Supreme Being involves duties which to you are superior to those arising from any human relation.

Question 3: Explain how, when, and from whom or from what source you received the training and acquired the belief which is the basis of your claim . . .

Whoa! How could anyone trace the development of a belief system to a specific source? What was I to answer—a bolt from God, who I wasn't sure existed? The Methodist minister in Center, who didn't understand how anyone could question the existence of God or refuse to "serve his country" with a rifle? Or how about Martin Luther King Jr., whose "Pilgrimage to Nonviolence" in *Stride Toward Freedom* certainly influenced me?

In September I had filed away the SSS Form 150 and went on with the business of putting out a newspaper and pursuing Miss Garretson. But this new "Order to Report for Armed Forces Physical Examination"—this was a serious threat I couldn't ignore.

We got the *News-Herald* to press late Wednesday. I spent Thursday recuperating and sketching out a work plan for the following week's issue.

Then I spent the whole damn weekend responding to the draft board's SSS Form 150—not by completing it, but by banging out a five-page, single-spaced letter that rephrased the questions and detailed my beliefs that proved I was a conscientious objector.

The whole question of conscientious objection was cast in the context of participation in war. But SSS Form 150 skirted the key issue: *killing*—specifically, *killing human beings*. That was the basis for my claim. I believed it immoral to kill another human being.

Ironically, the incident that had sealed my conviction didn't involve a human at all. It was seared into my soul by a rabbit, a female jackrabbit, an innocent doe. Like most farm kids in Center, I spent many an hour in the fields near our house with my .22-caliber Remington rifle, tracking "big game"—rabbits, magpies, tin cans, and beer bottles. One fall weekend in high school, I zeroed in on a sprinting rabbit and dropped it on a dead run. I sauntered over and knelt to inspect my trophy. She lay there panting, blood pooling, but not yet dead. Her eyes were wide open, red, pleading with me. *How could you?* they said. *Why would you?*

I never hunted again.

I didn't include that story in my response to SSS Form 150. The three men on the draft board—a farmer and two small business owners from the nearby towns of Del Norte and Monte Vista—were, like my father, World War II veterans. They had "served their country." They all belonged to the VFW. They owned guns. They hunted. I imagined myself meeting with them in person, relating that story. They'd look at me in disbelief: *A rabbit? Jesus, kid, your dad was a fine man, well respected in this county. What the hell happened to you?*

In my response to SSS Form 150, I bypassed the issue of killing. I answered in their terms, not mine, pointing out nuances that made it impossible to write simple responses. Too many nuances, too many shades. And here was the kicker that caused me heartburn—the SSS Form 150 required claimants for CO status to sign one of two statements:

(A) I am, by reason of my religious training and belief, conscientiously opposed to participation in war in any form. I, therefore, claim exemption from combatant training and service in the Armed Forces.

(B) I am, by reason of my religious training and belief, conscientiously opposed to participation in war in any form and I am further conscientiously opposed to participation in noncombatant training and service in the Armed Forces. I, therefore, claim exemption from both combatant and noncombatant training and service in the Armed Forces.

I couldn't sign either. I rejected the draft on moral grounds, not religious ones. I wrote:

Under present law, no provisions are made for those like me who claim conscientious objection on moral grounds; thus, my appeal for such classification seems fruitless. However, I cannot be loyal to myself and submit to the draft. I am prepared to accept the penalties for violation rather than sacrifice my principles.

I feel obligated to inform you that I will not report on Nov. 18 to the Court House in Del Norte, Colo., as directed by SSS Form 223: "Order to Report for Armed Forces Physical Examination."

So on the first workday of the month—2 November 1964—I was at the Glendale post office the moment it opened. The hassle with my draft board was no longer a penny-ante annoyance. I needed written proof they had received my response. I paid an extra twenty cents to send my letter by certified mail. That, too, pissed me off.

20

The Dreaded M-Word

Ann

Thursday, November 5, 1964, Glendale. I arrived at La Cocina ahead of Terry for a change and chose a booth toward the back, the latest issue of the paper tucked under my arm.

Two days before, on Election Day, he had vanished into the *News-Herald* and worked late. That marathon day extended into Wednesday night: thirty-six hours straight.

When he slid into the booth next to me, his eyes were red and he sprouted a two-day beard. But our recounting of Johnson's stunning landslide over Goldwater sent him soaring again. Our shoulders rubbing, we thumbed through the paper, and he recounted the dramatic turnout in Precinct 4: "I monitored it all day. Most voters waited in line more than three hours," he said, as we pored over his front-page photo. "At one point the line snaked clear across the railroad tracks, and . . ."

Midsentence, he paused and turned to me. A goofy grin spread over his face. "It's past time. We need to get married."

His words hovered in the air like a helium balloon waiting to be caught. Or popped.

Surprisingly, I didn't freak out. The bonds we had cemented by working together on his editorials and articles, my lesson plans, and our Arizona Constitution class—and by exploring Arizona many a weekend—had wrapped us ever closer. They would have squeezed out all doubt but for one issue. The draft.

His intransigence had me tied in knots. I didn't disagree with him philosophically. But I had labored to tone down his preachy responses on the conscientious objector form, as well as testing his clarity on key nuances like the distinction between combatant and noncombatant service. And I pushed him to get a lawyer—what good would come from going to jail?

When Terry refused to take the army physical, I feared they'd haul him off any moment. That worry wedged itself between every lesson plan, every paper I graded, every waking moment. Terry was equally apprehensive. If I wanted to talk to him, I had to call, let it ring twice, hang up, call back, ring once, and hang up again—just like at CU with the Atkins fiasco.

In the midst of my inner tumult, I had been drawn to Jack's more mainstream thinking. Despite the wound his "c'est la vie" letter had inflicted, I still loved him. I fixated on that letter. He'd opened with "Dearest Ann," signed it with "Love." *Should I blow on the embers and nurse them back to life?*

No, I had concluded, life with Jack would force me to battle different demons.

Terry and I hadn't mentioned the M-word since Labor Day. But now, our physical play outstripped springtime in Boulder. Good-night kisses began hours before he left my apartment. We explored each other's bodies shamelessly. It seemed absurd to end each day with Terry trudging off to that roach-infested cottage. Or not once waking up to the joy of being side by side in bed together. Clearly, we were on our way to that act I had reserved for the man I married. I teetered at the precipice, wrestling with my own desire and trying to rein his in.

Physical intimacy aside, marriage no longer seemed the Rubicon I had envisioned it to be. Terry hadn't inhibited my freedom or stifled my creativity. He had enhanced both.

As for the draft, I didn't have an answer. I knew only that I couldn't allow some distant draft board to decide whom I would or would not marry.

"Yeah, we should," I said. "And soon." It just popped out of my mouth.

For a moment, we sat there stunned, my last bite suspended midway to my mouth.

"Yes?" he said. "You said yes?" He started to hug me, but I warned him off with my eyes. Glendale was still a small town. And I was still a new teacher, out in public.

"Yes. Yes. Yes!" I squeezed his knee. "Do you need it in writing?"

Terry

Friday, 6 November 1964, Glendale. A Marshall-Garretson wedding at last? After all that heartache over Annie's devastating *no* the first weekend in September? How could that be?

No simple answer. We never had a single aha moment. I didn't sink to one knee and propose, nor did Annie dissolve into tears and sob, *Yes, of course I will, Ter, of course I will.* Our touches didn't, at some magical moment, ignite fireworks that lit up the future. She didn't wake up in the middle of the night to a heavenly command: *Now is the time. Marry that man!* It wasn't a bolt of lightning at all, but a thousand sparks artfully compressed into a mosaic of colorful memories like these:

Weekend tennis: I go to her place each Saturday morning at seven. She shoves aside a pile of student papers. We work up a sweat on the municipal tennis court, then splash in the Maryland Club Apartments' modest pool. We eat lunch on her tiny backyard patio. And on rare occasions, our weekly hour-long tennis class turns into an all-day romp.

Dawn one Sunday: We drive eighteen miles to the famed Goodyear Blimp's winter quarters. The *News-Herald*'s ad manager has finagled a ride for the three of us. In unearthly silence, we float over lush cotton fields and citrus orchards framed by the stark desert of central Arizona.

A Saturday afternoon: I drop next week's editorial on her kitchen table. "The idea's good, but you don't have to attack everyone in town," she says. She splatters the draft with red marks. I dress the bloody wounds. Monday, the publisher reads it: "Great job, Marshall. Well put!"

Meals together: We dine at her place on a Thursday. Or a Monday. Or whenever. Annie concocts a quick meal—ground beef, slivered onions and potatoes, and I work up a fresh fruit salad. After dinner, she washes, and I dry. Then it's back to grading papers or lesson planning for her and a night meeting and writing for me.

So what changed her mind?
She shrugged. "It was time. That's all. With your best friend, you just know."

Ann

Friday, Teachers Convention Day, November 6, 1964, Glendale. I hadn't joined the Arizona Education Association, so I had the whole day off. I took a deep breath and spent the day writing and rewriting a couple of long-postponed letters.

First, to Mom and Dad.

Pages one and two: updates on my classes—vignettes of student antics, snippets from English lit, discipline woes, and life in the Maryland Club Apartments.

Pages three and four: I worked up the nerve to tell them I planned to marry Terry and I wanted their approval. I laid out my case. Extolled his virtues. No question, he was the one.

Page five: My clincher, "We don't believe in long engagements." This was one of Mom's aphorisms: *Long engagements breed too much familiarity* (translation: premarital sex). I used her words to soften the shock of my next line. "We plan to get married over Christmas."

Yikes. We had six weeks to pull off a wedding. I sealed the letter before I got cold feet.

Next letter: Break the news to Jack. Ironically, I had just received a "Dearest Ann" note with his "momentous" news—he had interviewed with the foreign service. The head of the panel told him they "needed his type." I was delighted, both with their endorsement and with this positive hook I could use to start my letter. I hadn't written since his "c'est la vie" letter. The tidal wave of lesson plans and papers to grade had swept away time to respond.

In his note, he apologized for not writing sooner and then hit me with "I rather thought you'd decided against communicating for some reason." This new gibe stung as much as his quirky complaint of a year earlier about shooting the mail clerk and saving a bullet for himself—gentle but cutting rebukes of my own shortcomings as a letter writer. He said he'd visit me on his way to Vietnamese language training in California. He signed it, "Love."

I couldn't simply toss a breezy adios over my shoulder. Not to this man who had loved me without reservation, despite my erratic letter writing, the rivalry from Terry, his disappointments in our love life. He forgave my shortcomings, accepted my love without judgment, and even trusted me with his beloved Sting Ray.

He had also taught me more about the military than I had ever learned as an army brat. At the German-Czech border, he showed me what it meant to fight the Cold War, how essential it was to defend freedom with military might. And he gloried in the joy of living a cross-cultural life. He'd demonstrated that you didn't have to hate a former enemy. He had never been an American soldier "occupying" Germany, but rather, a fellow human with shared goals who had steeped himself in German culture and language and become a better person because of it.

Peeling our lives apart was as painful for me as I imagined it was for him. "I'll always love you," I wrote, "but I know now I cannot be the next generation of my mom. My behavior in the Landshut social scene was contrary to the inner me. I'll never be able to fill Mom's spiky heels or wear red lipstick or laugh politely at the general's ribald jokes."

I reread my final draft, signed and sealed it.

Then I folded up and cried.

Terry

Saturday, 14 November 1964, Glendale. We set another pot of coffee to percolate and spread out our draft wedding invitation—a four-page mini-newspaper, *Las Dos Animas* (The Two Souls). News stories, headlines, an editorial, letters to the editor, classified ads, a full-page photo spread. No traditional invitation on pretentious stationery for us. No "Colonel and Mrs. Ralph Bonner Garretson Sr. request the honor of your presence at the marriage of their daughter . . ." This wedding would capture the essence of our beings.

First, we banged out an editor's note:

You may not believe it, but this newsletter is a wedding invitation.

In a way, we're sorry we're not sending fancy, engraved announcements. They generally bring friends by the score and loot by the ton. We like both. But our little newspaper is more in keeping with our personalities. We're a little more informal than many.

Even if you aren't getting the customary engraved note, we still want you to drop in on the ceremony if you're in the area. (We don't expect you to make a special trip for it.) Or you can drop in for a sandwich and a swig of booze (milk if you prefer) afterward.

In place of loot, though, why not drop an extra five-spot into United Fund or your church collection plate or send a check to the United Nations. Or you might send a book to someone in the Peace Corps. All we want is a card saying hello, with a word about what you have been thinking and doing. We have everything else we need.

Then my thoughts turned to the draft board. I whipped out a letter to the editor:

Dear Editor:

We recently heard the news. But it won't work. We know as well as you do that your only reason for getting married is to avoid serving your country.

Enclosed is Form 339271803: "Order to File Real Reasons for Marriage, and to Report for Physical Exam, Induction Ceremony, Basic Training, and Shipment to Fort Misery." Fill out in triplicate and return within three days. Remember, Uncle Sam will get you.

Fiendishly,
Your Local Draft Board

And it was on to the classified ads. We tossed out ideas like shiny beads, snapped up those with promise, and brought them to life on the typewriter:

For sale: One used copy *How to Win Friends and Influence People.* Carefully read, but ineffective. See at newsroom of *Glendale News-Herald.*

For sale: One slightly used copy *Sex and the Single Girl.* Mint condition. Make offer. A. Garretson. Box 00.1, Glendale.

For rent: Tiny, bug-infested studio cottage with one broken window and warped door. No heater. Faulty air conditioner. Close to barking dogs, railroad tracks, and 7-Eleven. Bring bug spray and apply at 7409 N. 61st Avenue. Late nights only.

We camped out at Annie's kitchen table, ignoring the thunderheads of ungraded student papers and next week's editorial commemorating the first anniversary of President Kennedy's assassination. After lunch, we laid aside silliness to explain to our friends—and ourselves—how our friendship had turned to love.

I recounted last summer's climb up Kendall Peak where I "looked out at the world around me, the mile after mile of endless mountains, and asked, 'Who are we, so small, to stand here?'" I described my "biting loneliness" while Annie traveled Europe. Then we wrapped up our newsletter-invitation with this summary:

We marry now to destroy that loneliness, yes, but also to share the mutual joy in a sunset, the common pride in a well-prepared classroom lecture, the common hopes and desires and ambitions, the common sorrows and disappointments.

We remain lost, for we have not yet found the answer to "Who are we to stand here?" that I had asked so often in Silverton. We still search for our answer—and many times, for the right questions. But in marriage, we search together. That should make the difference.

Late afternoon, Annie pushed back from the table. "Enough already. We've turned Saturday into another workday. We're getting married. Let's celebrate."

We fixed cheese and crackers, opened her only bottle of wine—a Mateus rosé—pulled chairs onto the patio, and gloried in another dazzling Arizona sunset.

Though we had agreed to get married the day after Christmas, we hadn't done anything about choosing a church. We were sitting there, sipping wine, when it became obvious. We'd get married at sunset, somewhere in the desert near Glendale. No church needed.

Over dinner and margaritas at La Cocina, we let our fancies roam free. We'd fly to Mexico City for a grand eight-day honeymoon. We'd stroll the Zócalo. Wander Chapultepec Park and explore the National Museum of Anthropology. Climb the pyramids at Teotihuacan. We'd search out the murals of José Clemente Orozco, Diego Rivera, and David Alfaro Siqueiros. And we'd spend at least one night in Cuernavaca, the city of eternal spring.

The perfect end to a roller-coaster year, no?

21
Land Mines on the Road to Silverton

Terry

Monday, 16 November 1964, Glendale. Today, a shot over the bow from the draft board, short and to the point, dated November 12:

> The information submitted does not warrant reopening your classi-fication. Your Order to Report for Physical Examination mailed on October 26, 1964, to report on November 18, 1964, is still in effect.

Thursday, 19 November 1964. I didn't report for the physical. I spent the day at the *News-Herald*, pounding out stories under deadline—and looking over my shoulder, half expecting the military police to storm the building and haul me off to jail.

Since my move to Glendale in August, when I sent the draft board my new address, a nasty premonition had been skittering through the recesses of my mind like a midnight scorpion. In October, it had morphed into a coyote, stalking me in the shadows. Now it was a diamondback, coiled beside my bed, poised to strike.

Ann

Wednesday, November 25, 1964, Glendale. I had looked forward to Thanks-giving for weeks. I needed a break from my daily planning-teaching-grad-ing grind. Bonner flew into Phoenix from Washington, DC, to "keep me company" on my drive to Albuquerque. I hadn't seen him since August. Having cleared the air on the Hofbräuhaus episode before I left Germany, we devoted the first two hours of our trip to Albuquerque that November day to happy brother-sister talk. Then he took the wheel and smoothly sailed the car through the twisty Salt River Canyon—and the conversation into an ambush. "Are you really going to marry that guy? What's his name, the letter writer?"

"Yep, we decided it was time to get off the dime. Nice, huh?"

"He's not right for you."

"How would you know? You've never met him." Under my calm exterior, my demons whipped up a blistering attack: *Whoa, you're the guy who knocked up Gretchen and threw her away. Who are you to counsel anyone on love?* I didn't say it.

Marrying Terry would besmirch our family honor, he said, our religion, our folks' sacrifices for us, and the army. He extolled Jack's qualities as if they were ribbons on a four-star general's chest.

I countered with praise for Terry, our long friendship, his talent, and his values. I'd never won a debate with Bonner. He was too quick-witted, too articulate, too unflappable. But I couldn't help thinking his arguments seemed too well-honed. Had our folks sent him to talk me out of marrying Terry? Or had he come on behalf of Jack? I tensed up. "We're in love, Bonner. We're getting married. End of discussion."

"Yeah, if that's how you feel, you should. But you shouldn't have trashed Mom like that. That was nasty, Sis. Just plain nasty." He spit the words like shrapnel.

"'Trashed Mom'? What are you talking about?"

"'I can't be the next generation of my mom, wearing red lipstick, trying to fill her spiky heels,'" he whined in a snarky imitation of me. "Talk like that shouldn't go outside the family."

A prickly sweat crept up my neck. Those *were* my words—from my letter to Jack! Angry retorts boiled in my head. *So where'd you get that little nugget, big brother? How dare you read my mail! And you, Jack: You showed him my letter? How could you?*

Bonner had navigated the entire Salt River Canyon before I could squelch my internal invective. "Okay, let's step back a bit," I said at last. "This was my toughest decision ever. Jack will always be special to me—in more ways than *you* can possibly know." Bonner may have read my mail, but he couldn't read my mind! "I'm finally coming to terms with who I am. I'm not geared to be an army wife. As for Mom, defining my own path and becoming my own person is hardly 'trashing' her. They raised us to be independent. I'm affirming their success."

That was the opening skirmish in a weekend of sorties. On Thanksgiving Day, Mom and I were talking about my job as we got dinner ready. Out of nowhere she said, "Annie, teachers need to be above reproach. You shouldn't let Terry hang around your apartment so much. It doesn't look good."

"Jeez, Mom, where'd that come from?"

"Well, you are quite a catch. You can command *the very best*, so beware of getting indoctrinated by screwball ideas."

I nearly dropped the casserole. "Mom, I love Terry. He loves me. We're getting married. Please find some way to come to grips with that."

I said it calmly, but it hurt us both. Her eyes welled up. Mine too. She turned away, busied herself with the salad. Minutes passed. She turned back. "Would you ask Ralph to set the table, honey? Tell him we'll be ready in half an hour."

That was it—truce by avoidance. We prodded and poked and implied this or that, but at the least sign of resistance, we retreated.

Thanksgiving dinner went off as if we were the Nelson family in *The Adventures of Ozzie and Harriet*. Stories about my classes, my students, Arizona's glorious fall climate. Bonner's new assignment at Fort Belvoir, his readjustment to life in the States, his new girlfriend. Jimmy's prowess as a pole-vaulter, his classes at Sandia High. Mom's and Dad's joy in "finding a home" in a neighborhood church, Dad spearheading a drive to pave the church parking lot. We emptied two bottles of wine. Dad, Bonner, and Jimmy talked sports over the TV football games. Mom and I cleaned up, babbling as if we were still at the ranch and I was back in high school.

Friday evening, as I was fluffing my hair before we went out for dinner, Mom said, "How about a French roll? They're so elegant. And you do attract men by your grooming."

"Mom, I'm not trying to attract men. I'm engaged. Remember?"

"Yes, my darling, but may I add one more thing?"

I said nothing, steeling myself.

"Be sure this is really *love*. There has to be a *real thrill* for a marriage to work. A lively gift of gab, being buddy-buddy, and sharing the same likes and dislikes are important, but not as important as that all-consuming thrill that tells you this is the one."

I fixed my eyes on hers, forcing her to look at me. "Know what, Mom? You're right." I wrapped my arms over my breasts in a tight self-hug, effected a sultry look, and gave a throaty whisper, "Let me tell you how he thrills me. How lovingly he can—"

She clapped her hands over her ears. "Oh, no, honey! Please, no!" She dropped into a silly knee-knocking Charleston dance—her way of apologizing. "Oh, Annie, I'm sorry. As the song goes, 'Deary, please don't be angry. It's 'cause I'm lovin' you.'"

Such a goofy look. I had to smile. "I know, Mom, but let's call a cease-fire."

Later, she pulled me aside. "Honey, if this is the man you really love, you have our blessings for all the happiness in the world. I do hope you'll wait until summer, though, both to be really sure and to allow time to plan a proper wedding."

Saturday morning, November 28, 1964, Albuquerque. I gripped the wheel of my Bel Air and limped out of town, my spirits bruised and aching. All my life, my family had been a bulwark of support. But the harder they pushed against Terry, the more I dug my heels in.

They hoped for a proper princess doll, forever at her well-heeled husband's side—an army officer, a lawyer, a doctor, some high-paid professional. I wanted to be a free spirit. They wanted me to build my teaching career one gray concrete block on top of another. I wanted to join the Peace Corps and make the world a better place, initiating a future molded by travel and experiences I hadn't yet imagined. They wanted me to embrace the conservative politics that permeated military life. During their campaign to tug me back into the fold, Mom had sent me *A Choice Not an Echo*, a right-wing tract promoting Goldwater for president. It pained me she thought such tripe worth reading.

But those were the least of my worries that blustery morning. As I began the descent into the Salt River Canyon, snow driven by howling wind obscured the hairpin turns—not a place or time to dwell on family jousts over my future. Then my radio sputtered out, so no friendly announcer to override my thoughts. Soon after, one by one, the heater, the defroster, and the wipers died. With what turned out to be a cold coming on, I began

shivering and coughing. Suddenly, ka-thunk, ka-thunk. A flat tire! Where
was Bonner when I needed him? By the time I dug out the jack and spare,
my sneakers and thin jacket were soaked.

Finally, a man stopped. Didn't say a word. Seemed angry at me for making his day worse. But he changed the tire. I thanked him profusely. He
shrugged. By the time I reached Globe, about a hundred miles from home,
everything was closed except a grubby one-man gas station. "Electrical system," he said. He fixed it with duct tape and chewing tobacco. It got me home.

That and the angry Samaritan were the only bits of good news all day.

Terry

Saturday, 28 November 1964, Glendale. Aside from the fact I'd been alone
the entire holiday—including my birthday on the twenty-fifth—and the
painful void that Annie's pilgrimage to Albuquerque made in my Thanksgiving, this turned out to be a bellwether day.

I was home alone, but I was no longer alone in my battle with the draft.
Back on November 18, after we'd gotten the *News-Herald* to press, I put
together a packet of my correspondence with the draft board and wrote to
the Central Committee for Conscientious Objectors in Philadelphia, asking for advice. Now, ten days later, I heard back from the CCCO's execu-
tive director, Arlo Tatum:

> *Your letter to the local board of 31st October is truly excellent. It makes
> me wish that you could be a test case to challenge the constitutional-
> ity of the requirement that conscientious objectors be religious in or-
> der to obtain that classification—assuming we have success with the
> Seeger case now before the Supreme Court. However, you would not
> have much of a court case unless you "exhaust all the administrative
> remedies" and this includes the taking of a physical.*

He warned that since I hadn't shown up for the physical exam, I was
now liable for "a delinquency notice." The draft board could issue that notice and order me to report for immediate induction. They could screw up
my life—and sabotage my marriage!

Tatum added:

If you are ordered to report for induction on the basis of a delinquency notice, you could not then marry your fiancée and cause the induction order to be cancelled. If you took your pre-induction physical exam, and were ordered to report for induction, you could marry and cause the induction notice to be cancelled.

Contact a lawyer—immediately, Tatum said. He referred me to one in Phoenix.

Okay, Arlo. Annie had been pushing me anyway. She was right—it was time to talk to an expert.

Ann

Late Saturday, November 28, 1964, Glendale. Two nights after Thanksgiving, I slumped on my sofa, barking like a sea lion, too sick and too tired to move. Slowly, the road vibrations dissipated. "Oh, Ter, the trip home was miserable. The whole darn weekend was miserable!"

I dribbled out my sad tale of Thanksgiving, starting with the wretched drive back. I couldn't stop hacking. He found some cough drops, fixed me a cup of hot chocolate, cozied me in my down comforter, eased down beside me, and held my hand.

To protect the open wounds beneath the Garretson armor, I didn't divulge the worst details, not wanting to prejudice him against my family. We planned to marry for life, to hold our families close. So somewhere at the bottom of Salt River Canyon, I had swallowed the most cutting words—*gift of gab, indoctrinated, real man,* and *command the best.* All I needed to tell him was that they didn't want us to get married.

"I don't know, Ter. In some ways, their opposition makes me want to barrel ahead. Get married in Mexico City. The heck with them all."

"Elope?"

"Why not? Mom and Dad did. Talk about just deserts. You didn't know that, did you? And here's why—her parents rejected him. They were hardcore Baptist teetotalers. A man who had a sip of liquor now and then—which Dad did—wasn't fit to marry their daughter.

"But I'm not serious about eloping, of course. We want a simple wedding, a meaningful ceremony in a setting that inspires us . . . Right?"

He nodded and kissed my hand.

"And we want to share our joy with friends and family."

But reality told us we'd have a heck of a time pulling off a wedding by Christmas, now less than a month away. We had drafted our clever invitation but hadn't printed it. We had no location. No minister. No wedding dress. No ring. No plans for a rehearsal dinner. Nothing.

"What do we need to rehearse anyway?" Terry asked. "A wedding's a snap: Walk down the aisle. Say 'I do!' and 'Me too!' Then kiss the bride. And dive into bed."

"TERRRRRRY!" That set off another coughing fit.

"Or we could live together in sin. Easier and more Bohemian." He snickered.

I ignored him. "Let's see how much we can pull together in a week. And then we can decide."

Terry

Wednesday, 6:10 p.m., 2 December 1964, Glendale. So far, a banner week. I had called Arlo Tatum's CCCO lawyer in Phoenix first thing on Monday. He had agreed to meet Thursday morning. At work, we put the week's issue to bed in the late afternoon. Immediately after, the publisher called me in for an early Christmas present—he promoted me to editor. I'd take over January 1. The gang and I were celebrating with a rousing toast as Annie scooted into our booth at La Cocina.

By eight-thirty, everyone else had gone home, and it was just the two of us.

"How you coming on the wedding plans?" Annie asked, her voice still raspy from her cold.

"Got a letter from Allen in Silverton. He's thrilled to be best man. He's not hot on driving over, though—it's eight hours. Plus, Christmas week is tough. He's got a lot of printing to do. He wants to fly—if we'll foot half the fare. It's steep: $36.75. Other than that, nothing. But jeez, today's only Wednesday. When was I supposed to—"

"Me too. Christmas is impossible. We'll never make it. And I got another epistle from Dad. Listen to this: 'It was nice having you here, but we hated to see you leave unhappy. I am sure you realize, Ann, that you can

do as you please in this matter and we won't think any less of you—because
we do love you.'" And then I got to the crux of the letter:

> *All we are asking is that you wait until summer. You have obligations
> to those you work for as well as to yourself. We are not prejudiced
> and will make ourselves compatible with whatever choice you make.
> However, it would really be a burden on you, Sis, to take on a hus-
> band in the middle of the year. If you waited until June you would
> have the whole summer to get adjusted.*

"So you're thinking what? Buckle under? Put it off till summer?" I asked.

"No. They're hoping that if we postpone it, I'll 'come to my senses'
and call it off. But I'm stymied, Ter. No church. No minister. What now?"

I pulled out Nossaman's letter. "Here's an idea from Allen: 'Why in the
hell don't you two get married in Silverton? Jim Price says he'd be happy
to officiate.'"

We stared at each other, eyes wide, as if we'd witnessed a miracle.

To Annie's folks, our plan to get married in the desert—in the shadow
of a saguaro rather than a cross—was blasphemy. Her mom had written
her, "Annie, you simply have to have it in a church. It's not a campout. It's
a wedding. It's holy matrimony—a marriage before God."

Not only was Jim Price one of our Silverton gang, he was an ordained
minister, with a church. And it would be in the town we loved. "Why not?"
I said. "Why the hell not?"

Annie nodded. "Yes, indeed. Let's do it."

Back at Annie's apartment, we studied her school calendar as if it were
a newly discovered Dead Sea Scroll. Rodeo Holiday, March 11–14, was the
only break between Christmas and the end of the school year. That was it.

As soon as I got home, I fired off a letter to Allen. "You're on. We've postponed the wedding. We'll do it in Silverton. How does March 13 sound?"

Ann

Friday, December 25, 1964, Albuquerque. For Christmas, my folks invited
family members who lived in New Mexico—my aunt and a swarm of first
and second cousins—plus Grandma, Bonner, and me (fifteen in all). We

gathered in klatches around the house, swapping stories of what we'd been up to, as Dad circulated, lubricating our conversations with short quips and his bottomless wine decanter. My aunt and cousins plied me with questions about Glendale. Mom would have called the gathering *convivial*, her highest compliment.

Disappointing would have been a better word. After the flurry of shopping, decorating, baking, cooking, gift giving, and dinner preparations, no one at the Christmas gathering—no one—asked about Terry. Not a word. Had Mom warned everyone the topic was off-limits? Probably not. She wouldn't have disclosed our nuclear family's strife to the assembled relatives. And they were too polite to ask if I even had a boyfriend. By day's end, we all collapsed in front of our first-ever *color* TV and oohed and aahed at the novelty of it.

What really bothered me? With Thanksgiving still a raw memory, I didn't have the heart to quash my folks' joy at my decision not to marry at Christmas. I simply didn't bring it up.

When I got back to Glendale, I wished I had broken the news that we *were* getting married—in March—so they would have had time to help me plan. I should have talked it through with them as a family, answered their every doubt.

But I didn't. In a gutless effort to reestablish family unity, I bottled it up. I joined in the festivities, laughed and joked, and let the holiday slip by, leaving my parents in the dark about the looming wedding bearing down upon us.

Terry

January 1965, Glendale. The new year pranced in like a beneficent fairy godmother. I was editor of the *News-Herald* now, writing editorials, making assignments, and beginning to shape the paper into a Pulitzer Prize winner. I'd be the next William Allen White, and the *News-Herald* a modern *Emporia Gazette*. I was still single, but Annie and I had a wedding date.

My attorney had bought me time with the draft board. I still had to get the physical exam, but I could do it in Phoenix, not Colorado. It was set for February 8. The downside: The draft board had refused to change my classification. I was saddled with I-A, "Available for Military Service," which meant that the board could—in spite or on a whim—draft me at any moment.

I had lived with that fear since November 18 when I refused to report to the courthouse in Colorado. To stave off the army, I'd quit answering my phone. I would take a different route to and from work every day and vary my coming and going times, always checking the neighborhood for cars I didn't recognize to make sure the MPs hadn't staked out the house. Some days I didn't pick up my mail. I let it sit for a couple of days—hoping that any new orders from the draft board would spontaneously combust in the Arizona sun.

Friday, 15 January 1965, Glendale. Getting home after dark, I gathered the mail, unlocked the door, and rapped on the wall to scatter the roaches.

On Monday and Tuesday, I had interviewed the mayor and city council members—all seven of them, one by one—and stitched together a story that filled a third of the front page. "Where is Glendale going in 1965?" I asked. "What are our goals? What are our problems? How are we going to resolve them?"

I knew the problems before I asked. Housing crunch. Declining business district with a shrinking tax base. A population that had doubled between 1950 and 1960 and was on a trajectory to double again by 1970. I had spent my Friday fine-tuning an editorial calling on councilmen to pull their heads out of the sand and raise taxes. We couldn't build a city of the future on the resources of the past.

First the mail, then I'd heat up a Banquet Chicken Pot Pie for dinner. Bank statement. Latest issue of *Saturday Review.* A nine-by-twelve envelope stamped with "Peace Corps Official Business." The envelope looked like an oversized passport that had circled the globe, and in the process, it had crawled through the mud and been beaten up by thugs and run over by a semi. It had been forwarded to both places I lived in Boulder my last semester at CU and then rerouted to Center and finally to Glendale.

My hand shook. Inside, a letter from Sargent Shriver—the Peace Corps director himself. He said—oh my God!—"You have been chosen to train for a Peace Corps assignment overseas."

The envelope included a canary yellow four-page brochure, "Thailand

Peace Corps Program Description." Shriver had invited me to Thailand. He wanted me to teach English there.

I didn't even finish. I called Annie. "Hey, how about dinner at La Cocina? My treat."

"It's a little late, isn't it?"

"Yeah, but today's a holiday. Besides, you shouldn't be working on Friday night."

"A holiday? Which one, pray tell? Saint Baloney's birthday?"

"Yep, that's it. It's also an excuse. I want to see you. Isn't that enough?"

Silence. Then, "Okay, give me ten minutes. You'll pick me up?"

Between bites at La Cocina, we combed Sargent Shriver's invitation. It was dated December 11—five weeks earlier. "Oh shit, listen to this: 'Fill out the Invitation Acceptance Form and get it back to us within ten days.' That was December 21. It's too damn late."

Annie studied it. "Yeah, but it's not your fault. His letter proves they haven't blackballed you, even after you turned down Venezuela." She took another bite of her quesadilla and paused mid-chew. "You wouldn't accept, though, not without me, would you? Don't we have some kind of party or gala or something coming up? A whatchamacallit . . . *a wedding*?"

My mind was floating. Thailand! Wasn't that Siam? Wow, Yul Brynner in *The King and I*. Me riding an elephant—they did that in Siam. The colorful brochure had a picture of a guy riding one. No doubt a Peace Corps volunteer. And a picture of a school complex with palm trees. I'd need to buy a hammock. "They want me to teach English," I said. "Imagine that. We'll have classrooms next to each other. We'll use the same lesson plans. We'll—of course I won't go without you. I'll tell Shriver, 'You messed up with the mail. Send me two tickets.'"

"Yeah, you do that," Annie said. "Tell him he *owes* us two tickets. Preferably first class. We'd better go home right now and start packing."

I wrote a letter to Sargent Shriver over the weekend and mailed it Monday morning. I couldn't accept, I told him, but only because Annie and I were about to be married, and we wanted to join as a couple. I explained the mail mix-up—nicely, no poke in the eye—urging him to give us another shot. Anywhere he wanted to send us. At the end, after thinking long and hard, I added another paragraph:

> *If for some reason my fiancée and I do not get married this summer,*
> *I would like to enter training alone. The Peace Corps is too impor-*
> *tant to me to risk losing the opportunities you have given me to join.*

I didn't show Annie the final draft. I hoped it wouldn't come to that. But I had to cover my bases. If I turned down the Peace Corps yet again, I'd never get another opportunity.

Ann

January 1965, Glendale. The new year flattened me like a steamroller. I had to write final exams and submit them to the principal the first week of the year. I was wiser now about essays but totally underestimated the time and energy needed to write short-answer exams—so many questions, so many ways to make them too hard or too easy. Then hours and hours of marking 140 tests, and a two-day marathon calculating semester grades.

As if that weren't enough, I had rashly agreed to sponsor Glendale High's chess club, which called for my supervision at weekly meetings and at the citywide tournament two full Saturdays in January. And I had finals for my own college classes. I crammed too late for the Arizona Constitution exam and was stung by my first-ever D. For Transformational Grammar, I squeezed the answers to my take-home final into the few remaining slivers of time in the last week of the term. That effort yielded me an A.

Soon after, I was blindsided by yowls from four seniors who flunked my class. English was required for graduation. One girl and her siblings lived with their father, who demanded everything of the kids and gave nothing back—so said the school counselor. Her mother was in the hospital charity ward, and the church was feeding the kids. With an F in English, the girl reportedly said, "I'll quit school and get a job. At least my sisters can take lunch to school."

The counselor insisted I change her grade. I couldn't. Several other students were as close to passing as she was. How could I favor her over them? Word would get around, and I would be inundated with pleas for other changes. I told the counselor, "The most important thing I can teach is *responsibility*—changing my students' grades won't do that. Besides, it's dishonest!"

But wasn't their failure my failure? Distress over each failing student shredded my daytime focus and invaded my herky-jerky sleep. So did recurring worries about Terry, the draft, and our impending wedding—which I still hadn't mentioned to my folks.

Terry

Monday, 6:30 a.m., 8 February 1965, *Phoenix.* There I was at the Armed Forces Examining Station, with a hundred other conscripts, all barefoot and in our undershorts, shuffling along colored lines from one corpsman to the next: Ears—check. *Next station, please.* Eyes—check. *Next station, please.* Mouth. Teeth. Heartbeat and pulse. Balls—*turn your head and cough.* Penis—*yep, you've got one. Next station, please.* Feet . . .

"Marshall, Terry Lee," I said at each stop.

We were not a crowd or group or friends or even people at all. We were disembodied parts on an unstoppable slow-moving conveyor belt. Some recruits seemed eager, bursting with the pride of joining the army and fighting for their country. None knew I wasn't one of them. We didn't talk. We didn't laugh. We didn't even acknowledge each other. We followed orders. *Next station, please.*

At morning's end, a soldier at the last table handed me a slip of paper and pointed to the exit. I trundled past and read it outside. Form DD 62, "Statement of Acceptability." Beneath my name and address, a checked box: "Found fully acceptable for induction into the Armed Forces." Signed by Bruce A. Cunningham, 2nd Lt., AGC. No salute needed.

Thanks, Lieutenant.

Chilling words. The only cheer I could muster was that no MPs stood guard at the last table. No one was on hand to shanghai me that very day.

At my car, I paused and reread the form. Twice. My hands shook. My knees felt weak. I had passed their damn physical, but here was the catch-22: Now my draft board had a new weapon—primed, sighted in, and ready to fire. Their next step could be an order to report for induction. If they did, my lawyer advised me to report. Once there, he said I should refuse to cross the line, refuse to take the oath. That's when he would step in to take on the legal battle.

At that point the whole game would change: With the CCCO and a lawyer on my side, we would transform my personal struggle into a national one. If we won that war, we would eradicate the policy that religious belief was the only legitimate basis for conscientious objector status. We would change not only my life, but the life of every man whose conscience would not permit him to kill another human being.

These were heady stakes. Despite the indignities of the physical itself, I had won a small victory here—I'd taken an essential step toward confronting this odious draft law head on. But today I had obeyed every order the army medics made—*next station, please.* Did I have the guts to actually refuse to step forward when the time for induction came? I dreaded the thought.

A half hour later, as I pulled up to the *News-Herald*, I realized I no longer had to fear that the MPs would haul me out of the office or smash down my door in the middle of the night. All I had to fear was the daily mail.

Ann

Early February 1965, Glendale. After I turned in semester grades, I carved out an hour to go shopping for Jack's birthday, coming February 19. He liked books, loved art, so I got him *The Agony and the Ecstasy*, about Michelangelo. I mailed it the same day. Less than two weeks later, he sent back a thank-you on a Valentine's Day card, saying he had read it and planned to see the movie adaptation of it that weekend. He noted that he had visited my folks on his way to California and left the promised wedding-gift bowls with them. In passing, he mentioned he would leave for Vietnam in two months. He signed the card, *"Auf Wiedersehen."*

Clearly, he had decided against visiting me in Glendale. I dropped his valentine on the table, pulled the vase from its place of honor on my shelf, and ran my fingers over the luscious curves and swirls. What a princely farewell. *Yes, farewell to you, too, my more-than-friend.*

By contrast, Terry's 1965 valentine wish to me was simple, whispered over a quesadilla at La Cocina, "May this be your last Valentine's Day as a single woman."

Ten months earlier—in the spring of 1964—Terry had been the interloper in the romance Jack and I were nurturing. On April 19, 1964, Terry had given me a corsage on my birthday, taken me to dinner and a movie.

Jack had sent the handblown vase and the bouquet of a lifetime. I never imagined how things would play out, Jack keeping his promise to reunite the three pieces, even if I married someone else. I loved him for that.

Terry

February 1965, Glendale. As a relief in our harried lives, Annie and I spiced up our evenings now and then by stirring up dinner before our editing and lesson-planning sessions at her kitchen table. Each night, when we began to fade, we kissed good night, and kissed again, before I stumbled off to my cottage.

Late one weeknight, I stopped by her place after a contentious union meeting—I had to unload. We talked it through and next thing I knew, we were kissing, touching, and exploring. Over long minutes, piece by piece, our clothes fell away. Wrapped in each other's arms, I prayed silently she would allow my guarded, millimeter-by-millimeter exploration its full reign. She was fearful of getting pregnant, the trials of unwed motherhood etched in her psyche by Rachael, Gretchen, and Laura Lee. We took our time, no rush, and I made sure we were protected.

That night, gently, simply, we melted together.

Ann

February 1965, Glendale. One night after ten, my doorbell rang. It startled me. I hesitated, but opened the door a crack: Terry! He was stone-faced, eyes piercing.

"What's up? You okay?"

"We need to talk," he said. No greeting. "Garbage men are talking strike—the city fired the union president. At their meeting tonight . . ." His voice was as tight as piano strings. "Their working conditions are worse than disgusting! You gotta hear this."

"Okay, but take a deep breath. Quit pacing. Sit down and tell me."

Throughout the fall, Terry had reported on efforts by city employees to form a union—and on the city council's opposition. Now the council had fired the guy who started the union.

Smoldering with fury, Terry spun out a litany of complaints from the union meeting: The trash trucks had no hydraulic lifts. The men used brute strength to heft full cans to their shoulders and hoist them into the bed. They all had tales of slipped disks, torn muscles, or pinched nerves, as well as puncture wounds from glass shards, rusty nails, or jagged wood scraps.

"So what do the garbage men want?" I asked.

"The basics: decent working conditions . . . safe equipment . . . a grievance procedure, for crying out loud!"

"Are you doing a story? Tonight?"

"Can't. I promised them confidentiality. But soon. Our readers need to suffer the pain of their injuries. Feel the injustice when the city won't cover medical costs." He paused, searching for words. "And, yes, I want all of Glendale to take a deep whiff of the stench: putrid garbage, festering in metal cans in the Arizona sun. It's incredible that so many people dump unbagged crap into their trash cans—rotten meat, rancid cottage cheese, spoiled fruit and slimy veggies, an occasional dead cat. And dog shit. Lots of dog shit!"

"That's revolting."

He sat down at my kitchen table and thumbed through his reporter's notebook, spilling out heartbreaking stories from individual workers. Nearing midnight, I stood up and stretched this way and that, trying to banish the kinks from my back. His stories had both energized me and left me spent.

I moved to the sofa and patted the spot next to me. His eyes were bloodshot and hair frowzy. "Take a break, Ter. Let it evolve. You can't write it until it's ready."

He slumped down beside me and sighed. "It's late. I really should go."

"Yeah. You should," I said. But neither of us moved.

He looked sideways, leaned over, and kissed me. "Thanks for listening. It really helps."

I kissed him back. Next thing I knew, we were entwined together, kissing and hugging. We slipped from the sofa to the carpet. One thing led to another, and it just happened. We made love, right there on my living room floor, after all my months of holding back.

Was it bliss? Was I ecstatic? Actually, it was rather awkward. And scary. But thrilling too. And complete. It was more than simply having sex. It was the missing piece in the mosaic of our love.

"You know what else I think?" I said, wrapping my arms around him. "I'm proud of you. Of your passion. You care about people."

No question. We were meant to be.

February–March 1965, Glendale. I still hadn't written to my folks about our new wedding date, nor had I begun to plan. After the semester-end hump, I wrote my parents a double whammy:

> *We can no longer think of any good reason why we should wait until summer to marry. We plan to go to the Peace Corps this summer, which will involve more difficult adjustments, so we need time in between marriage and the Peace Corps. I fear you may not approve of the Peace Corps, but I must live according to my own conscience, and this is one thing I must do. I am sure. The best date for us would be March 13.*

I didn't mention that we planned to marry in Silverton—that came two days later when I called them. Silence at the other end of the line. I thought they'd hung up. In the end, they caved on Silverton and the imminent wedding date—by then five weeks away—and, in a series of letters, threw their weight against the Peace Corps specter:

February 9, from Mom: *We do hate to see you join the Peace Corps, taking things the hard way.*

February 10, from Dad: *I am wondering why you would take two years out of your life. I don't see where Terry figures he is going to toss a couple of years away.*

February 13, from Mom: *It's a shame for Terry to give up his job, now that he is editor, and for you to throw away your first year's experience to sacrifice two years of your lives to a venture that, while praiseworthy, will not advance you in any way. Think! Seriously, carefully, logically. You have too much at stake.*

This time, I didn't relent. And despite their objections to the Peace Corps and because the date was speeding toward us like stampeding horses, my parents jumped into wedding preparations with zeal. We were months behind any sane wedding planner's timetable. First, we had to print and mail our clever wedding invitation. That drew an immediate veto!

February 24, from Mom: *As for the invitations, we realize that Terry is clever and witty, and I'm sure his ideas were original and interesting. However, weddings are a once-in-a-lifetime affair (or should be), and a definite etiquette and protocol allow no deviation in the invitations. Rules specify this in no uncertain terms.*

Following that, she dropped a stone tablet of essentials on our toes: An acceptable wedding meant The Dress, shoes, jewelry, undergarments; something old, something new, something borrowed, something blue; honeymoon trousseau; maid of honor, bridesmaids, and flower girl, including their outfits; bride's mother's outfit; ring bearer, groomsmen, organist; photographer, and flowers; choice of a silver pattern; a post-wedding reception dinner-dance, with band and caterer. Oh, and don't forget color scheme and theme, seating chart, place settings, candles, centerpieces, favors, menu, drinks. And that pièce de résistance, The Cake. The list alone exhausted us.

Somewhere along the line, I had an epiphany. Weddings weren't for the bride and groom. They were for the parents. This relief valve turned some of Mom's "essentials" into comic relief: Protocol? Rules? Indeed! Who cared? In the end, Terry and I preserved the important stuff. Marriage before June. In Silverton. Followed, we hoped, by a two-year Peace Corps honeymoon in some exotic and faraway spot on the globe.

Mom ordered traditional invitations, embossed in a swirling wedding script on elegant stock. On February 24, I bought a simple wedding dress, by myself, in an hour, plus veil and white satin flats: $79.17. Mom picked up the invitations on March 1—twelve days before the wedding—and mailed them the next day. Over the next week, she fired off seven letters to me checking on music, ushers, gift list, corsages, boutonnieres, and champagne. She bought a special coat to get me from the church to the reception. She capped the frenzy with a lacy wedding-night peignoir with matching see-through robe. I smiled, taking it as final acceptance.

On March 4, Terry bought a suit: $86.27. On March 5, we combed the nearest mall for a wedding ring: $85.50. On March 8, we paid Loy G. Roberts, MD, $22.50 for Arizona's mandated syphilis exams. We passed.

In Silverton, Allen booked rooms for family members at the Grand Imperial, reserved the dining room at the Mill Creek Lodge for a reception, and got Jim Price's assurance that the church would be ours at 11:00 a.m. on Saturday, March 13.

I learned Mom had bought a book on wedding planning, which turned out to be doubly useful, since Bonner announced that same week in February that he planned to marry in May.

I suspect Bonner's news evoked more joy than mine. His fiancée was the daughter of an army general. And I was astonished that he'd found his life mate so quickly—after his still-secret, not-so-long-ago relationship with *Fräulein* Gretchen Schumacher.

22

Rodeo Weekend

Ann

Friday, March 12, 1965, Glendale. At long last, Rodeo Holiday—a three-day weekend. What rodeo? We didn't know. Didn't care.

Midmorning Friday, we landed in bright sunshine at the tiny airport in Durango, Colorado, where best-man Allen loaded us into his Scout. He negotiated the fifty-mile twisting, snow-packed pass through the mountains to Silverton as easily as if it were Kansas in summer—in advance of the glowering clouds and sloppy new snow that later greeted Mom, Dad, and Jimmy. As the temperature dropped, the highway turned slick, and they slid off a curve on Coal Bank Hill. Other motorists stopped to help jockey their car back onto the road. My folks were lucky—it could have been one of the precipitous turns with no railings, no shoulder, and a free fall into the Animas River a thousand feet below.

Terry bunked with Allen. We Garretsons checked into a three-room suite in Silverton's 1880s Grand Imperial Hotel, still exuding dignity despite her eighty-plus years' resistance to the elements, rowdy guests, and general neglect. Mom and Dad took the extravagant bed that stretched from wall to wall in one bedroom. Jimmy and I had separate beds in the other.

Our reunion was the antithesis of the Thanksgiving sparring match in Albuquerque. Dad clasped my shoulder, gave me his typical half hug, and then stepped aside. His posture and look shouted, *All this folderol over a wedding is the domain of women.* Mom greeted me like the quintessential proud mother of the bride: chatty, helpful, bursting with joy.

Late that afternoon, as we geared up to walk over to the church for the rehearsal, Mom breezed into my room from the shared bathroom. I had just taken my daily birth control pill from the monthly pack. She startled me. I flashed the telltale pack like a trophy and blurted, "Look, Mom, this is how the modern woman protects herself."

Her hand flew to her mouth. "Oh, Annie, no, you've already started!"

"Of course, Mom. You have to." I meant it as a bit of enlightenment, the fact that a girl had to begin taking these wondrous pills a full month before intercourse to be assured they would perform their magic. She didn't know. She saw the Pill as proof I was actively engaged in sex—in *premarital sex*—and no doubt with the vigor of a jackrabbit in heat.

She was right about one thing: I wasn't a virgin on my wedding day. For years I had held that, for me, sex before marriage was wrong. Sex was something so special I would reserve it for my husband. But in those past few months, I had come to realize that it wasn't premarital sex per se that was out of bounds. It was sex before I had formally committed myself to marriage. By February, Terry and I had made that pledge and set a wedding date.

But it was too late for a daughter-to-mother talk about coming of age in the sexual revolution. I shrugged, smiled, and flipped the offending pack of pills onto the bed.

Mom regrouped and rounded up Dad and Jimmy. We bundled up and walked the two blocks to the United Church of Silverton, our boots crunching on the icy residue of last week's snow. Terry and I had wanted simple for our wedding. This was it: a white clapboard church, red-brick chimney, and a steep, barnlike pitched roof. Inside, pews for fifty parishioners, wood floor, leaded glass windows, and unadorned pulpit. Built in 1881 by locals, it was as homey as a country store.

We met up with Terry's family and the wedding party and spent twenty minutes on the rehearsal—a snap once we agreed to forgo writing our own vows and to follow Jim Price's advice. "It's already a high-stress moment," he said. "Why complicate it by trying to memorize something you haven't even written? You'll like the vows I use."

We adjourned to the Grand Imperial for dinner. Wine flowed. We swapped tall tales from CU and the past two summers. We laughed. We hooted. Mom joined in like she always did—but with a hint of disappointment that only a daughter can read in the eyes of her mother. What was it? Disappointment that I had chosen someone whose politics and life goals were so different from theirs? Distress that her Christian daughter was a "fallen woman"? In any event, she and Dad shone as congenial parents of the bride, despite whatever underlying heartache burdened them. Mom engaged Terry's mother and sister in chat, and Dad talked agriculture in the San Luis Valley with a farming friend of Terry's family.

Saturday morning's bright sun and blue sky belied the temperature—not even warm enough to melt the ice designs on the windows. The little church filled with family and friends who came from afar, Allen's and Terry's local buddies, and random rubberneckers grateful for a break from the frozen solitude of a Silverton winter. When the pianist struck up "Here Comes the Bride," Dad pulled my hand through his elbow, held it an extra count, beaming as if I were marrying the famous West Pointer Pete Dawkins, and marched me to the arm of my chosen husband—a guy sporting a brand-new suit and tie, a fresh haircut, and a clean-shaven face.

When we turned toward Jim Price, his words about the joys of marriage floated past me as if they were murmurs in a snowstorm—none registered. Before I knew it, Terry and I were facing each other, and he was following Jim's cues in reciting the vows. And then it was my turn.

I, Ann, take you, Terry . . . to be my husband . . .

A regiment of fugitive tears formed. To keep them at bay, I opened my eyes wide.

. . . to be your loving and faithful wife . . .

The tears marched down my cheek, my voice cracked, and I squeaked out the last words.

. . . giving myself to you and you alone.

My meltdown at the altar was the only flaw in the day. In the reception line, one of the guests saved me by whispering, "The sun shines on a bride who cries at her wedding." Afterward, I raced for the bathroom to repair the damage—and was grateful she hadn't commented on my bright red nose.

Thanks to Mom's masterful management, the reception at the Mill Creek Inn, nestled in a forest meadow near Durango, went off without a hitch—complete with white tablecloths, red and pink decor, and name tags at each place setting. Mom outdid herself on The Cake. It was discretely elegant without too much gooey icing.

The inn itself set the tone for the informal gathering of friends—varnished log walls like a ski lodge, wrought-iron chandelier, Navajo rugs—normally a gathering place for men in Pendleton shirts and women in colorful patio dresses. And the show outside? Giant mountains framed blue spruces, their branches heaped with frosting-like snow, while new snowflakes the size of doilies fluttered past the lodge's wraparound picture windows.

Jack would have approved of the mountain setting, the simple ceremony, and the intimacy of the reception—if not my choice of groom.

Terry

Saturday, 13 March 1964, Silverton. Late that afternoon, Annie and I scrunched with Jimmy into the back seat of the Garretsons' white Riviera—like fifteen-year-olds being delivered to the prom. They dropped their only daughter off at the regal, turn-of-the-century Strater Hotel in Durango, bid their wistful goodbyes, and headed for home. Hand in hand, Annie and I bounded up the broad carpeted stairway to room 226—the honeymoon suite—without looking back.

An elegant four-poster bed dominated the room, positioned under a mirrored ceiling and bathed in a halo of muted light, the covers folded back. Two mints and a spray of white roses lay between twin pillows, and a pair of thick white robes rested side by side at the foot. The bed itself winked and whispered, *Welcome. I'm here for your pleasure.*

We showered and for some minutes stood at the broad, second-story window and gazed out over Main Street. Annie leaned back into me. One by one, the city lights flicked on, highlighting the falling snow, and I slid my hands over her breasts.

At last we were legal: freed from the moral restraint imposed by society's taboo against sex before marriage. Not only did it not matter that friends and family knew we were sleeping together, they expected us to. Eventually, we shed our robes, joined into a loving embrace, and, in the comfort of that old four-poster bed, recommitted to each other.

Room 226 was worth every cent of the $10.70 we shelled out, in cash, for our one-night honeymoon.

Ann

Sunday, March 14, 1965, Durango. We caught the midmorning Frontier flight back to Phoenix. That afternoon, we hauled over the rest of Terry's belongings from his scuzzy cottage, and that night I welcomed him to the Maryland Club Apartments with open arms. Never again would he have to slip out under cover of darkness.

The next morning, I reported in at Glendale High before seven-thirty and stunned one class after another with the news that henceforth they should address me as *Mrs. Marshall*, not *Miss Garretson*. The girls crowded around and examined the wedding ring. The boys let out a few ribald catcalls and then looked on with disinterest. The news traveled fast. Members of my third-hour class raced out and bought me a faux crystal cake plate and a card, signed by everyone in the class.

After school, at the *News-Herald,* the whole staff crowded into the newsroom the moment I arrived. We emptied two bottles of champagne and demolished an angel food cake.

That was it. No pomp and circumstance. No Arch of Sabers. No limo, band, or fancy dinner. A simple ceremony in a place we loved with a handful of friends and family. That's all we wanted.

Well, not all. We didn't get that leisurely honeymoon in Mexico City.

23

From Joy to Pain

Terry

Friday, 7:40 a.m., 14 May 1965, Glendale. I wasn't even halfway through my leisurely no-deadlines-Friday breakfast when the phone rang.

No doubt it was Annie, a quick call before her first class. "Forget something?" I asked.

"Terry or Ann Marshall, please." A woman's voice. Not one I recognized.

"Yes? I'm Terry."

"I'm . . ."—I didn't catch her name—"I'm with Peace Corps Placement in Washington. We have an assignment for you. For both of you."

I don't know what I said—probably something dumb, like "Great" or "Wow, really?" I listened and nodded and managed an occasional yes or okay, not thinking to take notes. This was a heads-up call, she said. They'd send us a formal letter, but she wanted to make sure we were still available.

"Yes, yes, of course!" I said.

After she hung up and I got my wits back, I scribbled everything I could remember into my reporter's notebook. They'd send us to the Philippines for two years. Together. We would teach English, either elementary or high school—they weren't sure which.

First, we'd train for ten weeks in California—classes 7:30 a.m. to 9:30 p.m., six days a week, Sundays off. Tagalog language lessons four hours a day. Teacher training three hours a day. Philippines history and culture another three hours. Also, classes in US history, world affairs, and health care—how to survive in the tropics. Plus PE—we'd have to run a mile and ace the Red Cross swimming test. Training would begin June 19. After training, they would fly us to Manila.

The Peace Corps at last! But we had barely a month to get ready.

I made it through the morning by shuffling papers and jotting notes for next week's stories, but I couldn't concentrate on work. After lunch, I slipped across the street to the town library. I couldn't wait to find out more about where we'd be for the next two years. No books on the Philippines, but the encyclopedia offered a cornucopia of exotic scenes: rugged mountains, stunning waterfalls, pristine beaches. A major volcano. Pineapple plantations, coconut palms, and ancient rice terraces; water buffalo and wild monkeys; half-naked hill tribes and leaf houses. Man, this was the tropics!

I left work early to make it home before Annie did and met her at the door. "Happy anniversary! Dinner out tonight? With champagne?"

She gave me her *what's-up-now-Terry?* look.

"Two months ago today—our first full day as a married couple."

Over dinner—and two margaritas each—I told her about the Peace Corps call. We talked for two hours at La Cocina and stayed up most of the night, imagining, dreaming, spinning out the possibilities that lay ahead, planning how to close out life in Glendale in a month.

Manila! Now, there's a honeymoon!

Ann

Sunday, May 16, 1965, Glendale. For weeks I had put off writing to Jack. Friday's Peace Corps call gave me the spur I needed. I wouldn't tell him that endless rows of faded yellow barracks popped onto my mental canvas when Terry said "the Philippines"—based on childhood recollections from army friends who had lived there. My unspoken reservations were best kept locked away, especially since I was so excited about our upcoming challenge.

But warriors loved to get mail from home. Jack would be happy to hear from me, and he'd be delighted with our news. Even though our romance was over, he would celebrate my happiness almost as much as if it were his.

I dug through my shoebox of his letters, found a snapshot of him, and propped it by the typewriter. Jack sitting in his Sting Ray, dwarfed by the tank behind—his tank. Big smile on the man with his muscle machines, doing what he loved. A mere three weeks after the wedding, while Terry and I were wrapped up in each other, buoyant with hopes and plans, Jack had plunged into war, fighting the Vietcong. In the jungle. At least he had his tank. He wouldn't be slogging through the muck, dodging bullets from AK-47s, risking trip wires of primitive but deadly booby traps we'd seen on TV.

The previous night's CBS news had given us glimpses of the national Vietnam War teach-in in Washington, where thousands had assembled to debate the war. American intrusion in Vietnam was deepening, as Jack had feared—and so was antiwar sentiment. No question which side Terry and I were on. We had to oppose this war, end America's meddling—and bring Jack and his fellow American advisers home.

But I couldn't figure out how to even start the letter: "Dear Jack"? Too intimate! How about just plain "Jack"? No, too drastic a demotion. *Jeez, how do I address you, dear Jack, now that I'm a married woman?* Not so many months ago it had been "Dearest Jack" and "My Dearest Jack." I could no longer *think* those words, let alone write them.

I settled on "Dear Jack" and wrote a newsy letter, the kind I'd write Mom. "Thanks so much for the crystal bowls—Mom has stored them safely in my bedroom closet." I told him about the Peace Corps. How ironic, I thought, that we would wind up on the same side of the Pacific—on such different missions. "We'll teach high school, possibly in Manila. If you ever have leave time, you should plan to come see us." I wanted to hear from him, to know what life was like on the front lines, to know he was safe. "By now you are in Vietnam, and every day as I read the news, I wonder what your part is. Do write, Ann."

Argh. The letter was too lightweight, but how did you write to a man who was dealing with life and death twenty-four hours a day? A man you loved as I loved Jack? Everything I wrote seemed trivial by contrast. I sent the letter anyway.

Terry

Monday, 24 May 1965, Glendale. It was official! We were in the Peace Corps. A letter from Shriver himself confirmed it. We each got a letter dated May 20. Training in Sacramento would start on June 27—not June 19 as they'd said on the phone. That would give us an extra week to get ready. We needed it.

We had to return an acceptance form within ten days. Then Shriver would write again with more details and plane tickets. He added a PS: "This invitation is contingent upon your passing your medical examination; therefore, we advise you to have your physical immediately."

After mailing our acceptance Tuesday morning, I called Dr. Roberts. He worked us right in, and we sent the medical form the next day. Both of us were in tip-top shape. Cleared to go.

Ann

Wednesday, June 2, 1965, Glendale. I shuffled home from school, mentally spent but grateful to have only five days left in the school year. I tossed the mail on the end table, changed clothes, and sank onto the sofa, resting a bit before fixing dinner.

As I thumbed through the phone and car insurance bills, I made a mental note to have our mail forwarded. To Manila! Terry would take care of that. A postcard from Dad, one of those free motel cards—*Hospitality House Motor Inn, Arlington, Virginia, 5 minutes from downtown Washington, DC.* Dated Sunday, May 30. Postmarked Monday.

Mom and Dad were there for Bonner's wedding. Good for him, finally committing himself after so many girlfriends. I wanted to be there—to wish him well and reknit the family unity unraveled by my marriage to Terry. I wanted to welcome this new woman into our family and get past my anger for how he had abandoned Gretchen. But I couldn't. Too much work to close out the school year. Too little time to gear up for the Peace Corps. Too expensive to fly to Washington.

I meant to skim the postcard—Dad's notes were always friendly bits of neatly scripted news, his way of telling me he cared about how I was—but this missive jumped off the card:

> *Dear Sis:*
>
> *This is the day before the wedding! Bonner got word yesterday that Jack was killed in action. It sure takes the joy out of the occasion. Bonner went up to Pennsylvania last night to see Jack's father.*
> *Love, Dad*

That was it: forty-one words on a postcard. Jack was dead.

Terry bounded through the door that evening. "Sorry I'm late. Got tied up with an interview over at—whoa, what's up?"

I was hunkered on the floor in the corner of the kitchen. Terry knelt and took my hands. "What's wrong? You sick? Hurt?"

I nodded, trying to take a deep breath. All I could manage was a gurgled sob.

He pried the postcard out of my hand. Tears rolled down my cheeks and neck.

24
Echoes of Vietnam

Ann

Early 1990s, Denver, Colorado. No one ever told me directly how Jack died. Or where exactly. I pieced it together over the years from letters I received from Bud, Jack's father; from the newspaper obituary and miscellaneous clippings Bud sent in his final years as he dispersed mementos of his only son to people he knew would care; and from a handwritten letter Major Raymond Battscalf Jr. wrote to Jack's mom two weeks after Jack was killed.

Major Battscalf, the adviser to the 4th Vietnamese Cavalry, arrived on the scene the day after Jack died. He interviewed Jack's men and wrote the official army report. Battscalf knew Jack—he had been Jack's English instructor at West Point. Tributes posted on various West Point websites, including a long, glowing one from my brother, added a few more pixels to my understanding of that terrible day.

But the fact is, I have no on-scene record of what happened. No war correspondents were on hand. No photographers or moviemakers. Jack died just a little more than a week after I had labored over my final chatty note to him. That twenty-eighth day of May 1965 was before the war heated up: six months before the Battle of Ia Drang Valley, almost three years before the battles of Khe Sanh, and Huế, and nearly a full decade before the South Vietnamese army's last stand at Xuân Lộc in April 1975.

In the scope of the Vietnam War, the battle that killed Jack was a minor skirmish—a small force of Vietcong dug in with antitank weapons in a tiny village near Quảng Trị.

Jack's troop went in to clear the village, but Jack, their American mentor, wasn't with them when the battle began. He'd gone to Da Nang that morning for a meeting with his fellow US Army advisers, and when he got back to Huế, his troop had been dispatched to engage the Vietcong near that hamlet. I knew Jack. I can see him in action:

I've got to join my men. How do I get there? That was Jack. Determine the facts. Then act. He got the coordinates. His troop had taken their tanks and armored personnel carriers. He couldn't hail a taxi into battle or drive a jeep pell-mell into the jungle, so he finagled a Huey for a lift to the action and dropped to the ground as it hovered. I can picture him, bent low, sprinting to the command APC, scrambling up, and dropping in beside the Vietnamese commander. They were a team, he and his counterpart.

Where's their firepower? No idle talk. They calculated enemy positions. Called in an air strike and then another. It was dusk, the light fading. Jack signaled him, *Let's take 'em!* He swung up behind the carrier's machine gun. Targeted a nest of persistent shelling. Raked the dug-in VC with fire. Waited. Watched. Hit them again. He zeroed in, concentrating on the task at hand. Focused.

The VC didn't return fire. He had them pinned down. But he was exposed, hunched over the machine gun. From his right flank, a machine gun volley sliced through the dimming light. "A burst from this gun walked up the side of the carrier," Major Battscalf wrote.

Walked? Absolutely not! This was war, not some Sunday stroll. Do bullets from a machine gun ping off the armor? *Zap? Sizzle? Ricochet? Walked* is too gentle. In my mental image, the burst from the machine gun *tore into* and *ripped* and *thundered* and *clawed* and *shrieked* up the side of the carrier.

Did Jack hear it? Of course. He was trained to be aware, to anticipate the unexpected. But bullets hit too rapidly to react to. It was too late to swing his gun around. Then, according to Battscalf's report, "A bullet struck Jack just below the bottom of his armored vest."

The bullet *struck* him. Blasted his unprotected underside. It *struck* him and sent him reeling, blood spurting. Or gushing. The armored vest protected his muscled chest, maybe the upper part of that chiseled stomach. But the enemy hit him below the belt.

By that time, it was too dark for a Huey. Besides, the battle raged. The nearest medical help was in Quảng Trị, an hour and a half overland. An armored personnel carrier wasn't an ambulance. Its top speed was forty-two miles an hour. But that was all they had.

They headed for Quảng Trị, Jack losing blood. His breath faltered. I can hear his final thoughts, *Damn, I should have anticipated that SOB . . . I should have had him.*

He was dead on arrival at the Quảng Trị aid station.

I learned of Jack's death on June 2, 1965, two days shy of one year after I'd skipped commencement to travel Europe with him. On that day, June 4, 1964, I had left a forlorn Terry on the steps of Hallett Hall. In June 1965, it was Terry trying to comfort me. But what could he say about the death of his former rival? What could I say to my husband about my loss? *Do you mind sleeping on the sofa for a while, Ter? I'm too torn up about Jack.* Obviously not. I was a married woman. The man I needed to mourn was not my husband.

Terry sympathized. He held me. Patted my shoulder. Mumbled, "Damn, I'm sorry."

It was so inadequate. But he couldn't know how I felt. Nor could he fix things. He'd never met Jack. He had no idea how close Jack and I had been, how much I really did love him. I'd never told anyone, especially not Terry. No one knew how close I came to marrying Jack—not even, I suspect, Jack. On that day in 1965, I grieved silently, but I didn't mourn.

Not then.

Terry

Spring 1993, Washington, DC. The polished black granite slabs of Maya Lin's wall at the Vietnam Veterans Memorial on the National Mall in Washington, DC, are silent on the details of the deaths of the 58,307 Americans killed in that war. The wall bears only their names. No hometown or rank. They all had death in common, but names alone tell us nothing of the uniqueness of each person.

The wall doesn't say "Captain Jack Sigg" (he was promoted before he went to Vietnam). Only his formal name is listed—"John C. Sigg"—though Annie always spoke of him as Jack.

They hadn't finished installing the wall before Annie and I and our two kids moved from DC back to Colorado in 1983. But on a trip there in

1993, I made two rubbings of Jack's name, carved on panel 1E, line 127. One for Annie. One for Bud.

Annie was meeting with one of her clients at the time, ironically a US Army lieutenant colonel charged with testing antiballistic missiles. Her job was to help the army with public communications. In the end, try as she might, she didn't stray too far from the corral after all.

Ann

Friday, August 23, 2013, our home in Las Vegas. After nearly five decades of marriage, Terry and I began recreating the past, working on a memoir to understand the Mad Hatter's ride that caused so much turmoil, heartache, and angst for all three of us—Jack, Terry, and me.

For years after Jack died, I kept my grief airtight. And then I went to the library at the University of Nevada, Las Vegas, where I borrowed an antique reel-to-reel tape player to digitize—and relive—Jack's taped letters. My goal: exhume buried memories of Jack to help tell our story. For four days, six hours a day, Jack came alive, forever twenty-six and "shivering with joy and hopes" for the two of us. "I want to spend the rest of my life . . . ," he says, pausing a full ten seconds to regain control of his voice, "with you."

Parked at a polished library table in a large open room, earphones on my head, I worked hard to keep a poker face around an impossible lump in my throat. *You can't dissolve here, Ann.*

Delayed grief, I discovered, is not a sudden deluge on a summer day that's over in a few hours, giving way to sunny thoughts. Rather, it builds up and sloshes around inside its sturdy canvas pouch until one day it's exposed to the air. After that, it dribbles its cargo at inopportune moments, too heavy to carry, too precious to abandon.

I have sometimes wondered, *What if* I had married Jack?

I would have been a widow at the age of twenty-three. Or would I? Had we married, would he still have gone to Vietnam? Yes, I assured myself—it was his duty.

But then I rediscovered a line in a letter he wrote in the fall of 1963. I had asked him about Vietnam. He wrote, "If my real hopes are answered,

I'll no more want to go to Vietnam than to the South Pole. But if 'we' fail to become 'us,' it would be a deathblow to my soul. And I would most likely volunteer for Vietnam. It would be a release to get away from it all for a while."

Apparently, by the time he left Landshut for the US after our summer together, he'd concluded that the "deathblow" had been delivered. He never asked me to marry him, not directly.

Or did I not hear him?

I'll never know.

Epilogue: Dare We Relive History?

Ann

Friday, May 2, 2014, en route to Germany. I'm on my way to Munich again, this time with Terry. The pilot begins his descent. No knots in my stomach, but oh, the butterflies! What forgotten delights will I remember from the summer of '64—and be reluctant to share with Terry? What dark memories will I dredge up as we travel the route I blazed with Jack?

Terry squeezes my thigh. "See anything familiar?" His hand calms the butterflies.

I take in every detail. Subdivisions encroach on a crazy quilt of small farms. Green plots give way to urban sprawl. A city appears, thick with leviathan red-roofed buildings, cathedral spires, gleaming office towers, broad squares and parks, multilane highways, a massive convergence of rail lines. Nothing's familiar. Frankly, I barely noticed Munich that first trip, my mind on the guy waiting for me in the airport—Jack Sigg, splendid in army greens, so clean-shaven his skin glowed, with a smile that nearly swallowed his face.

I remember also that jolt of guilt at my parting view of Terry, slumped on my dorm steps, sweaty and disheveled, with his Fu Manchu mustache, lamb-chop sideburns, and hair scruffing over his collar. He still has a mustache, but it's white now and more or less tamed.

I cover Terry's hand with mine. "Don't recognize a thing. Have we been here before?"

His reply is immediate and deadpan: "One of us has. But it wasn't me. Remember?"

He betrays no regret, merely stating a fact. He's long past his persistent probing to wring from me every detail of each moment I spent with Jack, especially on our grand tour.

That's history. I zero in on the adventure before us. *We're* descending into Munich—Terry and I—fifty years after I made this flight to be with Jack. *We're* about to replay my summer of 1964, though I know it will be different. Times have changed. Europe has changed. My companion is my husband. But I have longed to etch a new set of European adventures into my shared life with Terry. Do I have qualms about retracing with my husband a trip I took with my boyfriend fifty years ago? Of course. That summer was an amazing adventure, but ghosts of heart pain still lurk.

We don't speak German, though that isn't new for us. Some decades ago in faraway Taiwan, Terry and I arrived in the late afternoon in the city of Taichung, with no hotel reservations or guide book, no knowledge of Chinese. We wanted a local hotel, not a Hilton. We wandered the streets until we were exhausted, our backpacks weighing heavier and heavier. At last, we found a small, nondescript place that seemed to fit the bill. We asked for a room for the night.

The clerk's response: a blank stare.

We asked again. We pantomimed. We gestured.

The clerk unleashed a flood of Chinese. He pantomimed. He gestured. Finally, we got his message: "Our rooms rent only by the hour."

Oh! We wanted a night's rest, not a quickie. Red-faced, we shook our heads and slipped out the door.

We survived, found a room, and spent a memorable week in Taiwan— the third leg of a monthlong journey full of similar miscues and discoveries in Hong Kong, South Korea, and Japan, on our way home from two years as Peace Corps volunteers in the Philippines.

We settled in Madison, Wisconsin. I worked as an editor for the American Society of Agronomy while Terry went to grad school. When he finished, we moved to his hometown of Center and lived for four years in the Chicano barrio—Terry as Head Start director and I as a community organizer and later as deputy director of a new clinic we helped establish. Our daughter, Leslie, spent her infancy in a basket at farm worker rallies and community meetings in Center.

But even after another stint in grad school, this time for both of us, and two more years in Center, we never lost our Peace Corps dream. In 1977, we plunged again into the Peace Corps, this time as country co-directors of programs in the Solomon Islands, Kiribati, and Tuvalu. We lived for three years on Guadalcanal, where our son, Shawn, was born on July 4 and Leslie spent her elementary years running barefoot through the jungle. From the South Pacific, we settled in Washington, DC, and Terry worked for two years at Peace Corps headquarters.

The Peace Corps implanted service and international travel into our DNA. As country co-directors, we stayed many a night in Fiji, Tuvalu, Kiribati, and Nauru, with multiple excursions in the Pacific—the Marshall Islands, Papua New Guinea, Malaysia, Thailand, New Zealand, and Australia—plus, believe it or not, Morocco. During our ten years in Denver and seven in Carlsbad, New Mexico, we explored Southeast Asia; Italy, France, and Spain; Puerto Rico, Cuba, Antigua, and Central and South America.

Throughout those later years, I worked as a consultant to the US Environmental Protection Agency and later the Energy Department—at several Superfund sites in Colorado, Montana, and Utah; and at nuclear waste sites near Carlsbad, Las Vegas, and Los Angeles. Terry turned to writing, publishing several books, a major sociological study, and numerous short stories, essays, and articles. Since 2000, he and I have called Las Vegas home.

Now, in 2014, we're arriving for the first time together in Germany. We can do this.

"We're here, *old buddy*," Terry says. "Let the fond memories flow."

Monday, May 5, 2014, Landshut, Germany. These, I remember: the Isar River at city's edge; the arch in the twelve-foot-thick red brick wall, guarded by dual parapets, a reminder that Landshut started as a fortress in 1204; and downtown storefronts in a rainbow of soft pastels.

On this hushed afternoon, the only sound is the tap-tap echo of my flats on the hard tile of the former US Army Bachelor Officers Quarters, where Jack and Bonner lived, now vacant. We talked a man in a hard hat into unlocking a chained door for us. It's about to be remodeled into a college dorm.

I peek into the open doorways of officers' former suites. Barren rooms all. No furniture. No posters. No hint of previous occupants. Rows of open doorways gape blankly from both sides of the empty hallway. The vacant rooms dissolve into history. Jack and I cuddle in his cozy sitting area, listening to Miles Davis. His desk, stereo, and speakers artfully shield his tidy bunk, a bath connects to another suite, and a shared kitchen is down the hall. Jack rails about BOQ-mates who don't clean up after they've cooked.

Like Monopoly hotels, two identical rows of these dusty-yellow, three-story structures have withstood the ravages of World War II, the Cold War, and the ensuing fifty years. Today, no lieutenant is on hand to welcome me. It's as spooky as a graveyard on a gloomy afternoon.

Later, we find the former officers' club. No MPs on duty, rifles at the ready. A brass plaque identifies the building as Städtische Musikschule Landshut, the Landshut Music School. Below that, another brass plaque verifies that it was indeed the officers' club.

The front door is unlocked. We creep in. No receptionist. No soldiers in dress greens. From far down the hall, a single flute plays—not a German Jean-Pierre Rampal, assuredly, but not a rank beginner, a simple melody, not one we recognize. It stops. Starts again, same passage. This isn't the free-flowing club I remember. The interior of this military facility has been sliced and partitioned; rows of doors lead, apparently, to tiny practice rooms, all locked.

What am I looking for? A whiff of reminiscence, perhaps? The thrill of a recaptured memory that I can wrap in a tissue paper of words and safely stow for the future? Or is this an inquiry into the fragility of human institutions? Where now are those hale warriors who guarded the borders of human freedom? Long since gone . . . every one.

We find no bar. No dining room. No pool or Ping-Pong tables. In the hour we explore, we hear only our footsteps, our whispers, and that flute. An army officers' club, this quiet? In some ways, it fits. As Terry says, "They've beaten swords into ploughshares—and tanks into flutes."

Terry

Wednesday, 7 May 2014, Frauenau, Germany. Through the rain, we drive the Crystal Road, a two-lane highway that shadows the Czech Republic border from the south at Passau to Neustadt an der Waldnaab in the north. This is the heart of Bavaria's handblown glass industry. We've cruised small towns and scoured crystal shops, showing them our eight-by-ten photos of the blue vase Jack had bestowed on Annie that year—and the matching bowls he gave us as our wedding present. Fifty years ago, Annie visited the studio where they were made, but none of these small towns or crystal outlets look familiar to her.

"Where did these pieces come from? Who made them?" we've asked. No one knows.

In Zwiesel, we stop at an information center.

"They don't make those anymore," the attendant tells us. "They're out of style."

No, we don't want to buy one, we explain, but merely find out where they came from. We try a few circumlocutions but can't get the idea across. Clearly exasperated, the agent sends us to Frauenau, a small town down the road. You'll find a glass museum there, she grunts. Ask them.

It's only seven kilometers to Frauenau, but it's 4:00—can we make it before closing? It's still raining, and the road is a lane-and-a-half-wide twisted and looped ribbon through the hills. We pull up to the *Glasmuseum* at 4:30.

Inside, the receptionist is intrigued by our photos. "Wait!" She picks up the phone. Moments later, the museum director descends a broad staircase from a block of glass-enclosed offices on the second floor. She ushers us through the entry stile, waives the fee, and leads us to an exhibit with several Palatinate-blue crystal pieces. Same brilliant blue, but different style. "I can't be sure about your vase. We have nothing like it. Maybe it is from near here, Bavarian Zwiesel, or further south, toward Passau," she says.

By now it's 5:15, past museum closing time. She asks, "Where are you staying tonight?"

We have no idea. An hour ago we'd never heard of Frauenau, let alone thought about where to stay. We tell her we prefer small family-owned guest houses, not fancy hotels.

"I know the perfect place. The senior chef was a master glassblower. If anyone knows the vase, it would be him." She calls Pension WaldKristall, reserves a room, and directs us there.

At WaldKristall, we show our photos to the owner, Michael Kapfhammer. He is fluent in English and has spent time in Las Vegas. "Leave the photos with me," he says. "I'll ask my father."

The next morning, Michael greets us, "My father asks if you would like to look at his work. He's waiting in his showroom."

We dash a half block in the rain to Michael's personal residence, where he leads us to the basement and into a sixty-foot-long rectangular store-room, shelves four high on every windowless wall, every shelf filled with gleaming crystal—a bedazzling array of vases, bowls, stemware, decanters, flacons, tumblers, and goblets in a rainbow of color—all handblown and cut by master artisan Sigfrid Kapfhammer, Michael's father.

The guy is built like a fullback and still looks in good enough shape to play Division I ball, though we know his choice would be soccer, not football. He's strong, with hands of seasoned leather, and next to him, I look like the water boy.

Sigfrid studies our photos and delivers a monologue. Michael translates: "He says your vase probably came from Nachtmann Riedel in Weiden."

I look at Annie and she looks at me. We are both thinking: *Where the hell is Weiden, and how do we get there?*

Michael continues, "But he's not sure of the artist. No one makes these anymore. People want machine-made pieces. They're cheaper."

Sigfrid shrugs. What can we say? It's true everywhere, about so many things. We look at Sigfrid and nod in empathy.

He sweeps his hand around the room, gesturing at the full shelves. "This is my life's work," Michael translates. "You are welcome to look."

This basement is a fine arts gallery. We go shelf by shelf, piece by piece. Each has a small silver sticker with tiny red print, *"Das Glas mit,"* and to the right of those words is a red heart labeled *"Herz"*—"Glass with Heart." In the center is *"Echt Waldkristall"*—"Authentic Forest Crystal," Sigfrid's brand.

The shelves hold only a few blue pieces, but Annie spots a pair of slen-der Palatinate-blue vases with vertical rows of the same transparent silvery ovals as on Jack's vase, topped by filigree designs in the flared rim, delicate as spider webs. "Will he sell these?" she asks.

"Ja," Sigfrid says, nodding. *"Ja!"*

We select a matched pair of banana-boat bowls, replete with silvery ovals and swirls, as heavy as . . . well, as heavy as lead crystal. And a tall, cylindrical vase, artful as a totem pole. We assemble them on Sigfrid's worktable. He examines each and totals them on a slip of paper. Writes, "Euros 250." He steps back, goes to the shelves, selects a teardrop-shaped vase, same Palatinate blue, same swirls and ovals, and sets it with the oth-ers. Says something to Michael.

"That one is his gift to you," Michael translates. "He is honored that you value his work."

Annie holds the vase in one hand and caresses it with the other, running her fingers, dare I say, sensuously over the ovals and swirls. Then with eyes sparkling, she pings the edge with her fingernail. "Listen. Its peal is as crisp as a morning in the forest. Of course. *Waldkristall!*" She nestles it in my hands. It fits perfectly. The feel is exotic and, yes, sensuous. Also familiar—a first cousin to the vase and bowls we have used almost weekly at home for fifty years.

We take photos all around: Sigfrid with our purchases; Annie and Sigfrid; Sigfrid and me; Sigfrid, Michael, and me. We thank Sigfrid and offer a hearty goodbye.

As he clasps my hand, he slaps his other hand on my shoulder. He's teary-eyed. So am I.

Outside in the car, Annie and I realize that our quest is over, no need to find Weiden. Sigfrid is a surrogate connecting us to a time and place that no longer exists. He has given us an indelible memory of how much his art—so much of it now languishing in a dark basement—means to an artist of his talent.

Moreover, he has drawn me into that intimate circle that links Jack to Annie and her summer of '64. That summer is now my summer as well as theirs.

Ann

Sunday, May 11, 2014, Badenweiler, Germany. After graduating from law school in Buenos Aires, our Argentinian "daughter"—a Rotary exchange student who lived with us her senior year of high school—spent two years as a nanny in Germany and Switzerland. She went so she could learn German. She also gained another "favorite mother": Antje Marcantonio. Like a new-found sister, Antje welcomes Terry and me into her home in Badenweiler.

Over several wine pairings, we feast on scrumptious pasta—handmade by her husband, Rocco. And drink. And talk. And drink. Antje and I share love stories: Antje tells me about vacationing as a coed in Italy, about meeting a suave Italian lifeguard, and their whirlwind romance—pursued in languages the other didn't understand; of his dream to open his own espresso shop. I tell her about flying to Germany to rendezvous with my dashing warrior—no, not Terry, I tell her—and about my torment as I wrestled with the anguish of loving two men.

"And the soldier, when did you fall out of love with him?" Antje asks.

For a moment, I'm speechless, just staring at her. Then these words spew unbidden from some previously locked vault in my heart: "I didn't. I still love him, even today, fifty years later."

Antje's jaw drops. Mine, too. We exchange glances, my mind racing.

In the living room, Terry and Rocco carry on like diehard fans as they watch a soccer match on TV, hands flying, voices animated, stuttering along in Spanish, the only language they have in common, neither of them fluent. They're fully engaged. Neither heard me.

"So it's no wonder," I stammer, "that I had such a hard time deciding what to do."

"But how?" Antje is more puzzled than I am.

Yes . . . I remember now. That's what I told Jack fifty years ago—that I would always love him, but I couldn't marry him and become an army wife. My breath is coming in small puffs. I want to explain it to her, but the memories are at full flood.

It would take me another ten months to explain it to myself: That I locked it away in my heart for five decades. That it doesn't mean I've loved Terry any less, but rather that I loved them both deeply.

Acknowledgments

With gratitude to Mary Lou, Heidi, Marian, Allen, Fran, Susan, Gary, Bonner, Jim, Pam, Greg, Randall, Kathy, Michael, Jon, Earl, Lois, and Charles, who all played important roles in our story.

To our folks—Ralph and Dorothy Garretson, and Charles and Margaret Marshall—and Ann's grandmother, Alice Courts, who raised us in love and patience, even after we chose paths they would have preferred we had never discovered.

To Laura Lee Christiansen, who changed Terry's life in 1963; she remains a dear friend to both of us, and gave us valuable feedback on key sections of our manuscript.

To our high school teachers, Julia Speiser and David Judy; and to our university professors, A. Gayle Waldrop, John Mitchell, Bob Rhode, Floyd Baskette, and William Markward, our initial tutors in writing and literature.

To Greg Blake Miller and Hope Edelman, excellent writers, superb mentors, skilled coaches, astute literary critics, and patient advisers. In their critiques of several versions of our complete manuscript, both of them, in different ways, helped us better structure our story, sharpen our prose, and turn our experiences into a coherent memoir.

To Tim Bascom, B. K. Loren, Marc Nieson, Nancy McGlasson, Alan Brody, Magda Montiel Davis, Amy Turner, Dag Scheer, Sarah Conover, Ann Green, Sue Ade, Tim Hillegonds, and Diana Hovey for their thoughtful comments, critiques, and suggestions at various stages of our manuscript.

To Cynthia Carbajal for her creative initial book cover and travel maps, which gave visual life to our words.

To Jared and Julia Drake, who helped us present our work to a world beyond our own backyard, and who linked us to Sandra Jonas.

To our publisher Sandra Jonas, who believed in our project, who asked the tough questions to help us refine our story and characters, who served as our editor extraordinaire, and who did the hard work to bring the book to fruition and to the reading public.

To Jill Tappert, who read our manuscript with a sharp eye tuned to the smallest errors, historical inconsistencies, word repetitions, and passages in need of massaging for clarity.

To Jack's parents, Bud and Peggy Sigg, who embraced Ann as a family member and shared the best fresh corn to be found; and to Jack's cousins, Gregory Sigg Murphy (who shared numerous family photos with us), Pam Sigg, Lin (Sigg) Morgan, Jack Quinn, and Jean Quinn.

To Jack's and Bonner's West Point and other military comrades, especially Colonel Tom Fintel and French Lieutenant Jacques d'Achon, who provided us with photos, insights, encouragement, and background information on various events in Jack's professional years. Lieutenant d'Achon also shared a trove of his own photos from the German-Czech border.

To the UNLV Special Collections Library for their assistance in setting Ann up with the equipment to listen to and digitize Jack's many reel-to-reel taped letters to Ann.

And finally, to the digital geniuses who designed and shared Google Search, Wikipedia, and Facebook, which enabled us to connect with key people in the United States and France who informed our knowledge of the Cold War in Europe. These tools also made it possible for us to find details such as key rail and auto routes through Europe, phases of the moon, times of specific sunrises and sunsets, hamburger prices, and scores of obscure facts and figures that added color to our story.

A Note on Memory and Sources

We have done our best to tell our story with authenticity. To aid our memory and to reconstruct conversations and thoughts, we combed our extensive collection of personal letters, notes, news clippings, and audiotapes. We don't claim to remember the exact words of every conversation, but the dialogue and narrative represent our interactions as faithfully as we can—even when they are painful or reflect poorly on us.

Now, fifty-plus years later, we still ache as people and events rise from the spent wick of our youth in an eerie séance with our current selves and passions. All of us have behaved imperfectly at some critical junctures, a fact that in no way diminishes our love for our families and friends, then or now. We have long since forgiven past injuries, theirs and ours. We hope our readers, and our adult children, will do likewise.

All the people herein are real, not composites or constructs. We have, however, used pseudonyms for key people to protect their privacy: Sarah Abrams, Rachael Goldman, Laura Lee Christensen, Geoff Jordan, Gretchen Schumacher, Stefanie Wiercinski, Angelica Archuleta, Bobby Marks, Cindy Gomez, Dr. Wagner, Dr. Perini, and everyone identified only by a first name. Further, for simplicity, we have used the family name "Bonner" for Ann's older brother, Ralph Bonner Garretson Jr. His friends and colleagues knew him as Ralph. Finally, Smoky Point, Colorado, and Huntersville, Nebraska, are pseudonyms for real towns.

Some of the people have since died, including our parents, Bonner, Allen Nossaman, and Sarah Abrams; we miss them. Others have remained dear friends throughout our lives, including Gary Althen and the people presented as Laura Lee, Angelica, and Ann's "high school boyfriend." Ann also corresponded, visited, and exchanged occasional gifts with Bud Sigg, Jack's father, until he died in 2005. And over time, we have made serendipitous connections with six of Jack's cousins, including Jack Quinn, who contacted Ann within hours after hearing her 2018 Memorial Day tribute to Jack Sigg in an interview with NPR's Ari Shapiro. Jack Quinn has since died.

We lost touch with Gretchen, and despite efforts by an archivist in Landshut and a private detective in the US, we have been unable to locate her. Ann kept her secrecy promise to Jack for forty years before she shared it with family members, some of whom want to meet their previously unrecognized relative, Gretchen and Bonner's daughter. If Gretchen should ever read this account, she will recognize her story despite the pseudonym, and we want her to know that we would welcome a reunion with her.

A Rendezvous to Remember is more than the adventures of three people and assorted friends and family. We also wanted to show how the chaotic early 1960s, awash in Women's Liberation, the Sexual Revolution, the Cold War, the Civil Rights Movement, and the Vietnam War, affected our lives and the lives of our generation.

To reconstruct this era, we did extensive research and interviews with others who lived through those heady times. Ann sought out Jack's and Bonner's West Point classmates and fellow officers to learn more about life on the German-Czech border in 1963–64 and interviewed two men who served there with them: an American, Colonel Tom Fintel, and a Frenchman, former Lieutenant Jacques D'Achon. Mr. D'Achon, who has since died, gave us several dozen photos taken on the border, and Ann still corresponds with his daughter, Cecile. Colonel Fintel, now retired, related actions on the border the day President Kennedy was assassinated.

Although Jack and Bonner were two of the main actors in Colonel Fintel's story, Ann hadn't heard it from either of them. The story stuck with her, and we concluded that we needed to tell it to convey a little-publicized potential "near-miss" on that fateful day in the shadow of the Iron Curtain. So, with deep gratitude to Colonel Fintel, Ann reimagined Jack telling the story to Colonel Ed Kirtley, officer to officer. Colonel Kirtley was serving in Verona, Italy, when Jack and Ann visited him and Edna Mae there in July 1964.

On a final note, what became of Terry and the draft?

We assume Terry had some kind of deferment while we were in the Philippines—though they never told him. At the time, Peace Corps volunteers didn't receive an automatic deferment.

After the Peace Corps, the board reclassified him I-A (available for military service), setting off another long series of attempts to get him reclassified as a CO, including the hiring of another lawyer when Terry was a grad student in Wisconsin. He appealed. The board turned him down.

Terry met personally with the board in mid-August of that year. After they denied his appeal, he appealed the local board's decision to a five-person state appeal board. That board also denied it, and classified him I-A again in November 1967.

The battle continued.

The board wrote Terry a letter in July 1968 reaffirming his I-A classification, but they said that the draft wasn't currently taking men over twenty-six, so they were going to stop working on his appeal. The following spring, they classified him II-S (student deferment) and in December of 1969 reclassified him II-A (occupational deferment other than agricultural and student).

There the correspondence ends. We believe they simply buried Terry's case in the back of a filing cabinet and left it.

Photo Album

The Garretsons (*clockwise from left*): Ralph Sr., Dorothy, Bonner (Ralph Jr.), Ann, and Jimmy, 1956.

Ann, cheerleader, Livorno American High School, Camp Darby, Italy, 1957.

The Marshalls (*from left*): Terry, Randy (now goes by Randall), Margaret, Greg, Charles, and Pam, 1958.

Colorado's winners of the Ford Teen-age Press Conference:
Terry in 1958 and Ann in 1959.

Terry, 1958.   Ann's passport (to Germany) photo, 1964.

A man and his "horses": Jack Sigg, his Corvette Sting Ray, and his tank, Landshut, Germany, 1964.

Jack Sigg, West Point cadet, 1961.   Captain Jack Sigg, Vietnam, 1965.

Silverton, Colorado, as seen from Molas Pass, 2015.

Surviving Black Bear Pass. This isn't Allen Nossaman's 1958 Scout, but it is the route we traversed in chapter 8.

A mountain wedding: Terry and Ann, married at last, 1965.

Jack's birthday vase to Ann—designed, crafted, and delivered to her dorm in Boulder, Colorado, from Bavaria, Germany, 1964.

About the Authors

Terry Marshall grew up on a farm in Center, Colorado. Ann Garretson Marshall was an army brat who spent her childhood on military bases in the United States and Italy.

After they graduated from the University of Colorado Boulder—Ann with a degree in English and Terry in journalism—Ann taught high school English in Glendale, Arizona, while Terry worked as a reporter and then as the editor of the *Glendale News-Herald*. Following their marriage, they both taught English in the Philippines as Peace Corps volunteers.

Terry earned an MS in rural sociology from the University of Wisconsin and a PhD from Cornell University in sociology of development. He has worked as a community organizer and activist, including three years as a Peace Corps country co-director in the Solomon Islands, Kiribati, and Tuvalu; two years in the Peace Corps headquarters in Washington, DC; and six years organizing on behalf of Chicanos in his hometown. Terry has studied, analyzed, and written both fiction and nonfiction works on discrimination, poverty, rural development, foreign language learning, and intercultural relations.

Ann earned an MS in communication arts from Cornell University. She worked side by side with Terry as a Peace Corps country co-director in the Pacific and as a community organizer and activist in Colorado. She has thirty years' experience as a writer, editor, and organizer helping the US government involve local communities in the cleanup of hazardous contamination and nuclear waste. Ann is also a trained mediator.

The couple live in Las Vegas, Nevada. They have two adult children.

50

149

550

● OURAY

● TELLURIDE

● SILVERTON

149

160

550

DURANGO

160

84

151